100 Hikes in™ OREGON

100 Hikes in™ OREGON

Rhonda and George Ostertag

© 1992 by Rhonda and George Ostertag

All rights reserved

5 4
5 4 3 2

No part of this book may be reproduced in any form, or by any electronic, mechanical, or other means, without permission in writing from the publisher.

Published by The Mountaineers
1011 SW Klickitat Way, Seattle, Washington 98134

Published simultaneously in Canada by Douglas & McIntyre, Ltd., 1615 Venables Street, Vancouver, B.C. V5L 2H1

Published simultaneously in Great Britain by Cordee, 3a DeMontfort Street, Leicester, England, LE1 7HD

Manufactured in the United States of America

Edited by Lisa M. Nicholas
Maps by Elizabeth Duke
Cover design by Watson Graphics
Book layout by Nick Gregoric
Typography by Typeworks

All photographs by the authors except as otherwise noted.
Cover photograph: Beargrass and rhododendrons; Mount Hood in the distance, Mount Hood National Forest, by Kirkendall/Spring.
Frontispiece: Oregon white oaks tower above Mount Pisgah Summit Trail

Library of Congress Cataloging in Publication Data

Ostertag, Rhonda, 1957–
100 hikes in Oregon / Rhonda and George Ostertag.
p. cm.
Includes index.
ISBN 0-89886-298-1
1. Hiking—Oregon—Guidebooks. 2. Oregon—Description and travel—1981– I. Ostertag, George, 1957– . II. Title.
III. Title: One hundred hikes in Oregon.
GV199.42.070844 1992
917.95'043—dc20 92-18750
CIP

CONTENTS

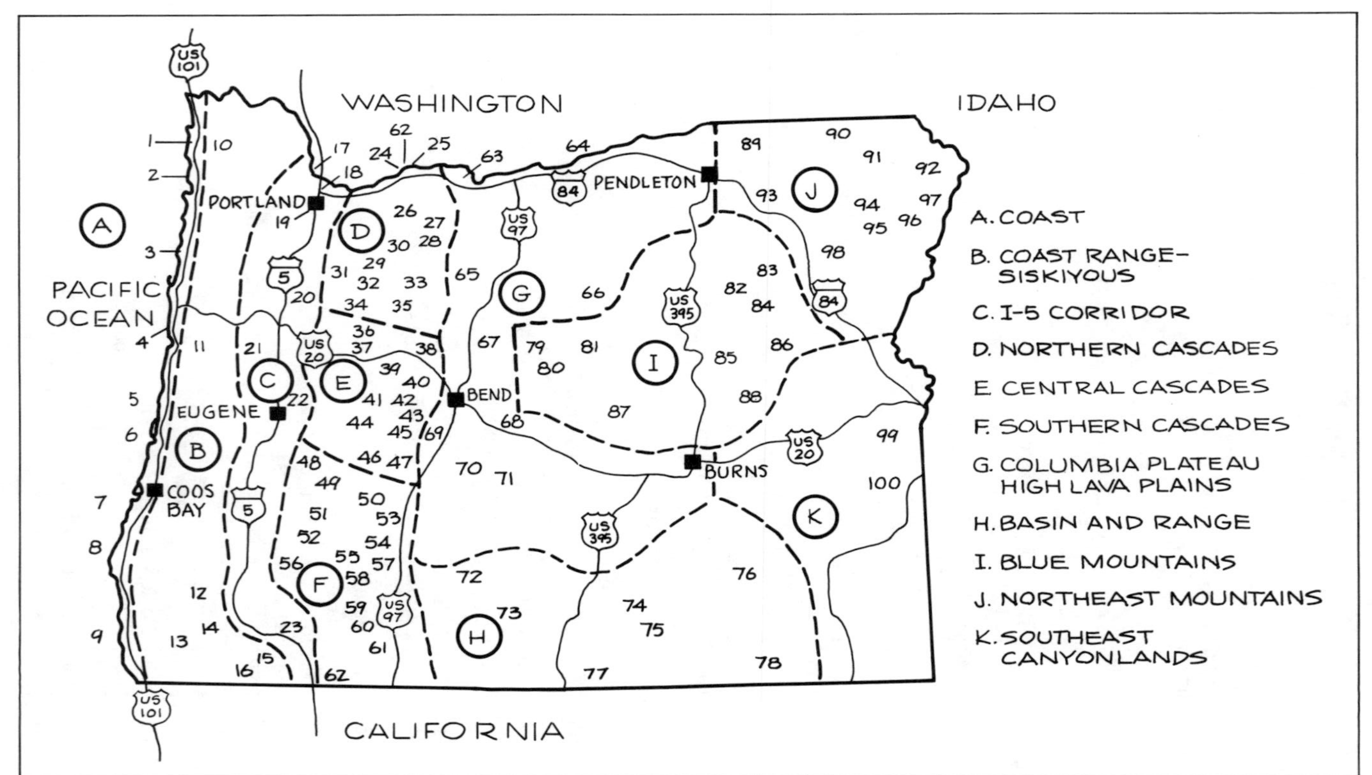
WASHINGTON
IDAHO
PACIFIC OCEAN
CALIFORNIA
PORTLAND
EUGENE
COOS BAY
BEND
PENDLETON
BURNS
US 101
US 97
US 20
US 395
5
84
A. COAST
B. COAST RANGE–SISKIYOUS
C. I-5 CORRIDOR
D. NORTHERN CASCADES
E. CENTRAL CASCADES
F. SOUTHERN CASCADES
G. COLUMBIA PLATEAU HIGH LAVA PLAINS
H. BASIN AND RANGE
I. BLUE MOUNTAINS
J. NORTHEAST MOUNTAINS
K. SOUTHEAST CANYONLANDS

PREFACE

While exploring Oregon, we found no shortage of interesting trails. They offered all kinds of adventures in all kinds of terrain. The challenge was to select a representative mix that hailed the diversity and spotlighted the unique, that saluted the recognized and applauded the little known, and that featured the accessible yet dispersed visitor stress from the popular. As hikers and environmentalists, we face a dilemma: The use of an area is often our strongest voice for ensuring its protection, yet the use of an area may, ironically, threaten or degrade the very qualities in which we rejoice. With responsible use of all our wild areas and a tempered use of our most sensitive, most frequented lands, we can mitigate this dilemma.

Along the trail, we have met people who mentioned their annual trips to their favorite haunts. When those haunts lie close to population centers and receive excessive foot traffic, a break with tradition may show the fondest admiration for the land. Going every three or four years and instead exploring new areas may best ensure that our favorites remain unspoiled for years to come. New favorites await, and the wanderlust can prove contagious, once we've broken with the familiar.

Off-season visits, opting for day trips instead of backpack trips, hiking in smaller parties, and limiting the overnight stays, too, can reduce the stress to certain areas.

Over the years, with innovative materials and designs, hikers have become spoiled, being able to port comfort, convenience, and even luxury into the wilds. The time has come now to revive the old concept of "roughing it." Lawn chairs, coolers, and radios have no place in the backcountry. If you cannot live without the comforts of home, then perhaps wilderness trekking is not for you. Let's not confuse the sacred separation of wilderness and home.

We appreciate individuals, both private citizens and agency personnel, who, in the past, carried the banner for recreation and for the protection of our natural resources. Now, our own ranks must rise to the challenge and build on that legacy, ensuring pristine environments, thriving wildlife populations, and prime recreation lands for future generations to enjoy. In addition to lobbying for adequate budgets to maintain, improve, and add to our recreational facilities comes a call for greater volunteerism. It's a system that works, and in our travels, we have benefited from its effectiveness. Central Oregon riding clubs have annually cleared the winter downfalls from the trails to Lookout and Round mountains. The twice annual beach cleanup has made tidepool viewing more productive and barefoot strolling a carefree enjoyment, and volunteer-constructed trails and footbridges have opened up new avenues for discovery and eased the going.

But the call for user responsibility, stewardship, and volunteerism should not be considered a dismissal of our public agencies' roles in preserving our state's natural habitats and promoting recreation.

The environmental-recreation commitment made by agencies and political leaders needs to be more than just a headline-maker or a collapsible running platform that's stored in a closet between elections. Our land-management agencies must demonstrate a genuine commitment from the top down—with lands, money, and personnel dedicated to the creation, overseeing, and protection of both natural and recreation lands. Without this commitment, the willingness heard at the agencies' local levels is crushed out.

In recent years, we have witnessed the first wobbly steps toward recognizing that recreation has a value, just as watersheds and wildlife do, and that forests and trees have a value that is not measured in board feet. Let's not let our political leaders and managing agencies stumble now that they've tried their legs. Keep the steadying hand of public pressure applied through comment at open hearings and letter campaigns.

Today, more than ever, there is a need for a cooperative spirit among recreationists, land stewards, and developers, as well. In Bend, Oregon, that spirit led to the creation of Newberry National Volcanic Monument—just think what other great things it could hold in store for the state of Oregon. For a small investment of time, energy, and cooperation, the return is the great outdoors.

LEGEND

ACKNOWLEDGMENTS

We would like to acknowledge the many people who helped bring this book to its conclusion: the staff at The Mountaineers Books, the personnel at the managing agencies who fielded our many inquiries, and the people we met along the way who shared their experiences, who aided our travels, and who suffered our requests for photos. Our thanks.

Rhonda and George Ostertag

Ground squirrel beggar, Iron Mountain

Pine needles, Kalmiopsis Wilderness

INTRODUCTION

This guidebook features a statewide sampling of both backpack- and day-hike-length trails that challenge, excite, and engage hikers. Oregon is a vast state celebrating a diverse terrain, open expanse, and natural splendor. Within its borders, Oregon houses prized beaches, rich forests, mountain ranges of distinct character, deserts, lava lands, and canyon country. In many of these areas, state and nationally protected waterways serve as natural discovery corridors. Some of this treasury is well-known, but great expanses remain little tapped. Limited to 100 hikes, this book can only brush the possibilities for outdoor adventure. Assembled within these pages are trails that appeal to the hiking enthusiast and to the casual hiker. We've featured a mix including a few well-tracked favorites and some less explored routes. While some trails unveil prized destinations, others are passageways to discovery and adventure. For year-round hiking enjoyment, the mix includes both high-country and low-elevation routes.

Use of the Book

We have structured the book to aid in the trail selection process. First, the trails are grouped by geographical region. Second, to discover the trail character at a glance, each write-up begins with a summary list identifying distance, elevation change, degree of difficulty, seasonal considerations, maps, and the source or sources for additional information.

For each hike, the selling points of the trail are described: what makes it special, the natural history, seasonal surprises, and the rewards and disappointments of the trek and/or destination. From this, hikers can determine whether the trail matches their present interests and time considerations, and they can make comparisons and selections when multiple trails bid for their attention.

Detailed directions to the trailhead follow, along with a description of the trail's progress, which draws attention to special features and alerts hikers to obstacles and potentially confusing trail junctions. Using the directions given in conjunction with the appropriate agency map(s) is the best bet for a "no-fuss" trip to the trailhead.

For use of the summary list, an explanation of some terms is in order to avoid any misinterpretation:

Distance measures represent pedometer readings of round-trip distance, with the exception of the one-way, car-shuttle hikes which are clearly specified. For the most part, backpacking excursions—sometimes dictated by distance, sometimes by attraction—are left to the hiker's judgment.

The elevation change notes the difference between the elevation extremes, providing a clue to the minimal demands of the trail.

The classification of the trails as easy, moderate, or strenuous is subjective. Easy hikes are generally short (under 5 miles), and have an elevation change less than 500 feet. Moderate hikes usually fall within the distance range of 5 to 12 miles and carry a maximum elevation change of 1,500 to 2,000 feet, and strenuous hikes are all those with a distance exceeding 12 miles and carrying an elevation change greater than 2,000 feet. Overriding considerations to these general guidelines include trail condition and grade, obstacles, and, to a lesser degree, exposure to the elements.

Absent from the summary lists are estimations of hiking times, as personal health and physical condition, party size, the interest of the trail features, and weather and trail conditions all may influence the time spent on the trail.

Hikes and trail lengths should be personalized for individual interest and physical ability. The fact that a trail continues does not mean the hiker must. Much of the enjoyment comes in passing along the way. Similarly, just because the write-up concludes doesn't mean the hiking excursion must come to an end as well. Interlocking loops, side trails, and alternative destinations often invite further exploration.

In examining the book's maps, the introductory map shows the eleven geographical regions defined by terrain and natural history that give structure to the book. The code numbers identify the general locations of the trailheads within those eleven regions and relative to key routes and towns.

The maps included within the text are not intended to replace the more detailed area maps. They do supply basic information about the place and the trail's character, but they fail to communicate specific information about the route(s) to the trailhead, neighboring landmarks and features, secondary or alternate routes, and other vital decision criteria.

Outdoor Primer

For most, wilderness trekking is a revitalizing experience, but for a few, it is an ordeal. Adequate preparation can mean the difference between returning from the wilds refreshed and full of praises for the adventure, or returning footsore, dehydrated, and irritable.

The enjoyment of nature's wonder sometimes involves sacrifice and some degree of discomfort. Sun, wind, rain, dust, insects, steep terrain, and brush exact a toll.

Prepared hikers learn to anticipate such evils and take measures to eliminate or minimize their effects. Learning and heeding the regulations for backcountry use, becoming familiar with the area and its maps, and properly equipping for the demands of the trail and the climatic conditions will smooth the way to a pleasurable outing. Matching the hike to the willingness and ability of the hiking party further ensures that end.

To protect and preserve the privilege of a quality outdoor experience, hikers must show responsibility for both themselves and the environment. The following "basics" lay the cornerstones to that end.

Preparation

Outdoor experts have assembled a list of Ten Essentials for meeting and surviving the challenges that nature and the unexpected may hold for the backcountry traveler. Attending to these items provides a head start to a safe and rewarding outdoor adventure:

1. Extra Clothing—more than is needed in good weather
2. Extra Food—so that something is left over at the end of the trip
3. Sunglasses—especially important for alpine and snow travel
4. Knife—for first aid and emergency fire building (making kindling)
5. Firestarter—a candle or chemical fuel for starting a fire with wet wood
6. First-aid Kit—the hiker should also have basic first-aid knowledge, with CPR skills a plus
7. Matches—in a waterproof container
8. Flashlight—with extra bulb and batteries
9. Map—the right one(s) for the trip
10. Compass—with knowledge of how to use it

Clothing. The amount and the types of clothing worn and carried on a hike depend on the length of the outing, the weather conditions, and personal comfort requirements.

Layering is the important concept to remember when selecting clothes. Wool is the fabric of choice for cold or wet weather, and for changeable weather conditions. It serves the hiker by retaining heat even when wet. Cotton is the fabric of warm summer days.

Hats are a light-weight article of clothing that provide a major service. In the summer, they shield the eyes, face, and top of the head from the sun's intensity. In winter, wool ones preserve body heat.

In much of Oregon, a clothing necessity is a good suit of rainwear: jacket and pants (or chaps). Most hikers agree the comfort provided during a major cloudburst easily compensates for the added weight, especially with the light-weight, compact, water-resistant fabrics of today.

Footgear. Sneakers are appropriate for short hikes on soft earthen trails, if conditions are dry. For long hikes and hikes on uneven terrain, boots are preferred for both comfort and protection. While the light weight of sneakers may be appealing, after a full day on the trail, that appeal departs with the throbbing memory of each stone encounter.

Sock layering, with a light undersock worn next to the foot and a second, ragg wool sock worn atop, helps prevent rubbing, provides cushion to the sole, and allows for the absorption of perspiration. Avoid buying and wearing ragg socks with a large cotton content, as they are cold when wet and slow to dry.

Food. The guideline for food is to pack plenty. Hiking demands a lot of energy. Strive to maximize the energy value of the food for its weight, particularly when backpacking. With Oregon's wet weather, it's also a good idea to select foods that come in moisture-resistant wrappers or repackage the items in reusable plastic bags. Cardboard and paper do not fare well in the rain.

Food helps fend off fatigue, a major contributor to accidents on the trail.

Equipment. The quantity and variety of equipment carried in addition to the Ten Essentials will depend on the length and nature of the hike and on the season, but a good pack for transporting that gear is a must. A day pack with padded straps, a reinforced bottom, and side pockets for water bottles is appropriate for the short outing. For backpacking, it is important to select a pack that carries the weight without taxing the hips and shoulders or creating a strain on the neck.

As backpacks represent a major investment, we recommend the newcomer first try renting a backpack. One cannot adequately evaluate a pack in the store with only a few sandbags for weight. A trail test delivers a better comfort reading, plus it demonstrates how well the unit packs with one's personal gear. Check to see if your backpacking store will allow the charge of one rental to be applied to the purchase price of a new pack.

Camera equipment, binoculars, and nature guidebooks are optional gear that may enhance the trip.

Map and Compass. Taking the time to become familiar with maps and their reading in conjunction with a compass will increase one's enjoyment of the outdoors. Maps are important tools. They provide an orientation to the area, suggest alternative routes, present new areas to explore, and aid in the planning and preparation for the journey.

Several maps serve the outdoor enthusiast, each with its own mix of useful information:

1. United States Forest Service (USFS) maps provide a wealth of information. They show the roads and road surfaces, the maintained trails (at the time of the map making), land ownership, campgrounds, waterways, and major landmarks. What most of these maps do not show is the topography of the land; wilderness area maps are the exception.

Although the nonwilderness maps are a good single source for gaining an overall picture of the area, they provide limited information about the character of the trail.

Forest Service maps are available at the Ranger District Offices, Forest Service Headquarters, and outdoor shops.

2. United States Geological Survey (USGS) topographic maps (or topos), are necessary for any cross-country excursions and prove a valuable aid for reading the progress of the trail. Topos indicate the elevation change, suggest the terrain and vegetation, and show primary and secondary trails, watercourses, and the works of man. The USGS offers them in two sizes: the 7.5-minute series and the 15-minute series.

The drawback with these maps is that they are often dated. Trails have been abandoned or re-routed, new trails and roads have been added, and so forth. But they continue to deliver useful information about the terrain.

Topos are available at most outdoor and mountaineering/ski shops or by writing to the USGS, Western District Center, Federal Center, Denver, Colorado 80225.

3. *Green Trails* maps are a relative newcomer to the outdoor market. Produced by a Bellevue, Washington, company, these easy-to-read topographic maps contain more up-to-date information than their USGS counterparts. They are truly designed for the hiker, with bold green lines

View from Coffin Mountain

spotlighting the trails and with the incremental distances and key elevation points plainly specified. They also indicate winter recreation routes and have summarized trail information on the back.

The drawback is that not many of these maps have been produced. Presently, the *Green Trails* maps for Oregon show only quadrants in the northern Cascades. But their more current information and ease of reading make them worth mentioning. These maps may be purchased at many outdoor/mountaineering stores.

4. The Blue Line Quads, available at the district offices of the Bureau of Land Management, show roads, trails and jeep trails, watercourses, the land's ownership and management status, and major features and landmarks. While these quads fail to show the elevation contours and provide only minimal information about the terrain, they prove an invaluable tool for navigating remote BLM areas.

As a reminder, for proper map reading, a magnetic declination of the compass is necessary, as true north does not equal magnetic north. For Oregon, the mean declination is 20 degrees east. For specific locales, the declination may vary one to two degrees. Most topos indicate the declination on the map's bottom border.

Taking to the Trails

Reaching the Trailhead. Backcountry roads demand greater respect than city roads, where services and assistance are readily available. Keeping the vehicle in good repair, topping off the gas tank before entering the backcountry, carrying vehicle emergency gear (jack, usable spare, tire inflator, jumper cables, and chains—for foul weather), carrying basic survival gear for the unexpected (water, blanket, food, matches, first-aid kit, and a flashlight), and carrying the maps for the area you are visiting all promote safe backcountry travel.

Pacing Yourself. Adopting a steady rhythm or pace allows the logging of distances with greater comfort. Psychology comes into play while climbing. When steps grow belabored and eyes train on the top of the hill, the task and the physical exertion become amplified. Taking in the surroundings, maintaining a steady pace, and freeing your thoughts from the task at hand will surprisingly speed and ease the climb.

Taking short rests at moderate intervals helps guard against overexhaustion.

Crossing Streams. A dry crossing is preferred, but when stream conditions prohibit it, stage the crossing at the widest part of the watercourse, where the current is slower and the water more shallow. Sandy bottoms suggest a barefoot crossing, while fast, cold waters and rocky bottoms require a surer footing. This calls for boots.

Before beginning a boot-clad wade, shed your socks. That way, when you resume the hike on the opposite shore, you'll still have dry socks to help keep your feet warm inside the wet boots; this is when the outer wool sock truly shows its thermal value. Hiking in wet boots may be uncomfortable, but it's a minor discomfort compared to a possible dunking. Depending on weight considerations and the number of stream crossings, carrying a pair of lightweight sneakers for the purpose of wading may be justified.

Hiking Cross-country. Cross-country excursions, save for short distances, are not for the beginner. To travel cross-country safely, one must have good map and compass skills, good wilderness skills, and good common sense.

Steep terrain, heavy brush, and the many downfalls both physically and mentally tax the hiker. With the added energy expenditure involved in cross-country hiking, the potential for injury goes up. This, of all hiking, should not be attempted alone. Even know-how and preparation cannot fully arm one against hiker fallibility and the unpredictability of nature.

Beach Hiking. Before taking a long hike, study the tide tables to learn the times of high and low tide. To avoid the danger of becoming stranded, make sure there's adequate time or adequate beach property to complete the hike or reach safety before the incoming tide. "Sneaker" waves—those unexpected, irregular-sized waves that can knock you off your feet—occur along the Oregon Coast. Beware: Drift logs do not provide a safe haven from the incoming waves. The force of the surf can shift, roll, and lift a log, tumbling, striking, and even crushing the unsuspecting rider.

Wilderness Courtesy

Trails. Keep to the path, as shortcutting, skirting puddles, walking two abreast, and walking along the bench of a recessed trail all contribute to erosion and the degradation of trails. To further protect them, report any trail misuse or damage.

Permits and Party Size. Oregon, too, has come to the realization that an open-door policy in regards to our prized wilderness areas can no longer be maintained. Trampled lakeshores, too many campsites, and visitor excess have dictated a new permit policy for backpackers and day hikers entering the Mount Jefferson, Mount Washington, and Three Sisters wilderness areas.

As the permitting system is relatively new and subject to change, it is best to contact the managing ranger district before beginning your trip. At present, the policy calls for backcountry users to secure permits at the ranger stations or visitor centers, while day-use hikers may secure their permits at the trailhead.

Permits are required between Memorial Day weekend and October 31. Presently, no fees apply, but they may be collected in the future; an enforced cut in visitor numbers may accompany that action.

When planning a backcountry outing, particularly to any wilderness lands, keep your party size small and adhere to any regulations restricting party size. If you're unfamiliar with an area's rules and policies or if you haven't visited an area in some time, it's a good idea to contact the managing agency for this information prior to a visit. Rules do change over time, as the tenuous balance between serving visitor needs and protecting the integrity of the wild shifts.

Pets. While pets are enjoyable companions and part of the family, their presence is inappropriate in the wild. Owners should strictly adhere to posted rules for pets. Controlling animals on a leash is not just a courtesy reserved for times when other hikers are present; it is a responsibility to protect the wildlife and ground cover at all times.

Camping. With more and more people enjoying the outdoors, low-impact camping should be the goal of every hiker. Wherever possible, select an established campsite and don't rearrange it by removing ground cover, bringing in logs for benches, banging nails into trees, or digging drainage channels around the tent. The clues that a hiker passed this way should be minimal.

Reduce the number of comforts (as opposed to necessities) ported into camp.

Carry a backpacker's stove for cooking. When a campfire is necessary, keep it small, and heed the regulations on campfires and wood gathering. Wood collection is limited to downed wood. Snags and live trees should never be cut.

If there are no pre-established campsites, select a site at least 200 feet from the water and well removed from the trail. Delicate meadow environments should be avoided, as the foot traffic alone, in and to camp, can cause severe damage, scarring these areas for years to come.

Courtesy also comes into play with site selection. While a camp placed on an overlook or beside a special trail feature may be beautiful for you, the camp and its legacy may deprive others of an appreciation for that same view or natural offering.

Sanitation. For human-waste disposal, select a site well away from the trail and at least 300 feet from any watercourse. There, dig a hole 6 to 8

Log crossing, Cow Creek National Recreation Trail

inches deep for the disposal and burying of the waste. This biologically active layer of the soil holds organisms that can quickly decompose organic matter.

Tissue poses a greater problem, particularly in drier regions. If fire poses no danger, touching a match to the tissue will prevent its becoming nest-building material for a rodent or garbage scattered by salt-seeking deer.

If the ground prohibits the digging of a hole of the specified size, dig as deep as possible and cover well with gravel, bark, and leaves.

Litter. "Pack it in, pack it out" is the rule. Any litter that does not completely burn should be carried out. This includes aluminum foil and cans, as examples.

Orange peels and peanut shells are pack-it-out garbage. It takes six months for nature to reclaim an orange peel, and the animals do not eat them.

Disposable diapers have become a nuisance and a contaminant in the wild. It is wonderful that hikers are sharing the outdoors with their children at such an early age. But they should also remember their wilderness responsibility to "pack it in, pack it out."

Burying garbage is not a solution. Animals may be attracted to the smell, which means torn up vegetation and garbage spread to the winds. Also, the metals and other materials used in the containers and packaging may contaminate the soil.

As filter-tipped cigarette butts take ten to twelve years to decompose, smokers should field strip cigarette butts and pack out the paper and filter for proper disposal. Gum chewers should pocket wrappers and the package pull string.

Washing. Bathing and washing dishes should be done well away from the lake or stream. Water should be carried to the washing site and biodegradable suds used sparingly. Biodegradable soaps, despite their many benefits and their ecological-sounding name, still present a threat to water. Whenever possible, select a rocky wash site, removed from vegetation.

Noise. Nature's quiet and the privacy of fellow hikers demand respect. Hikers are guests in the wild.

Safety

Backcountry travel entails unavoidable risks that every traveler assumes and must be aware of and respect. The fact that an area is described in this book is not a representation that it will be safe for you. For while the book attempts to alert users to safe methods and warn of potential dangers, it is limited—nature is continuously evolving, and man is a fallible creature. Too, each hiker brings to the trail a different set of skills and abilities that can change with time. Independent judgment and common sense remain the hiker's best ally.

When traveling the backcountry, hikers assume risk, but they also reap the rewards.

Water. Water is the preferred refreshment for the hiker. Drinks with caffeine or alcohol are diuretics which will dehydrate and weaken the hiker.

Drinking water taken from lakes and streams should always be treated. Today, even clear, pulsing streams in remote reaches may contain *Giardia,* a protozoan that causes stomach and intestinal discomfort.

Bringing water to a full boil for ten minutes offers the best protection. Water purification systems that remove both debris and harmful organisms offer a satisfactory alternative to boiling. But be forewarned, these filters come in varying degrees of sophistication. Make certain the selected system strains out the harmful organisms. Iodine tablets offer better protection against *Giardia* if used appropriately, but they are not considered safe for pregnant women.

It is best to carry some water on all excursions; sources can dry up or become fouled. Even on short nature hikes, water is a good companion. If thirsty, one cannot enjoy the trail's offering.

Getting Lost. Being stranded or injured in the wild poses a great problem; prior to any outdoor adventure, it is critical to notify a responsible party of your intended destination and time of return. Notifying the informed party when you return completes the safety procedure.

If lost, it is best to sit down and try to think calmly. There's no immediate danger, as long as one has packed properly and followed the notification procedure. If hiking with a group, all should stay together.

Conducting short outward searches for the trail and returning to an agreed-upon, marked location if unsuccessful are generally considered safe. Aimless wandering would be a mistake.

If the search meets with failure, whistling or making loud noises in sets of three may bring help. (Combinations of three are universally recognized as distress signals.) If it's getting late in the day, efforts are best spent preparing for night and trying to conserve energy.

Normally, unless one has good cross-country navigational skills, conserve energy. Aid the rescuers by staying put and hanging out bright-colored clothing.

Hypothermia. Hypothermia is the dramatic cooling of the body that occurs when heat loss surpasses body-heat generation.

Cold, wet, and windy weather command respect. Attending to the Ten Essentials, eating properly, avoiding fatigue, and being alert to the symptoms of sluggishness, clumsiness, and incoherence among hiking party members remain the best protection. Never underestimate the unpredictability of weather.

Should a party member display the symptoms of hypothermia, it is critical to stop and get the member dry and warm. Dry clothing, shared body heat, and hot fluids all will help restore body temperature.

Heat Exhaustion. The strenuous exercise of hiking combined with summer sun can lead to heat exhaustion, an overtaxing of the body's heat regulatory system. Wearing a hat, drinking plenty of water, eating properly (including salty snacks), and avoiding fatigue are the safeguards against heat exhaustion.

For those who are sensitive to the sun, hiking in the early morning and evening hours with midday rests proves beneficial. Wearing wet bandanas about the temples and around the neck and wearing wet wrist bands introduces coolness to the pulse points, further minimizing the impact of heat and sun.

Poison Oak and Ivy. The best way to avoid contact with these plants is to learn what they look like and in what environments they grow. A good plant-identification book will supply this information.

Scientists are working toward creating creams or vaccines that will inhibit the plants' poison. Meanwhile, should these plants come in contact with the skin, rinse off in cold water, and avoid scratching the area of contact as it will only spread the oils. Exposure to air and time remain the best medicines.

Stings and bites. The best armor against stings and bites is again knowledge. It's important to become aware of any personal allergies and sensitivities and to become knowledgeable about the habits and habitats of snakes, bees, ticks, and other "menaces" of the wild and how to deal with the injuries they may cause.

In the case of a tick bite, after removing the tick watch for signs of redness and swelling, which could be an early indication of Lyme disease. Consult a physician whenever wounds show signs of infection.

Bears. In dealing with bears, use basic common sense. Food should not be stored near camp and especially not in the tent. If clothes pick up cooking smells, they should be suspended along with the food from an isolated overhanging branch well away from camp.

Sweet-smelling creams or lotions also may prove enticing to a bear and should be avoided.

Trailhead Precautions. Hikers are a vulnerable lot. Their vehicles (and frequently their valuables) are left unattended for long periods of time in remote trailhead parking areas—a virtual invitation to the trailhead thief.

As a safeguard, while enjoying the wilderness experience, heed the following precautions:

- Whenever possible, park away from the trailhead at a nearby campground or other facility. A car left at the trailhead parking area says "my owner is gone."
- Do not leave valuables. Carry keys and wallet, placing them in a remote compartment in the pack where they won't be disturbed while on the trail.
- Do not leave any visible invitations to the thief. Whenever possible, stash everything in the trunk. If that's not possible, be sure any exposed item advertises that it has no value.
- Be suspicious of loiterers at the trailhead. Some thieves have become creative. With a pack in tow, they sit at the trailhead, presumably waiting for a ride. This allows them to observe easily the unloading, the stashing of items in the trunk, and the hiding of valuables. It also allows them to engage the hikers in conversation naturally, learning where they are going and when they'll return. It's easier than taking candy from babies; hikers won't squeal until they return to the vehicle.

For more detailed information about outdoor preparedness, there are many good instructional books and classes on outdoor etiquette, procedure, and safety. Even the outdoor veteran can benefit from a refresher, as field experts find better approaches to enjoy the outdoors safely, while minimizing the impact of user presence on the wild.

Note About Safety

Safety is an important concern in all outdoor activities. No guidebook can alert you to every hazard or anticipate the limitations of every reader. Therefore, the descriptions of roads, trails, routes, and natural features in this book are not representations that a particular place or excursion will be safe for your party. When you follow any of the routes described in this book, you assume responsibility for your own safety. Under normal conditions, such excursions require the usual attention to traffic, road and trail conditions, weather, terrain, the capabilities of your party, and other factors. Keeping informed on current conditions and exercising common sense are the keys to a safe, enjoyable outing.

The Mountaineers

Coastal forest

1 TILLAMOOK HEAD NATIONAL RECREATION TRAIL

Distance: 6 miles one way
Elevation change: 1,200 feet
Difficulty: Easy to moderate
Season: Year round
Map: None
For information: State Parks, Tillamook Regional Office

This national recreation trail (NRT) follows a historic Indian route across the headland. In 1806, an Indian youth guided William Clark and twelve others from the Lewis and Clark Expedition along this route—the first white men of record to visit Tillamook Head. The January 7, 1806, entry in Clark's journal describes the headland's nearly perpendicular sides, its cloud cap, the difficulty of the climb, and the fine view.

Clark named Ecola (Whale) Creek for a beached whale on a shore nearby—the quest of his headland journey. Rumors of the whale's demise prompted Clark to set out to obtain blubber and oil, vital for the expedition's return east.

Today, this trail is part of the greater Oregon Coast trail system. It travels a mostly forested inland route and offers views of Seaside, Cape Disappointment in Washington State, the mouth of the Columbia River, and the offshore 1880s-built Tillamook Lighthouse—a high seas- and weather-wrought rocky outpost, now abandoned to time and the will of the sea.

The northern trail terminus is found at the south end of Seaside. From South Holladay (US 101), turn west onto Avenue U, crossing the Necanicum River. At the northwest end of a golf course, turn south (left) onto Edgewood, which turns into Sunset Boulevard. Continue south to the end of Sunset for the marked trailhead.

The southern terminus lies in Ecola State Park. From the north end of Cannon Beach, turn west off US 101, following the signs for the state park. Trailheads are found at Indian Beach parking (closed in winter), or at Ecola Point parking (the southernmost area), adding 1.3 miles to the hike. The trail leaves from the north end of each parking area.

From the trailhead off Sunset in Seaside, the route journeys south through the Elmer Feldenheimer Forest Preserve before entering Ecola State Park. It tours a rich forest of western hemlock and Sitka spruce with an understory of mixed ferns, salal, *Maianthemum,* and salmonberry, thimbleberry, and huckleberry. A thick mossy carpet spreads beneath the profusion. The gradually climbing trail is rock-studded in places.

Between 0.6 and 1.2 miles, switchbacks advance the trail. Marshy areas dot the route even in early summer. The climb then eases, as the trail passes beneath an alder canopy. In an area long ago logged, salmonberry bushes hug the path.

By 2 miles, the trail settles into an easy rolling course, passing through a forest of mid-sized hemlock with a few old-growth Sitka spruce. Oxalis blankets the floor. The trail then travels a corridor with

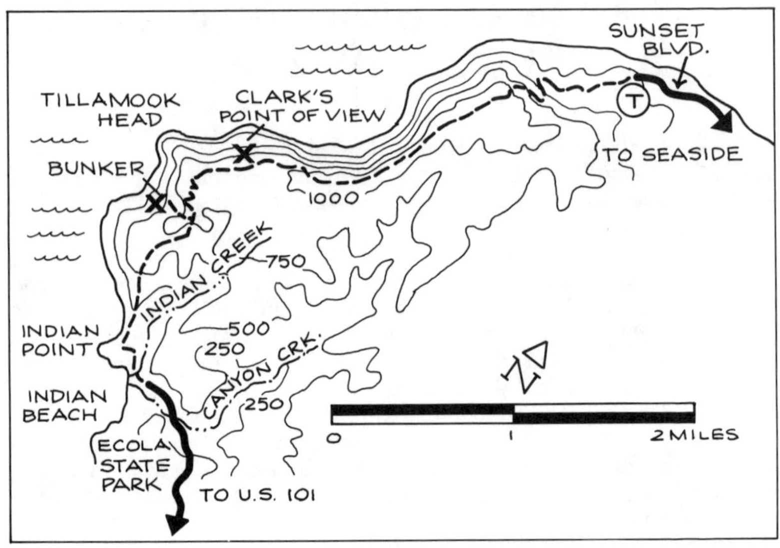

alder and clearcuts on one side and ocean cliffs and limited vistas on the other. The roar of the wind and the surf are strongly audible from here.

At the 2.4-mile mark, the trail affords an open ocean vista of the headland and Tillamook Rock and Lighthouse; tree-filtered views follow. Less than a mile farther is a 60-foot detour to Clark's Point of View—the standout vista of the trek. It features a long-distance view to the north. Beyond the vista, choked forest and salmonberry thickets frame the trail's descent.

The trail arrives at Tillamook Camp, an open area with tables and a pit toilet, at 4.4 miles. A detour west from the camp leads to a World War II gun-encampment bunker. Exploration of this moss-decked concrete bunker requires a flashlight. To the west of the bunker is a coastal vista including Tillamook Rock and Lighthouse, a black sandy beach far below, and the offshore rocks where seabirds nest.

Forgoing the detour, the NRT continues its descent from Tillamook Camp, passing through forest, dense coastal thicket, a fern meadow marked by large alders, and a Sitka spruce forest close to the ocean cliffs. Along the way, a few more lighthouse views are available through the thick branchwork.

Approaching Indian Creek, the trail offers a view of Indian Beach, an inviting strand wrapping along a large cove. Offshore rocks punctuate the sea off Ecola Point to the south; wind-whipped trees top the point. The headland trail then crosses Indian Creek and descends to Indian Beach parking. A side trip to the beach finds shell mounds recording the early Indian occupancy of this area.

From Indian Beach parking, hikers may continue south along the Oregon Coast Trail to Ecola Point.

2 NEHALEM SPIT HIKE

Distance: 4-mile loop (optional tour possibilities)
Elevation change: Minimal
Difficulty: Easy
Season: Year round
Map: None
For information: State Parks, Tillamook Regional Office
Nehalem Bay State Park

The Nehalem Spit offers coastal beach, bay shore, and vegetated, reclaimed dunes hiking with beach–bay, inland–beach, and inland–bay circuits possible. Hikers find trip-planning flexibility when confronting tide, wind, and weather and when considering the degree of effort and the potential for discovery. The spit's vegetated interior provides some foul-weather protection; the ocean beach offers the easiest walk.

The park provides access to an extensive, open beach stretching north from the Nehalem River mouth to Oswald West State Park. Much of the way, the beach features a wide, relaxing, sandy strand bordered by high dunes. The spit tour samples only the 2-mile southern tip. Beachcombers looking to lengthen their visit need only to look north.

For the bay tour, an old pair of sneakers and a carefree attitude toward mud and water prove helpful. Crab boats often work the bay; during low and minus tides, clammers probe the sinking shore for soft-shelled clams. The fish runs on the Nehalem River attract an enthusiastic following of harbor seals. Agates washed down from the coastal mountains entice the baycomber.

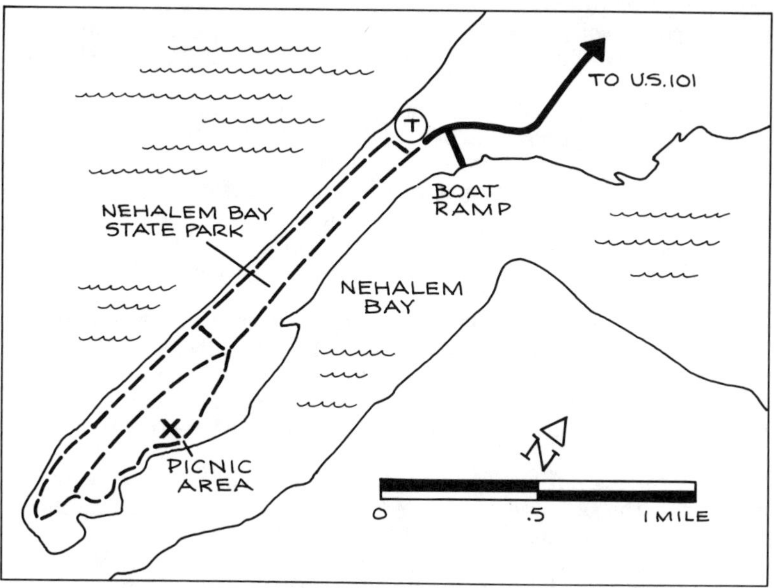

Nehalem Spit beach and Neahkahnie Mountain

The Nehalem Bay estuary and the ocean shore host sandpipers, scoters, western grebe, and a variety of ducks. Several hundred bird species occupy the bay area, including hummingbirds (seen along the reclaimed dune of the spit) and bald eagles (sometimes seen in flight or in the treetops overlooking the bay).

To reach the spit, from US 101, 3 miles south of Manzanita, turn west at the sign for Nehalem Bay State Park. The trailhead is located at the day-use parking area: The ocean–beach route journeys west from the comfort station, the bay access lies just to the north at the park boat launch, and the interior route leaves the south end of the parking area.

The inland route and a horse trail merge, touring a corridor of Scotch broom, shorepine, a few small spruce, and dune grass. Side paths branch to the ocean and bay; farther along, the scrub grows too thick for any off-trail navigation. Beds of loose sand work the legs.

At 1.2 miles, the track splits: The horse trail branches west to cross the foredune to the beach. The left fork crosses the reclaimed dune to reach a picnic site overlooking the bay in 0.5 mile. Stay on the central path continuing south toward the river mouth. At 1.7 miles, looking east finds a small seasonal wetland often active with birds. Near the end of the spit, the trail again forks: The right branch ventures toward the drift-log litter of the ocean–bay beach; the left branch journeys eastward toward the bay.

Opting for the left branch, at 2 miles, hikers reach the bay with the riprap from the jetty and its big sandy bar. Gulls, cormorants, and shorebirds frequent this site where fresh and salt water meet.

The bay route continues the loop traveling the 0.25-mile stretch of riprap upstream, passing between the previously mentioned wetland and bay. Be quiet upon leaving the riprap, as harbor seals, in numbers upward to 100, haul out on the beach to sun; bring binoculars and maintain a respectful distance.

From the end of the riprap, look for a cedar post atop the dune to the west. The post marks the location of the picnic site with tables and a pit toilet. Hiking the 2-track away from the picnic area returns to the 1.2-mile junction.

The return along the bay completes the 4-mile inland-bay loop at the state park boat launch. This option requires the tide's cooperation, but normally a fair strip of beach exists for most of the tour.

Wind-blown dune grasses and shorepines vegetate the ledge above shore. On the opposite bank, small communities intersperse the second-growth–forested hillsides. The damp, sinking sand provides a fun workout.

Midway along the bay, the trail passes an old boat launch constructed of big tree trunks. Past it, the beach is littered with rock cobbles and remains so to the end of the bay tour.

Returning from the end of the spit by oceanside is relaxing, with the wind, the surf, and simple discoveries along the way. Horseback riders share the beach.

To the north, Neahkahnie Mountain (elevation 1,631 feet) presides over the stage, often being masked and unmasked by the fog.

3 HART'S COVE TRAIL

Distance: 5.4 miles round trip
Elevation change: 600 feet
Difficulty: Moderate
Season: Year round
Map: USFS Siuslaw
For information: Hebo Ranger District

This trail travels a portion of the 9,670-acre Cascade Head Scenic Research Area, created in 1974. The designation recognizes the headland's beauty and value as a natural laboratory. Along the headland's south border, more land is being brought under public ownership in order to return the Salmon River estuary to nature's hand, further adding to the area offering.

Cascade Head rises 1,800 feet above the ocean. The site features both ancient and second-growth coastal forests of western hemlock and Sitka spruce, alder-lined drainages, vertical cliffs, and native prairies. The prairie meadows support such rare plant species as the catchfly and the hairy checker mallow and prove a vital hatching site for the rare silver-spot butterfly. The headland is so named because it houses three creeks which pass through deep-cut gorges to cascade some 60 to 80 feet to the ocean.

Hart's Cove Trail applauds many of these headland features. When bathed by the sun, the trail's relaxing meadow destination invites the kicking-off of boots and the use of the day pack as a pillow. At other times, veils of drifting fog; a stinging, chill breeze; and the piercing cry of an oystercatcher awaken the senses.

From November to March, during the gray whale migrations, the meadow site serves as an ideal watch post; the glistening heads of sea lions may be spied at any time. A bald eagle often roosts on a snag above Hart's Cove, where Chitwood Creek cascades to the ocean. The fortunate may even discover a puffin among the passing seabirds. Binoculars are worth their portage.

On US 101, travel 3.5 miles north from the US 101–OR 18 junction or 3.3 miles south from Neskowin, and turn west onto gravel FR 1861 (Cascade Head Road). Trailhead parking is at the road's end in 4 miles. The route bypasses the Cascade Head Nature Conservancy Preserve; signs mark the junctions.

The trail begins with a set of relatively steep, quick downhill switchbacks passing through an alder stand and a choked second-growth hemlock forest. The noise of Cliff Creek precedes its appearance. Salmonberry now grows thickly along the trail and down the slope to the creek. At 0.75 mile, the trail crosses Cliff Creek bridge to enter an old-growth gallery of fabulous stout, tall Sitka spruce with their scenic outstretched arms.

The forest bursts with beauty and diversity. Snags riddle the multistoried grove, harboring secret bounties of living organisms. Ferns deck the floor. Periodic mileage markers record the hiker's progress.

The grade of the trail flattens with the rounding of the slope. Some fine examples of witches'-broom (irregular, matted, fanning boughs) punctuate the hemlock canopy. At 1.2 miles, the sound of the surf and the barking of sea lions confirm that this is indeed a coastal trek. For the most part, the forest thickness defies views. To the south, sea lions sometimes

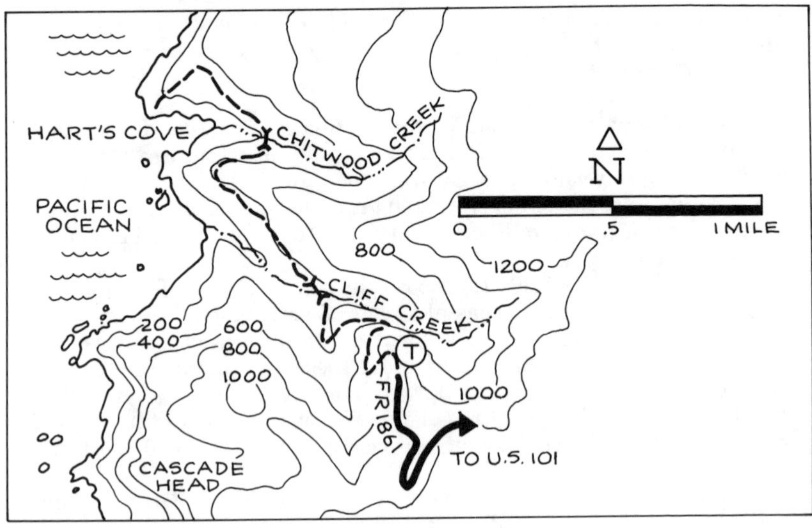

Sitka spruce above Hart's Cove

haul out on an inaccessible beach at the base of the cliffs. The abundant salmonberry amid the coastal scrub turns back those who would venture off trail for a glimpse.

By 1.5 miles, the trail is touring a steep, forested slope above the ocean. An interpretive sign ahead announces the Neskowin Crest Research Natural Area. Through forest succession, western hemlocks will slowly replace the area's 250-year-old spruce trees that have survived past fires.

The bench at Hart's Cove Viewpoint invites a brief stop for a view of the grassy headland destination footed by steep, dark cliffs. Branches intrude on the view.

Gulls, red-tailed hawks, pigeon guillemots, and woodpeckers provide variety for bird-watching. The barks of the sea lions grow faint, as the trail drifts inland to round Hart's Cove. Dense salmonberry with sword ferns and an occasional massive Sitka spruce frame the path. Across Chitwood Creek, the forest briefly opens up, but big trees again house the trail before it reaches the meadow-topped headland.

The now-narrow trail descends through the meadow, offering southern views of Two Arches, an offshore rock with side-by-side ocean gateways, and an overlook of Hart's Cove with its steep moss-decked cliffs, cascade, seascape, and nearby weather-shaped trees. Views to the north feature Capes Kiwanda and Lookout and a large offshore island. Explorations across the grassland add a western vista, overlooking the offshore rocks with their various seabird and shorebird nesters and visitors.

Return as you came.

4 SOUTH BEACH HIKE

Distance: 9 miles one way
Elevation change: None
Difficulty: Easy to moderate
Season: Year round
Map: None
For information: State Parks, Tillamook Regional Office

This central Oregon coast trek is characteristic of the beach explorations that neighbor the state's coastal communities—a broad, sandy strand of tension-erasing walking, marred occasionally by rooftops and the noise of US 101. Along the way, ample opportunity exists for the solitary appreciation of surf and sand. The hike travels from Yaquina Bay's South Jetty to Seal Rock, interrupted by Beaver Creek near Ona Beach.

The 0.5-mile long, 1880s-built South Jetty was the first of its kind constructed on the Pacific Coast. Jetty views feature the Yaquina Bay Bridge, the fishing boats exiting the bay, and the year-round channel residents: gulls, grebes, sea lions, and seals. Near the hike's start, the Oregon State University Marine Science Center invites a detour with its displays and information on marine life, coastal geology, tides, and estuaries.

The cliffs of Seal Rock Head present an imposing "stop sign" to the journey. Here, a ledge of partially submerged rocks parallels the coastline; the highest rises 20 feet above the water. In the late 1800s, these rocks attracted great numbers of seals and sea lions, hence the site's name.

Multiple access points just off US 101 serve the hiker. At Newport, from the south end of the Yaquina Bay Bridge, take the turn marked for the Hatfield Marine Center–South Jetty and follow 26th Street west to the Jetty Road or park at Bridgehead Day Use, and walk to the jetty. South Beach, Lost Creek, and Ona Beach state parks likewise offer easy access to this beach route.

Beginning a north to south tour, hikers find sands from the dunes have drifted against and over the top of South Jetty. Scattered cobbles, shell fragments, and a few fossilized shells litter the beach. Waves rushing to shore break at irregular intervals. Sandpipers and gulls are commonly viewed, with wintering loons less so.

At 1 mile, a broad break in the foredune signals the arrival at South Beach State Park; it provides access to a comfort station, picnic area, and day-use parking area.

The trek crosses four main creeks en route to Lost Creek State Park; most are easily negotiated via rock hops or easy wades as they fan out to the ocean. Henderson Creek, at 1.5 miles, marks the transition between the dunes and the 20- to 30-foot-high bluffs.

At 2.1 miles, the beach hike passes a low dip in the hillside where shore pine and Sitka spruce come down to the edge of the beach. In another 0.5 mile, the cliffs undergo a change: Now, a dark, eroding sandstone cliff with embedded fossils lines the sandy avenue.

Ahead, the route rounds a small point. Especially high tides may turn

Boulders revealed at low tide near Seal Rock

hikers back or suggest a wading. Over-the-shoulder views find Yaquina Lighthouse.

At 3.5 and again at 5 miles, patches of beach gravel draw the agate collector. From the second gravel patch, the fence to Lost Creek State Park is visible atop the bluff ahead; Seal Rock Head rises to the south. At 5.25 miles, a 0.1-mile path travels up a coastal-scrub corridor to the Lost Creek picnic area.

Across the rocky drainage, the beach trek continues traveling the wide strand below an orange-hued sandstone cliff. Wind-sculpted spruce and pine accent its top. A dune border replaces the bluffs as the hike arrives at the shore of Beaver Creek (6.75 miles). The usual collection of gulls gather at this freshwater site. Continuing the tour usually requires a detour to US 101 and Ona Beach State Park for a footbridge crossing of the creek to return to the beach; fordings are possible when waters and tides are low.

By 7.25 miles, occasional rock outcrops punctuate the strand, followed by a chain of bedrock tidepools with some eye-catching, round boulders revealed at low tide. Anemone, barnacles, eelgrass, fish, and fossils are among the secluded treasures of the pools.

At 8 miles, the trail passes a small beach access at the community of Seal Rock. After this, the route crosses tiny Deer Creek. Scoters ride the surf. From 8.5 miles to 9 miles, low tides and the parallel, sometimes water-isolated rock ledges create a snug cove leading up to Seal Rock Head with its surf-carved hollows. Beware the tide when exploring this arm of beach; it's a steep climb up the cliff to safety.

Although an unauthorized footpath does angle to Seal Rock Wayside atop the headland, return to the public access 1 mile north to spare the cliff from further erosion.

5 HECETA BEACH TO BAKER BEACH HIKE

Distance: 6.4 miles one way
Elevation change: None
Difficulty: Moderate
Season: Year round (though the influence of high tide and high waters in Sutton Creek may suggest two separate beach tours)
Map: USFS Siuslaw
For information: Mapleton Ranger District

This south to north beach hike ties together the civilized Heceta Beach and the wilder Baker Beach with a Sutton Creek fording. Part of the greater Coos Bay Dune Sheet, Baker Beach offers just a smack of the setting found along the premier dune fields and beach strips of Oregon Dunes National Recreation Area to the south.

Sutton Creek estuary

The Heceta Beach portion of this hike spans northward from the Siuslaw River mouth at North Jetty. Located between bay stillness and ocean surf, North Jetty offers calm-seas strolling with an even walking surface for its first 300 yards; beyond lies a rock jumble with filled-in cracks. Sea lions make splashy dives upon a hiker's approach. Harbor seals venture closer, conducting their characteristic wide-eyed study of the jetty passersby. Gulls dot the rocky tongue.

Both Heceta and Baker beaches offer broad, flat, sandy strands mostly bordered by low, grass-capped dunes. Northward-looking views include the Heceta Beach community, Heceta Head, its lighthouse, and the cliffs and headland at Sea Lion Caves. The dune buffer to Baker Beach invites side trips for investigation, play, and beach overlooks. This deeper dune field holds rounded 10- to 20-foot-high mounds with dips, rises, and shallow depressions.

Sutton Creek marks the start of Sutton Creek Recreation Area. Spreading to the east, its twelve habitats, including dunes, a darlingtonia bog, and coastal lakes, nurture a wildlife diversity of some 300 species. Beach-goers witness the varied birdlife attracted to the estuary.

To reach Heceta Beach, at the OR 126–US 101 junction in Florence, go west on 9th Street. At the T-junction with Rhododendron Drive in 0.9 mile, turn right following the signs to Siuslaw estuary and ocean beaches. After traveling 2.8 miles north, turn left onto Jetty Road to find beach parking in another mile.

To reach Baker Beach, on US 101, go 5.6 miles north of Florence, and turn west onto the 2-lane, gravel Baker Beach Road. A broad, undeveloped beach parking area is at the road's end in 0.4 mile. A 0.3-mile footpath winds through the coastal scrub and around and over the dunes to arrive at the beach; beware an invading, unyielding spiny shrub amid the vegetation.

A northbound trek from North Jetty begins along a relatively unspoiled beach. The softer sands near the low dunes hold a changing art show of wind patterns; the wave-washed sands promise easier walking. The thin veil of receding water tosses back perfect reflections of the ever-darting shorebirds, while the washed sands reveal the countless holes of unseen crustaceans. Shell fragments dot the beach.

By 0.8 mile, the rooftops of Heceta Beach rise above the dunes. Going another 0.5 mile finds a Lane County beach access and parking area at the north side of Driftwood Shores. While the neutral-colored beach houses that line this strip are not overly intrusive, they do steal from the feeling of escape.

At 2.3 miles, hikers reach the mouth of Sutton Creek. For most, the warm days and low waters of summer alone suggest a fording for a continuous beach tour.

On the opposite shore lies a drift log–littered flat between the ocean beach and Sutton Creek estuary. A wilder, little-traveled beach strip awaits. By 2.7 miles, low, rolling dunes shield the estuary from the beach. At 3.7 miles, the tops of the wind-sculpted spruce on the east shore announce Holman Vista, an estuary overlook. From atop the dunes, hikers can see the observation deck. Here, too, finds the end of the creek's parallel course to the beach.

Horseback riders have access to Baker Beach. Occasionally hikers will see a solitary rider and horse splashing along the tide line—a postcard silhouette, when looking into the bright afternoon sun.

In another half mile, the angle of the cliffs block the views of Heceta Head Lighthouse, and beginning at 5.1 miles, pole markers signal routes across the dunes to the Baker Beach access parking. Ahead finds the outlet to Lily Lake. It requires a fording to tour the final mile of beach to the coastal cliffs. The sight and sounds of US 101 intrude here.

From the foot of the cliffs, backtrack to the Baker Beach access markers and travel across the dunes to the parking area.

6 THREEMILE LAKE–TAHKENITCH DUNE LOOP

Distance: 6.5-mile loop
Elevation change: 400 feet
Difficulty: Easy to moderate
Season: Year round

Map: USFS Oregon Dunes National Recreation Area
For information: Oregon Dunes National Recreation Area

This circuit provides a snapshot of the 32,000-acre national recreation area (NRA): a playground of "living" sands, freshwater lakes, a dune–

Trail sign on foredune overlooking beach

transition conifer forest, and open beach. The dunes offer exploration closed to off-road vehicles (ORVs), while the beach portion remains open to them.

Although off-season encounters with the machines are rare, between tides their tracks leave a lingering record. Still the beach tour is pleasant with findings of kelp tangles, clam shells, jellyfish, and crab parts and the passings of cormorants and gulls. The surf races to shore in lined-up breakers of threes and fours.

Threemile Lake is a long, isolated freshwater lake pinched at its middle. The trail approaches but does not suggest a lakeshore access; that's left to the hiker's device. While no formal backcountry camps ex-

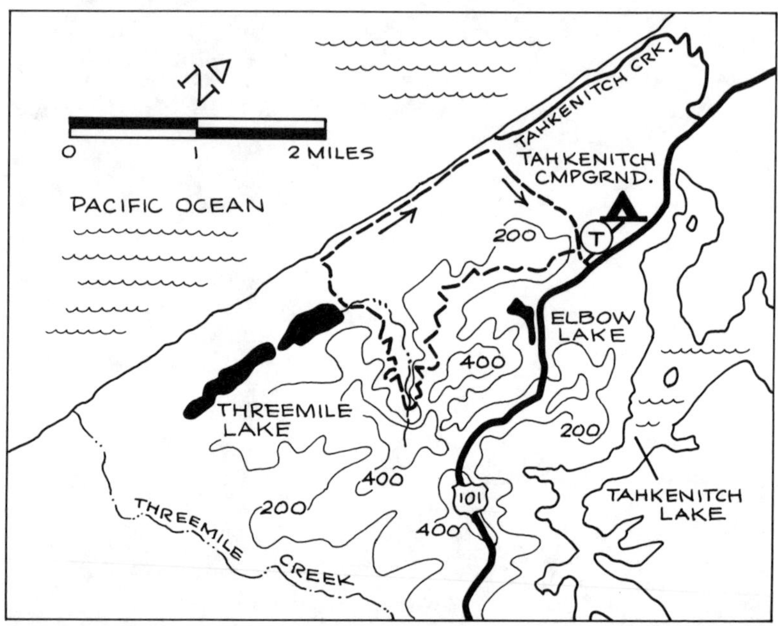

ist, no-trace camping is allowed near the lake.

The open dunes between the lake and the beach and Tahkenitch Dune, farther north, offer natural fun and discovery. The coarse beach grass whips designs in the sand, while the winds shift, mold, and remodel the dunes. The tracks of mice and deer and lacy insect signatures ornament the ever-changing canvas.

The transition forests house the greatest variety of NRA wildlife—some 145 species. Hummingbird, towhee, woodpecker, varied thrush, and olive-sided flycatcher are commonly spied. The area's older forests shelter deer, coyote, and eight species of salamander.

On US 101, travel 7.7 miles north from the US 101–OR 38 junction in Reedsport or 12.5 miles south from Florence, and turn west for Tahkenitch Campground. The marked trailhead and day parking area are found at the southwest corner of the campground.

A wide trail of easy grade ascends a corridor of thick coastal vegetation to reach the 0.25-mile trail junction. A clockwise loop begins via the lake trail.

Noise from US 101 accompanies the hiker on the first stretch of this tour, as it wraps around and over the rolling terrain passing through forests of second-growth western hemlock, young Douglas fir, and classic choked, second-growth Sitka spruce. Red and black huckleberry, salal, and sword fern form the understory. Red alder and salmonberry claim the drainages.

At 0.5 mile, a bench overlooks Elbow Lake, a large, bowed coastal lake. Soon after, the trail crosses the slip face of a U-shaped dune with its loose, wind-deposited sands. It then returns to forest. A bench at 1.4 miles offers a forest-gap view of the advancing surf, the wide beach, and Tahkenitch Creek mouth. The sound of the surf rides to this remote post.

At 3 miles, spring-fed rills announce Threemile Lake. A quarter mile beyond the outlet footbridge, the lake trail ends on the crest of a vegetated dune overlooking the lake, the dunes, the beach, and ocean.

For the next 0.5 mile, the circuit follows the blue-banded cedar posts west across the open dune. At the deflation plain, hikers may continue to the beach and follow it north to Tahkenitch Creek or follow the less-traveled deflation-plain trail north through the coastal scrub, avoiding the chance encounter with ORVs.

Opting for the beach route, hike 1.25 miles north. Where the dune border flattens prior to reaching the Tahkenitch Creek mouth, keep a sharp eye for the blue-banded post on the rise to the east signaling the Tahkenitch Dune Trail. (Hikers touring counterclockwise need to be especially alert, as the small, brown hiker sign marking the inland turn from the beach to Threemile Lake is easily bypassed and has no landmark.)

A side drainage may separate the beach from the dune trail at 5 miles, but an informal log-and-plank bridge usually allows a dry crossing. Before heading inland, hikers may wish to linger at Tahkenitch Creek, a good place to view both shorebirds and songbirds.

Across the drainage, the deflation-plain spur enters from the south; the dune trail continues east passing through shore pine-scrub to travel the open sand at the south end of Tahkenitch Dune—the major dune ridge spreading north. Beach grass, seashore lupine, and coast strawberry anchor patches of the shifting sand.

As the trail enters the forest, a bench affords a farewell look at the dunes and beach. A wonderful canopy of hemlock, cedar, and fir above a bountiful, green-bursting understory with rhododendron creates a mood different from the dark Sitka stands seen earlier.

Noise from US 101 returns as the loop draws to a close at the initial trail junction. Return downhill.

7 ESTUARY STUDY TRAIL

Distance: 3.6 miles round trip
Elevation change: 300 feet
Difficulty: Easy to moderate
Season: Year round
Map: Estuary Study Trail brochure
For information: South Slough National Estuarine Reserve

A southern extension to Coos Bay, this drowned river mouth is home to the nation's first ever estuarine reserve—South Slough. Established in 1974, it houses 4,400 acres of natural laboratory. The estuary habitat (where fresh and salt water merge) is among the world's most vital and productive, nourishing vast fisheries and wildlife populations.

South Slough pilings

The forested uplands shelter bobcat, raccoon, deer, and eagle. The open channels feed fish and invertebrates, while the tidal flats nurture shellfish, shrimp, and worms. Salt-tolerant plants, including grasses and pickleweed, filter the estuary waters.

Over time, more than half of the area's estuary wetland has been filled in, drained, or otherwise claimed. The South Slough area itself has been used for logging (with a railroad to carry the logs to the open water for rafting to mills), ranching, and farming. The reserve's Valino Island housed a casino where loggers passed their time and spent their money. By the 1930s, though, this estuary had begun its return to nature's hand.

Today, the reserve's goals of research, education, and low-impact recreation serve the naturalist well. The sanctuary is open year round. Except holidays, its center is open 8:30 A.M. to 4:30 P.M. weekdays (daily in summer). Films, displays, self- and interpreter-guided walks, a canoe trail, and the study trail introduce the slough's features. Trail and slough brochures are readily available; routes are well marked.

From North Bend–Coos Bay on US 101, go west on Cape Arago Highway toward Charleston. At the east end of Charleston, turn south on Seven Devils Road (a sign indicates this route to the reserve). The visitor center is in 4 miles.

At the Interpretive Center hilltop, the 10-Minute Nature Trail introduces the coastal scrub community and launches the Estuary Study Trail—a self-guided interpretive route, the reserve's longest trail.

At a marked spur, the study trail leaves the nature trail and descends the canyon hillside. En route to the slough, it tours a scrub corridor of salal, waxmyrtle, and huckleberry; a choked second-growth hemlock and cedar forest; and a more open, mixed forest.

At the 0.75-mile junction, bear left on the narrow dirt road to continue toward the slough; the path heading uphill leads to the trailhead off the visitor center spur road.

Taking either path at the 0.9-mile junction eventually finds South Slough pilings. The trail to the right follows the Hidden Creek boardwalk downstream passing through a skunk cabbage bog. The cupped yellow bloom and pungent scent of the cabbage are the first heralds of spring. Its leaves can measure up to 4 feet long, amazing bog visitors well through the summer.

Ahead, a second boardwalk crosses a salt-marsh meadow to reach the slough observation tower set amid a stand of ancient Sitka spruce. This post at 1.3 miles holds the nicest overlook of the slough mudflats, open water, and rimming forest—a picture that changes with the tide.

At the junction near the tower, the route bears right ascending the hillside via the Tunnel Trail. This snaking footpath passes through thick, young forest to arrive at the Slough Overlook (1.7 miles), which holds only a strained look at the slough. A nonflush toilet is found nearby.

From the vista, descend the hilltop to reach the Timber Trail near the spur to Rhode's Dike. Going right leads to the South Slough pilings and the end of the trail at 2.1 miles.

The boardwalk of Sloughside Dike offers the best up close look at the slough. Here, the main slough body features mudflats, tidal channels,

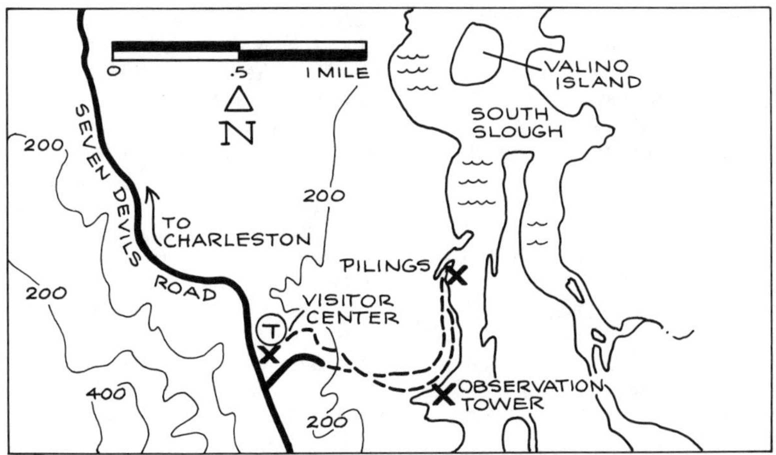

and saltwater marsh. The pilings record the former railroad-logging days and serve as lichen- and moss-coated roosts for gulls, herons, and other birds. Osprey, caspian tern, sandpiper, merganser, vulture, kingfisher, yellowlegs, canvasback, and brant goose provide varied sightings through the binocular window.

The patterns of the water's rise and retreat etch the face of the mudflat. Bubbles pass through a system of burrows rising to the mud's surface. Animal tracks and otter slides may sometimes be spied along the banks. Opportunities for nature study and relaxation abound along the shore of the slough.

To return to the center, follow the 1.5-mile Timber Trail from the slough. Along the way, a brief leafy tunnel claims the path, and a marked patch of sundews—low-growing, insect-eating plants—suggests a stop.

8 NEW RIVER BEACH HIKE

Distance: 19 miles round trip
Elevation change: None
Difficulty: Strenuous
Season: Year round (BLM may post area closures during critical nesting time, April–August)
Map: Unnecessary
For information: Coos Bay District BLM

Isolated by river and private ranch property, this long, sandy strip is presently only accessible via small craft, paddling across the New River, or by hiking north 3.25 miles through undeveloped Floras Lake State Park on an unmarked trail. The river approach holds the most straightforward access to this coastal strip—Oregon's wildest stretch of beach.

Created by pioneers to make pastureland, New River is less than 100 years old. It flows 10 miles north from Floras Lake to enter the ocean. In summer, the flows in sections of this river grow minimal.

The New River, with its drained floodplain and sandy meadow, is returning to a viable coastal dune-estuarine ecosystem. In 1989, the Nature Conservancy signed an agreement with the Bureau of Land Management (BLM) to protect this area, assisting in the purchase of private lands in order to preclude development and keep the area natural.

New River, an Area of Critical Environmental Concern since 1983, supports a wildlife diversity that includes both threatened and endangered species: the western snowy plover, American and Arctic peregrine falcons, the Aleutian Canada goose, and the bald eagle. The planned natural area would include some 9 miles of coastline between Bandon State Park and Floras Lake.

From the New River access, the primary hiker route journeys south past Floras Lake to conclude where the cliffs and sea suggest a turnaround, offering a solitary stroll along an unspoiled avenue of sand.

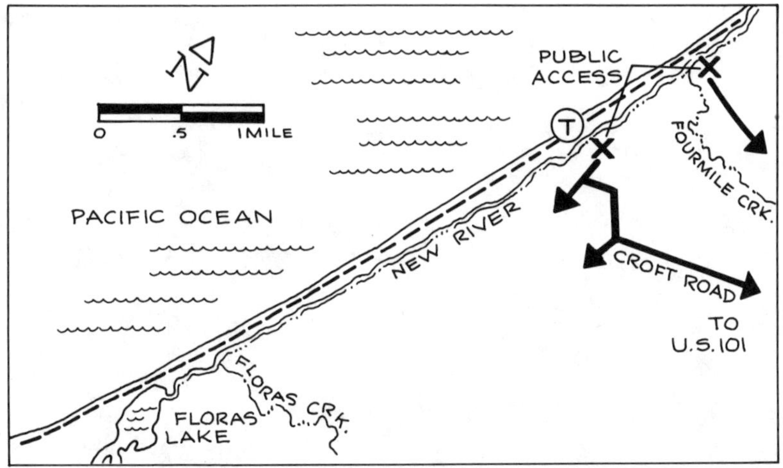

Views feature Blacklock Point and Cape Blanco Lighthouse.

For the easiest river access, from US 101, 8.8 miles south of Bandon, turn west onto Croft Road. After going 1.5 miles, bear right on the 1-lane gravel road, soon entering BLM property. At the T-junction in 0.8 mile, go right to reach the boat launch site in another 0.2 mile.

After rowing across New River, a long-distance hike awaits to the south. The winter surf whips up and deposits trails of foam along the tide line, passing swans and "V"s of geese draw the eyes skyward, and the ocean backwash creates a comforting hush. Ahead the tour passes a BLM sign indicating no motor vehicles on the beach—the official endorsement to a wilderness trek.

The intermittent low dunes allow cross-views to the coastal mountains. Approaching the dunes, hikers can overlook New River, which sometimes displays a marshy character and shows a few islands. The numerous bird and animal tracks and insect signatures record the vital wildlife habitat of the dune area, but avoid traveling this area—the rare silvery phacelia grows here and shorebirds nest along and on the dunes.

Beginning at 2.5 miles and continuing much of the way to Floras Lake, the beach consists of rolling, loose sand. The curled lip or slope of the beach adds to the workout and tests the ankles. Over-the-shoulder looks find Bandon Rocks; farther south, the eroding cliffs, Blacklock Point, and Cape Blanco Lighthouse come into view.

In places, strings of broken shells, washed rocks, and agates invite combers to kneel and look closely; the occasional whole sand dollar rides to shore. Deer crossing the low dunes provide surprise encounters. Between 7.25 and 7.75 miles, the dune border gives way to a log-littered flat between the ocean and the river for additional views of the coastal hills. In the early morning, owls and hawks call from places beyond, in the low dunes or on the far shore.

Sea kelp graveyards, drift logs, sneaker waves, and loose, dark sand

Beachcomber, New River beach

await as the beach tour rounds the sloping base of a 10-foot-high dune ridge. Ahead lies the dune breach to Floras Lake (8 miles). Floras Lake is a large, coastal lake with grassy points and a dune and Sitka spruce shore. It attracts swans, geese, ducks, and more, while marsh hawks patrol its grassy rim.

As the hike continues south from the lake, eroding sandstone bluffs frame the beach; weathering has given them bizarre faces. Larger cliffs rise above the beach and offshore rocks punctuate the surf, as the avenue of sand becomes precariously reduced by sea and cliff. This is the turnaround point for the southern tour.

For a northbound trek from the river access point, hikers must continue to port a flotation device for the dry transport of selves and/or gear across the mouth of New River in about 2 miles. Low tides and the reduced waters of summer alone may permit wading or swimming across the river.

Once across, hikers find the rustic beach-goers' "Hilton," a fine campsite of character. The northern stretch of beach becomes increasingly "civilized" as it approaches Bandon State Park and Face Rock Wayside, but it holds grand vistas of both nearshore and offshore rocks.

9 OREGON COAST TRAIL

Distance: 10.3 miles one way
Elevation change: 400 feet
Difficulty: Strenuous
Season: Year round
Map: USGS Brookings, Carpenterville; USFS Siskiyou
For information: State Parks, Coos Bay Regional Office
Boardman State Park

This snatch of the extensive Oregon Coast Trail provides an encapsulated look at the offerings of this premier trail system: rugged headlands, secluded beaches, shifting sands, ocean and shoreline vistas, and coastal wildlife sightings. The trail tours meadow, thicket, alder grove, and Sitka spruce forest, as it dips deep into canyons and marches sharply up the headlands. Brief US 101 interruptions punctuate the route.

Gulls, storm petrels, murres, auklets, and puffins nest on the offshore rocks, part of Oregon Islands National Wildlife Refuge. Natural bridges, arches, and blow holes are among the scenic rock features.

Multiple day-use picnic and parking areas west off US 101 access this trail segment. Points of access begin 4 miles north of Brookings and 15

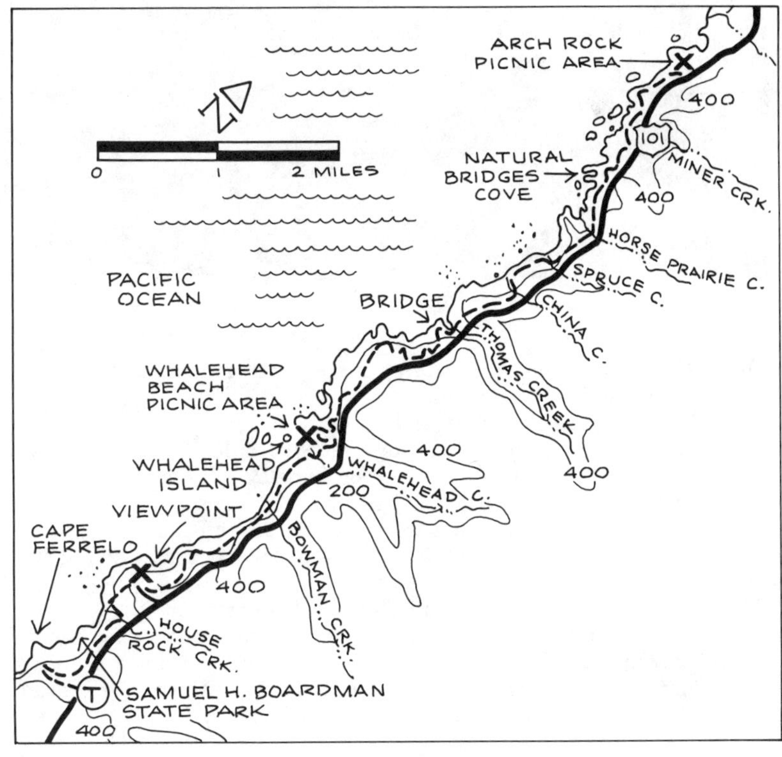

Whalehead Cove

miles south of Gold Beach, providing hikers with numerous short and hopscotch-shuttle hike opportunities.

Cape Ferrelo, at the southern end of the trail, invites a headland detour before the journey north. Hiking south 0.5-mile across the grassy summit meadow finds a vista overlooking Lone Ranch Beach and spanning the coastline north to south from Natural Bridges to Goat Island—an oceanscape of coves, beach parcels, headlands, offshore rocks, and ceaseless blue water. During winter migrations, whale spouts signal offshore pods. Winds often buffet the summit.

The main tour of the Oregon Coast Trail heads north, passing through coastal meadow and scrub and touring forest to find tree-rimmed House Rock Viewpoint in 1.3 miles; finer views await. At 1.9 miles, a rocky ridge affords a northward-looking view of the ragged shore, Whalehead Cove, and distant Humbug Mountain.

Soon, the trail bears west leaving a section of old abandoned road to switchback down a grassy headland to arrive at the beach at 2.5 miles. Posts mark the trail. The route then follows north the boulder-strewn beach isolated by a vegetated, spruce-topped cliff. Fall and winter storms deposit kelp tangles, jellyfish, and seabird casualties on shore. Skunk and deer tracks mingle with those of seabirds. Just past the Bowman Creek crossing, the cliff shows a narrow cave hollow.

Wading Whalehead Creek, the hiker finds the Whalehead Beach Picnic Area at 3.3 miles. The often photographed Whalehead Island occupies center stage offshore. This rocky islet is so dubbed because a hollow on its seaward side and a hole in its top create the effect of a whale spout when the surf is just right.

The trail resumes uphill, near the junction of the picnic area road and US 101. It climbs the headland touring a shady Sitka spruce forest. Pale orange monkey flowers are the accents of late fall. At 3.5 miles, a side trail leads onto an open headland arm, a quiet retreat with a grand north-south coastal vista. Ahead, the main trail unfolds views of rocky channels, islands, and surging waters.

At 4.5 miles, the trail tags the edge of Indian Sands, a bluff outcrop of compacted and shifting sands, which drops away to the ocean in steep cliffs. Where the forest meets the sands, trail posts guide hikers northward. Thomas Creek Bridge commands the view. After the trail encircles a loose-sand bowl behind a tree island, it overlooks a fingery cove to the north.

It then descends into this dramatic, squeezed canyon. The opposite wall's stark, eroding cliff contrasts with the scrub-vegetated wall traveled by the trail. A steep ascent leads to US 101 and a short trail segment, before the Thomas Creek Bridge crossing.

En route to China Creek Beach, the trail drops into a dark, choked forest of Sitka spruce. At 6.7 miles, it arrives atop the grassy bench overlooking the wilderness strand; atop the bench is a nice campsite.

The trail then heads north along China Creek Beach. Deep drainage furrows mark the vegetated slope, and the offshore rocks create a natural sculpture garden. Low tides allow a rounding of the cliff (7.1 miles) to Spruce Creek Cove; a zigzag trail then connects Spruce Cove to US 101.

Still more US 101 trail interruptions occur near Horse Prairie Creek Canyon. The trail then settles into a longer coastal forest tour to reach the overlook of Natural Bridges Cove (8.3 miles), where natural gateways in a rock-arm extension of the cliff admit the sea to the cove in a wondrous display.

The trail continues north offering multiple looks at Thunder Rock, a similar rock outcrop with arch openings. After a forest and thicket tour, the trail arrives at Miners Creek Cove (9.2 miles), with its small beach looking out at a magnificent collection of bare and tree-capped offshore rocks.

The trail offers more coastal views as it draws to a close at Arch Rock Picnic Area (10.3 miles). Gulls pass by at eye level.

10 SADDLE MOUNTAIN TRAIL

Distance: 5.9 miles round trip (with spur)
Elevation change: 1,600 feet
Difficulty: Strenuous
Season: Spring through fall
Map: USGS Saddle Mountain
For information: State Parks, Tillamook Regional Office
Saddle Mountain State Park

Bald-topped Saddle Mountain (elevation 3,283 feet) affords one of the best vistas in Oregon's North Coast Range, spanning two states—Oregon and Washington. From the summit, the visitor has views of the Northwest volcano chain. Mounts Rainier, Saint Helens, Adams, and Hood punctuate the east with snowy crowned elegance. To the west, a clear day holds views of the Pacific Ocean, Astoria, and the Columbia River mouth. Temperature inversions add a dance of veils to the spectacle, as waves of fog drift inland to claim the river valleys.

While the vista is the primary draw, Saddle Mountain is also a noted botanical area, boasting some 300 flora species, including the rare crucifer, Saddle Mountain saxifrage, and Saddle Mountain bittercress, which grow only in this limited province. More common species which add color to the summit are Oregon iris, cinquefoil, nodding onion, and yellow fawn lily.

Saddle Mountain is one of three "islands" in the North Coast Range secluding rare alpine flora; the other two are nearby Onion Peak and Sugarloaf Mountain. Saddle Mountain offers a public window to this rare floral museum.

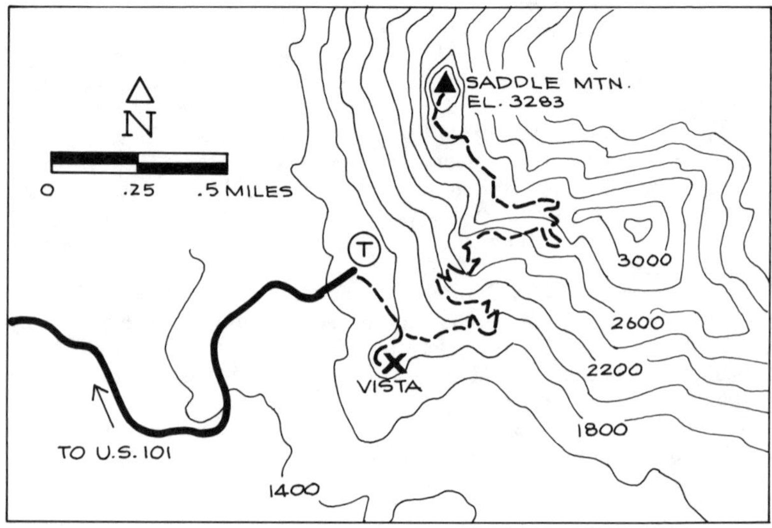

Saddle Mountain

Saddle Mountain figured in Native American legend explaining the creation of thunder and lightning, and it appears in the journals of Meriwether Lewis and William Clark. From its lookout, the Tillamook fire of 1933 was first reported; the lookout has since been dismantled.

Approaching from the coast, from the junction of US 101 and US 26, south of Seaside, travel 20 miles east on US 26. Arriving from the east via US 26, go 17.8 miles west past Jewell Junction. A sign for Saddle Mountain State Park marks the north turn. Go another 6.9 miles on winding, paved road to reach the park at road's end.

On summer weekends, spillover parking lines the road entering the park—a testament to the trail's popularity. Midweek and off-season visits promise a more peaceful encounter with the mountain.

Departing from the east side of the parking area, the trail begins as a wide, paved swath eventually becoming a foot trail. In 0.2 mile, a side trail branches to the right for a nice 0.25-mile side jaunt to an outcrop affording the first vista of the journey: a good look at Saddle Mountain, its pronounced volcanic dikes (raised rock veins), and the surrounding Coast Range.

Past the 0.2-mile junction, the main trail remains mostly shaded. Second-growth fir and alder stands reign above a varied undergrowth of cow parsnip, maidenhair fern, false Solomon's seal, vine maple, and thimbleberry. A steady stream of hikers courses over the trail, as groups of all ages challenge the summit.

At 1.1 miles, the trail pulls into the open. Shade now is prized; carry plenty of water. The trail becomes gravelly and riddled by shortcuts. Keeping to the trail protects vegetation and avoids adding to the problem of erosion.

The trail then tops the ridge at 2 miles, offering views to the north. Its open, thin-soiled meadow parades much of the springtime bounty: prairie smoke, Siskiyou fritillary, Indian paintbrush, and monkey flowers. The steep south-facing slope of Saddle Mountain houses a rare rock-garden community.

Unstable, crumbly rock slows and confounds the final 0.7-mile charge to the summit. Although the trail has undergone repairs to stabilize its bed, this stretch is not for the sneaker wearer; it's easy to lose your footing or twist an ankle.

The summit view rewards the effort. The grandeur of the volcano and ocean vistas is mediated only by broad sweeps of clearcut and the mostly denuded Humbug Mountain (save for the part which belongs to Saddle Mountain State Park). The park land spreading from the summit features mostly second-growth forest. Glass fragments hint at the one-time lookout site.

Return as you came, allowing adequate time for the first precarious leg of the descent. Do not stray from the path for better footing; the summit plantlife is fragile and must be protected.

11 HORSE CREEK TRAIL

Distance: 5.5 miles one way (when Drift Creek can be forded)
Elevation change: 1,200 feet
Difficulty: Moderate
Season: Year round
Map: USGS Tidewater; USFS Siuslaw
For information: Waldport Ranger District
Drift Creek Wilderness Area

This 5,800-acre wilderness represents one of the last bastions of untouched, ancient rain forest in the Coast Range. It seduces with old-growth tranquillity and the rushing beauty of Drift Creek. The rich multistory forest is an orchestration of texture, shape, color, and lighting. Douglas fir and western hemlock dominate the forest, red alder and bigleaf maple reign creekside, and everywhere cascading greenery dresses the forest floor.

Forest management practices spared this area from the saw blade and the road cut, by first designating it as a primitive area—not for development, then as a roadless area, and finally in 1984, as a wilderness area. The trail bears the unlikely name "Horse Creek Trail," as it is a fragment of the old forest-management trail of that name.

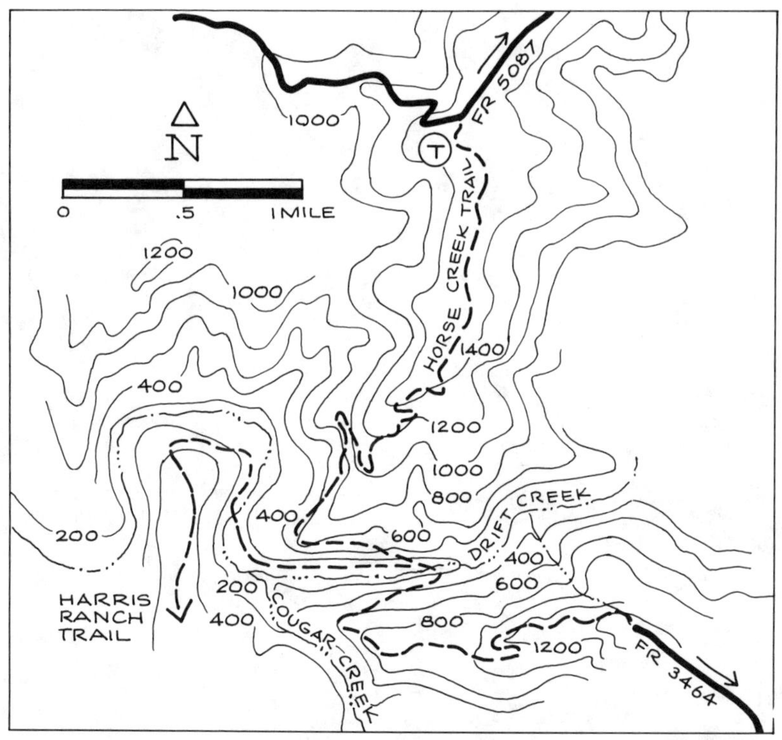

Drift Creek boasts wild runs of steelhead and coho and chinook salmon, as well as a resident population of crayfish and trout. Dippers dive into the chill waters.

The normally driving waters of Drift Creek isolate the two Horse Creek Trail fragments; only during late summer does the creek allow their linkage. During low waters, an alternative hike also presents itself, tying together Horse Creek Trail (north) and the Harris Ranch Trail. Each of these three interlocking trail fragments offers a slightly different window to the wilderness.

To reach the northern trailhead, from US 101 near Ona Beach State Park, turn east onto North Beaver Creek Road (County 602). After going 3.8 miles, turn right onto North Elkhorn Road, FR 51; look for the turn just past the Beaver Creek crossing.

Continue east on FR 51 for 5.8 miles to where the road comes to a T. There, turn left onto FR 50. At the trail sign in 1.3 miles, turn right onto FR 5087 (an improved-surface road easily passable for conventional vehicles). The marked trailhead is in 3.4 miles.

Entering from the south, from the US 101–OR 34 junction in Waldport, head east on OR 34 for 7.3 miles. After the Alsea River crossing, turn left onto Risley Creek Road, FR 3446, and continue another 7.3

Fungi, Drift Creek Wilderness

miles. At the trail sign, turn left onto FR 3464. The trailhead is at the end of the road in 1.6 miles.

When hiking north to south, the trail begins with an even grade, working its way along a ridge; the thick forest denies vistas. Elk usage of the trail shows in the breaking away of the soft shoulders and the occasional ruptures in the trail bed itself—a slight impact compared with the reward of the presence of elk.

By 1.2 miles, the trail has abandoned its even course for a zigzagging one down the south flank of the hillside. Well-designed switchbacks slow descent, without introducing tiresome, unnecessary distance.

At 2.5 miles, a steep, unmaintained side trail branches right to meet the north end of the Harris Ranch Trail at Drift Creek. Keeping to the main trail finds a junction at 3 miles. Going to the left finds a creekside camp, the end of Horse Creek Trail (north), and the beckoning (or forbidding) trail sign for the hike's continuation on the opposite shore.

After a Drift Creek fording, following the well-trampled angler path upstream leads to a large tree-sheltered campsite in 0.1 mile, while

Horse Creek Trail (south) quickly pulls away from Drift Creek.

In spring, the strong aroma of the skunk cabbage announces the small, moist drainages along the bottom half of this fragment; salmonberry blooms farther up slope envelope the trail with a rich, heady smell. Whatever the season, the tall straight Douglas fir towers create a soothing rhythm of pattern—a balance to the understory chaos of greenery. Rain showers present the old-growth forest in all its finery.

Throughout the journey, the trail exhibits a steady, comfortable uphill grade, allowing a leisurely appreciation of the wilderness. At 5.5 miles, the hike ends at the trailhead on FR 3464.

For the Horse Creek (north)–Harris Ranch Trail hike, go right at the 3-mile junction on Horse Creek Trail (north). This begins a tour of the northern segment of the Harris Ranch Trail, a 0.7-mile bench trail framed by alder, bigleaf maple, and salmonberry leading to the bank of Drift Creek.

When Drift Creek permits fording, the southern portion of the Harris Ranch Trail continues on the opposite shore, touring meadow and climbing through wilderness forest to reach the trailhead on FR 346 for a 6.2-mile shuttle. (From OR 34, east of Waldport, turn north onto Risley Creek Road and travel 4.1 miles. At the sign for Harris Ranch Trail, turn left. Go 0.7 mile on FR 346 and bear left for the trailhead.)

12 ROGUE RIVER TRAIL

Distance: 47 miles one way
Elevation change: 700 feet
Difficulty: Strenuous
Season: Year round

Map: USGS Galice, Marial, Agness; USFS Siskiyou
For information: Gold Beach Ranger District, Medford District BLM
Siskiyou National Forest

This 47-mile national recreation trail journeys alongside 40 miles of the Wild and Scenic Rogue River, a captivating waterway. It travels a former mining trail of dreams and disappointment and passes Zane Grey's Cabin and two National Historic Places: the Rogue River Ranch and Whiskey Creek Cabin. The trail boasts exciting river views of narrow gorges, white water riffles, and yawning passages; crosses scenic creeks with beckoning swimming holes; and offers great wildlife viewing with deer, otter, osprey, blue-tailed skink, salmon, ring-tailed cat, mink, and bear (so exercise proper care with food).

Along the north canyon wall, the trail alternately tours high above and right next door to the river, offering various impressions of the Rogue. It crosses steep forested flank, woodland hillside, and river bench and bar. Around each bend, vegetation changes vary the mood. Solitude abounds.

The trail is accommodating to backpackers. Shuttle services for rafters also serve hikers allowing a one-way tour of the trail without a second vehicle. The river corridor holds plentiful campsites and rest stops, and hikers even have the luxury of buying iced drinks at Paradise Bar Lodge.

The forest service distributes a Rogue River Trail booklet with area history. Though presented from a river-traveler's perspective, it serves hikers, too.

Grave Creek is the gateway. From I-5 north of Grants Pass, take the Merlin exit, head north 0.2 mile, and turn left onto Merlin– Galice Road. Travel 22 miles, cross Grave Creek bridge, and turn left for the boat ramp and trailhead. Overnighters must park along the road.

The trail begins rounding the north canyon wall well above the river; mixed conifer and deciduous trees shade its path. At 2.1 miles, a side trail descends to Rainie Falls. At times, the arched backs of salmon break the water's surface.

From Whiskey Creek bridge, a 100-yard side trail leads to Whiskey Creek Cabin with its abandoned apple orchard and the rusting remnants from its heyday. The trail continues its rolling, slope-wrapping course passing through mixed forest. Beware of the poison oak.

At 8.7 miles, the trail overlooks Slim Pickens, a river narrow. At 17.5 miles, Kelsey Creek beckons with its deep swimming holes—a favorite with hikers and rafters. At the trail split beyond the creek, take the branch leading to the river.

Approaching Ditch Creek, the trail winds through an ash- and oak-studded grassland right above the river. The next stretch is often hot and dry, so top the water jugs. By 20 miles, the steep, unstable canyon slope forces the trail uphill around slide areas.

At Quail Creek, a sandy bar on the river suggests a stop to cool the feet. After crossing the creek, follow the trail branch heading toward the river. At 23.7 miles, the trail enters Quail Creek fire zone, where, in 1970, fire jumped the river burning 2,800 acres.

At the Rogue River Ranch, the path bearing left leads to campsites and Mule Creek; the uphill fork to the right leads to the publicly owned ranch and the trail's continuation. Top the water jugs at Mule Creek. Past the ranch, at 27.7 miles, the trail meets and bears left on an open road for 2 miles; a 2.5-mile–long basalt-bench tour follows. Here, a churning Coffeepot—the narrowest passage on the Rogue—catches hikers' attention. Although the elevated bench holds grand vistas, the heat-radiating rock can be unpleasant. At 32.5 miles, alder-lined Blossom Bar Creek with its deep, shimmery pools proves a siren.

From Paradise Bar Lodge (33.8 miles), the trail heads uphill, passes through a gate, and travels the length of a grassy runway to resume its downstream trek well above the river. Later, it follows a rocky cliff nearer the river to reach the woodland flat of Brushy Bar, which has campsites but an unreliable creek.

From the bar, the trail climbs bypassing the marker for Captain Tichenor's defeat and skirting gravel mounds from the placer mining era. Near Clay Hill Creek private residences dot the route. After an open trail segment across a grassland-oak hillside, Flora Dell Creek at 42.5 miles beckons with its 30-foot falls and shady setting.

The summer sun takes a harsher toll on the creeks along the final leg

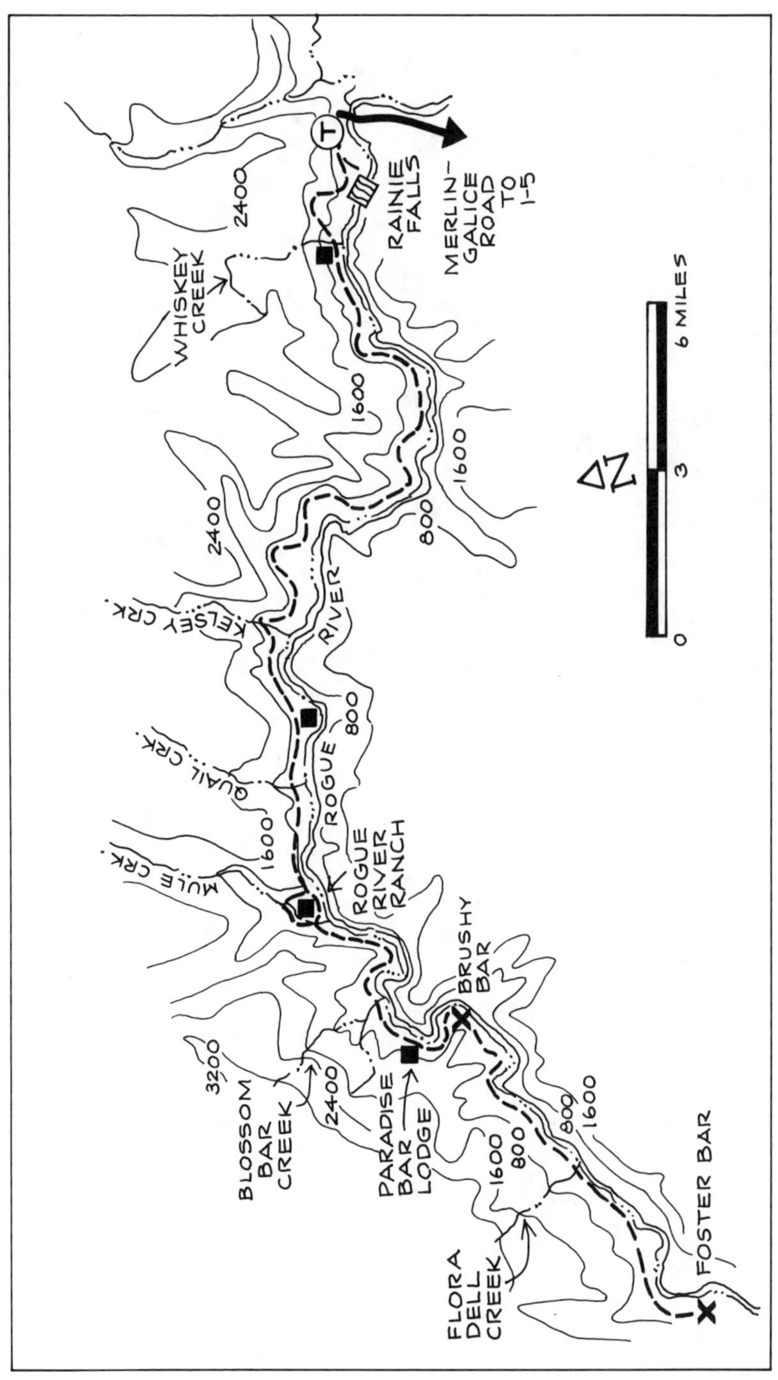
MERLIN-
GALICE
ROAD
TO
I-5
RAINIE
FALLS
WHISKEY
CREEK
2400
1600
800
N
0
3
6 MILES
KELSEY CRK.
RIVER
ROGUE
QUAIL CRK.
MULE CRK.
ROGUE
RIVER
RANCH
BRUSHY
BAR
3200
BLOSSOM
BAR
CREEK
PARADISE
BAR
LODGE
FLORA
DELL
CREEK
FOSTER BAR

Deer along Rogue River Trail

of the tour. While there's water for the jugs, the tempting pools are absent, and river access is limited. The trail concludes touring the open field of Big Bend Pasture to reach Foster Bar Trailhead.

As shuttle services generally park vehicles at the Foster Bar boat launch, from the end of the trail, hike downstream via FR 3700.300 and County 375 to reach the parking area and your vehicle in about 0.3 mile.

13 JOHNSON BUTTE TRAIL

Distance: 12.6 miles round trip
Elevation change: 600 feet
Difficulty: Moderate
Season: Spring through fall
Map: USFS Kalmiopsis Wilderness
For information: Chetco Ranger District
Kalmiopsis Wilderness Area

This less-traveled ridgeline route affords solitude and unfolds grand wilderness vistas that include the Dry Butte–Johnson Butte Ridge, Boulder and Box Canyon creek drainages, Quail Prairie Lookout, Pearsoll Peak, and Eagle Mountain. It also offers overlooks of Valen Lake, glimmering from its steep-sided forest basin.

The open-canopied trail travels the evergreen-deciduous diversity of the Siskiyou transition forest. Along the way, it tours an old fire zone, where knobcone pines will once again flourish. In this arid climate of extremes, fire is a critical player in forest renewal releasing seeds from their weather-tight cones.

The *Kalmiopsis leachiana,* an ancient member of the heath family, lends its name to the wilderness and decorates spots along the route with spring blooms. Out-of-season blooms are commonly spied as well. From May through July, water lilies color Salamander Lake. When in bloom, the azaleas rimming this lake envelope the area in sweet perfume.

Protected since 1946 (with wilderness protection coming in 1964), the 180,000-acre Kalmiopsis Wilderness Area is noted for its rugged terrain, rare botanical species, and mining legacy. A single-site camp at Red Prairie on FR 1909 provides a quiet base for exploring the wilderness.

From Brookings, go east on the North Bank Chetco River Road, County 784/FR 1376 (pavement becoming gravel). In 15.7 miles, turn right onto FR 1909 and stay on it, following the Kalmiopsis Wilderness signs. In 12.3 miles, the route passes Red Prairie camp on the left. At the

Manzanita

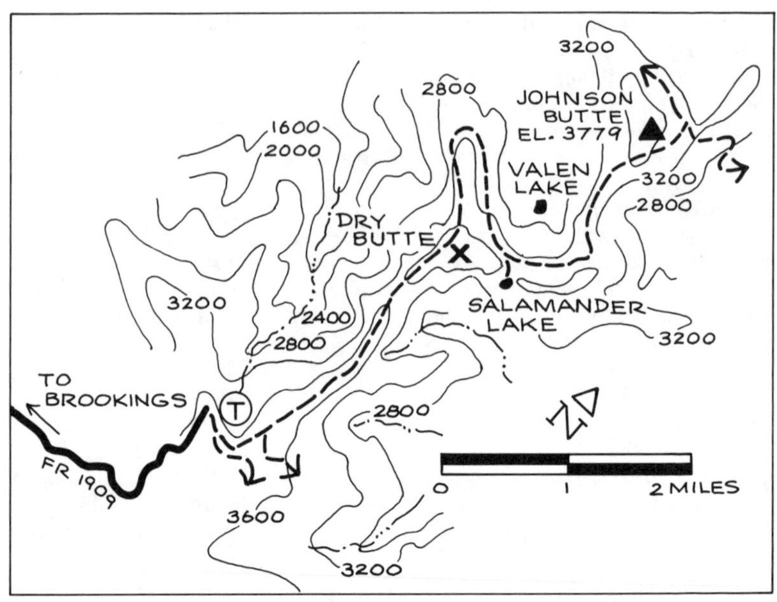

road fork 0.7 mile farther, bear left still staying on FR 1909 to reach the Vulcan Lakes–Johnson Butte Trailhead in another 1.7 miles.

During the wet season (fall–winter), FR 1909 will be closed due to slide danger. An alternate route to the site begins after the South Fork Chetco River crossing at 15.7 miles, following FR 1917 to Quail Prairie Lookout and past the Upper Chetco Trailhead to connect with FR 1909 above the danger area.

At the 100-foot trail junction, the Vulcan Lakes Trail heads uphill to the right; the butte trail journeys straight via an old, cobbled road that once led to the eastern chrome mines. Boots prove their value in this rocky terrain.

Port Orford cedars along with Jeffrey, whitebark, and western white pines line the hiking corridor, while kinnikinnick, bear grass, and patchy arid shrubs embroider the trail's edge. Arriving at the 0.75-mile trail junction, continue straight for Dry and Johnson buttes.

Crossing over the saddle finds views to the northwest and east. Atop the ridge, views of Dry Butte greet the hiker. A foot trail replaces the old road by 1.6 miles.

At 2 miles, the trail crosses to the west side of the ridge overlooking the Boulder Creek drainage. As the trail travels the saddle approaching stark-faced Dry Butte, the kalmiopsis plants first appear.

Passing below the false summit, the trail rounds to the back side of this butte, touring a fire zone, where young knobcone pines are renewing the forest. The view extends west to Quail Prairie Lookout and the ocean fog bank. Glassy serpentine rocks litter the route.

As the trail comes out of a bend at 3.25 miles, it overlooks the cobalt waters of Valen Lake; no trail leads to this isolated water. The crowns of Pearsoll Peak and Eagle Mountain show above the Dry Butte–Johnson Butte Ridge. More kalmiopsis plants add color.

On clear days, hikers can see the dramatic fog-filled Illinois River drainage rimmed by blue ridges to the north with Big Craggies rising to the northwest. Douglas firs command the moist north-facing slopes with the rare weeping spruce appearing in the mix. Snags dot the slope below the rock slides of Dry Butte.

At the 4-mile trail junction, the path to Salamander Lake and a campsite branches right. Just over the ridge is the pine-shaded site; a steep 300-yard descent leads to the lake—a small lily pond with a wet meadow border—named for its number-one resident.

The main trail, framed by rhododendron, continues rounding the ridge above the Boulder Creek headwaters before changing direction. It then points toward shrub-cloaked Johnson Butte, descending to a saddle. At 5.1 miles, a 250-yard trail descends the right-hand side of the saddle to a spring.

Ahead, the trail tours a shady Douglas fir–bracken fern corridor with tall tree-like tanoak, chinquapin, and live oak. Birds rustle in the bushes. Where the trail again descends, a moist, shady draw with abundant bear grass encloses it. The hike concludes at a forested flat (suitable for a campsite, but lacking water) at the Upper Chetco Trail Junction (6.3 miles).

From here, hikers may continue their wilderness exploration via the Upper Chetco Trail: To the right finds Box Canyon camp, Taggarts Bar, and the sparkling Chetco Wild and Scenic River. To the left, a northwest trek leads to the Tincup Trail; it requires a dual fording of Boulder Creek and the Chetco River.

14 ILLINOIS RIVER–BALD MOUNTAIN LOOP HIKE

Distance: 24 miles round trip
Elevation change: 3,100 feet
Difficulty: Strenuous
Season: Spring through fall
Map: USFS Kalmiopsis Wilderness
For information: Galice Ranger District

This hike samples a portion of the Illinois River National Recreation Trail, offering overlooks of and access to the Illinois Wild and Scenic River. The trail tours the floral diversity of the Siskiyous, which is greater than that found in any U.S. mountain range other than the Great Smokies of Virginia. Along the way, it crosses York Creek Botanical Area, which houses some rare *Kalmiopsis leachiana,* in bloom from April to June.

Its loop visits a beautiful riverside grassy bench (the former Weaver Ranch site), and tags Bald Mountain summit, "podium" for regionally

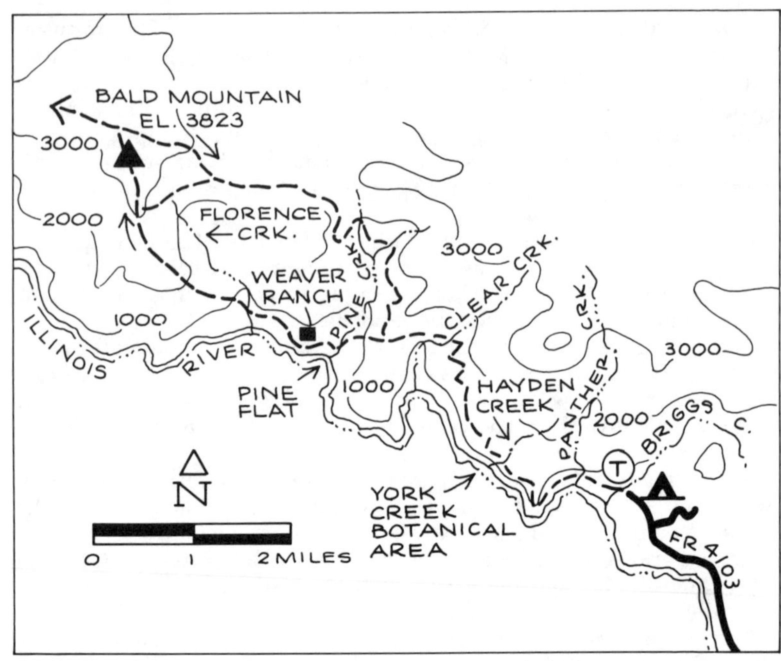

noted conservationist Lou Gold, who began his mountaintop vigil in 1983, protesting the construction of Bald Mountain Road. Bald Mountain has a precarious boundary with its south flank in protected wilderness, its north flank on public forest land open to logging—the ideal sermon line.

From US 199 at Selma, turn west onto the Illinois River Road (County 5070/FR 4103) heading toward Store Gulch. It begins as a 2-lane, paved, and winding road and becomes a 1-lane gravel road with some rough stretches (pickup or 4-wheel-drive vehicle recommended). In 16.7 miles, bear right staying on FR 4103; the road worsens. Briggs Creek campground and trailhead are in 1 mile.

The trail tours a transition forest of ponderosa and sugar pine, cedar, madrone, fir, and oaks. Near its start, spurs branch to the river. After entering the Kalmiopsis Wilderness, the trail wraps around the rugged north canyon wall finding open views of the Illinois—flowing wide, clean, and crystalline. The south wall parades a similar thin-soiled forest and deep side canyons. Slides mar the steep mountainsides.

Hayden Creek marks the entry into the small York Creek Botanical Area. From 3.25 to the ridge at 5.25 miles, the trail tours a richer, mixed forest secluded from river views. Beside tumbling Clear Creek (4.5 miles) is a restful campsite.

At the ridgetop junction, the Illinois River Trail to Bald Mountain journeys slightly uphill to the right. A clockwise loop follows the Pine

Flat Trail straight ahead for a steep, switchbacking descent on a wooded slope to the river bottom. A morning dance of fog lifts from the river. Where the trail forks on the rocky, oak-fern flat, bear right and cross Pine Creek. Campsites dot the area; a boulder-bar scramble leads to the river.

The trail now travels the edge of the boulder bar past a reed drainage to duck into the forest near a moss-decked oak. At 6.9 miles, it reaches a beautiful homestead meadow with broken fireplace, rusting equipment, and some old cans. While the open, grassy river flat dotted by a few pines and oaks may prove inviting, pitch no-trace camps off the meadow.

Hikers and anglers find easy river access between Pine Flat and Florence Creek, as the trail rounds the slope just above the river. At 7.7 miles is the Florence Creek fording; at its bench campsite, a small sign signals the Florence Way link to Bald Mountain—a steep, narrow path streaking up the hill.

Traveling the ridge above Florence Creek canyon, this trail, on an irregular maintenance schedule, offers a greater challenge: downfalls and faint or overgrown stretches in the burn areas. Where the trail fades, stop and scan the hillside to discover the next identifiable portion—never far from sight. Beautiful hollow oaks punctuate the burn.

At 10 miles, the trail crosses an open slope offering a deep-canyon view of the Illinois far below and the Klondike and Yukon creek drainages. Soon after, the trail travels the dividing ridge between Florence and Sulphur creek canyons—essentially a fire line.

At the 10.7-mile junction in a brushy clearing, going right meets the Illinois River Trail 2 miles east of Bald Mountain; going straight leads to the Bald Mountain summit (elevation 3,823 feet).

At 11.5 miles, scorched bushes and trees rim the summit knob of Bald Mountain. Its views sweep the river canyon and the opposite wall.

Following the grassy footpath bearing left (west) away from the summit leads to the Illinois River Trail (12 miles). A turn right begins the homeward trek. (Counterclockwise travelers should be alert for the summit junction, as the signs face away from them.)

The trail travels a scorched forest with bear and other perennial grasses, Oregon grape, and bracken fern. Mushrooms grow up the tree trunks; woodpeckers drill off the charred bark. Touring an impressively steep slope marked by cliffs, the trail offers views of the wildly rugged Silver Creek canyon.

Framed by reseedings, the next downhill segment affords views of the controversial Bald Mountain Road. Later, the trail parallels the road. By 14.5 miles, the slope-contouring trail leaves behind the burn.

At 16.5 miles, the trail rounds a small ridge and descends more rapidly. It crosses the forks of Pine Creek and offers clearing-area views of the Illinois River canyon, before arriving at the ridgetop junction with Pine Flat Trail, closing the loop. From there, retrace the river trail east to Briggs Creek trailhead.

15 STERLING MINE DITCH TRAIL

Distance: 17 miles one way, plus access spurs
Elevation change: 800 feet
Difficulty: Strenuous
Season: Year round, except during low-elevation snows
Map: BLM Sterling Mine Trail System brochure
For information: Medford District BLM

This trail tours a remnant from Oregon's colorful prospecting era. Placer gold strikes in the early 1850s led to the founding of Jacksonville; the 1854 Sterling Creek discovery skyrocketed the area to fame. Tales of four hundred dollar daily takes fueled the fever, sending waves of prospectors scouring the foothills above Little Applegate River.

In 1877, miners fashioned an artificial creek to draw water from the Little Applegate River to the mineral-rich Siskiyou mountainsides. The 26.5-mile-long, 3-foot-deep ditch was completed in six months' time; it remained in use until the 1930s. Now, a stream of hikers flows along the ditch canal.

The historical route passes through deciduous-evergreen transition forest and across open oak-grassland hillsides. In the spring, a wildflower showcase features scarlet fritillary, yellow fawn lily, shooting star, monkey flower, and more, but beware, the poison oak is also at its peak. Common wildlife sightings include deer, grouse, and ravens.

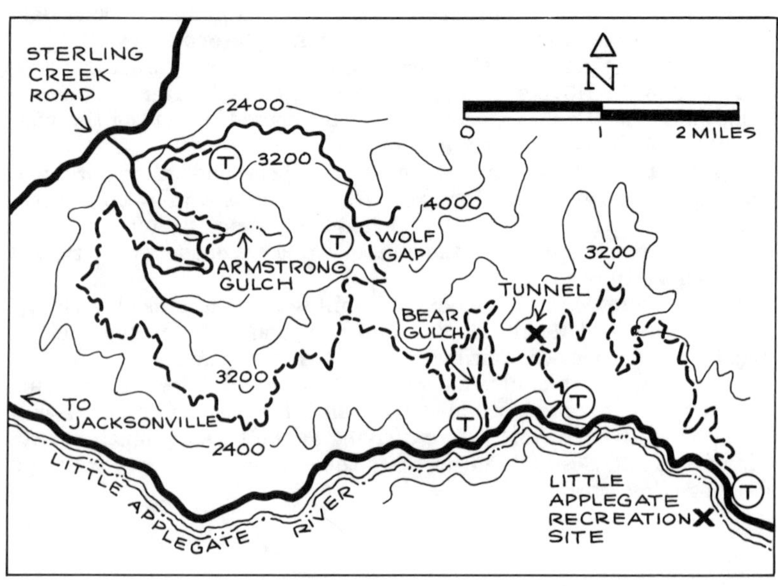

Upper Applegate River Valley

From Jacksonville, drive south 7.3 miles on OR 238 and turn left onto Applegate Road at Ruch. In 2.8 miles, turn left onto Little Applegate Road (a paved and gravel route). Signs indicate the way to the trailheads, with Little Applegate Recreation Site (in 11 miles) being the easternmost one.

The westernmost trailhead for the ditch trail is at Deming Gulch: From the junction of Little Applegate and Sterling Creek roads (5.5 miles southeast of Ruch), go 2 miles north on Sterling Creek Road, and turn right onto Armstrong Gulch Road. At the road fork, bear left, and go about 0.7 mile on BLM 39-2-8 to find a direct access to the ditch trail on the right side of the road.

If time is limited, the eastern sampling holds the better offering. At Little Applegate Recreation Site, a 0.5-mile spur accesses the ditch. Elsewhere, the access spurs measure between 1 and 1.75 miles long, with Wolf Gap (off Grub Gulch Road) having the longest, most difficult approach. Multiple trailheads allow for customized hikes; a 4-mile loop knits together the Tunnel Ridge, Sterling Mine Ditch, and Bear Gulch trails with a brief road segment.

The east-end spurs ascend moist gulch drainages and white oak hillsides to reach the ditch trail. Early views feature the Little Applegate

Valley with its alternating oak and evergreen slopes. In the distance, the river rushes.

Touring the levee above the ditch, the trail is mostly flat. Where the ditch passes through private properties, the trail charges up and around them.

Despite the passage of time, the ditch remains defined but not detractive. Small bushes and grasses have softened its banks and invaded its bottom. Wooden retaining walls, many in disrepair, and a 30-foot-long, 3.5-foot-high tunnel penetrating a ridge 5 miles west of the ditch's east end record the construction effort.

Frequent vegetation changes occur along this hillside-wrapping route, providing visual stimulation. White oak grassland, scrub forest, manzanita-buckbrush chaparral, and ponderosa pine–madrone-fir forest take turns framing the route. Below Wolf Gap, a rich ancient forest encloses the trail. Balsamroot, strawberry, yarrow, and poison oak weave amid the grasses and needle mat.

The trail segment between Wolf Gap and Armstrong Gulch includes a 4-mile central stretch through a recovering fire zone. The degree of the burn varies, and interesting discoveries about forest renewal await. Within the burn, woodpeckers abound, and raptors patrol overhead. Views of Little Red Mountain, Sevenmile Ridge, and Yale Creek drainage invite the eyes to stray from the scorched forest.

On either side of the burn is thriving transition forest. Heading west from the burn, the trail unfolds views of Negro Ben Mountain, Mount Baldy, Burton Butte, and Little Applegate and Applegate river valleys, before entering a moister mixed forest en route to Armstrong Gulch. Along the final trail leg to Deming Gulch, the surrounding clearcuts steal from the shade and the view.

Seasonal changes alter the look of the trail. Winter reveals abandoned nests amid the spiny, unclad deciduous branches, while fog lies in the valley. The route's varied microclimates applaud the arrival of spring with floral diversity. In summer, the deciduous trees bring fullness and shade; in autumn, pine cones line the trail, and golden-brown leaves drift in the breeze and crackle underfoot. The trail's flatness welcomes a leisurely study of all its offerings.

16 COLLINGS MOUNTAIN LOOP

Distance: 11.5-mile loop
Elevation change: 1,500 feet
Difficulty: Moderate to strenuous
Season: Spring through fall
Map: USFS Rogue River
For information: Applegate Ranger District

En route to the California gold fields, a party of Willamette Valley prospectors found favor with the Applegate River Valley. Although claim markers and placer tailings (rubble from mining) are ever present

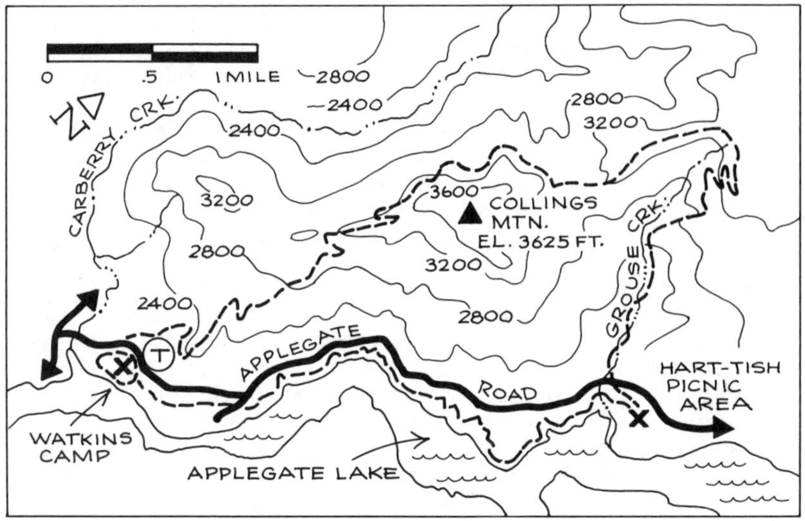

in this region, the true wealth mined from these slopes is the tranquillity of the trails.

This loop weaves its way up through the mixed transition forest of Collings Mountain to travel along the ridgetop. It offers limited California and Oregon Siskiyou vistas and overlooks of the Carberry Creek drainage and Applegate Valley. After touring the Grouse Creek drainage, it contours the open-forested slope above the Applegate Reservoir to swing to a close.

From Jacksonville, travel 8 miles south on OR 238 to Ruch; there turn left onto Applegate Road following the signs to Applegate Reservoir. Stay on Applegate Road rounding the west side of the reservoir to reach Watkins Camp and the southern trailhead for Collings Mountain Trail, in about 18 miles.

Beginning on the opposite side of the road from Watkins Camp, the trail climbs through the young manzanita and madrone of a recovering burn area dotted by scorched snags. An osprey nest tops one. Where the trail enters the living forest, monstrous ponderosa pines preside.

In varying combinations, ponderosa pine, Douglas and grand fir, white and live oak, madrone, and sugar pine frame the route as it tours the east flank of Collings Mountain. At times, sections of choked, small-diameter firs enclose the trail. By 0.7 mile, it enters a designated wildlife unit cleared of brush and seeded for browsers. Spring annuals burst from the needle mat.

As the trail dips, climbs, and wraps, it introduces microclimate pockets which hold quick changes in lighting, texture, and mood. On this little-used route, the trailbed is at times matted with needles and cones. By 1.8 miles, the incline of the slope grows steeper, and by 2.1 miles, the semi-open forest allows southeastern views.

Topping a small saddle and climbing the ridge, the forest fullness again denies views. Rock outcrops dot the forest. At 2.4 miles, the trail passes beneath a rock overhang before crossing over the ridge to begin its descent.

On this steeper, more rugged flank, the understory is brushy and grassy; live oaks thrive. From a rock outcrop at the first switchback, hikers obtain limited looks at the Carberry Creek drainage.

At 3 miles, the trail passes over the faint line of an old road. In spring, be alert to the possibility of ticks amid the tall grasses which sweep the pants legs. Beware poison oak, whenever venturing off the trail.

Ahead, the grade levels out for easier walking. In another mile, the trail tops a saddle at a junction of old, abandoned roads. Here, the loop continues north along the ridgetop, soon crossing over to the Applegate side of the mountain. A full-canopy forest shades the path.

At 4.9 miles, the trail drops via quick, steep switchbacks, before settling into a steady, more even-paced descent. The loose rock of the slope supports few ground plants. Clearings provide looks at the Grouse Creek drainage and the Applegate River area.

By 6 miles, the trail is following Grouse Creek downhill. During drought years, the creek is reduced to mere puddles even in winter, but a thick moss ornaments its banks and the trunks of nearby oaks. Soon, the trail bypasses an old mining adit; do not approach as it is hazardous. Where the trail crosses Grouse Creek on a built-up rock path, the grade again eases.

At 6.5 miles, the trail skirts an old hand-split-shake cabin, wheezing in the wind. It then crisscrosses the creek before climbing to Applegate Road at 7 miles.

Across the road, go left to enter Hart-tish Picnic Area. There, the route descends the paved path through the picnic grounds to meet and follow the Da-Ku-Be-Te-De Trail to the right, beginning its reservoir journey south to Watkins Camp.

Fir, oak, and madrone with a few pine frame the path. Looks to the north feature the dam. Ducks occupy the more isolated arms and bays of the reservoir. At 9.8 miles, the nearness of the road intrudes on the hike. After touring a brushy slope below the road, the trail offers views of the reservoir that hint at its river origins; riffles now appear in the watery arm. At 10.7 miles, the trail crosses the Copper Ramp access road to travel a dry, open slope. Beautiful, twisted brick-red manzanita capture the eyes' attention.

At 11.2 miles, the trail enters an inviting, shady forest stretch, despite its proximity to the road. At the upcoming footbridge, the hiker finds Watkins Loop. Either way delivers the hiker to the campground; going right is the quickest route. The loop tour concludes at the small camp which has walk-in sites, toilet facility, and water.

17 WARRIOR ROCK LIGHTHOUSE TRAIL

Distance: 7 miles round trip
Elevation change: Minimal
Difficulty: Easy
Season: Year round
Map: ODFW Sauvie Island Wildlife Area brochure
For information: Oregon Department of Fish and Wildlife

Some 16 miles long, Sauvie Island is the largest island on the Columbia River; it features lowland fields, oak–ash woodlands and cottonwood groves, marshes, lakes, seasonal ponds, and sloughs. The Lewis and Clark party named it "Wap-pa-to," the Indian name for arrowhead, a wild potato. In the 1830s, the island was the site of Fort William, a Hudson's Bay Company trading post. Warrior Point, at the north end of the island, houses the remains of a World War I shipyard.

Warrior Rock, a jut on the Columbia River shore, sports a lighthouse.

Riparian forest, Sauvie Island

The rock owes its name to a tense moment recorded in George Vancouver's journal where Lieutenant Broughton unexpectedly found himself encircled by some twenty-three canoes bearing war-clad Indians. Although the meeting ended peacefully, the significance of the moment suggested the name for the landmark.

The island offers premier bird-watching. At the peak of fall migration, it houses a concentration of some 300,000 waterfowl, some 2,000 to 3,000 tundra swans, and some 2,000 sandhill cranes. Bald eagles winter here feeding on the weakened fowl. In late-afternoon, the birds peel from the waters in an extravaganza of beating wings, but better waterfowl viewing opportunities exist on island trails other than this one.

Deer, raccoon, and aquatic mammals also may be spied by hiker and canoeist.

From Portland, take US 30 west to reach the Sauvie Island Bridge, crossing the Multnomah Channel. On the island, turn left on Sauvie Island Road. The right turn for Reeder Road is in 2.6 miles, but visitors may wish to detour to the headquarters, only 0.25 mile beyond, to obtain visitor information and restrictions. The trailhead lies at the end of Reeder Road in 12.9 miles.

A wildlife area day-use parking permit is required; they are easily purchased at convenience stores along US 30 or at markets on Sauvie Island. Hunting season finds parts of the island closed to hikers.

The trail begins its journey north with a fence crossing to follow the open, grassy path along a dike. To one side lies the river; to the other is a grassy field with cottonwoods and blackberry brambles.

The sandy, tide-washed beach offers an alternative, low-tide route. In a few places, the strand is absent or crowded with branchwork forcing the stroller to mount the bank. The honking of geese breaks the morning still.

At 0.25 mile, the primary hiking route enters a cottonwood grove via a jeep trail, which soon forks near a small high-voltage station. Bear right on the leafy, smaller jeep track to tour the woodland edge of the Columbia River beach. The route can sometimes be miry.

Barges and recreational boats cut the waters; blue herons, cormorants, and gulls are skyway travelers. The Washington shore holds a similar woodland setting.

At 0.5 mile, take either fork as they soon merge. Here, the trail travels a broad corridor between the river and an area with a lake and seasonal ponds; in winter, the leafless cottonwoods allow limited lake views. Moss and licorice fern deck the trunks, while snowberry, small ash, and willows weave through the woodland. By 1.3 miles, the path opens up, touring the bench above the river; the entire trek affords easy river access. Soon Warrior Rock lighthouse pulls into view. At the 2.4-mile trail fork, again bear right staying along the river.

The path once again forks at 2.75 miles only to rejoin at 3 miles. Blackberry brambles line the route as it nears the lighthouse. At 3.2 miles, looking down shore across a line of old pilings, hikers gain a photo point on the lighthouse, now absent its beacon dome. A small light remains. At the upcoming fork, bear right.

At the 3.4-mile fork, bear left to reach Warrior Rock lighthouse and a nice sandy strand; the path to the right leads to private land. When exploring, please note that the lighthouse is Coast Guard property and off limits to the public.

Warrior Rock affords a good downstream view of the river and shoreline pilings; mosses deck the rock. Beyond the rocky lighthouse point, a wide strand of beach extends down river, inviting a stroll.

Along the beach, deer and skunk tracks record the passersby of last night and early morning. As the beach tour continues downstream, hikers gain cross-channel views of St. Helens with its scenic old town. In 0.4 mile, the strip narrows forcing hikers to turn back or ascend the steep bank to find still more pilings in another 0.1 mile, hinting at the World War I shipyard. For the return trek, retrace your steps.

For additional hiking, the 3-mile Oak Island Loop (reached by turning north onto Oak Island Road NW from Reeder Road) tours some of the island's large inland lakes and the oak groves where the eagles roost in winter. It offers the better opportunity for waterfowl viewing.

18 WILDWOOD NATIONAL RECREATION TRAIL

Distance: 26.3 miles one way
Elevation change: 600 feet
Difficulty: Moderate to strenuous
Season: Year round
Map: Portland Parks Bureau trail map
For information: Portland Parks and Recreation Department, Hoyt Arboretum

This noteworthy metropolitan trail explores some of the natural habitats cached within Portland's city limits. It is ideal for those times when business or homelife ties the hiker to the city—a convenient escape from the pace and routine, as well as a good leg stretch.

The Wildwood Trail is a family trail, one for all ages. It invites a morning jog and the exercising of leashed pets. Multiple access points allow hikers to customize the length of their tour. A number of side trails connect to and explore outward from this major hiking artery. The junctions, for the most part, are well marked, allowing hikers to navigate loops and side tours easily with the use of the park's trail map.

Alder and bigleaf maple woodland, second-growth Douglas fir–western hemlock forest, and an arboretum forest house the trail. Seasonal changes alter the discovery. On the forest floor grows a variety of springtime blooms; in autumn, the abundant deciduous trees and shrubs color the slopes in yellow and orange.

The trail crosses fire lanes and city streets and tours the natural buffers amid the area's residential tracts. For the most part, the Wildwood

Balch Creek

Trail has a 3-foot-wide, defined bed and a comfortable grade for its rolling, slope-contouring journey.

This well-used trail is remarkably free from litter. During heavy rains though, it can become muddy in a few places.

At the southern terminus, there's ample parking near the World Forestry Center. From US 26 in west Portland, take the indicated exit for Washington Park and the zoo and follow the well-signed route north to the World Forestry Center. Hike north from the Center to the Oregon Vietnam Veterans Memorial Area trailhead.

Skyline Boulevard, a major route through Portland's northwest hills, strings together multiple signed access-spurs leading to the heart of the Wildwood Trail.

To sample the northern end of the trail, take the indicated turn for N.W. Germantown Road off N.W. St. Helens Road (US 30), just north of the St. Johns Bridge. N.W. Germantown Road holds three trailheads; the marked trailhead in 1.7 miles has a parking area for five to six vehicles and offers a pleasant forest tour to the south.

Presently, the trail's northern terminus lies just beyond N.W. Germantown Road on Newton Street. Proposals call for additional trail miles to be added beyond it.

From south to north, the Wildwood Trail passes through the prized parks of Portland's northwest hills for a more "civilized" tour. It ventures through broad woodland corridors and journeys across the open lawns of the developed parks. Road noises and rooftops occasionally intrude, yet even here, pockets exist where the forest succeeds in filtering out city reminders.

Touring the Hoyt Arboretum segment of the Wildwood Trail, hikers enter a planned forest uniting native Northwest trees, shrubs, ferns, and

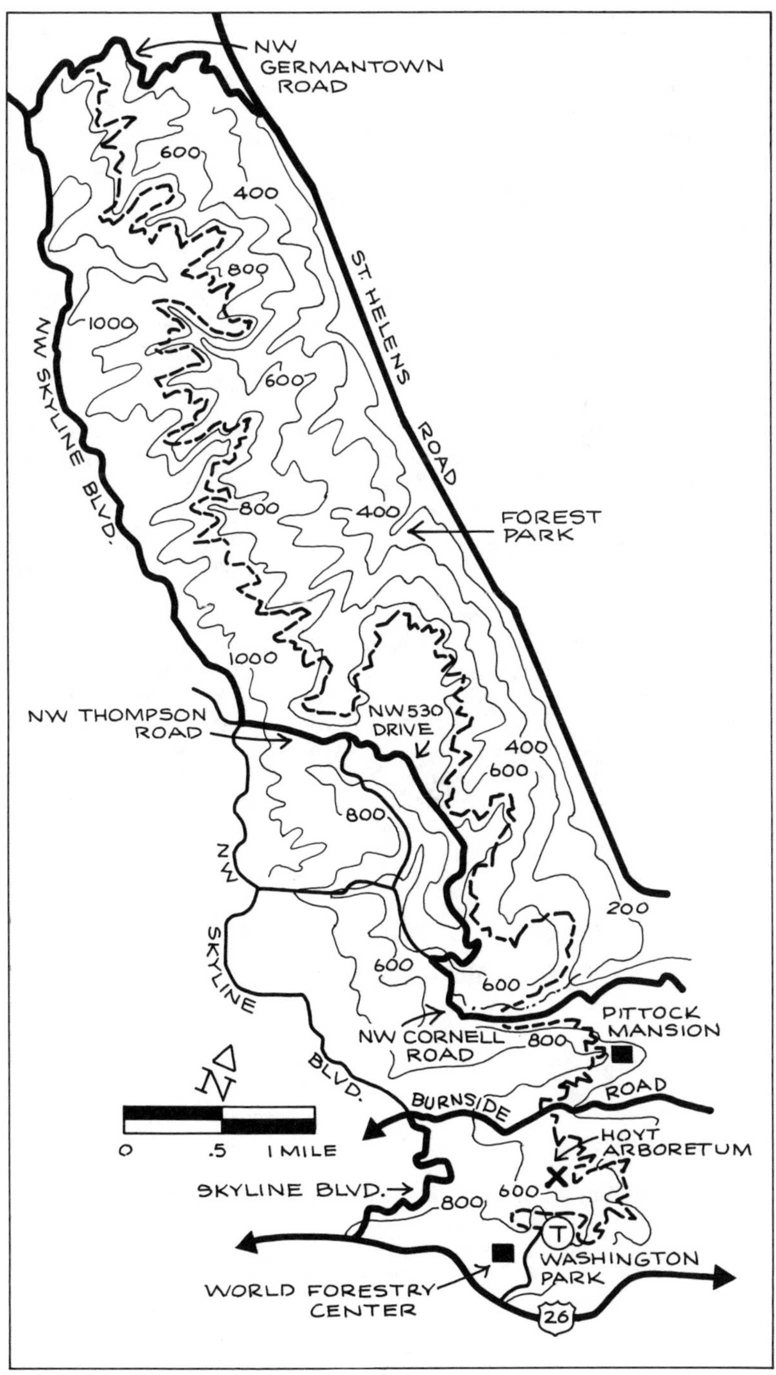
NW GERMANTOWN ROAD
ST. HELENS ROAD
NW SKYLINE BLVD.
600
400
800
1000
FOREST PARK
NW THOMPSON ROAD
NW 530 DRIVE
200
NW SKYLINE BLVD.
NW CORNELL ROAD
PITTOCK MANSION
BURNSIDE ROAD
HOYT ARBORETUM
0
.5
1 MILE
SKYLINE BLVD.
WASHINGTON PARK
WORLD FORESTRY CENTER
26

wildflowers with more than 675 tree species from around the world. The Arboretum's own 9.8-mile trail network is organized by tree family/class; small plaques identify the species. Staying on the Wildwood Trail alone, visitors sample the pine–conifer and redwood planting schemes.

Where the trail passes through woodland corridors, bigleaf maple and alder primarily comprise the overhead canopy; a few Douglas fir and western hemlock pierce the leafy roof. Sword fern, salal, and red huckleberry contribute to the understory, while vine maple, hazel, and cascara add to the midstory. In places, ivy invades the treetops and forest floor.

Vistas along the route are few. Perhaps the best is secured at Pittock Acres (3.8 miles). A short detour to the hilltop finds the French Renaissance mansion which once belonged to newspaper magnate Henry Pittock. The hilltop affords an overlook of the city and the Willamette and Columbia rivers with the Cascades in the backdrop. The grounds are open (free) to the public.

Cornell Road at 5 miles marks the dividing line between the refined tour and the more remote and wild stretches of the Wildwood Trail. Beyond Cornell Road, the route probes deep into Portland's wilderness park, Forest Park, traveling mostly through second growth. Here, greater numbers of evergreens intermix with the bigleaf maples, which still remain dominant. Douglas and grand fir, western hemlock, and western red cedar are well represented. This deeper, multistory forest displays a richer texture. Sword, lady, and maidenhair fern, Oregon grape, salal, trillium, twisted stalk, and other low-elevation forest species flood the understory; thickets of salmonberry crowd the small drainages. Lichen, moss, and licorice fern adorn the trunks and branches.

The northbound tour now stays in a similar setting all the way to Germantown Road. The shadow-and-light play created by the overhead abundance adds to the relaxation of the tour.

Whether it's for a short walk or a long-distance tour, the Wildwood Trail well serves the city-bound hiker.

19 "HIKER LOOP" TO IRON MOUNTAIN BRIDGE

Distance: 3 miles round trip
Elevation change: 100 feet
Difficulty: Easy
Season: Year round
Map: Tryon Creek State Park brochure
For information: State Parks, Portland Regional Office

Tryon Creek State Park is a 631-acre natural preserve cached within the Portland city limits. It occupies the former 1849 homestead, mill, and logging site of pioneer Socrates Hotchkiss Tryon.

In the 1880s, this creek canyon was logged; the forest has since regrown naturally. Today, it displays a rich deciduous canopy with red al-

"Hiker Loop," Tryon Creek State Park

der, bigleaf and vine maple, hazel, and cascara—a wonderful visual tangle of texture and greenery. Tall Douglas fir and western red cedar punctuate the forest. In places, ivy rules the floor and climbs the tree trunks.

The park is noted for its treasury of trillium, which bloom between mid-March and mid-April. Along the canyon's moist drainages grows the pungent yellow skunk cabbage. The pencil-point cuts of the beaver mark the banks of Tryon Creek; songbirds and woodpeckers are commonly spied.

When conditions tie hikers to the city, this family park offers an ideal outdoor retreat. Insulated from much of the noise and chaos, the park retains a sense of remoteness. Only the numbers passed along the trail betray its proximity to civilization. Some 8.5 miles of hiking trail web the park suggesting a variety of tours. Separate trails serve bicyclists and equestrian users.

The park is located on Southwest Terwilliger Boulevard in Portland. From I-5, take the Terwilliger exit, and follow the park signs. At 1.7 miles, bear right rounding the curve, staying on Southwest Terwilliger. The park turn is at 2.5 miles, just beyond the Northwestern School of Law.

Trail maps are available at the Nature House, which also holds exhibits and a fine botanical library; be sure to pick up a map to clarify route choices at the many junctions.

This tour begins on the path to North Creek Hiking Trail, traveling away from the Nature House. Licorice fern, lichen, and moss color the tree trunks and snags. Near the house, the trailbed is surfaced. Away from it, wet weather can turn the trails miry and slippery. For leisurely strolling, the dry season is preferred.

A fairly quick, steep grade delivers Tryon Creek. For the hiker loop, cross High Bridge at 0.4 mile. Salmonberry thrive in the creek canyon; alders overhang the water. With winter rains, the creek runs silty.

At the junction just beyond High Bridge, going left on the Creek Hiking Trail continues the loop. The now narrower footpath follows the rolling bench above Tryon Creek, but the alder network denies views. Cedar stumps record long ago logging; notches indicate the use of springboards in cutting.

At the 0.6-mile junction, turn right for the loop, quickly crossing West Horse Loop to continue the woodland tour. Lady ferns abound in the understory.

The trail then ascends the canyon side. Stairsteps cut into the slope aid the climb. After the trail levels, another junction follows; go left staying on the hiker trail again crossing over the West Horse path. Here, some

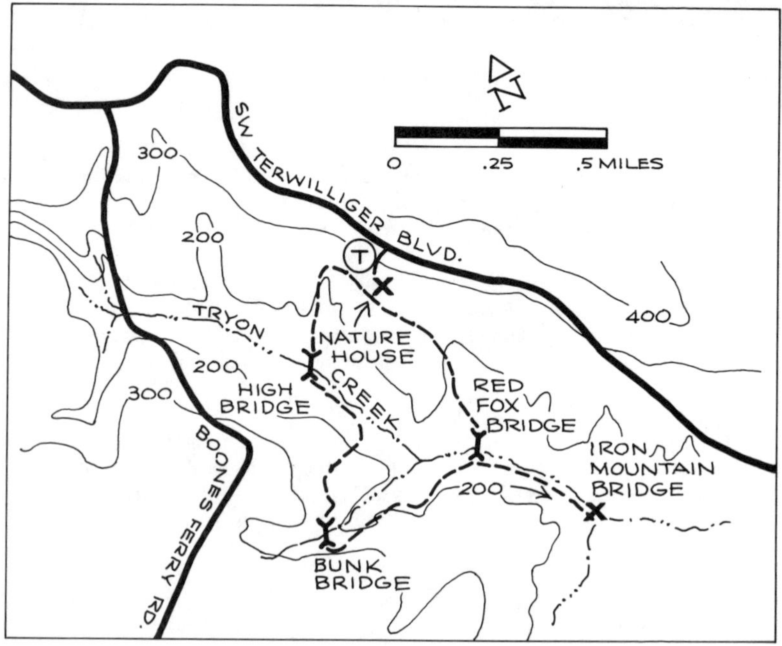

nice cedars preside. Many more cedars line the trail as it descends to Bunk Bridge.

The trail next follows the slope above a side creek passing the Englewood Drive junction to follow the route indicated for Red Fox Hiking Trail. A meandering descent into the canyon finds an unnamed footbridge, from which the trail rolls and dips approaching Red Fox Bridge.

Just before Red Fox Bridge, a 0.4-mile detour heads right for a nice extension to the hiker loop visiting Tryon Creek via the South Creek Hiking Trail. This nice all-weather stretch of trail tours the canyon slope downstream, collecting a few creek overlooks.

Some hemlock and the occasional fir mark the cedar forest, while stumps hint at the ancient cedar forest that once stood here. Blackberry bushes and horsetail reeds line the trail as it nears Iron Mountain Bridge. From the bridge, hikers gain the best view of slow-moving Tryon Creek.

From Iron Mountain Bridge, backtrack upstream to the hiker loop and cross Red Fox Bridge (2.4 miles). The route now weaves up slope through a rich evergreen stand of even-aged fir with a few deciduous trees. The forest introduces a change in lighting and mood not previously witnessed. The ivy is well entrenched.

A right returns to the Nature House via the quickest route. Wider, wood-shaving trails and benches indicate the route's nearing the house and the close of the loop.

20 SILVER CREEK CANYON LOOP

Distance: 9-mile circuit with spurs and interlocking small loops
Elevation change: 400 feet
Difficulty: Moderate
Season: Year round

Map: State Park flier
For information: State Parks, Portland Regional Office
Silver Falls State Park

Country roads wrap around orchards, tree farms, and fields to deliver this surprising destination—a pocket of old-growth forest along Silver Creek Canyon, which houses ten major waterfalls. The falls measure between 27 and 178 feet high, with five falls plunging more than 100 feet. Headward erosion by Silver Creek carved out this canyon showcase. Where the cliff basalts were weakest, the water's force sculpted cavernous hollows behind the falls and scenic amphitheater bowls.

The canyon is most commonly viewed in summer, but seasonal changes add to this dramatic stage: Springtime charges the greenery with brilliance and sprinkles wildflowers across the forest floor; autumn paints the canyon bottom in yellow, gold, and brown; and on occasion, winter creates a fantasy-scape of rushing water, blue ice, and threateningly beautiful icicles.

At this 8,000-acre Willamette Valley boast, deer are commonly seen

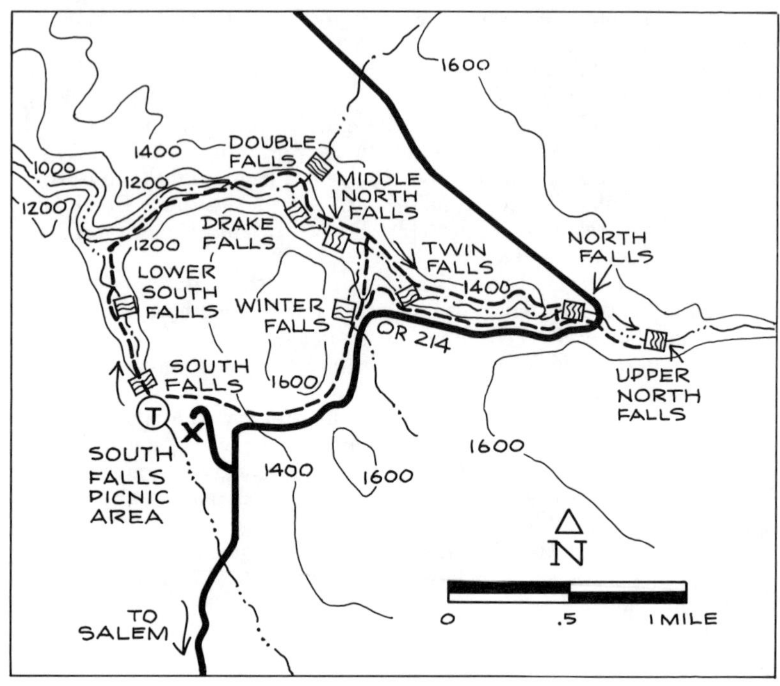

grazing the lawns or bounding for wooded shelter. Huge ant mounds dot the woodland of the canyon rim, providing interesting discoveries from a distance.

To reach the park, from OR 22 about 12 miles east of Salem, take the exit for Silver Falls State Park. Signs mark the junctions, as OR 214 twists its way northeast to the park in 15.5 miles.

Multiple trailheads found at the day-use areas and along OR 214 access this hiking circuit; map boards dot the hiker route and mark trailheads, aiding navigation. The park's campground (open mid-April to late October) offers hikers a pleasant overnight base.

From South Falls Day-use Area "A," a paved and forest path descends to South Falls, the most visited and photographed falls in the park. The 177-foot veiling waterfall is examined from top, sides, back, and face. The cliff hollow behind the falls allows hikers to pass behind the spraying chute for an unusual perspective.

Waterleaf, miner's lettuce, salmonberry, and grasses adorn the cliff. Bigleaf maples accent the canyon.

Bypassing the bridge below South Falls, the loop tour continues downstream. It travels a rich cedar–fir–maple canyon with cascading greenery and offers views of the clear-coursing South Fork. At 1 mile, the loop unfolds side views and outward-looking views from behind the 93-foot watery curtain of Lower South Falls.

Soon after, the trail curves away from Silver Creek's South Fork to follow the North Fork upstream passing Lower North, Drake, Middle North, and Twin falls, with the option of a side trip to Double Falls at 2.3 miles. Double Falls is a seasonal falls with reduced waters in summer; Middle North Falls (106 feet) is one of the prettiest waterfalls in the gallery.

At 4.1 miles, the trail delivers multiple perspectives on the 136-foot North Falls. Again, hikers may pass into the gaping mouth of the cliff to peer out through the thick droplet veil. As the trail climbs away from North Falls and out of the canyon, beware the trail's stone steps may be slippery when wet, especially when temperatures drop. Mosses and ferns adorn the canyon's steep rock walls.

As the trail levels out, it offers overlooks of the scenic pools and swirling cascades of North Fork Silver Creek. Looking over their shoulders, hikers can witness the simultaneous quick drop of both the trail and the water into canyon.

Bypassing the trail junction for the loop's canyon rim tour, hikers find a 0.3-mile upstream trail leaving the northernmost parking area. This spur probes still deeper into the moist canyon of North Fork Silver Creek, ushering hikers to an Upper North Falls vista. This broad falls enters its canyon slipping over a rocky bowl for a 65-foot drop into a circular pool. The water's force fans the boughs of nearby cedars; the chill spray defies a lengthy up-close viewing.

After backtracking downstream, hikers resume the loop bearing left at the junction above North Falls for the canyon rim tour. This is a fast segment with minimal grade change, touring a corridor of Douglas fir and cedar between the rim and the park road.

A switchbacking downhill detour from the Winter Falls Viewpoint turnout holds one final look at the plunging waters that bring this park fame. This look pairs the 134-foot shimmery veil of thin streamers with a bold view of the steep, moss-mantled basalt canyon wall.

The long days of summer allow a comfortable completion of the 9-mile circuit with time for detours and an unhurried appreciation of all the falls.

21 MILL HILL LOOP

Distance: 2.5 miles round trip
Elevation change: 100 feet
Difficulty: Easy
Season: Year round
Map: Willamette Valley National Wildlife Refuges brochure
For information: William L. Finley National Wildlife Refuge

Purchased with duck stamp monies, this 5,325-acre tract is part of the greater Willamette Valley refuge complex set aside for wintering "duskies"—a rare subspecies of Canada goose, which summers along Alaska's Copper River. When the geese congregate at the refuge, all areas are closed to hunting, and much of the refuge is closed to visitors to minimize the human disturbance to the birds. The duskies' wintering season runs from the end of October through mid-April.

The refuge is named for William L. Finley, the early-day naturalist who encouraged President Theodore Roosevelt to set aside such lands for wildlife protection. The refuge celebrates the diversity of plant and animal life found in the transition zone between the Coast Range and the Willamette Valley. Oak woodlands, mixed forests, meadows, marshes, ponds, and farmland create a habitat diversity for the migratory and resident waterfowl and shorebird populations.

Some 222 bird species have been identified at the refuge. Ruffed grouse, California quail, red-tailed hawk, mourning dove, red-winged blackbird, and woodpecker are commonly sighted residents. Binoculars and bird identification guides enhance a stay.

In late spring–early summer, the refuge microclimates show a rich variety of wildflowers: Oregon iris, buttercup, adder's-tongue, dwarf star tulip, larkspur, camas, and more. Late-summer hikers must contend with clinging dried grass seed.

Hiker routes follow foot trails and closed gravel roads.

To reach the refuge, from Corvallis, go 10 miles south on OR 99W and turn right onto Finley Refuge Road. In 1.3 miles, the route turns south into the refuge, reaching a kiosk with a map display and brochures in another 0.8 mile. From the kiosk, continue south 1.8 miles to arrive at the trailhead parking area opposite the maintenance yard.

From the wooden gate at the west end of the wire-mesh fence, a trimmed-grass swath guides hikers around a closed area near the pond

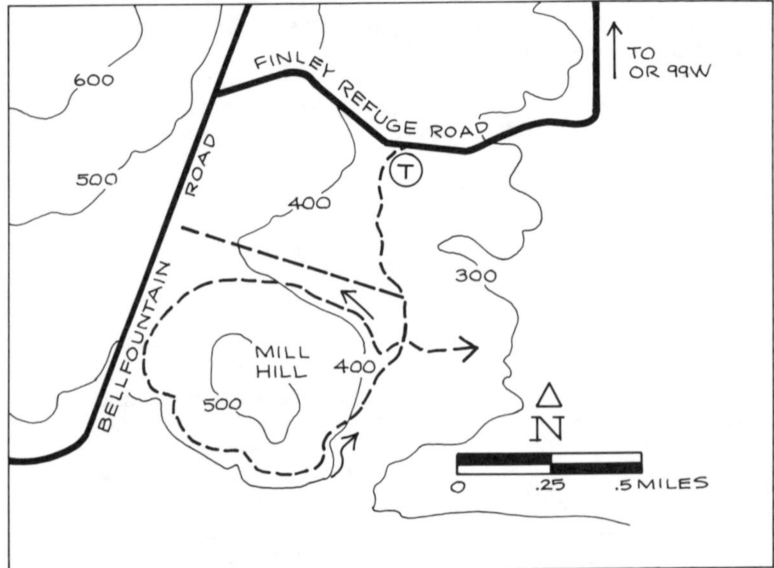

Oregon white oak

and maintenance yard. Swallows dart and swoop, while low-flying hawks patrol the open field. Poison oak is abundant along the trail; be alert when making off-trail investigations.

In 0.3 mile, the trail meets a gravel road. At this point, an unmaintained 0.5-mile spur branches to the right, travels a bush-lined path to an abandoned orchard, and ends at Bellfountain Road near milepost 10—a detour offering additional opportunity for bird, small mammal, or even deer sightings. The primary hiker route follows the gravel road to the left.

Going a short distance along the road locates the 0.1-mile access spur to the Mill Hill Loop, on the right. A counterclockwise tour of the 1.5-mile circuit introduces a mixed woodland with many oaks and maples and an extraordinary number of galls littering the path. Birds scratch for food in the undergrowth, but seldom reveal their identities.

Departing the woodland, the trail then tours an open meadow of inviting grasses and wildflowers. Free from poison oak, the meadow is engaging. From the meadow, the trail travels the bench above Gray Creek Swamp, but offers only teasing glimpses of the wetland through the branchwork. The loop then draws to a close.

With the return to the road, hikers have the option of extending the hike during the time the interior refuge is open for hiking: April 15 to October 30.

Going to the right finds the Ponds Loop in about a quarter mile. The loop trail visits Beaver and Cattail ponds, which occasionally seem to boil with leaping bullfrogs.

Beyond the ponds' circuit, routes branch to additional trail options for all-day outings: The Pigeon Butte Trail climbs to the summit of the refuge's most prominent feature (elevation 543 feet) for a refuge–Coast Range–Willamette Valley vista. The Muddy Creek Trail explores a riparian environment and holds the potential for such wildlife sightings as wood ducks, mergansers, and rollicking otters.

As signs are few and junctions many, it's a good idea to carry the refuge brochure. Trail maps are available at the refuge office or at the entrance kiosk; check the bulletin board for current regulations and information.

22 MOUNT PISGAH SUMMIT TRAIL

Distance: 3.2 miles round trip
Elevation change: 1,000 feet
Difficulty: Moderate
Season: Year round, except
For information: Lane County

Map: None
during extreme fire danger
Parks Division
Howard Buford Recreation Area

This trail ascends a classic grassland–Oregon white oak woodland of the Willamette Valley hills to reach the summit of Mount Pisgah (elevation 1,516 feet). The broad summit overlooks the Willamette Valley floor, the Springfield–Eugene area, the Coast Range, and the near and distant Cascade peaks.

A variety of wildflowers dot the grassland slope. Here, yellow monkey flower, fawn lily, spring queen, woolly sunflower, daisy, thistle, field mustard, and Oregon iris bloom. Wildlife sightings may include deer, rabbit, hawks and other raptors, western tanager, jays, and woodpeckers.

Set aside in the 1970s, this 2,244-acre natural park houses an ecologically diverse land rising above the Coast and Middle forks of the Willamette River. Mount Pisgah was a traditional hunting-harvesting ground for the Calapooya Indians.

Old fire roads and footpaths lace the higher slope presenting loop-tour options. Routes probing the southwest portion of the Howard Buford Recreation Area suffer the intrusion of clicking overhead powerlines.

At the base of the hill, interconnected, short trails explore Mount Pisgah Arboretum with its riparian, marsh, forest, and grassland habitats.

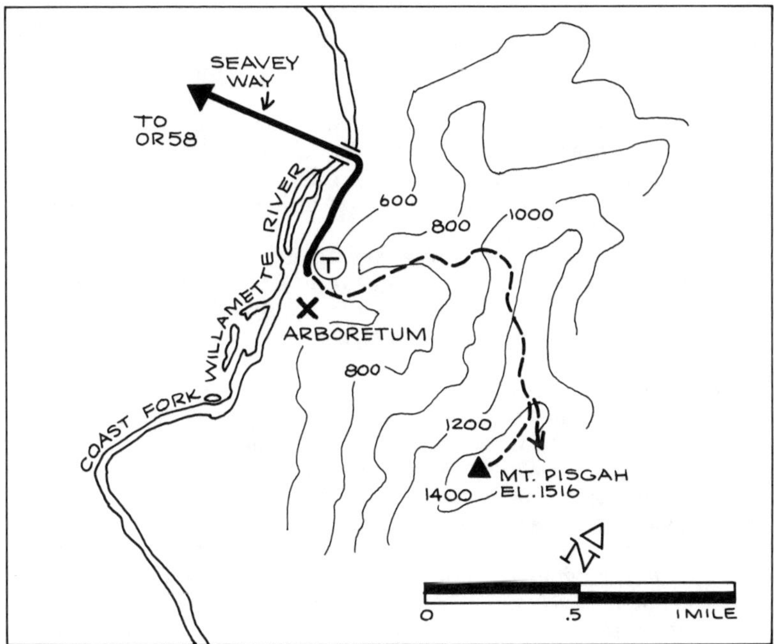

Some of its oaks and maples are more than 200 years old. Trail and natural history brochures are available at the Arboretum for a nominal fee.

From OR 58, 0.25 mile east of I-5, go north on Seavey Loop Road. A sign for Mount Pisgah marks the turn. At the T-junction in 1.8 miles, turn right on Seavey Way, following the brown road signs for Buford Park and the Mount Pisgah Arboretum. The park lies less than a half mile ahead; the trailhead is found at the Arboretum parking area at the end of the park road.

From the hiker gate above the parking area, the trail climbs, passing beneath utility lines. As it rounds a natural oak–grassland slope with a few Douglas fir, it overlooks the Arboretum. Ferns, wildflowers, and poison oak interweave the grasses, while mistletoe and lichen accent the crooks of the oaks.

The hike follows a former road, which shows time-softened edges and a steady climbing grade. It offers a wide hiking lane for this popular summit trek. At 0.1 mile, a footpath intersects the Mount Pisgah Summit Trail; continue straight ahead. Early views of the round-topped mountain soon greet the hiker. Below the trail is an intermittent, gurgling creek. At 0.5 mile, a secondary trail breaks away to the left to mount and cross a nearby low saddle. A detour to the saddle finds an overlook of the farmland along the Middle Fork Willamette River and Potato Hill.

The summit trail continues its open grassland tour. Oaks claim the rises, while a few blackberry brambles patch the grassland. Hawks circle overhead.

Soon, the trail offers views of the confluence of the Coast and Middle forks of the Willamette River, the valley fields, the Coast Range, Spencer Butte, and the Springfield–Eugene area. A cloud bank moving in from the coast is a common sighting.

At 0.8 mile, the trail crosses under the wires one last time, as it enters a turn to travel the west face of Mount Pisgah. The view now spans 180 degrees west. The trail tops the summit ridge at 1.8 miles, entering an oak grove. Along the ridge, spring queen blooms in late winter–early spring.

Where the trail forks at 1.1 miles and again at 1.2 miles, take either path as they again merge in short distance. Boulders just off the trail invite hikers to pause and enjoy the view. As the trail tours the ridge grove, a few maples and some scenic snags divert attention from the oaks.

At 1.4 miles, take the uphill path to the right to tag the mountaintop. The summit throws open a window to the east featuring the distant snow-capped Three Sisters. Atop Mount Pisgah, a bronze monument shows the topography of the immediate area. Its carved base records the mountain's geologic evolution. Trails crisscross the broad summit unfolding a 360-degree view.

Return as you came, or return to the 1.4-mile junction and take the other fork, swinging a loop around the mountain. The tour travels oak–grassland and passes beneath powerline corridors to arrive at the foot of Mount Pisgah above the Coast Fork of the Willamette River. It returns to the trailhead via the Arboretum.

23 UPPER AND LOWER TABLE ROCKS TRAILS

Distance: 3 miles round trip (Upper Table); 5 miles round trip (Lower Table)
Elevation change: 700 feet (for each)
Difficulty: Moderate
Season: Spring through fall
Map: The Table Rocks brochure (produced by The Nature Conservancy and the BLM)
For information: Medford District BLM

These two landmark mesas towering some 800 feet above the Agate Desert and the snaking ribbon of the Rogue River bear protective status as a Nature Conservancy Preserve (Lower Table Rock) and a Bureau of Land Management–designated Area of Critical Environmental Concern (Lower and Upper table rocks). Public access to the summit of Upper Table Rock is a courtesy of the Rogue River Ranch.

The Rogue River Valley and its tablelands were the long-time home to the Takelma Indians. Then in 1853, the Rogue River War erupted pitting

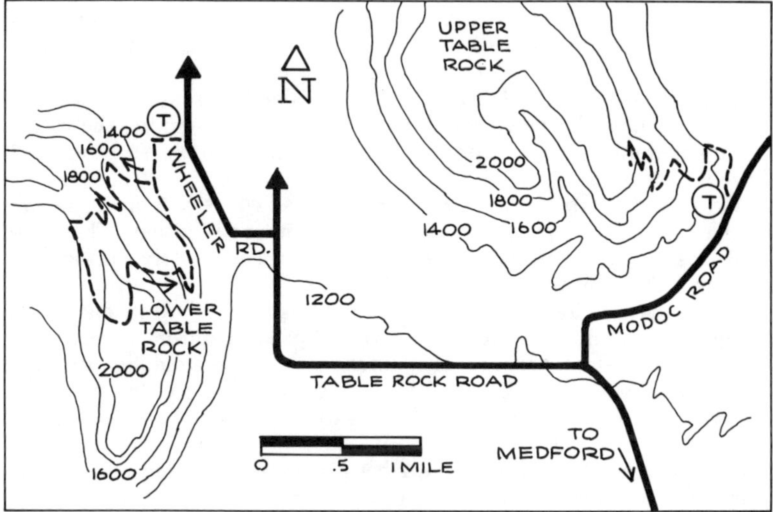

the Takelmas against the white settlers and soldiers. The land surrounding the rocks was the battle stage; at its outcome, Lower Table Rock became the site of a short-lived reservation.

The tablelands feature basalt rims above skirts of older sandstone. The mesas were isolated by erosion over a period of some 10 million years. Today, erosion continues to whittle the rock slowly.

The terrain suggests various microclimates with mixed evergreen–deciduous woodlands, oak savannas, and valley chaparral. Native bunchgrass carpets much of the floor. The summits display grassy moss mounds, a low rock studding, vernal pools, and a springtime wildflower show (March to June), with goldfield, widow's grass, lupine, clover, and a species of meadowfoam that grows atop these rocks and nowhere else in the world.

Hikers commonly spy black-tailed deer, quail, meadowlarks, acorn woodpeckers, flickers, towhees, turkey vultures, and hawks. Rattlesnakes and whipsnakes are among the eight snake species found at the rocks, though they are seldom encountered.

To reach the rocks, from I-5 at Central Point, take exit 32 and head 1 mile east to Table Rock Road. There turn north, and go 5 miles. A right turn onto Modoc Road finds a large, marked gravel parking pad on the left in 1.5 miles, Upper Table Rock trailhead.

For Lower Table Rock trailhead, continue along Table Rock Road, another 2.4 miles from the Modoc Road junction. Turn left onto Wheeler Road at the sign and go 0.8 mile to find the trailhead on the left.

The Upper Table Rock Trail is a good, steady climbing earthen trail, which can become miry following rains. It travels a white oak savanna–grassland and a mixed pine–oak woodland with madrone, manzanita, deerbrush, and poison oak. Mistletoe hangs from the oak branches, while lichens dress the trunks. At 0.2 mile, the trail passes a couple of large, mossy rock outcrops which afford Rogue River Valley overlooks.

At 0.5 mile, either trail fork leads to a wooden bench atop a low knob. The ascent expands the view to include the foothills rimming the valley and the distant Cascades. The trailbed is now rocky in places; some road noise echoes up the slope.

At 1 mile, the trail enters a thicker woodland where tall madrone and black oak are dominant. A shaded bench welcomes a breather. Where the trail crosses a time-healed fire-break road, trees effectively squeeze out all views. The trail tops the mesa at 1.5 miles.

Hikers may explore the private land of the summit with its patterned ground vegetation, tree islands, and vernal pools. Strolling the footpath and old jeep trails radiating to the plateau rim, hikers gradually unravel the 360-degree vista, featuring Lower Table Rock, the patchwork of the valley fields, the Siskiyou foothills, and the lower rocky shelves within the plateau canyon. Return as you came.

The Lower Table Rock Trail begins traveling a fenced corridor along an oak grove for 0.4 mile. There, it enters a woodland of black and white oaks, madrone, and manzanita. Ahead lies a junction: The main summit route ventures straight uphill; the bench route journeys right for a counterclockwise loop.

The bench trail weaves along an oak terrace to pass a wooden bench at 1 mile. The trail then switchbacks up through a more congested, mixed evergreen–deciduous forest with a brushy midstory topping a ridge of moss-covered rocks at 1.5 miles. Here, hikers gain views of the far plateau of horseshoe-shaped Lower Table Rock.

En route to the summit, the rocky trail now descends a brushy corridor and crosses a rock field where poison oak thrives. At 1.7 miles, it meets an old road. A left continues the loop, heading uphill passing through private property. The open corridor proves hot summer hiking; keep to the roadway to avoid trespassing. At the hiker gate, the trail enters the summit Area of Critical Environmental Concern. At 2.25 miles, the trail tops the plateau. The summit offers valley, foothill, and Upper Table Rock vistas with an opportunity to explore the grassland, vernal pools, and wildflower myriad.

The loop follows the grassy swath north from the end of the summit runway to find an earthen trail at the plateau's oak and manzanita fringe. The main summit trail then descends the slope via stretches of steep, rugged old road and groomed foot trail.

Similar mixed woodland–oak savanna habitats with a grove of beautiful madrone at 3.5 miles frame the route. The branchwork allows only limited valley and table rock views. The loop closes in another mile. Retrace your steps to the trailhead.

24 GORGE TRAIL

Distance: 25.3 miles one way (Bridal Veil to Eagle Creek)
Elevation change: 1,500 feet
Difficulty: Strenuous
Season: Year round, except during low-elevation snows
Map: USFS Trails of the Columbia Gorge
For information: Columbia Gorge Ranger District

In 1986, the Columbia Gorge officially became a national scenic area. Throwing open the doors to many of the Oregon attractions is the burgeoning Gorge Trail, which incorporates new and existing trails and abandoned segments of the old scenic highway. It will one day link Portland with the town of Hood River, some 65 miles east; presently, it's complete between Bridal Veil and Cascade Locks.

This main hiking artery travels just above or below the front cliffs of the gorge, stringing together a prized collection of trails. Together, they explore the drama of the Columbia River Gorge: its sheer basalt cliffs carved by an ancient roiling river, the silver threads of a host of major waterfalls, temperate Douglas fir rain forests, celebrated vistas, narrow canyons, and crystalline creeks. In addition to long-distance hiking, the Gorge Trail provides a variety of loop hikes as well as access to the Columbia Wilderness trails.

Its main drawback is the noise intrusion from the interstate highway, rail, and river transportation routes that likewise probe this corridor. The fire in the fall of 1991 improved the health of the overall forest, eliminating brush and snags from cut-over areas and sweeping unevenly through the fuller forest, opening it to greater diversity.

The Gorge Trail enjoys multiple access points off the 7-mile western segment of the Old Scenic Highway (US 30). From Portland, travel I-84 west and take the Bridal Veil exit. Trailheads are found near the Bridal Veil junction, at the vista turnouts farther east, and at Ainsworth State Park. Additional access points are found at John Yeon State Park near Warrendale, at Wahclella Falls Trailhead south of Bonneville Dam, and at Eagle Creek Campground.

Beginning at the trailhead just east of the Bridal Veil junction, the Gorge Trail strikes uphill, touring a temperate Douglas fir-bigleaf maple rain forest on its eastward journey. At 2.2 miles, a side trail to the left leads to Angels Rest atop the gorge wall for a grand wind-swept vista looking downstream.

At 4.8 miles, the trail tags a view of the mystifying headwater springs which immediately give rise to the full-coursing Wahkeena Creek. The hike then descends along the creek offering views of the falls. Farther east, the Gorge Trail reaches the Multnomah Falls area. Downstream from the Multnomah Creek crossing, a short spur to the left leads to a platform vista atop the falls. The main trail switchbacks down slope to a junction. Going left (west) finds a stone bridge with a square-on view of

Multnomah Falls

the upper falls and a top-view of the lower falls. At 620 feet, Multnomah is the fourth tallest falls in the nation. Downhill from the bridge is Multnomah Lodge (8.3 miles).

Continuing eastward from the bridge vista, the Gorge Trail tours multistoried forest, rounds cliffs, and crosses over scree slopes en route to Oneonta Gorge (about 10.5 miles). Oneonta is an impressively narrow chasm, richly decked in mosses and ferns—a designated botanical area. A side trip uphill finds Triple Falls in 1 mile, three side-by-side 100- to 135-foot falls. Beyond Oneonta, the Gorge Trail continues its forest and cliff tour passing behind Ponytail Falls. After skirting above Ainsworth State Park, the trail exits at the old scenic highway.

The route then follows the frontage road east to Dodson, where hikers find signs pointing them back onto the trail. The hike resumes touring forest, requiring creek fordings, and wrapping along the gorge wall,

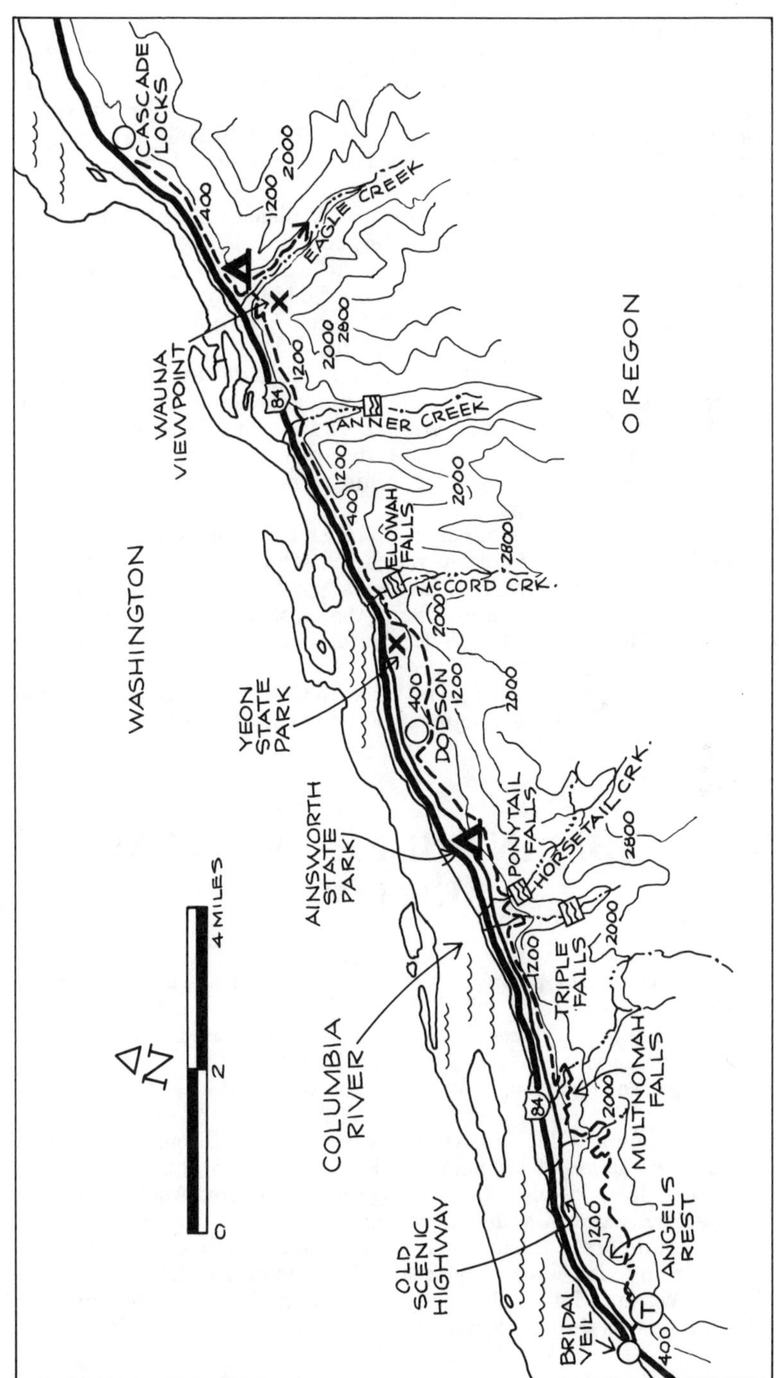
CASCADE LOCKS
EAGLE CREEK
WAUNA VIEWPOINT
TANNER CREEK
OREGON
WASHINGTON
ELOWAH FALLS
McCORD CRK.
YEON STATE PARK
DODSON
AINSWORTH STATE PARK
PONYTAIL FALLS
HORSETAIL CRK.
TRIPLE FALLS
MULTNOMAH FALLS
COLUMBIA RIVER
ANGELS REST
OLD SCENIC HIGHWAY
BRIDAL VEIL
84
T
N
0
2
4 MILES
400
1200
2000
2800

while drifting away from the freeway.

From Yeon State Park (at about 17 miles), the trail heads east into a rich Douglas fir forest. In less than 0.5 mile, a right leads to the Upper McCord Creek Falls. Going left toward Elowah Falls advances the Gorge Trail leading to a footbridge vista of this pretty falls spilling through a cleft in a cliff. Bypassing picnic sites, the trail alternately travels forest and across scree to the Moffett Creek fording.

Along the next stretch, the forest setting is pleasant, but the trail is far too close to the freeway to be completely relaxing. Utility corridors, here and elsewhere, steal from the tour. A brief stretch via an old two-track and a right on the downhill path finds the old highway leading to Tanner Creek and Wahclella Falls Trail at 21.4 miles. A 1-mile detour upstream from the gated road finds this elegant falls.

Bypassing the falls trail, the Gorge tour continues east toward Eagle Creek, traveling beneath the bigleaf maples and alders of a second-growth forest, following old two-tracks, and crossing forest roads. Nearing the Wauna View Point junction, the trail passes across a fern and scree slope, where pikas pipe from hiding. The view point suggests another detour for a gorge vista.

Rich, ancient forest surrounds the hiker on the remainder of the trip to Eagle Creek. In fall, hikers can watch the salmon wriggle upstream to spawn in the clean gravels of the creek. From the day-use area (25.3 miles), Eagle Creek Recreation Trail—the most popular entrance to the Columbia Wilderness and itself a waterfall showcase—calls hikers away from the front wall tour.

The Gorge Trail continues east 3 miles to Cascade Locks, often traveling via the time-healed old highway. Farther east, the trail is under construction.

25 HERMAN CREEK–WAHTUM LAKE LOOP

Distance: 26.2-mile loop, plus optional side trips
Elevation change: 4,100 feet
Difficulty: Strenuous
Season: Late spring through fall
Map: USFS Trails of the Columbia Gorge
For information: Columbia Gorge Ranger District
Columbia Wilderness Area

This Columbia Wilderness circuit travels mainly through forest as it ascends the canyon of Herman Creek, tags pretty Wahtum Lake, and crosses and descends the ridge housing Benson Plateau. Ancient Douglas fir forest richly woven with bigleaf maples yields to a congested forest of high-elevation firs at the upper reaches. A cedar swamp and a bonanza of diverse spring- and summer-flowering flora add to the journey.

Above Wahtum Lake, Chinidere Mountain beckons for a detour. This side trail travels through forest and up a talus slope to a top-of-the-world

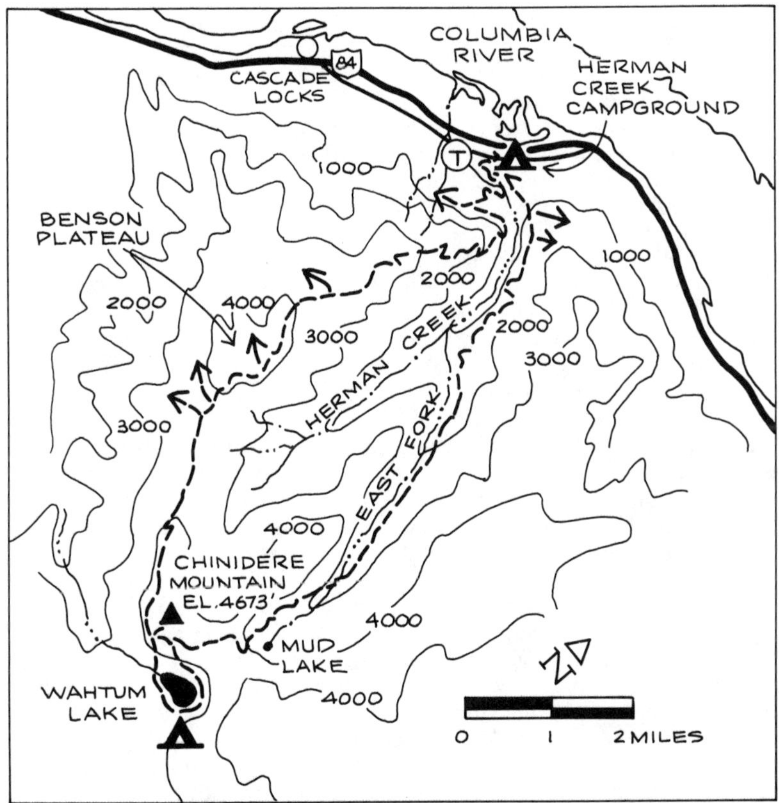

360-degree panorama. Views applaud the Columbia Wilderness and offer looks into Washington. As the route tours the ridge, meadow openings and forest gaps bring additional views.

To reach the loop, from I-84, take Cascade Locks exit 44. At the town's east end, follow Forest Lane (the frontage road along the freeway's south side) toward Oxbow Hatchery. Going 1.7 miles finds a work center and the turn for Herman Creek Campground and Trailhead. Trailhead parking lies 0.4 mile uphill. In winter, the gated road requires hikers to walk this distance or hike the access spur from the center.

The hike's first 2 miles offer little, but roll by quickly. After short uphill switchbacks, the merging of the Work Center Trail (0.1 mile), and the crossing of a utility-corridor road at 0.25 mile, the trail briefly enters a nice, forested stretch, as it bypasses the Herman Bridge Trail Junction.

A closed dirt road continues the route passing through semi-open second growth. Marked routes branch from it; keep to the roadway, which narrows to a footpath at 1.9 miles. A fuller forest now encloses the trail. Fern, pathfinder, duckfoot, wild rose, and twin flower weave a rich forest mat.

The trail climbs, rounding mossy rock outcrops and oak-shaded points to enter the wilderness at 2.8 miles. Cascading creeks and intermittent waters accent the trek and mark distance; some require wading. Deep in the canyon flows Herman Creek.

At 4.1 miles is the Casey Creek Camp. An unmarked, steeply dropping, 0.6-mile secondary path leads to the camp's water source—the confluence of Herman Creek and its east fork—both driving waters with mossy, boulder banks. From the camp, the trail follows the East Fork Canyon upstream.

At 7.1 miles, the route crosses a skunk cabbage bog nestled in a moist forest. Ahead, the Cedar Swamp Shelter occupies a grand ancient cedar grove. The loop then continues through moister forest to reach the East Fork crossing, followed soon after by Noble Camp.

As the trail climbs, the forest shows smaller fir and hemlock as it naturally thins with the gain in elevation. Past the Mud Lake Trail Junction (9.2 miles), the trail tops out.

Several trails now work their way to Wahtum Lake. At 10.2 miles the hiker finds the Anthill Trail Junction; stay on the Herman Creek Trail. In another mile, the Herman Creek Trail comes to a T-junction with the Pacific Crest Trail (PCT). Bear left to reach Wahtum Lake. Bear grass and huckleberry bushes fill the understory. A primitive, walk-in camp is above the south shore of the lake.

Rounding the lake clockwise to the Lower Chinidere Trail Junction, go right, cross the log-jammed outlet, and head uphill to again reach the PCT (13.5 miles). The loop resumes bearing left. An early detour follows the Chinidere Mountain Trail, climbing 0.3 mile and 400 feet. The summit view features the deep drainages and high ridges of the wilderness, Wahtum Lake bowl, and Mounts Adams and Hood.

Forgoing the detour, the PCT follows the ridge, touring true fir forest and talus slopes. Manzanita, bear grass, and kinnikinnick spread beneath the tightly bunched firs; lichens adorn the trunks. Openings offer views of the Eagle Creek drainage and Tanner Butte to the west; Herman Creek drainage, Tomlike Mountain, and Woolly Horn and Nick Eaton ridges to the east.

At 15.5 miles, a side trail leads to a vista atop a cliff rim. It overlooks the Herman Creek drainage, Tomlike Mountain, Mount Adams, and the Columbia Gorge. Soon lower-elevation flora enters the mix.

From the Eagle–Benson Trail Junction, the PCT flattens as it travels north along the eastern edge of forested Benson Plateau. By 19.2 miles, the trail steeply descends from the main plateau. Near Benson Way Junction, hole-riddled snags mark the forest, and the trail switchbacks down to Tea Kettle Spring (20.8 miles). Campsites occupy the junction flats.

At 22.3 miles, the trail enters a steep, open wildflower meadow with limited views toward Washington. With more downhill switchbacks, the trail leaves the Columbia Wilderness. Douglas fir and vine maple shade its route; the understory grows more profuse.

At the 24.3-mile junction, the loop continues downhill to the right via the Herman Bridge Trail, passing through forest, touring below cliffs, and crossing scree slopes to Herman Creek bridge. Climbing from the creek, the loop closes at the Herman Creek Trail. Go left to find the trailhead in 0.7 mile.

26 TIMBERLINE TRAIL

Distance: 40.7-mile loop
Elevation change: 4,100 feet
Difficulty: Strenuous
Season: Mid-summer through early fall
Map: USFS Mount Hood Wilderness
For information: Zigzag Ranger District

This heavy-duty hiker trail constructed in the 1930s by the Civilian Conservation Corps applauds the rugged beauty of Mount Hood. Along it, hikers dip deep into chiseled drainages, ford glacial streams, cross rocky slopes, bypass glaciers and snow-melt falls, and tour high-elevation forest and inviting alpine meadows. In places, snowfields linger into summer. Stream crossings are best accomplished in the morning, when waters are lowest; some may prove impassable at times.

Mount Hood (elevation 11,235 feet) is a strato-volcano, which had four minor eruptions in the 1800s. A buried forest along the tour hints at the mountain's explosive nature. A harsh environment of thin soils, changeable weather, and hefty winds claims the mountain. Spreading outward from the volcanic peak is the Mount Hood Wilderness Area, measuring 47,000 acres.

Mid-July and August find a wildflower showcase in the high meadows with bear grass, lupine, paintbrush, penstemon, and phlox. Vistas feature the many faces of Hood, its forested neighborhood, Mount Jefferson and Trillium Lake to the south, and Washington's Mounts Adams, St. Helens, and Rainier to the north.

One of the most-climbed glaciated peaks in the United States, Mount Hood represents a technical climb; the first full ascent came in 1845. The Timberline Trail ties together the popular climbing routes along with a couple dozen side trails, welcoming both day hikers and backpackers.

This trail is most easily accessed from Timberline Lodge. From US 26 east of Government Camp, turn north onto Timberline Road and go 5.2 miles to the lodge and ski area. The Timberline Trail and Pacific Crest Trail (PCT) are one in this area; the trail begins behind the lodge.

Other accesses lie off Lolo Pass Road (FR 18). Follow FR 1825 and 1825.100 to the Ramona Falls Trailhead, or take FR 1828 and 1828.118 north for 7 miles to reach the Top Spur Trailhead. For an easy access off OR 35, turn west onto Cooper Spur Road and follow FR 3512 through the Cloud Cap–Tilly Jane Historical District to trailheads near Cloud Cap Inn.

A clockwise tour from Timberline Lodge passes beneath the ski lifts to visit alpine forest and meadow, and spare, open slope. Mount Jefferson

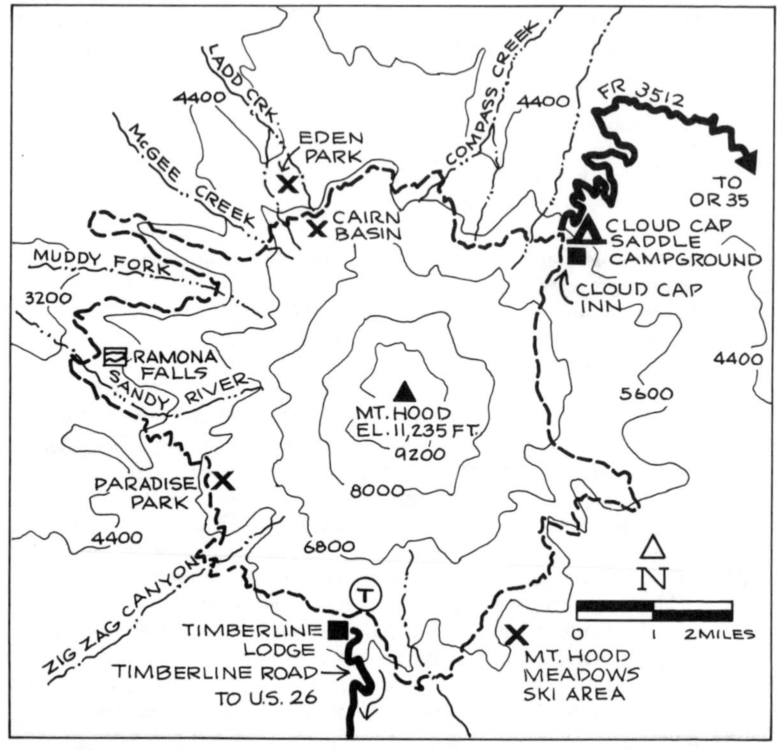

commands the view to the south. At 2.2 miles, the rollercoaster journey tops the open east ridge overlooking the rugged volcanic cut of Zigzag Canyon with Mississippi Head.

The trail then slips in and out of Zigzag Canyon, passes through Paradise Park, crosses creeks, and tags waterfall vistas. By 7.4 miles, it offers views of Slide Mountain and overlooks of Rushing Water Creek. The Sandy River crossing follows; cairns mark the route.

Approaching Ramona Falls (10.2 miles), the route briefly follows Old Maid Flat, a lahar (a ridge of rock and debris) formed during a Mount Hood eruption some 200 to 250 years ago. A small-stature lodgepole pine forest, uncharacteristic to the western slopes of the Cascades, houses the trail. The falls is a beauty, broad and spreading, splashing over moss-capped basalt. The trail continues rounding the untamed flanks of Hood.

At 13.3 miles, the Muddy Fork requires two stream crossings, but the overhead view rewards with Hood, Yocum Ridge, Sandy Glacier, and McNeil Point. Much of the way, the trail tours old-growth hemlock and true fir forest with lichen-brushed tree trunks. Huckleberry and bear grass dominate the floor. Winds wash up the slope in a bluster and circulate clouds near the crown.

The trail then switchbacks below McNeil Point, gains overlooks of the Lost Lake Basin, rounds meadow bowls and seasonal ponds. At the Cairn

Basin rock shelter (19.4 miles) the trail forks: The trail to the left continues the circuit to Eden Park; the right fork shortens the hike by 0.4 mile.

Beyond Elk Cove, the creek headwaters often house scenic, broken blue-glacier chunks. The views build featuring Washington's Mounts Adams and Rainier, the Langille Glacier and Crags, a ghost forest, Barrett Spur, the Hood River Valley, and Cloud Cap Inn. Along the stream cuts grow pearly everlasting, fireweed, mountain ash, and lupine.

At Cloud Cap Saddle Campground (27.5 miles), fill the water jugs. Water sources ahead are limited, as the trail next travels above timberline.

White River Canyon, Mount Hood

A detour east finds the inn. The Timberline Trail continues, bypassing a stone shelter en route to the crossing of Lamberson Spur—the highest point along the trail (elevation 7,320 feet).

The trail continues its rising-dipping course, fording creeks and touring forest, meadow, and open slopes. At 38.3 miles, the water level of White River may suggest an upstream crossing. Before long, the PCT (North) and Timberline Trail merge. A leg-taxing, loose sand trek follows, as the trail ascends the dividing ridge between the White and Salmon river drainages.

At the plateau where the ascent calms, hikers overlook the desolate headwater bowl of White River Canyon. Here, the last eruptions some 200 to 250 years ago buried the forest. Over time, wind and rain have revealed a few upper tree limbs.

From the ridge, the trail continues west, crossing the headwater drainages of the Salmon River, touring open, wildflower-dotted slopes and patchy, snag-pierced alpine forest to return to the lodge.

27 BADGER CREEK NATIONAL RECREATION TRAIL

Distance: 12.2 miles one way
Elevation change: 3,100 feet
Difficulty: Strenuous
Season: Spring through fall
Map: USGS Badger Lake, Flag Point; USFS Mount Hood
For information: Barlow Ranger District

This popular creekside trail explores the southeast arm and heart of 24,000-acre Badger Creek Wilderness. While the wilderness area enjoys relative ease of access, the trail affords great solitude.

Long-ago glaciers carved out the steep-walled, U-shaped valley drained by Badger Creek. The canyon boasts a transition forest, blending both east and west and high- and low-elevation species.

The southeast extension of the wilderness houses a drier habitat of white oak and ponderosa and white pine with a grassy, annual-sprinkled floor—a favored habitat of wild turkeys. With a gain in elevation, hemlock and true fir forests command the stage. From late June through July, the wilderness meadows have colorful wildflower blooms.

Cradled in the creek's headwater bowl is Badger Lake, tree-rimmed and dammed. A slope of silver snags and scree rises above one side, but the dam steals from the natural setting.

Good roads access the southeast trailhead. From OR 35 north of Barlow Pass, turn east onto FR 48, following it toward Rock Creek Reservoir. Or, from US 197 at Tygh Valley, turn west at the sign for Rock Creek Reservoir; the county road becomes FR 48 at the forest boundary.

East of the reservoir, turn north off FR 48 onto FR 4810 and follow FRs 4810 and 4811 north and west to reach FR 2710 in about 3 miles. Turn

Badger Creek

right for Bonney Crossing Campground. The trail begins opposite it, where FR 2710 crosses Badger Creek; park at the camp.

Following the north bank of Badger Creek upstream, the journey begins amid Douglas fir, oak, and pines. Trees blanket the north-facing slope; a rocky savanna claims the higher reaches of the south-facing slope. The transition habitat features such floral species as columbine, vanilla leaf, wild rose, twin flower, bracken fern, and chaparral lily. A mossy mat is absent.

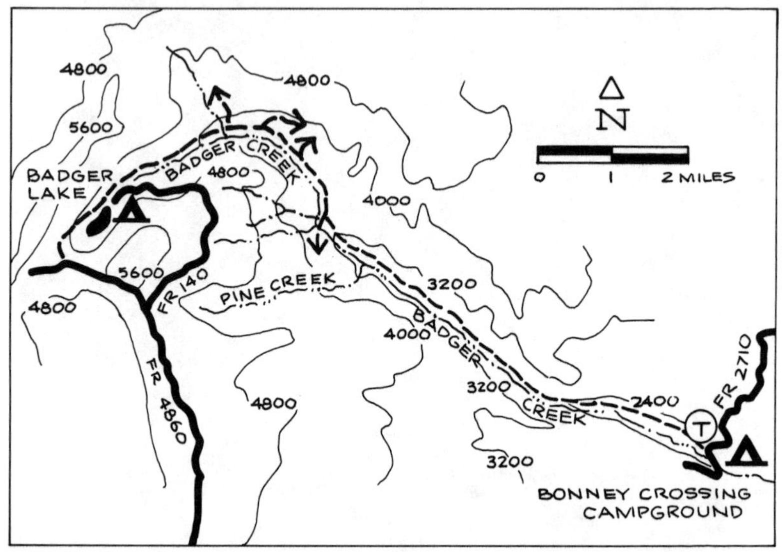

The early miles of the journey afford the best acquaintance with Badger Creek—clear and riffling, spilling over a rocky floor. Upstream, the trail offers only tree-filtered views.

Despite the full forest, the canopy remains semi-open. Hazel grows in the midstory. Moss-mottled boulders add character to the trail.

The 3-mile mark finds a small, dry, creekside meadow shaded by oaks and showered with lupine. With uphill switchbacks, the trail tours a drier slope. By 5 miles, the oaks have departed the mix. The trail slips farther from Badger Creek, losing all views of it.

The rise in elevation introduces a true mid-elevation Cascade forest of Douglas fir and hemlock with a few cedar, spruce, Pacific yew, and maple. At 7 miles is the Post Camp Trail junction; all junctions are well-marked. Beyond it, the National Recreation Trail (NRT) bypasses a nice campsite overlooking where moss-painted rocks pinch the creek forming deep pools and cascades.

At 7.6 miles, the hiker finds the Cut-off Trail junction; stay on the NRT. It is ever peaceful with filtered lighting. Bracken fern grow in the dry clearings.

After 9.5 miles, the trail again affords limited creek views. Here, the creek appears as a broad, dark-flowing banner. White riffles swirl around the rocks. The banks hold a wealth of greenery with many cedars.

The trail crosses numerous small drainages, but remains dry during all but the heaviest runoffs. Snags rise amid the mature, multistory forest. A congestion of vanilla leaf, bride's bonnet, lady fern, and more crowd the floor.

At 10.5 miles, a 0.1-mile side trail crosses the footbridge over Badger Creek and continues upstream to quiet Badger Camp, which is also accessed via forest road. Following the road uphill finds the main portion of the campground above man-made Badger Lake, a medium-sized lake, ringed by a tree stump–dotted, gravel beach when water levels drop.

Bypassing the camp spur, the NRT ascends from the broad canyon bottom reaching the primary lake access at 11 miles. Beyond it, the NRT travels a choked fir–spruce forest with many even-sized trees and a few large ones. Limbs scatter the floor.

At 11.3 miles, a regal spruce with a split trunk presides, marking the end to the choked forest. Gaps in the tree cover allow limited last looks at Badger Lake.

By 11.8 miles, huckleberry bushes border the open-cathedral path. The trail narrows, becoming rocky as it nears the trailhead on FR 4860 (a high-clearance-vehicle road). Lichens dress the tall straight trunks.

Round-trip hikers return as you came.

28 TWIN LAKES HIKE

Distance: 7.6 miles round trip
Elevation change: 800 feet
Difficulty: Moderate
Season: Late spring through fall
Map: USGS Mount Wilson; USFS Mount Hood
For information: Bear Springs Ranger District

This hike strings together three mountain lake basins, that of Frog Lake and Lower and Upper Twin lakes. It may be extended by a 0.9-mile side trip to Frog Lake Butte (elevation 5,293 feet), which finds a disappointing ridgetop harvest unit webbed by former roads, but a clear view of Mount Hood. En route to the summit, the trail gathers views of Mount Jefferson, Three Sisters, and Olallie Butte.

A mixed forest of hemlocks and Douglas and true fir with a few lodgepole and white pine shades much of the hike. Bear grass and huckleberry are the primary understory species.

Lower Twin Lake is the larger and deeper of the two hike-to lakes. Its fast-dropping shore suggests places to swim or fish. Trout can be spied weaving through the clear, green water. Forest rims the lake; a trail encircles it, tagging the well-spaced campsites.

The shallow waters of Upper Twin Lake draw fewer overnighters, promising the quieter retreat. The snowy crown of Mount Hood just peeks over its forest rim. A footpath similarly rounds the upper lake. Following the winter snowmelt, mosquitos are a nuisance at both lakes; be sure to carry insect repellent.

From the OR 35–US 26 junction, go southeast on US 26 toward Bend and Madras. In 4.4 miles, turn east (left) for the Pacific Crest Trail (PCT) and Frog Lake Campground. Parking for the PCT is just off US 26. For this Twin Lakes hike, go right on FR 2610 for 0.5 mile entering the campground; the trailhead lies opposite site 25. Hikers use the separate day-use parking area.

Beargrass

The trail leaves the campground never touring the meadow- and forest-edged Frog Lake. Instead, it climbs immediately away, crossing a forest road and passing through a block of forest flanked by harvest units.

In early July, the creamy heads of the bear grass blooms blaze the cuts. At 0.3 mile, the trail briefly tours one, finding open views of Mount Jefferson and Olallie Butte. The hum of US 26 accompanies the early hike distance.

At 0.5 mile, the trail crosses a second forest road. Hole-riddled snags pierce the forest; woodpeckers are commonly spied making the rounds. The trail, rock-studded in places, maintains its moderate uphill grade, topping the ridge at 1.1 miles. At the trail junction, hikers can detect Mount Hood through the tree cover.

To the right, the Frog Lake Butte Trail climbs 0.6 mile to the butte's ridge where it bears right on an old road followed by a left at the road fork; a small cairn indicates the turn. In 0.3 mile, it tags the summit for open views of Mount Hood. When the bear grass is in bloom, the summit harvest is less detractive. Morning views of the volcano are best. Forest Road 2610.220 offers a high-clearance drive to the site.

Forgoing the detour, a left leads down the slope to Lower Twin Lake. The trail begins narrow and quickly dropping, then settles into a more measured descent. A tighter forest cloaks this slope; huckleberry bushes are thick. Large-diameter trees bring added appeal.

At 2.4 miles, the trail meets the shoreline of this large, clear, green mountain lake. Following the east shore to the right, the hiker finds the quickest route to Upper Twin Lake. At the open camp flat in 0.2 mile, strike uphill to the right quickly arriving at a junction. The Wapinitia Trail circles left, traveling the west slope above the lake to meet the Pacific Crest Trail. Angling back to the right continues the lakes tour.

The trail makes a moderate ascent. The full forest absent of ground cover soon gives way to a forest rich with vine maple and a mixed floral

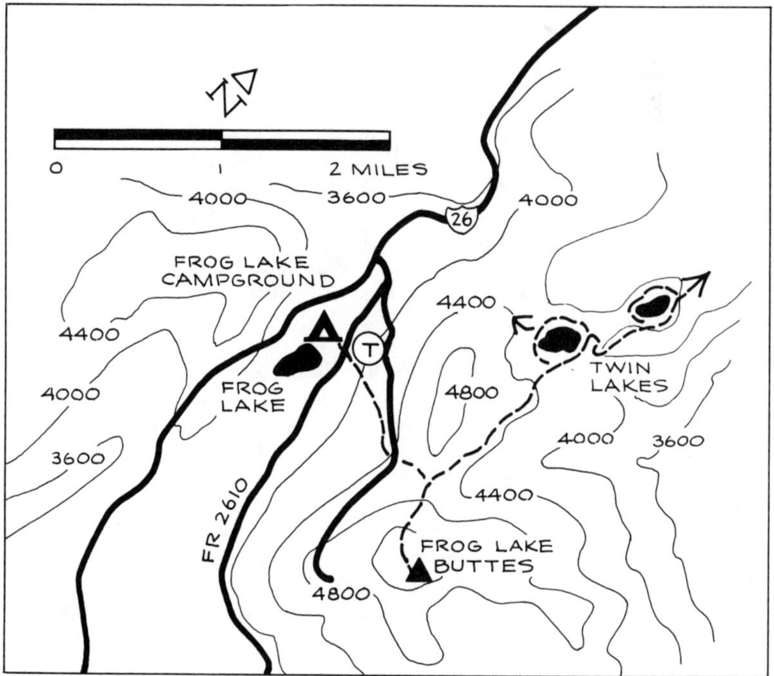

carpet. At 3 miles, the trail contours the slope overlooking the drainage linking the Twin Lakes.

At 3.25 miles, the trail arrives at the brownish green, shallow waters of Upper Twin Lake. Near the outlet, cross-lake views feature the upper crown of Mount Hood, rising above the evergreen rim of this nearly circular lake.

A 0.6-mile lake circuit hugs the shore, stitches together three or four campsites, and bypasses the junction for Palmateer View, which holds additional discovery for backpackers and all-day hikers. The west shore is less traveled with some leg-slapping shrubs.

From the outlet, retrace the route to Lower Twin Lake, descending to the open camp flat. There, go right along the lakeshore for a west bank tour, adding new perspectives.

At the junction in 0.7 mile, return as you came, crossing the ridge to Frog Lake basin and campground.

29 CLACKAMAS RIVER TRAIL

Distance: 7.8 miles one way
Elevation change: 400 feet
Difficulty: Moderate
Season: Year round, except during low-elevation snows
Map: USGS Fish Creek Mountain; USFS Mount Hood
For information: Estacada Ranger District

The pulsing, clear waters of the Clackamas Wild and Scenic River, a side trip to an unexpected waterfall, and remnants of old-growth splendor recommend this tour. In spring, when the water is high, kayakers and rafters ride the watery trail of the river. Gulls, kingfishers, dippers, and herons are the year-round co-travelers of the corridor.

This trail follows the southwest bank, touring a low-elevation ancient forest of fir, cedar, and hemlock with brief sections of post-harvest and post-fire second growth and utility-corridor meadows. The rolling route alternates from the slope to the river bench, offering river overlooks and approaches. Scattered, primitive camps welcome day hikes of various lengths. Mostly, the trail escapes the intrusion of nearby OR 224.

From Estacada, go southeast on OR 224, entering Mount Hood National Forest. Near Fish Creek Campground, turn right onto FR 54 to find the marked trailhead and a large, developed parking area near the bridge. To reach the trail's southeast terminus, stay on OR 224 and turn right onto FR 4620 for Indian Henry Campground. The trailhead lies opposite the camp.

From FR 54, an upstream journey tours a mixed old-growth forest. For a brief time, the trail surrenders to an old nature-reclaimed road. Twin flower, yellow violets, sword fern, trillium, oxalis, and Oregon grape add to the lush understory tangle. Between 0.3 and 0.5 mile, the trail serves up excellent river views before entering the first climb of its roller-coaster journey.

Osprey nest

At 1.4 miles, the trail reaches a campsite, but the noise of OR 224 intrudes. The trail is often rock-studded; a few seasonal falls streak the moss-decorated cliffs rising above the trail. For the next mile, OR 224 remains visible.

A nicer campsite lies at the 2.5-mile mark. It occupies a beautiful river flat with many cedars and snags and an abundance of moss, ferns, and oxalis. Opposite the Roaring River confluence, the trail switchbacks up the forested slope.

At 3.75 miles, nearing the descent to Pup Creek, a side trail branches to the right, touring the forested bench overlooking Pup Creek before a switchback up the slope.

This 0.25-mile footpath leads to a vista point which features the spectacular, though unannounced, Pup Creek Falls. This 200-foot showery drop begins as a 100-foot veil, feeding a tall, spreading, tiered falls, feeding a shorter basalt-hugging drop. Vine maple and cedar color the canyon. Yellow lichens etch the basalt of the cliff.

Beyond the falls detour, the river trail continues upstream with a crossing of the scout-built Pup Creek footbridge, which can be slippery when wet. The creek is a scenic tumbling water swirling around moss-capped boulders. Alders line its bank. For round-trip day hikes, Pup Creek marks the midway point.

Past the creek, the trail travels a long utility corridor with an open bracken fern meadow and alder fringes. At 4.4 miles, look for the osprey nest atop a riverside tree. Ahead finds a nice, rolling forested tour above the river.

At 4.7 miles, a side-creek crossing leads to a pleasant campsite on a forested bench above the river. Another utility corridor follows, before the trail switchbacks down to an overlook of the Narrows—a basalt-rimmed river channel (5.2 miles). Beyond it, a campsite welcomes a picnic lunch or a riverside stay.

The trail then passes through a mature cedar grove interspersed by fir and hemlock, a second-growth forest, and yet another utility-corridor meadow to arrive at an area of scenic cliffs and ancient forest.

Thick moss and succulents soften the jagged rock; spring enhances the cliffs with seasonal waterfalls and weeping walls. At 6.3 miles, the trail passes beneath a ledge and behind one of the ribbony intermittent falls. Bigleaf maples thrive near the cliffs.

By 6.5 miles, OR 224 rounds the slope below the trail, but remains out of sight; a generator noise intrudes. The trail next tours a forest of smaller trees in an area culled by fire this century; a few charred monarchs carry the tale.

After a footbridge crossing at 7.3 miles, the trail climbs and wraps around a forested slope to reach the FR 4620 trailhead. Cedar, fir, and hemlock house the path.

30 SHELLROCK TRAIL TO ROCK LAKES LOOP

Distance: 13.8 miles round trip
Elevation change: 1,000 feet
Difficulty: Strenuous
Season: Late spring through fall
Map: USGS High Rock, Fish Creek Mountain; USFS Mount Hood
For information: Clackamas Ranger District

This sometimes rugged, roller-coaster trail visits mountain lakes and a high meadow and tops Frazier Mountain (elevation 5,110 feet). The mostly shaded trail tours forest of both western and mountain hemlock and Douglas and true fir. Bear grass and huckleberry command the floor. A wealth of rhododendron claims the slope above and near Serene Lake.

The trail snags brief but splendid looks at Mount Jefferson, Olallie Butte, Mount Hood, and Washington's volcano line-up of Adams, St. Helens and Rainier. Other vistas include Serene Lake and the headwater drainage of the South Fork Roaring River below Indian Ridge.

Lake basin visitors and overnighters will want to come well-supplied with insect repellent, especially for trips following the snowmelt. Early season hikers may also have to contend with downfalls on the route.

The trail begins at Hideaway Lake. From Estacada, go southeast on OR 224 for 15.7 miles to take FR 57 east for 7.4 miles. There turn left onto FR 58, followed by another left in 3.1 miles onto FR 5830. In 5.3 miles, go left on the campground entrance road, FR 5830.190, to reach the camp and trailhead in 0.2 mile.

The hike rounds the northwest shore of Hideaway Lake to reach the Shellrock Trail junction in 0.2 mile. It then travels a low forested rise above the lake, skirts a meadow, and crosses FR 5830 reaching an alternative trailhead and parking area for the Shellrock Trail at 0.6 mile. A large, open harvest unit with small evergreens, bear grass, and huckleberry claims the next 0.4 mile.

The trail re-enters a full forest for a short, mild descent to Shellrock Lake, a beautiful, large lake at the base of Frazier Mountain's forest and scree slope. Alder and huckleberry flourish along the lake. Go right, crossing the outlet creek to round the lakeshore. Here, bunchberry, bride's bonnet, and wintergreen shoots add color. Gray jays and woodpeckers are passersby.

From the camp flat at 1.5 miles, follow the flagged route angling uphill to the right. This steep, rugged segment, sometimes rocky and marshy, works its way up the inlet drainage. At 2.4 miles, the trail arrives at a T-junction, the start of the loop tour.

A left begins a clockwise tour along the abandoned jeep track heading toward Cache Meadow. High-elevation trees, open, rocky stretches, and volcano vistas mark the loop. By 2.7 miles, the trail begins touring a full forest thick with huckleberry atop Frazier Mountain.

At 3.25 miles, the route leaves the dirt lane, turning left for Grouse Point Trail; a footpath resumes with a hefty forest descent to Cache Meadow, 4.25 miles.

A narrow footpath enters the moist meadow with its ponds and shrub hedges. Where the path fades, curve right, entering the forest to find a lean-to shelter. Frogs and newts populate the ponds; blueberry bushes, globeflowers, buttercups, and shooting stars ornament the grasses. The blazed trail continues along the forest fringe of the meadow. Spruce enters the mix.

At the unmarked three-way junction at 4.4 miles, take the fork to the right to continue the loop; do not cross the creek. The trail strings along the forest-meadow fringe to 4.75 miles, where it climbs away. At 5.4 miles, it tops and tours a ridge.

A detour into the small cut at 5.6 miles finds the finest vista of the hike—a four-volcano view with Mounts Hood, Adams, St. Helens, and Rainier. Deep in the basin rests oval Serene Lake. A rugged cliff outcrop towers above it. The loop skirts the cut, following the ridge for a slow descent. Rhododendrons add color in July.

At the 6.3-mile junction, go right to enter the Serene Lake Basin. In 1 mile, the trail reaches a superb lakeside campsite with a table. Fish snatch at insects from the latest hatch. The loop travels left to cross the outlet. Ahead, a low rise separates the trail from the lake; spurs branch to the water.

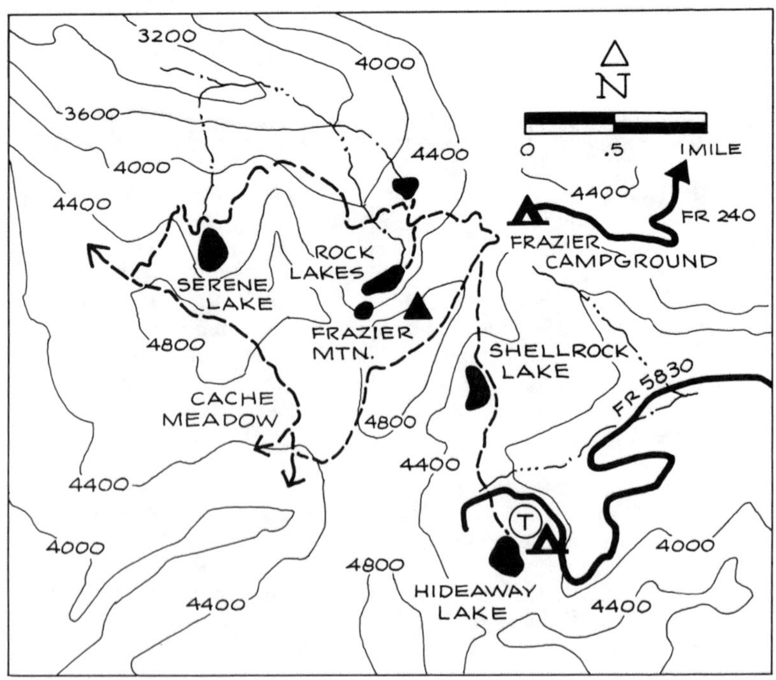

The trail next tours a steep slope marked by forest and talus stretches. Cedars claim the moist drainages. At 9.5 miles, the trail crosses the South Fork Roaring River, a log and rock crossing.

At 9.7 and 10 miles the hiker finds the short spurs to Lower and Middle Rock lakes, respectively. Lower Rock Lake is a good-sized, shrub- and forest-rimmed lake below Indian Ridge. The large, deep Middle Rock Lake rests below a steep, rugged flank of Frazier Mountain. Its gurgling outlet adds to the appeal.

Beyond the lakes, a wider trail continues uphill to primitive Frazier Campground (11.25 miles). Tables, grills, and pit toilets serve campers and hikers.

From there, the loop heads uphill to the right following the closed jeep track indicated toward Cache Meadow. Where the loop closes at 11.4 miles, go left following the 2.4-mile Shellrock Trail to end the hike.

31 TABLE ROCK WILDERNESS TRAIL

Distance: 17.5 miles round trip or an 11-mile shuttle
Elevation change: 3,600 feet
Difficulty: Strenuous
Season: Spring through fall
Map: BLM Table Rock Wilderness Access Map
For information: Salem District BLM

This hike explores a 5,750-acre island of protected forest on a tableland feature rising above the heavily cut Molalla River drainage. The rugged terrain, the vegetation changes, and the sharp reliefs of the basalt outcrops and crests unite to create a rewarding wilderness tour. In spring, the rhododendron blooms particularly recommend the hike.

Where the trail claims the Table Rock summit (elevation 4,881 feet), hikers find views that span the Cascade volcano chain from the Three Sisters in the south to Washington's Mount Rainier in the north. Far-reaching views toward the Willamette Valley and Coast Range complete the panorama, while the nearby clearcut-scarred hillsides prove both halting and haunting, detracting from the grandeur.

The hike travels a segment of an old Indian-pioneer route that once linked the Willamette Valley to eastern Oregon. In recent years, the Youth Conservation Corps has rehabilitated the route to serve a new set of boots.

From Molalla's city center, go east on OR 211 for 0.6 mile and turn right onto South Mathias Road. In 0.3 mile, turn left onto South Feyrer Park Road. At the T-junction in 1.7 miles, turn right onto South Dickey Prairie Road, staying on it for 5.3 miles. There, cross over the river via South Molalla Road and go 12.8 miles to reach the Middle Fork–Copper Creek road junction.

For the lower trailhead, go right reaching the Old Bridge Trailhead in 0.1 mile. For the upper trailhead, go left on the gravel Middle Fork Road

Basalt cliffs of Table Rock

heading uphill for 2.7 miles. There, turn right onto Table Rock Road. The marked trailhead is on the right in 5.6 miles. The upper trailhead allows for shuttle hikes and a shorter round-trip tour to the Table Rock summit (4.5 miles).

Beginning from the lower trailhead, hikers sign on for a hefty uphill haul to the summit. Initially, the trail passes through a forest of big Douglas firs with a classic low-elevation understory mix of salal, Oregon grape, vanilla leaf, and oxalis. Patches of shoulder-high bracken fern interrupt the forest stretches. Vine maples display a midstory vibrancy.

By 2.5 miles, the trail is touring a drier slope with wild rose, ocean spray, and Jacob's ladder. In an open meadow, hikers snare the first view, an overlook of the Molalla River drainage. The trail then crosses the "Old Jeep Road" Trail and continues climbing, returning to a richer forest.

For the most part, the grade is steady, marked by a few steeper stretches. Where the trail traces the ridgeline, thick patches of rhododendron often crowd the path. Hemlocks, true firs, and bear grass dominate the higher slope.

At 5.3 miles, the grade eases as the trail rolls along the upper ridge, passing through forest and open, rock-studded flats. Hikers obtain views of the Three Sisters and Mount Washington to the distant southeast and the Molalla River drainage below.

At 6.3 miles is an unmarked junction. The faint trail ahead continues to Pechuck Lookout. The trail to Table Rock climbs uphill to the left crossing over the open saddle flat near Rooster Rock. In the fall, blue gentian abounds along the upcoming tour; lupine, ground juniper, and bear grass grow in the dry flat.

The trail then crosses to the opposite side for a steep, forest descent. Where it bottoms out in a shrubby meadow below Rooster Rock, thimbleberry, nettles, bracken fern, and false hellebore shower into the path hiding it from view. Continue rounding to the left traveling a line where the meadow and forest meet; the route passes a small camp flat at 6.8 miles.

The trail next climbs through forest to follow a semi-open ridge toward the base of Table Rock. By 8 miles, views of Mount Jefferson and Table Rock with its striking, vertical-ribbed basalt greet the hiker.

At the small, open camp flat at 8.25 miles, the path to Table Rock heads uphill straight ahead. The one to the upper trailhead descends to the left. Both are unmarked paths.

An open, shrubby slope first frames the hike to Table Rock; then forest stands offer intermittent shade. At 8.5 miles, a grand Cascade Mountain vista begins to unfold with Mounts Jefferson and Washington, Three Fingered Jack, and the Three Sisters. As the trail tops the tableland, the crowns of Mounts Hood, Adams, and Rainier join the lineup, with Mount

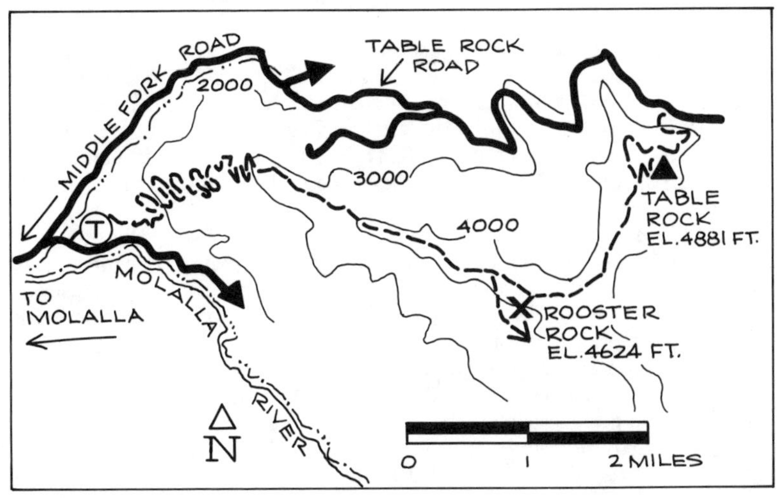

St. Helens completing the show. Clearcuts interrupt the green expanse.

Round-trip hikers, return as you came. Shuttle hikers, return to the camp flat at the foot of the rock and take the downhill path to the upper trailhead. The route adds new perspectives on Table Rock as it rounds the base touring a forest-shrub corridor to pass over a rock jumble below the cliffs. Alder, thimbleberry, and mountain ash color the slopes.

The trail then continues descending through forest, circling a lower rock feature, and contouring the hillside. At the 10.9-mile junction, continue straight ahead for Table Rock Road and the hike's end.

32 BULL OF THE WOODS–PANSY LAKE LOOP

Distance: 7.2 miles round trip
Elevation change: 1,900 feet
Difficulty: Moderate
Season: Late spring through fall

Map: USGS Battle Ax; USFS Mount Hood
For information: Estacada Ranger District
Bull of the Woods Wilderness Area

This trail tours an ancient forest, collects volcano and wilderness vistas en route to and at Bull of the Woods Lookout (elevation 5,523 feet), strolls wildflower-spangled ridgeline saddles, and visits modest, shallow mountain lakes. Pansy Lake derives its name from the area's old Pansy Blossom Copper Mine.

The wilderness covers nearly 35,000 acres. Early use of the area dates back to the 1880s with hunting, fishing, prospecting, and partaking of the area's hot springs—Bagby Hot Springs. A 75-mile trail system explores this wilderness; the interlocking routes welcome a variety of loop-hike options.

From Estacada, travel southeast on OR 224 for 25 miles to the junction of FRs 46 and 57. There, follow FR 46 south for 3.4 miles and turn right onto FR 63. Go 5.5 miles and again turn right, following FR 6340. Remain on FR 6340, bypassing the Dickey Creek Trailhead turn; in another 5.2 miles bear right onto FR 6341. The trailhead is on the left in 3.4 miles with parking for up to ten vehicles located across the road. Much of the route is paved.

The trail enters the wilderness, touring a rich forest of Douglas and true fir and western hemlock. Huckleberry, bunchberry, Oregon grape, twin flower, and bride's bonnet weave a mat beneath the large-diameter trees. Wisps of lichen cling to the trunks. The good earthen path shows a comfortable, climbing grade.

Past the hiker register at 0.3 mile, the forest shows a thick midstory of rhododendron and vine maple. At 0.75 mile, the trail crosses a side creek just above the point it drops in a small falls.

At the nearby junction, go left for the loop. A detour downhill to the right visits Pansy Basin Camp in 0.1 mile and continues left into the for-

Mount Jefferson vista

est arriving at a dry wildflower meadow and a square-on vista of the rock-slide slope on Pansy Mountain Ridge (0.25 mile).

Forgoing the detour, at 0.8 mile the hiker finds the loop junction; climbing uphill to the left begins a clockwise tour. Here, the hike bids farewell to many of the big trees, as the canopy opens up. Rhododendrons briefly abound, parading their pink pom-pom blooms in July.

The trail crosses the often-dry drainage from Dickey Lake and steadily ascends, touring a full forest of small-diameter, high-elevation firs. Bear grass dots the floor.

At 1.4 miles lies the 0.1-mile spur to Dickey Lake, downhill to the right. It is a scenic, green pool at the foot of Dickey Ridge. Snags mark the ridge; a thick border of alders and willows rims the lake. Newts ripple the lake's surface.

The loop continues, passing through a brief meadow patch with vanilla leaf, lupine, cow parsnip, and false hellebore, before returning to the high-elevation forest. Quick switchbacks lead to the trail junction at 2.1 miles. For the loop, bear right angling uphill. Where the trail passes above the talus slopes, it offers window-views of the Collawash drainage.

At 2.4 miles, the trail tops a saddle with views down the Dickey Creek drainage. Wildflowers add color splashes; ground juniper and small ce-

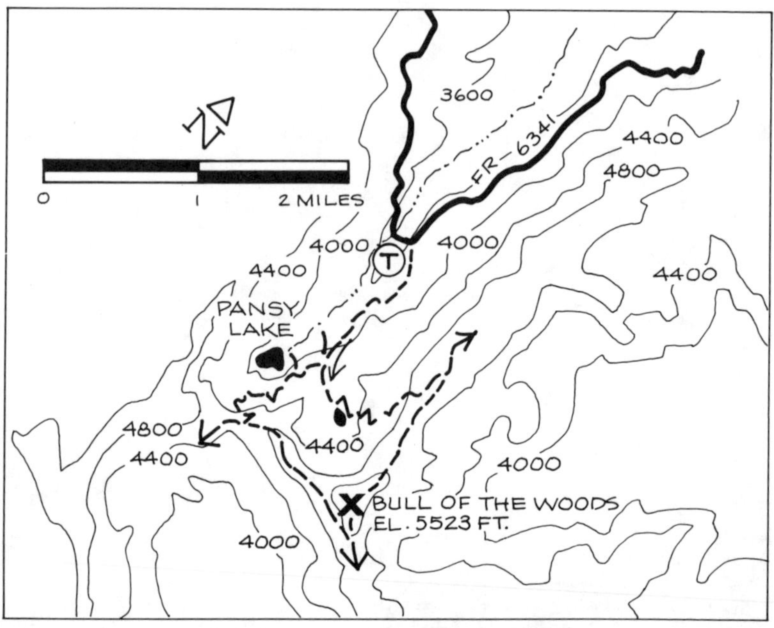

dar dot the ridge. A secondary spur to the left finds the first open view of Mount Hood. Touring below and along the ridge, hikers snare additional looks at Hood along with Mount Jefferson—bookends to a view that includes Olallie Butte, Big Slide Mountain and Basin, and the Elk and Welcome creek drainages.

At 3.1 miles, the trail arrives at the lookout, built in 1939. Views sweep the Mount Hood–Mount Jefferson expanse and broaden to include looks at Mother Lode, Battle Ax, Silver King, and Pansy mountains. Paintbrush, parsley, and bear grass ornament the site.

The Welcome Lake Trail then continues the loop, descending through a full forest of big fir and hemlock with a huckleberry-dominant floor. At the 3.75-mile junction, the loop follows the Mother Lode Trail to the right. An off-trail detour to the ridge finds one last look at Hood.

The route descends tracing a long contour across the steep, forested slope. At 4.3 miles, some cedars enter the mix, and forest gaps offer views of Mother Lode Mountain. In 0.5 mile, the trail offers a final look at Mount Jefferson. At the Pansy Lake Junction, go right.

The trail descends a mostly scree and talus slope into the basin. A sidearm ridge offers a Pansy Lake overlook. At 5.8 miles, going straight continues the loop; bearing left visits Pansy Lake, a square, shallow, brownish-green water ringed by gravel beach, shrubs, and forest. A nice forest-shaded campsite rests near the outlet.

From the 5.8-mile junction, the loop continues toward FR 6341, soon returning to a full forest with rhododendron. Where the loop closes at 6.4 miles, retrace the original 0.8 mile to the trailhead.

33 RED LAKE–POTATO BUTTE HIKE

Distance: 8.5 miles round trip or a 6.6-mile shuttle
Elevation change: 600 feet
Difficulty: Moderate
Season: Late spring through fall
Map: USGS Breitenbush; USFS Mount Hood
For information: Clackamas Ranger District
Olallie Lakes Scenic Area

This hike offers a sampling of the 11,000-acre lake-peppered region along the north-central Cascade Crest dubbed Olallie Lakes Scenic Area. It visits lakes and ponds, tours mid-elevation forests and prime huckleberry patches, and offers an area overlook from atop one of the low cinder buttes contributing to the bumpy skyline of the scenic area.

With the great number of lakes, lakeside solitude is always within striking distance, but early season hikers should come prepared for mosquitos. In the fall, this hike finds favor with the berry picker. "Olallie" is an Indian word for berries.

This trail leaves from Lower Lake Campground. From OR 22 at the west end of Detroit, turn north onto FR 46 at the sign for Breitenbush, Elk Lake, and Olallie Lake. For the best route into the area, go 22.3 miles and turn right onto FR 4690 at the sign for Olallie Lakes Scenic Area. At the T-junction in 7.8 miles, turn right onto FR 4220 to reach Lower Lake Campground in another 4.3 miles. A marked trailhead and day parking are found along the campground loop road.

The hike begins in a forest of true fir and hemlock. True and dwarf huckleberry and bear grass, with showings of arnica, lupine, bracken fern, and vanilla leaf, carpet the floor. At 0.25 mile, the trail arrives at Lower Lake, a 16-acre lake measuring some 73 feet deep—the deepest lake in the scenic area. This long, beautiful, blue lake rests below a low, forested hill. A few small alders, boulders, and the creamy floral heads of the summer bear grass accent its shore.

Numerous openings along the bank invite lake enjoyment and angler access. Where the trail leaves the lake at 0.5 mile is a junction: The trail to the far right leads to Triangle Lake and Olallie Meadows, the trail straight ahead goes to Fish Lake, and the one to the left finds Averill Lake and Red Lake, the hike's destination. Berry bushes abound near the junction.

The trail to Red Lake is rock-studded with rises and dips. Small fir and hemlock with the sporadic appearance of lodgepole pine form an open cathedral.

Atop the rise at 1 mile, hikers discover Middle Lake, a small pond, to the left. A talus slope rises above it. From the rocks, pikas squeak warnings. As the trail rounds Middle Lake, it offers looks across the shallow waters and up the basin at a small rocky butte.

Soon, the trail passes through a grassy meadow patch with a lily pond just beyond. The occasional rhododendron adds to the forest charm. At

1.8 miles is another shallow, forest-rimmed pond with a campsite near the trail. Just ahead is a junction: Going left leads to the Pacific Crest Trail; going right continues the hike to Red Lake.

The trail rounds shallow Fork Lake, the first of five in a line-up of larger lakes. Lodgepole pines now frame the path. Along the shore of Sheep Lake (2.1 miles) is the marked trail junction to Potato Butte. This 0.75-mile spur can be added now or on the return trek.

The Potato Butte spur meanders through an open lodgepole pine forest with bear grass, lupine, dwarf huckleberry, and blueberry. At 0.3 mile, it rounds a small, seasonal pond with invading grasses, after which it climbs rapidly in true "go-for-it" fashion.

Small-diameter firs, pines, and hemlock rise from the butte's red cinder slope; boulders litter its upper reaches. Gaps in the tree cover afford looks at Mount Jefferson to the south.

At 0.6 mile, the trail tops the mile-high feature and follows its rim to the summit vantage, finding a 180-degree view overlooking the forest expanse of the Breitenbush drainage to the north. Olallie Butte barely appears in the northeast corner of the vista; Sisi Butte Lookout lies due north.

Forgoing the spur, the trail rounds the large body of Sheep Lake with its scenic peninsula and a vista of Twin Peaks where the trail leaves the lake. Within 0.1 mile, the hike reaches Wall Lake, a large lake rivaling Sheep. Averill Lake at 3.1 miles is still another large lake with nice, little-used campsites along its shore.

Ahead, keep an eye out for the side trail to Red Lake on the left; it is unmarked, and the lake is well secluded by forest. A silver stump with a couple of protruding nails hints at a one-time marker near the turn. While much smaller than Averill, Red Lake proves a nice hideaway with a single-party campsite just off the spur. Gray jays materialize on the

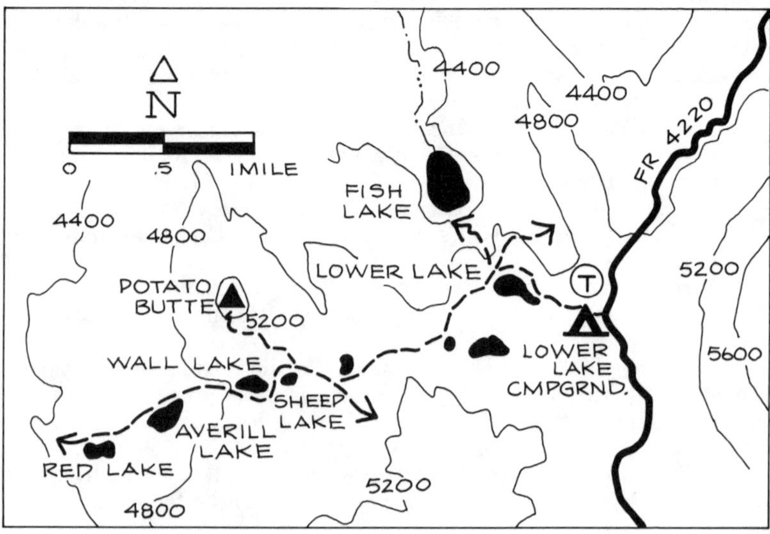

Angler on Lower Lake

tree limbs, as the lunch sacks open.

Round-trippers, return as you came; shuttle hikers, continue downhill to FR 4600.380, passing through a rich forest of lichen-covered, large-diameter fir and hemlock.

34 OPAL LAKE AND PHANTOM NATURAL BRIDGE HIKES

Distance: 4.2 miles round trip (combined)
Elevation change: 1,000 feet
Difficulty: Moderate
Season: Late spring through fall
Map: USGS Battle Ax; USFS Willamette
For information: Detroit Ranger District

This tour pairs up the 0.6-mile Opal Lake Trail and a 1.5-mile French Creek–Elkhorn Ridge hike to Phantom Natural Bridge. Together, they paint a vivid portrait of the old-growth debate, as they access the headwater lake and travel the overlooking ridge to the hotly disputed Opal Creek drainage.

This canyon represents the last untouched, unprotected ancient forest drainage in the Northwest. The neighboring drainages show extensive cutting.

Phantom Natural Bridge

From its mostly forested basin, Opal Lake shines up pleasant and blue. The footpath encircling it provides an up-close look at the old-growth habitat. Nearby presides Phantom Natural Bridge, which developed on the edge of a thick basalt flow, when the overhanging roof or shallow cave collapsed. The remaining arch snugged against the ridge measures some 40 feet across; it offers a tree-obscured window to the Opal Lake area.

From Detroit's west side, turn north off OR 22 at the west end of the bridge onto French Creek Road, FR 2223. Go 4.1 miles on the single-lane paved route with turnouts. At the Y-junction, go right on FR 2207; the route turns to gravel. On the left, in 5.5 miles, a spur trail leads to the French Creek Ridge Trail, beginning the Phantom Natural Bridge Hike; the trail sign shows Cedar Lake 0.25 mile. Going another 0.3 mile finds the parking turnout for the Opal Lake Trail, with the trailhead just beyond it; both are on the right.

Opal Lake Hike: The trail to Opal Lake travels steeply downslope for 0.3 mile, passing through a recovering cut. Small, second-growth mountain hemlock, true and Douglas fir, alder, mountain ash, rhododendron, and huckleberry frame the hiking corridor. Gouged by erosion, the trailbed is rocky and hard-packed, making footing difficult.

Entering the forested basin, the route levels. Meadow-shrub clearings interrupt the tree stands. At 0.5 mile, the trail passes through a grassy meadow, reaching the Opal Lake shore. Gentian dot the grasses; berry bushes rim the meadow.

The trail tags a narrow, shallow end of the lake where waterplants and cow lilies grace the surface. Ducks scurry into flight upon hiker approach. Uncommonly large Alaska cedar, fir, and mountain hemlock ring the lake; bald snags punctuate their ranks.

A path journeys left along the lakeshore, drawing hikers into the regal old growth. Near the outlet, the trail dies. Further discovery of the drainage requires cross-country travel. Return as you came.

Phantom Natural Bridge Hike: The spur to the French Creek Ridge Trail begins up a steep, old skid road, passing through an open second-growth forest. Over-the-shoulder views find Opal Lake and the Opal Creek drainage.

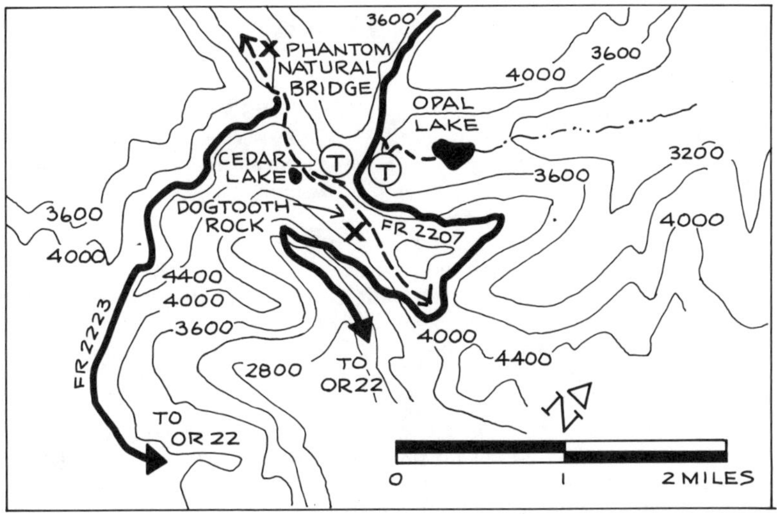

At 0.3 mile, the spur reaches the French Creek Ridge Trail near Cedar Lake; go right for Phantom Natural Bridge. Cedar Lake is an insignificant, small black pond semi-hidden in the trees behind the junction.

The trail continues with a hefty climb to top the ridge. A mature forest of mountain hemlock with an understory of huckleberry and bear grass frames the route. In the fall, the huckleberry bushes tease with plump prime berries that taste like vinegar. Over-the-shoulder views find Mount Jefferson and Dogtooth Rock.

As the trail rounds the slope at 0.6 mile, the view features Mounts Jefferson and Washington, Three Fingered Jack, Coffin Mountain, and Dogtooth Rock. Where the trail tops an open plateau, low cairns point the way across the flat-topped rock. The route then dips and rolls with the ridgeline, stitching together brief looks at the Three Sisters and Mount Hood. Sweet-tasting blueberries grow low to the plateaus.

At 1 mile, the trail steeply descends through another heavily eroded harvest site, crossing the end of FR 2223. From there, the hike heads up the Elkhorn Ridge Trail for a short distance reaching the spur to Phantom Natural Bridge.

From Elkhorn Ridge, hikers find grand looks back at Mount Jefferson rising above French Creek Ridge. To the south lies the heavily cut drainage of Sardine Creek.

The arch of Phantom Natural Bridge greets visitors at 1.5 miles. Treetops reduce the impact of the doorway view, but it's an interesting natural feature. The site itself offers good looks at Mounts Jefferson and Hood, Opal Lake, Three Fingered Jack, Battle Ax, and Coffin Mountain. When ready, return as you came to FR 2207.

35 PAMELIA LAKE–GRIZZLY PEAK HIKE

Distance: 10.4 miles round trip (permit required)
Elevation change: 2,700 feet
Difficulty: Moderate
Season: Late spring through fall
Map: USFS Mount Jefferson Wilderness
For information: Detroit Ranger District

This relaxing, old-growth tour visits a good-sized, though shallow mountain lake and claims the summit of Grizzly Peak (elevation 5,799 feet). Grizzly Peak affords perhaps the best close-up, square-on view of Mount Jefferson anywhere to be found. Views along the way include the Pamelia Lake Basin, the North Santiam drainage, Mount Hood, and Three Fingered Jack.

Due to its popularity, hikers should minimize the length of their Pamelia Lake stays and opt for day hikes instead of overnight outings. Midweek and off-season visits further reduce the strain on the area, while delivering a wilder, more private experience.

From Detroit, go 11.8 miles east on OR 22 and turn left onto FR 2246, Pamelia Road. Or from the community of Marion Forks, go 4 miles northwest on OR 22 and turn right. Follow FR 2246, a paved and gravel route, for 2.7 miles to the trailhead parking area at its end.

Paralleling Pamelia Creek upstream, the trail travels a dark, shadowy old-growth forest, entering the Mount Jefferson Wilderness at 0.25 mile. The skyline features cedar, fir, and hemlock with the occasional jagged-topped white snag. Winter 1990 upturned several of the big trees, giving a new look to the forest.

Oregon grape, prince's pine, bunchberry, and ferns accent the floor. While these forest plants may lack abundance, the mosses and lichens covering the ground, logs, and roots bring a richness to the surroundings.

At 0.9 mile, the trail reaches a trampled bank overlooking a scenic, tiered series of cascades and a small pool. Pamelia Creek is a clear, white-green water spilling between richly vegetated banks. Soon, more light penetrates the forest, and the buffer between the trail and the creek broadens.

A corridor of adult-high rhododendron next ushers hikers along the trail, but disappears before the trail junction at 2.25 miles. Here, the path straight ahead finds the lakeshore in 100 yards, the one to the left leads to the Pacific Crest Trail, and the one to the right begins the hike to Grizzly Peak.

Opting first for a lakeside visit, hikers quickly arrive at Pamelia Lake—a mostly shallow, big mountain lake, with semi-submerged logs. Rhododendron thread the forest perimeter set back from the open, rocky shore. In late spring and early summer, the bushes put on an outstanding color show. Pan-sized cutthroat trout attract anglers to the lake.

From shore, hikers find views of Grizzly Peak and Mount Jefferson. In the fall, the red-orange leaves of the vine maples blaze the ragged drainages on Jefferson.

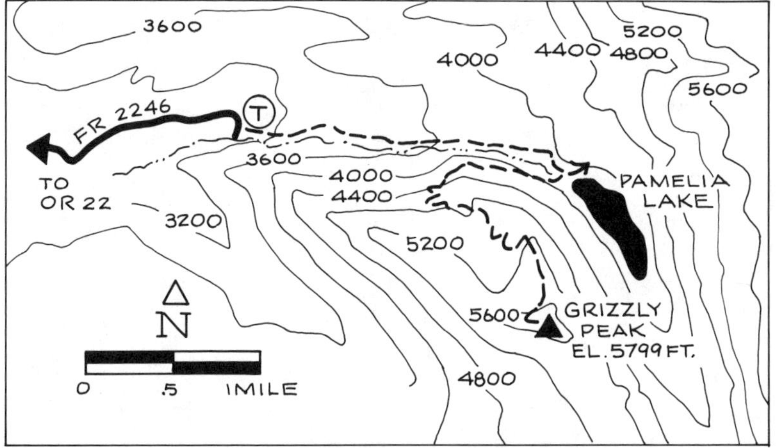

Returning to the 2.25-mile junction, follow the Grizzly Peak Trail southwest crossing over the rocky lake outlet. The trail then swings a long, downstream switchback above Pamelia Creek, before angling up the slope for a comfortable, steady climb.

A wonderful old-growth forest, filled with visual interest, cloaks Grizzly Peak. The thick midstory contains young trees, vine maple, rhododendron, and Pacific yew. Some bear grass dots the slope.

By 2.9 miles, the forest character undergoes a change as small trees and a bounty of rhododendron enfold the trail. A few switchbacks follow, and the trail setting again changes with the hike following a sunken grade through an open, high-elevation forest with bear grass and huckleberry.

After contouring a slope with some dominant big firs, the trail takes a turn finding an open view of Mount Jefferson and an overlook of the Pamelia Lake Basin; only a part of the lake is visible. Cathedral Rocks

Ancient forest

Mount Jefferson

and a glimpse at Goat Peak complete the view. A rumbling Upper Pamelia Creek echoes up from the basin.

Gaps in the tree cover afford additional looks at Mount Jefferson and a view of the North Santiam River drainage. At the trail bend at 5 miles, hikers spy the crown of Mount Hood, followed soon after by limited looks at Three Fingered Jack and the Three Sisters.

At 5.2 miles, the trail tags the summit at the site of a former lookout for a bold view of Mount Jefferson that spans a full 7,000 feet of its elevation from the Pamelia Lake Basin to its summit crest. Goat Peak is now fully visible; Mount Hood rises to the north.

A gap in the tree cover offers a Three Fingered Jack–Three Sisters view; another opening pinpoints Coffin and Bachelor mountains. While the mountain hemlocks rimming much of the site deny a 360-degree vista, the vantage on Mount Jefferson excuses the shortcoming. When ready to descend, return as you came.

36 COFFIN MOUNTAIN TRAIL

Distance: 3 miles round trip
Elevation change: 1,400 feet
Difficulty: Easy to moderate
Season: Late spring through fall
Map: USGS Detroit; USFS Willamette
For information: Detroit Ranger District

This hike climbs to the summit of a prominent, descriptively named skyline feature rising to the south above Detroit Lake. The route passes through old-growth and fire-denuded forest. In late July and early August, the summit ridge features a bear grass bloom extravaganza with thousands of the creamy-headed stalks showering the slope and saturating the mountain air with their intoxicating perfume.

Atop the mountain stands a fire lookout tower, staffed during the summer months. The summit view sweeps the Cascade Crest spotlighting Mounts Jefferson, Hood, and Washington; the Three Sisters; and Three Fingered Jack. Olallie Butte, Detroit Lake, and a neighboring former lookout site, Bachelor Mountain, add to the vista lineup.

With the trail being dry and often exposed, carry water.

From the Detroit Ranger Station, go 7.7 miles east on OR 22 and turn south onto Coopers Ridge Road, FR 2234. In 4 miles, turn right onto FR 1003 followed soon after by a left onto FR 2236. Go 2 miles on FR 2236 and turn left onto FR 130. Follow FRs 130 and 137 to reach the upper trailhead in about 1.5 miles. Look for the marked trailhead on the left-hand side of FR 137; parking is alongside the road.

The route to the trailhead travels paved and good gravel surfaces. This

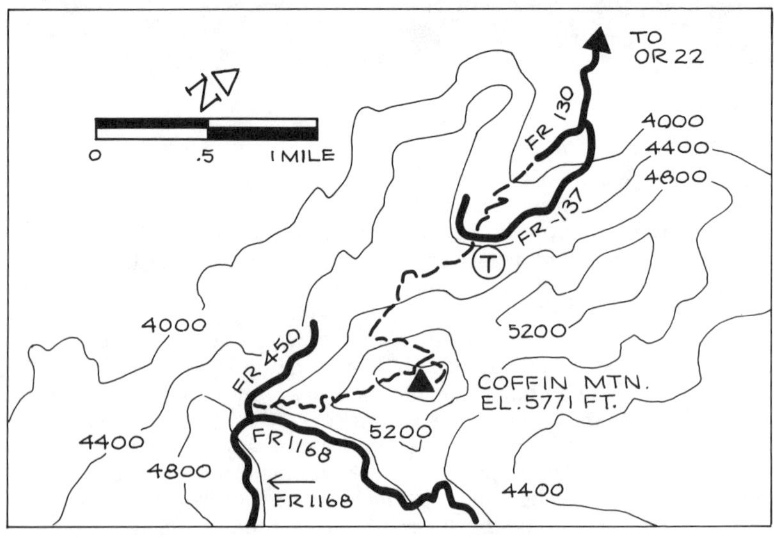

particular hike approaches the Coffin Mountain Lookout from the north. A second route arrives from the south off FR 1168.450; it involves a steeper climb on an unimproved walking surface.

Passing between two gate posts, the trail enters an old-growth stand of towering, large-diameter Douglas firs. Quickly, the number of big trees grows fewer as the forest complex shows a more mixed canopy of fir, hemlock, and spruce. The understory features a variety of species including bunchberry, bear grass, vanilla leaf, huckleberry, and rhododendron.

At the 0.25-mile trail junction, go left for Coffin Mountain Lookout. An unmaintained trail remains visible to the right.

The trail now climbs, pulling into the open. Here, silver snags record the 1967 lightning-started Buck Mountain wildfire. Small trees have returned along with bear grass and huckleberry. Summer wildflowers seen here include aster, fireweed, Indian paintbrush, lupine, pearly everlasting, and columbine; they present a showy display, while hummingbirds buzz from bloom to bloom.

From this exposed slope, hikers gather early views of the lookout and an overlook of the Blowout Creek drainage. Clearcuts mark many of the neighboring hillsides.

Along the upper reaches of Coffin Mountain, mountain hemlock, noble fir, and creeping juniper frame the trail. At the 1.25-mile junction, the path to the right journeys south across the summit ridge, before descending to the southern trailhead on FR 1168.450. A brief detour along this route finds an impressive sea of bear grass along with southern views of the Cascade Crest. For the lookout, go left along the ridge. Where the trail pulls into the open, the lookout looms ahead.

At 1.5 miles, the trail claims the summit (elevation 5,771 feet) for a grand look at the Detroit Lake area and the Cascade volcano lineup stretching from Diamond Peak to Mount Hood. The north and east sides of the summit feature impressive drop-away vertical cliffs.

When ready to descend the mountain, return as you came.

37 IRON MOUNTAIN TRAIL

Distance: 3.4 miles round trip
Elevation change: 1,500 feet
Difficulty: Easy
Season: Spring through fall
Map: USGS Echo Mountain; USFS Willamette
For information: Sweet Home Ranger District

Iron Mountain represents one of the premier wildflower showcases in the state of Oregon, bringing together ancient forest, alpine meadow, and rock ledge floral species. On July 4, the historical date marking the peak of the bloom calendar, wildflower aficionados from across the state make their annual trek to the mountain. Together with nearby Echo Mountain, this significant botanical area houses seventeen species of conifer and several rare plants.

Iron Mountain Lookout

The summit (elevation 5,455 feet) affords a grand vista of the Cascade Crest and the Central Cascade neighborhood. The 360-degree view features an all-star skyline with Mounts Adams, Hood, Jefferson, and Washington; the Three Sisters; and Diamond Peak. Cone Peak, Echo Mountain, Tombstone Prairie, and Browder Ridge comprise the immediate neighborhood, with the mountain's own rugged volcanic cliffs completing the panorama. A fire lookout sits atop the mountain.

Road noise from US 20 alone disturbs the trail's tranquillity.

From Sweet Home, travel 35.6 miles east on US 20 and turn right onto FR 15 at the sign for Iron Mountain Trailhead. In 0.3 mile, a large trailhead parking area with space for up to ten vehicles serves the hiker. The trail begins across the road from the parking area.

A forest of hemlock and true and Douglas fir with a diverse understory of bunchberry, false Solomon's seal, vanilla leaf, wild strawberry, lupine, huckleberry, and trillium frames the route. The tall, full forest affords wonderful shade. In 0.2 mile, the trail crosses US 20 to continue the climb; be careful at the crossing.

This popular hike enjoys a wide, groomed, well-graded trailbed, remarkably free from short cuts or other degradation. The old-growth habitat engages with its big trees, jagged snags, and midstory vine maples. In unique style, the woodpeckers, hummingbirds, and grouse announce themselves.

At 0.4 mile, the trail rounds a large, red volcanic-rock outcrop, striking both in size and the suddenness of its appearance. As the trail switchbacks uphill, it leaves behind many of the big trees.

At 0.7 mile, the hike draws into the open for the first view of the summit cliffs and lookout. The cliffs show a rich layering with a distinct red band. The trail then enters a steep meadow with bracken fern and tall floral species measuring 18 to 24 inches high. Sprays of blue, bell-shaped flowers top one species. While the slope steepens, the trail remains steady. At 0.9 mile is the Cut-off Trail junction. Here, a spur arriving from the trailhead on the forest road below offers a shorter hike to the summit—a popular starting point for the "Sunday hiker" set.

The smaller-diameter trees create an open overhead canopy. At the 1-mile junction, the Cone Peak Trail heads left, crossing over the peak's saddle; claiming its summit requires a cross-country effort. The Iron Mountain Trail heads right. Each switchback builds upon the view, introducing Diamond Peak, Browder Ridge, and looks at the heavily harvested neighborhood in its various states of regrowth.

The slope grows rockier with colorful wildflower displays of larkspur, Indian paintbrush, wallflowers, star tulip, lupine, columbine, waterleaf, and more. Islands of trees spot the rock and meadow slope.

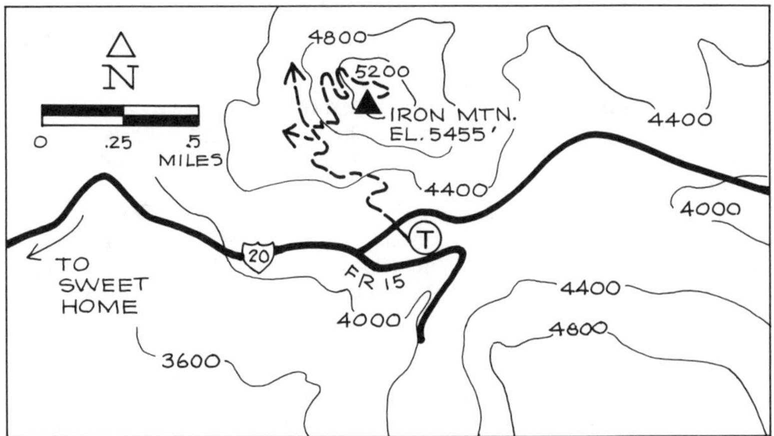

At 1.3 miles, the trail swings directly toward the imposing summit cliff for a dramatic look. Where the trail enters a turn, the view captures Cone Peak, Mount Jefferson's summit crown, and the lookout. Huckleberry bushes dominate the floor.

Soon, the climb adds the presence of Mount Hood along with the rounded top of Mount Adams. The 1.5-mile switchback finds a superb view of the Three Sisters overlooking Iron Mountain's ragged cliff. Overhead, hikers may spy an eroded, natural-arch window. Ground juniper, mountain hemlock, and small cedar hug the higher reaches.

Atop the summit ridge, a detour left onto the small point unfolds a sweeping vista of the Cascade volcano chain from Mount Adams to Diamond Peak, along with the immediate peaks and ridges and Tombstone Prairie. Penstemon and wallflowers accent the rock ledges below the post. Ground squirrels beg for handouts, while swallows circle the summit.

The lookout offers a different perspective on the setting and the finest look at Iron Mountain's own eye-catching, layered volcanic-rock cliffs. The return is as you came.

38 WEST BANK METOLIUS TRAIL

Distance: 14 miles round trip
Elevation change: 300 feet
Difficulty: Moderate
Season: Spring through fall
Map: USGS Whitewater River; USFS Deschutes
For information: Sisters Ranger District

This hike follows the Metolius Wild and Scenic River—a treasured state waterway—for an eye-engaging tour. Grassy mounds, small islands, and silvered logs accent the aquamarine water, which reveals various moods as it churns through deep trenches, riffles over stones, and slows to form deep, tranquil pools. To protect the wild fish, special fishing regulations apply to much of this blue-ribbon waterway.

Along the route, hikers can tour the grounds and operations of the Wizard Falls Fish Hatchery. A self-guided tour visits displays and holding ponds, with a favorite stop being the settling pool holding the "escapee" fish. Large splashes give clues to their size. Here, eagles, minks, and herons gather to feed.

From US 20/OR 126 northwest of Sisters, turn north on County 14 toward Camp Sherman. At the junction in 2.5 miles, go left on County 1419. In another 1.3 miles, head straight on FR 1420 toward Sheep Springs Horse Camp. Stay on FR 1420 for the next 4 miles; the road surface turns to gravel. Turn right onto FR 1420.400 to reach the Lower Canyon Creek Campground and the West Bank Metolius Trailhead in 0.7 mile. The trail leaves the end of the camp loop for a downstream tour.

The hike starts at the Canyon Creek–Metolius River confluence, a few miles downstream from the Metolius headwater. This river owes its origins to springs originating deep beneath Black Butte. The water emerges

Headwaters of the Metolius

at a fairly constant rate of 50,000 gallons per minute immediately launching a full-coursing river.

The hiker-only path begins along a natural river stretch free from development. Alders, Rocky mountain maple, and other shrubs overhang the water. Horsetail reeds, columbine, star flower, wild rose, lupine, and thistle color the thin meadow bank and the bitterbrush–grassland slope. Ponderosa pine, fir, and western larch shade the river corridor.

The trail closely hugs the course of the beautiful, fast-rushing, clear, wild water. Along the opposite shore at 0.3 mile, a series of low, spring-launched cascades bubble white over a mossy bank to the river. At times, the river appears shimmery black and mysterious; other times, it bursts into ice-blue riffles and eddies.

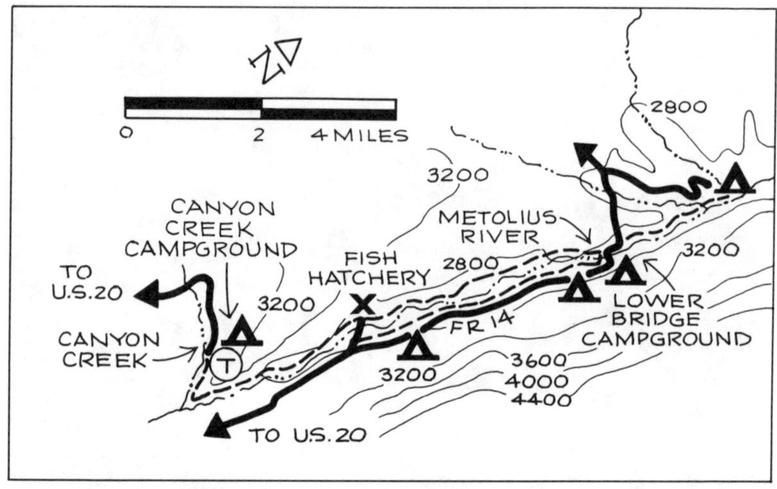

By 1.2 miles, a few side drainages create marshy spots requiring a stone-step negotiation. Soon, large vegetated islands split the river's flow. False hellebore, lupine, waterleaf, and mountain ash color the islands. In this area, Canada geese often rear their young. Farther downstream, underwater shelves and trenches again change the river's look.

By 2.25 miles, the trail climbs above the river approaching the Wizard Falls Fish Hatchery (2.5 miles). Where the trail forks, either path reaches the parking area. From there, hikers may detour for a hatchery grounds visit, or continue the hike which resumes along shore just above the bridge and below the facility.

En route to Lower Bridge (5.5 miles), the rolling trail tours a mostly dry, bitterbrush–grassland bank with some magnificent old-growth ponderosa pines. Grand river views continue.

On the earthen path, animal tracks record the nighttime river visits of deer, skunk, and raccoon. A beaver's wake may catch the river traveler's attention. Fly lines dance over the heads of anglers.

In the fall, the rotting flesh of the spawned-out Kokanee may lend a putrid edge to the crisp morning air—part of the natural cycle. Dippers bob on the rocks and skim the water's surface. From Lower Bridge, the West Metolius Trail angles left across FR 12 and resumes descending a steep slope. The trail from here to Candle Creek is at times canted, rock-studded, or eroded, fouling footing.

Reeds line much of the shore and more cedars join the mix. At 5.75 miles, the trail arrives at a primitive campsite—a nice place to stop, sit on a log, and admire the water. Ahead, the trail briefly tours a lusher, forested flat. Western tanagers are colorful companions; dark-eyed juncos flit from branch to shrub.

At 6.75 miles, the trail arrives at a nice, fast-rushing river bend, a potential ending point for the hike, but the trail continues across the Abbot

Creek footbridge to reach the Candle Creek Campground and trailhead at 7 miles.

For the return trek upstream, hikers may opt for an east-bank tour between Lower Bridge and the Wizard Falls Fish Hatchery bridge, thus gathering a different perspective on the river course.

39 PATJENS LAKE LOOP TRAIL

Distance: 6 miles round trip (permit required)
Elevation change: 500 feet
Difficulty: Easy
Season: Summer through fall
Map: USFS Mount Washington Wilderness
For information: McKenzie Ranger District

This little-demanding trail proves a nice family hike. The circuit tours a semi-open forest complex of high-elevation firs, hemlock, and lodgepole pine, bypasses a couple of long, narrow meadows, and visits the shores of the three shallow Patjens Lakes to conclude along the forested bench overlooking Big Lake. While not a vista hike, the tour does offer views of Sand Mountain, Mount Washington, the Three Sisters, and Hoodoo and Hayrick buttes. Mostly though, it's a relaxing, rolling, dry-forest tour.

Patjens Lakes bear the name of a turn-of-the-century sheepherder who had a summer range near here.

From US 20 at Santiam Pass, turn south onto FR 2690, Big Lake Road; there's a sign for Hoodoo Ski Area at the turn. In 0.9 mile, turn left staying on paved FR 2690 and continue straight for another 3 miles, bypassing Big Lake Campground, to reach the trailhead on the right-hand side of the road. The road ends ahead.

The hike begins paralleling FR 2690 southwest, traveling an open forest corridor with bear grass, lupine, and pearly everlasting. At 0.2 mile, the trail reaches the loop junction; there, it enters a truer forest of Pacific silver fir, hemlock, and lodgepole pine.

The bear grass understory presents a fine display of creamy blooms and sweet fragrance in mid-summer. The dried flower stalks continue to add interest to the forest in the fall.

A counterclockwise tour begins to the right; the good earthen path shows a minimal grade. Along the tour, hikers can witness forest succession as the small firs gradually replace the lodgepole pines. The forest has a congested look with many small trees, low branches, and downfalls.

Soon, the trail is traveling the forest fringe to a narrow, 0.4-mile-long wet meadow with rich, knee-high grasses, a buffer of blueberry bushes, and a cross-stitching of silver logs. It's a peaceful detour just off the trail. Larger firs and hemlocks rise overhead with yellow-green lichens dangling from the branches.

At 1.5 miles, the trail arrives at a junction: The trail to the right leads to Cayuse Horse Camp; the path straight ahead continues the loop with a climb.

Gaps in the tree cover afford looks at the Sand Mountain Lookout to the northwest. At 1.75 miles, the trail enters the Mount Washington Wilderness and crosses a saddle, where hikers capture quick looks at Mount Washington and the Three Sisters. The route then descends passing through drier forest and open bracken fern patches.

At 2.7 miles, the trail arrives next door to an oblong, shallow pond ringed by meadow. In another 0.5 mile, the rolling trail arrives at the first of the Patjens Lakes.

A short spur leads to this shallow, circular lake situated at the foot of a low, unnamed, forested butte. A few alders and ponderosa pines infiltrate the forest mix around the lake.

Following the forest fringe alongside another long, scenic meadow, the trail tags the second Patjens Lake at 3.5 miles. Meadow and lodgepole pines rim this slightly larger lake, which rests below the saddle of two buttes. Touring the west shore, hikers find a cross-lake view of Mount Washington, peeking over the forest rim.

In another 300 yards, the path to the right continues the loop; the one to the left leads to the last of the Patjens Lakes—the smallest of the lake

Big Lake and Hayrick Butte

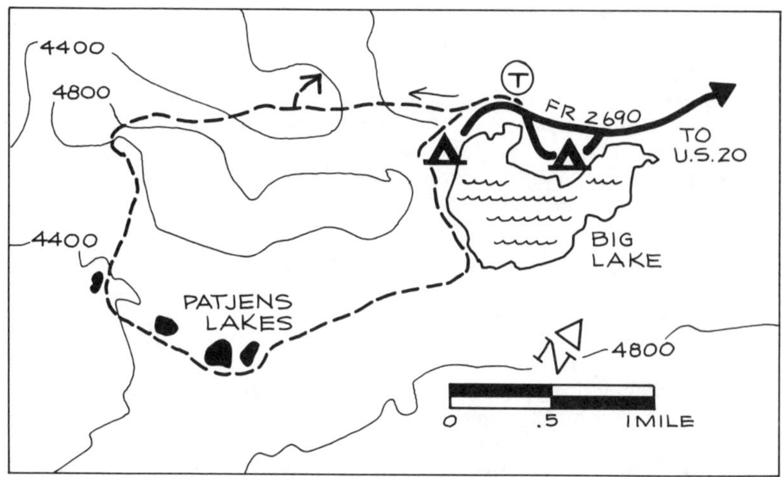

waters. It, too, rests below the saddle.

A dry, mixed-forest flat next claims the trail for a semi-open tour. At 5 miles, an unmarked, though maintained, trail branches right, while the loop continues straight ahead touring the forested bench along the southwest shore of Big Lake. Hoodoo and Hayrick buttes overlook the Big Lake Basin.

Narrow, sandy beaches below the trail sometimes invite a descent; small bays scallop the shoreline of this large, blue, mountain lake. The breeze rising off the water brings a welcomed refreshment after a hot, dusty tour. The fuller forest further improves comfort. Where the trail forks at 5.5 miles, the loop trail bears left to circle behind the shoreline bench. The downhill path to the right leads to the walk-in camp and a nice view of Mount Washington in 300 yards.

A forest tour brings the loop to a close at 5.8 miles. Bear right to return to the trailhead.

40 BLACK CRATER TRAIL

Distance: 7.6 miles round trip (permit required)
Elevation change: 2,300 feet
Difficulty: Moderate to strenuous
Season: Late spring through fall
Map: USFS Three Sisters Wilderness
For information: Sisters Ranger District

This rugged-climbing route claims the summit of Black Crater (elevation 7,251 feet) at the site of a former lookout for a striking, up-close vista of snowy-faced volcanos and stark lava flows. North Sister and Mount Washington rise up as imposing next door neighbors. Westward views applaud the Mount Washington Wilderness Area; eastward views overlook much of Central Oregon. Clear days find Washington's Mount Adams visible to the far north.

This is a dry trail; carry plenty of water. The upper mountain reaches are exposed, and the demands of the trail offer a good workout.

From the US 20–OR 242 junction at Sisters, go west on OR 242 for 11 miles to reach the marked trailhead and parking area on the left-hand side of the road. Be alert on this winding route. If you pass Windy Point, you've gone too far.

With a straight uphill charge, the hike enters the Three Sisters Wilderness Area, touring a mixed forest of fir, mountain hemlock, and white and lodgepole pines. A spare covering of grasses spreads beneath the trees. While the initial incline eases, a persistent, climbing grade remains throughout the journey.

A few bracken fern, lupine, prince's pine, and scraggly manzanita begin showing up amid the grasses. While the trees of this elevation are characteristically small in diameter and stature, the forest is full. Roots riddle the trail, but most are adequately embedded so as not to be obstacles. Tree-filtered views feature Mounts Washington and Jefferson and Three Fingered Jack.

After 1 mile, the trail passes through an open forest of lodgepole pines and fir, a meadowy area, and a fuller stand of mountain hemlock with lichen-brushed bigger trees and numerous small ones.

At 1.7 miles, the trail shows a brief climbing burst; it then settles into a switchbacking mode. In another 0.5 mile, the trail offers the first open

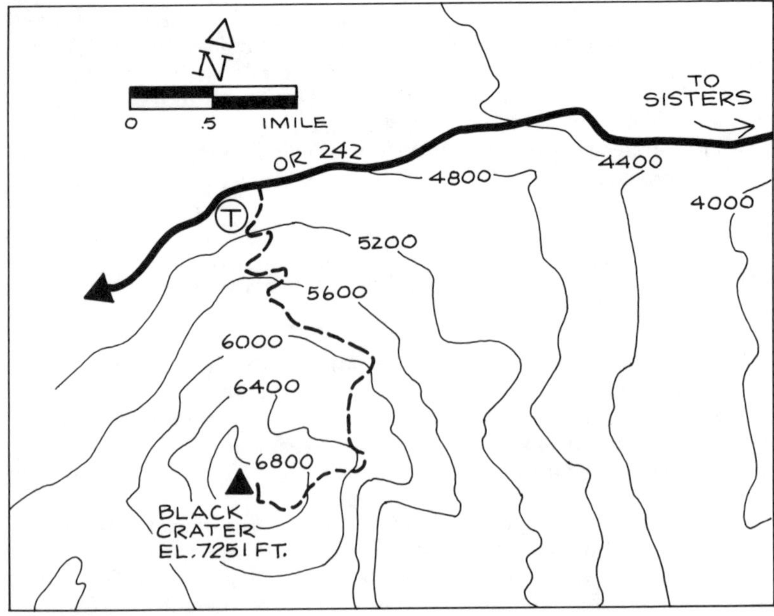

Black Crater summit

views of the hike presenting the nearby volcanic peaks. A few wildflower patches now interrupt the forest.

Ahead, the trail crosses over to the northeast-facing slope, making a brief descent above a bowl-like depression. A lupine-meadow spills into the bowl, while the forest shapes its rim.

An ashy floor and open forest now characterize the tour. At 2.3 miles, the trail offers a look at the summit destination. Afterward, the trail briefly rolls with easy dips and rises. When it again climbs, hikers gain looks at Black Butte.

The tour undergoes a character change at 2.8 miles, passing from a forest hike to mountain hike. As the trail crosses the open, high-meadow slopes, it offers eastern views of Black Butte, Smith Rock, and the high desert north of Bend. Red and black cinders blanket the upper crater.

At 3.3 miles, the trail switchbacks amid a patch of small mountain hemlock and whitebark pine. Where it tops the summit ridge, east–west views greet the hiker. Here, too, comes the first bold look at North Sister. It's a grand view featuring the snowy volcano, the craters at its foot, the extensive lava flows spilling from its flank, and the small tree islands isolated by the flow.

In another 0.5 mile, the trail tops Black Crater at the site of a former lookout. Rusted nails and melted glass hint at its one-time existence. This lofty post overlooks the peak's blown-out bowl, which often cradles snow well into summer.

Rising up at the heart of this Central Cascade volcanic country, Black Crater offers a prized 360-degree view. The Three Sisters, Black Butte and the Metolius River drainage, Dee Wright Observatory and the expansive flow atop which it sits, and Belknap and Little Belknap craters along with the peaks of the Cascade Crest amply reward the climb and suggest a lingering stay.

Return as you came.

41 McKENZIE RIVER NATIONAL RECREATION TRAIL

Distance: 26.5 miles one way
Elevation change: 1,800 feet
Difficulty: Moderate
Season: Spring through fall
Map: USFS Willamette, McKenzie River National Recreation Trail brochure
For information: McKenzie Ranger District

This first-rate addition to the national recreation trail system visits cold water springs, Clear Lake, the Upper McKenzie Wild and Scenic River, towering river falls, ancient forest, and lava flows. Some 3,500 years ago, a lava spillage from Nash Crater dammed the ancient McKenzie River and continues to influence the present-day river—a major tributary of the Willamette River.

A remnant of the historic wagon road that linked Central and Eastern Oregon with the Willamette Valley in the late 1800s marks the uppermost trailhead.

Multiple trailheads off OR 126 access this linear route for a variety of shuttle hikes. To reach the uppermost trailhead, from the US 20–OR 126 junction, go south on OR 126 for about 2 miles and turn left for the Old Santiam Wagon Road. The lowest trailhead lies 1.5 miles east of the McKenzie Bridge community.

Beginning at the uppermost trailhead, a downstream hike follows south the often-dry Fish Creek drainage to cross the footbridge at the head of Clear Lake. It then rounds the east shore to find Great Spring (1.5 miles). This cold water spring gives rise to a mesmerizing pool with exacting reflections, the 43-degree waters of Clear Lake, and the McKenzie River. Ospreys patrol the lake.

The rolling lake-tour continues crossing a crusty lava flow dotted with vine maple and juniper, passing beneath stout, old-growth Douglas firs, and rounding below Coldwater Cove Campground. Past it, the route travels an older flow through fuller forest, bearing left at the junction to cross OR 126 at 4 miles.

From the McKenzie River footbridge, the trail travels downstream along the west shore passing black pools and ice-blue cascades. At 4.5 miles, it overlooks the 100-foot Sahalie Falls plunging over a lava dam.

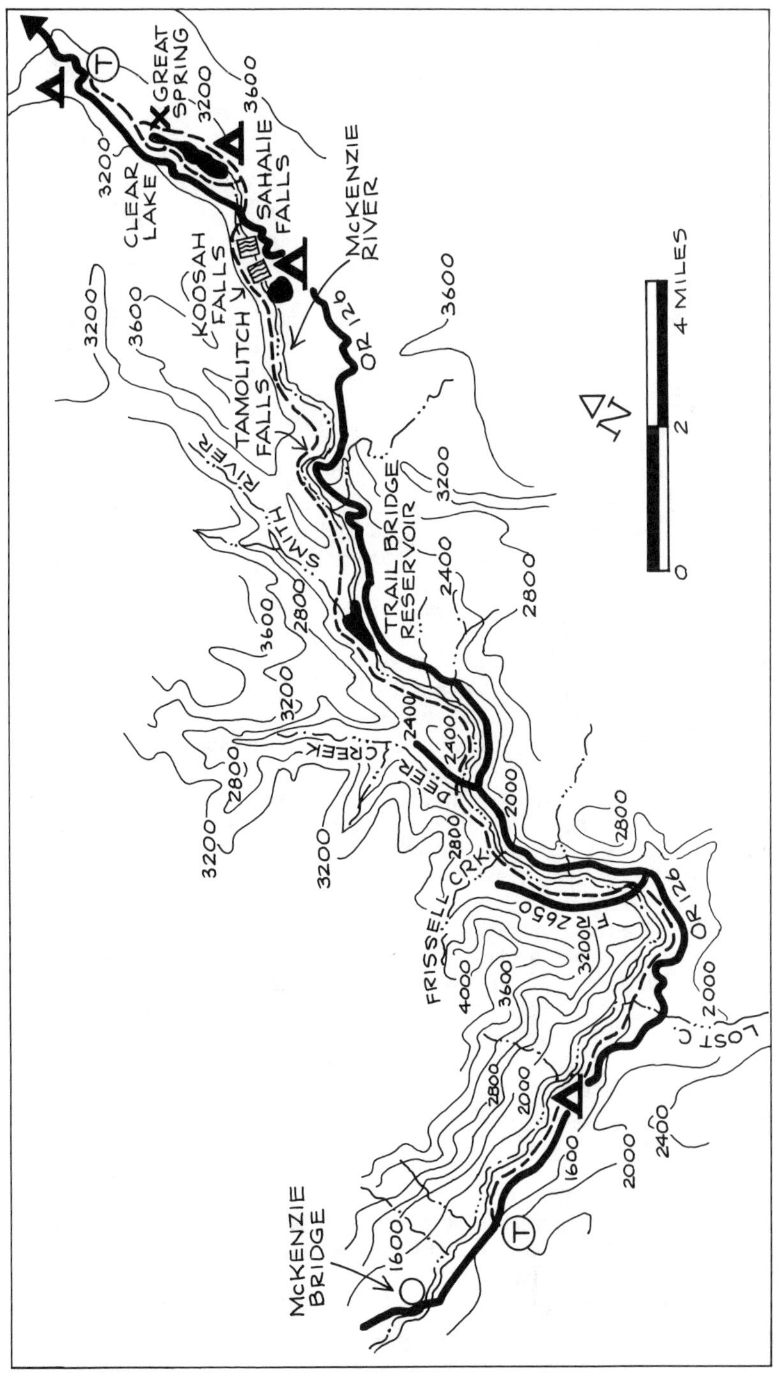
GREAT SPRING
CLEAR LAKE
SAHALIE FALLS
KOOSAH FALLS
TAMOLITCH FALLS
McKENZIE RIVER
OR 126
SMITH RIVER
TRAIL BRIDGE RESERVOIR
CREEK
FRISSELL CRK.
FR 2650
LOST C.
McKENZIE BRIDGE
0
2
4 MILES

Downstream finds Koosah Falls, a 63-foot, thundering, split falls. The trail then reaches Carmen Reservoir at 6 miles.

A fir–cedar–hemlock forest colored by vine maple, dogwood, rhododendron, and huckleberry frames much of the upper trail. Dippers dive into the river, while otters sometimes play in the reservoir. Beyond the reservoir, the river runs dry.

At 9.2 miles, Tamolitch Falls Viewpoint overlooks a 60-foot cliff and a site where the ground releases the river water. Upstream, the porous lava deposited some 1,600 years ago by Belknap Crater sucked the stream underground. At rare times, heavy runoffs rush over the flow sending a tumbling Tamolitch Falls over the cliff.

An older, overgrown flow with mosses and lichens, collapsed lava tubes, and tree casts next claims the trail; the tree casts are hollowed lava molds depicting the bases of trees standing at the time of eruption. By 10 miles, the trail enters a magnificent old-growth forest with an overflowing low-elevation Cascade flora. Such richness characterizes much of the lower tour.

At 11.5 miles, the route crosses FR 2672.655, and in another mile, it finds Trail Bridge Campground. Here, the trail descends toward the boat launch, crosses Smith Reservoir Road and the Smith River footbridge, and travels the west slope above Trail Bridge Reservoir, another small reservoir.

A long forested stretch follows. The McKenzie River is now much larger having passed the diversions of nature and human. More bigleaf maples frame the river corridor. At times, noise from OR 126 intrudes.

At 16.6 miles, the trail crosses Deer Creek Road, briefly touring a logged-over slope, before re-entering the rich ancient forest. An adjacent cut crowds the west side of the forested hiking corridor. In another mile, the trail crosses alder-lined Frissell Creek.

Young firs and alders signal the trail's upcoming arrival at FR 2650.610, where the route follows the road left for 0.2 mile. The trail resumes touring an ancient forest corridor returning to the river at 18.6 miles. Where the trail tours a bench alongside the river, the intrusion from OR 126 becomes both audible and visual, as the guard rail and road cut replace the natural bank. The river itself is wide and riffling.

At 19.9 miles, the trail heads left crossing the McKenzie River via the bridge on FR 2650 to begin a tour of the southeast bank. This relaxing, forested stretch travels mostly along the river with convenient access to the water, until the trail gets pinched up to OR 126. There, it passes a turnout and travels an abandoned paved road for a short distance before turning left to return to the ancient forest. At 21.6 miles, the trail crosses Belknap Springs Road. At 22.4 miles lies a junction: the river trail continues straight.

As the trail nears Lost Creek, it begins one of the finest segments of the entire tour. A rich, multi-textured deciduous–evergreen forest encloses the trail; a thick spongy moss cloaks the floor. Ahead, a log footbridge crosses the wide, fast-rushing Lost Creek leading to a picnic site on the opposite shore. The forest splendor continues.

At 24 miles, the trail crosses over the Paradise Campground entrance road near OR 126; Paradise is a scenic, forested riverside campground. From there, the trail alternately nears OR 126 and the river, remaining in forest and crossing over residential access roads to arrive at trail's end at 26.5 miles.

42 PROXY FALLS AND LINTON LAKE TRAILS

Proxy Falls Trail

Distance: 1.4 miles round trip (permit required)
Elevation change: Minimal
Difficulty: Easy
Season: Summer through fall
Map: USFS Three Sisters Wilderness
For information: McKenzie Ranger District

Linton Lake Trail

Distance: 3.2 miles round trip (permit required)
Elevation change: 100 feet
Difficulty: Easy
Season: Summer through fall
Map: USFS Three Sisters Wilderness
For information: McKenzie Ranger District

These two short hikes along OR 242, McKenzie Pass Scenic Highway, are easily paired for a peek in the door at the wilderness.

The Proxy Falls Trail serves up a visual antithesis to the spring-launched rivers for which Central Oregon is famous. Here, waterfalls seemingly dead-end. Actually, the porous lava at the base of the falls draws the water underground save for a small remnant pool that never overflows.

The Collier Crater lava flow formed the basalt dams on Proxy Creek creating the falls. It also deposited the basin lava which creates the spectacle of the disappearing water.

Nestled in a scenic bowl, Linton Lake offers a more traditional, quiet retreat where lava, forest, and meadow unite. Centrally showcased on the forested west-facing slope is a broad, whitewater section of Linton Falls. This scenic chute sets the lake basin apart from its neighbors. A lava flow dammed Linton Creek creating this wilderness lake.

From the OR 126–OR 242 junction 4.4 miles east of McKenzie Bridge, go east on OR 242. The roadside turnout for the Proxy Falls Trail lies on the right-hand side of the road in 8.5 miles. Going east another 1.4 miles finds the Linton Lake Trailhead and parking area, also on the right-hand side of the road.

Proxy Falls Trail: This trail mounts a lava flow to enter the wilderness. It then travels a forest-flow transition habitat with vine maple, alder, hemlock, Pacific yew, red huckleberry, Oregon grape, and salal. At the 0.3-mile junction, the path to the left leads to the upper falls in 0.1 mile; the path to the right finds the lower falls vista in 0.3 mile.

Upper Proxy Falls

To the left, the trail arrives at the base pool of Upper Proxy Falls for a good look at this 200-foot beauty. A mossy delta separates the white, lacy streamers spilling down the steep mountainside. The pool has no outlet, yet never overflows—it's nature's version of the magician's bottomless glass.

At Lower Proxy Falls, a vista platform offers a cross-canyon view at a second 200-foot waterfall, elegant and white, spilling over a mossy cliff and coming to a seemingly abrupt end. Here, too, the porous rock diverts the water's flow underground for an intriguing sight. Cedars fill the canyon; hemlock and rhododendron frame the vista.

Retrace your steps to the junction and return to OR 242.

Linton Lake Trail: This comfortable, rolling trail explores a vital, congested habitat of Douglas fir, western hemlock, vine maple, rhododendron, Oregon grape, and bunchberry, among other species. A few white snags pierce the overhead canopy.

At 0.25 mile, the trail crosses over the tongue of an old lava flow. At 0.5 mile is a more extensive flow hinting at the area's volcanic origins. Mosses, lichen, and small plants now claim the lava.

Ahead, the trail gently climbs, reaching a junction at 0.8 mile. Here, an OR 242 spur scheduled for abandonment enters from the left; the Linton Lake Trail curves right.

The trail now climbs along the front edge of the flow. A fuller midstory grows beneath the more open canopy of smaller firs and hemlocks. Bear grass, red huckleberry, and chinquapin spot the floor.

At 1.2 miles, the trail descends through a dark forest, where large-diameter trees claim the slope. In another 0.25 mile, the footpath loses definition, and side trails streak down the bank to the lake outlet. The lake is best reached by following one of these paths and crossing the outlet to arrive via the lava flow along the west shore.

Linton Lake, at 1.6 miles, is a deep, green, oblong pool in a forested bowl. Lava rubble, meadow, and forest rim the lake; above it, Linton Falls sparkles amid the tree cover. Return as you came.

43 TAM McARTHUR RIM TRAIL

Distance: 8 miles round trip (permit required)
Elevation change: 1,300 feet
Difficulty: Moderate
Season: Summer through fall
Map: USFS Three Sisters Wilderness
For information: Sisters Ranger District

This hike travels the forested slope above Three Creek Lake to tag Tam McArthur Rim, a prominent ridge spanning east from Broken Top. Views build along the way, stringing together an impressive line-up of Cascade volcano peaks.

From the rim, hikers gain an incredible up-close look at Broken Top and South Sister in their chiseled snow, ice, and lava wildness. The rugged, vertical rock of the rim itself provides a dizzying spectacle with Three Creek and Little Three Creek lakes dotting the forested basin at its foot.

The rim's name honors Lewis A. "Tam" McArthur, a former member of the Oregon Geographic Board and author of *Oregon Geographic Names,* a popular reference book for state enthusiasts.

From US 20 at Sisters, turn south onto Elm Street/FR 16 heading toward Three Creek Lake. In 13.7 miles, the pavement ends. In another 0.8 mile, bear right staying on FR 16 reaching Three Creek Lake in 1 mile. The trailhead lies on the left-hand (east) side of FR 16 across from the dam.

From the basin floor, Tam McArthur Rim rises steeply. As the trail climbs, the enclosing forest of lodgepole pine, mountain hemlock, and fir quickly swallows the rim view. A few lupine and grasses pepper the ash and pumice soil.

Soon the trail tops a saddle and begins mounting the rim proper. At 0.5 mile, openings reveal the crowns of Middle and North sister. A few feet beyond, the view broadens to include the Cascade volcano chain stretching north to Washington's Mount Adams. Belknap and Black craters and Black Butte add to the view.

Where the trail takes a turn at 0.7 mile, the emphasis of the view changes to the abrupt cliff of Tam McArthur Rim. By this point, the mountain hemlocks reveal multiple trunks, the firs show full skirts, and the whitebark pines are runty and twisted.

Atop the rim, at 0.8 mile, the trail enters an open pumice flat. Here, hikers find the first view of Broken Top and South Sister. Both the forest and the trail are generally open; a few alpine plants dot the rim.

By 1.4 miles, detours to the rim edge find sweeping views of the Tam McArthur–Three Creek Lake area, North Sister and the volcanos to the north, and the desert plain to the northeast. Just ahead, reddish-hued Broken Top commands the view, joined by Mount Bachelor. The route grows rockier with loose sand.

At 2 miles, the trail crosses the end of a pumice bowl that sweeps to the edge of the rim. Where the trail next tops a small rise, it affords a view to the southeast of Newberry Crater.

Beginning at 2.4 miles, side trails lead to an exciting bluff vista (2.6 miles). From this jut on the rim, the view applauds most of the Oregon landmarks named earlier, adding a dramatic look at and down Tam McArthur's own rugged, fast-dropping cliff. Three Creek and Little Three Creek lakes sparkle below.

Some visitors may opt to end the hike at the bluff viewpoint, but the trail continues along the rim. At 2.75 miles, it veers south passing

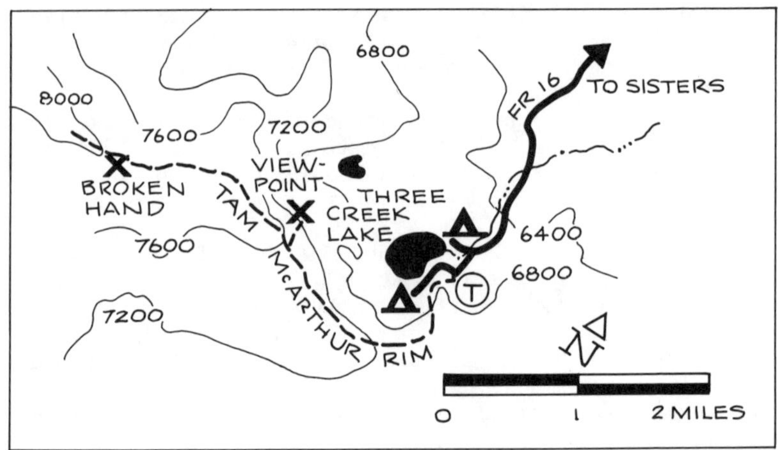

Tam McArthur Rim

across a pumice flat littered with volcanic rock and ringed by whitebark pines. The view features Mount Bachelor, Tumalo Mountain, and Cayuse Crater.

Bypassing the snowfields at 2.9 miles, the trail tours a cinder flat, followed by a boulder field. In another 0.5 mile, the trail arrives at the base of a snowfield that claims the trailbed in the early hiking season. From this snowfield, the route climbs to the saddle of Broken Hand, a cinder ridge offering grand looks at the dominating beauty of Broken Top and the Three Sisters.

Lava bombs—football-shaped molten rocks cooled in flight—dot Broken Hand. Some are quite large; all are intriguing records of this area's explosive history. At 4 miles, the trail reaches the end of the cinder ridge, marking a good point to end the hike and turn around.

Beyond this point, the trail grows rockier and more rugged. Where it fades, stay along the rim. To the southwest, the Cascade Lakes area soon comes into view.

By 4.25 miles, all hikers lacking the climbing skill and equipment to travel this rough mountain terrain of rock and ice should turn back. The return is as you came.

44 GRASSHOPPER–CHUCKSNEY MOUNTAIN LOOP

Distance: 10.9 miles round trip
Elevation change: 2,000 feet
Difficulty: Moderate
Season: Late spring through fall
Map: USFS Willamette, Three Sisters Wilderness
For information: Blue River Ranger District

Chucksney Mountain (elevation 5,760 feet) rises up at the center of a peninsula of land snugged between the Waldo Lake and Three Sisters wilderness areas. The circuit tours wonderful, low- and mid-elevation old-growth forests and open, dry meadows tagging the summit for views of the Three Sisters, the Three Sisters Wilderness Area, the South Fork McKenzie and the Roaring river drainages, and Hiyu Ridge. The return follows along Box Canyon Creek.

Chucksney Mountain bears the name of an Indian who once lived along the Middle Fork Willamette River.

From OR 126 about 5 miles east of the Blue River Junction, turn south onto FR 19 toward Cougar Reservoir. Stay on FR 19 for 25 miles and turn right entering Box Canyon Horse Camp. Follow the road spur to the right to reach the trailhead and parking area for the loop tour.

The hike begins following the Grasshopper Trail touring a rich, full, ancient fir-hemlock forest with vine maple, bracken fern, bunchberry, Oregon grape, and more. Above the horse camp, go right bypassing the Box Canyon Trail (which branches left) to reach the Chucksney Mountain Loop Junction at 0.3 mile.

A right begins a counterclockwise mountain tour with a steady uphill climb away from Box Canyon. Oregon grape now dominates the floor; where light penetrates, thimbleberries abound. At 0.6 mile, dogwoods claim the midstory, promising a floral showcase in late spring. After some switchbacks, the trail enwraps the slope.

At 1.25 miles, the trail tours a dry opening with limited views to the east overlooking the Roaring River. Changes begin occurring in the forest mix; enormous trees line the intermittent drainages.

The trail next rounds above a tributary drainage emptying into the

Roaring River. At 2.75 miles, it reaches a rock outcrop with limited views toward the northeast and South Sister. Beyond it, a wealth of vanilla leaf fans the trail.

At 3.2 miles, the trail climbs taking a couple of switchbacks to top the ridge at 3.4 miles, only to drop down again for an easy forest stroll. The transition between a low-elevation and a mid-elevation forest is now complete, with true fir, hemlock, and white pine forming the canopy. Small meadow patches, one with a vernal pool, now interrupt the forest stands. Lichen drapes the trunks.

By 4.1 miles, the trail eases into its climb toward the Chucksney Mountain Ridge. The forest opens up with a dry meadow spilling beneath and between the forest stands. Pearly everlasting, lupine, aster, paintbrush, and mountain ash spot color to the grasses. The trail briefly overlooks the area from which it came, and then, with a switchback, it tops the ridge at 5.1 miles.

The summit just ahead is little distinguished from the remainder of the ridge; its open top overlooks the rock-outcrop rim. The primary view lies to the east. Views to the west overlook the tops of small trees.

The neighboring rises on Chucksney Mountain, the forest–meadow–shrub drainage at its eastern base, the Three Sisters, and the Roaring River drainage shape the vista. To the east, one clearcut at the wilderness boundary interrupts the view of an otherwise protected, forested expanse.

Western views improve as the trail dips away from the summit touring the extensive, broad meadows on the mountain's west flank. The trail overlooks the Augusta Creek drainage and the forest-cut patchwork on

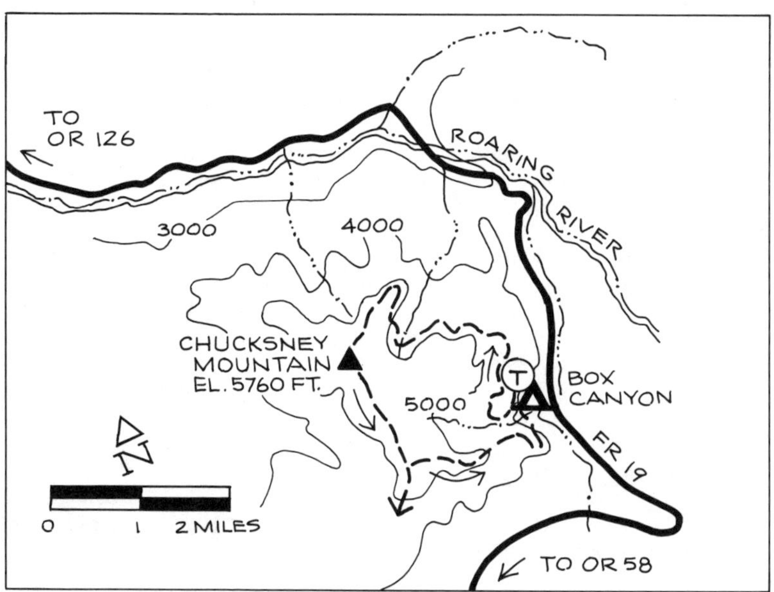

Grasshopper–Chucksney Mountain Loop

Hiyu Ridge, which houses Grasshopper and Lowell mountains.

The trail continues at about the same height rounding the slope, passing through dry meadows and forest stands. Bear grass and lupine dot the meadows.

At 6.1 miles, the trail enters a tight stand of mountain hemlock losing all views. At 6.6 miles is the junction with the Grasshopper Trail; go left for the loop traveling the steep slope returning to an old-growth fir habitat.

The trail wraps and descends the slope at a steady pace. At 7.4 miles, it passes through a meadow-shrub drainage area where lodgepole pines are again present. Wild strawberry abounds. Soon the trail travels above the Box Canyon Creek drainage amid a full forest with lower elevation Cascade flora.

In another 0.25 mile, the trail crosses the often-dry upper drainage via a footbridge. Where it again crosses over the drainage, tall bracken fern crowd the slope and the trail. Rhododendron, vine maple, and a few dogwoods now add a leafy midstory to the forest.

At 9.9 miles the trail takes a switchback working its way toward the Box Canyon Horse Camp. In another 0.6 mile, it crosses Box Canyon Creek. Maidenhair fern line the canyon; by September, the creek is quite small as it slips over the rocks.

Ahead the loop closes. Continue along the trail above the horse camp to return to the trailhead.

45 GREEN LAKES LOOP HIKE

Distance: 12.8-mile loop (permit required)
Elevation change: 1,400 feet
Difficulty: Moderate
Season: Summer through fall
Map: USFS Three Sisters Wilderness
For information: Bend Ranger District

This circuit links the less-traveled Soda Creek Trail with the popular Green Lakes Trail for a fine wilderness tour. Sandwiched between Broken Top and South Sister, the high basin of Green Lakes offers stunning, up-close volcano views. Three lakes dot the basin, presenting slightly different perspectives on this wildly rugged stage.

Often traveling along snow-fed watercourses, the loop tours lodgepole pine and mixed hemlock–fir forests, passes through bunchgrass–wildflower meadows, and crosses pumice ridges. Views of Mount Bachelor, North Sister, Sparks Lake, and Devils Hill add to the tour.

Due to the popularity of this destination, mid-week and off-season day hikes prove the responsible choices. Area backpackers should practice no-trace camping and select sites well removed from the sensitive lakes area.

In Bend, turn west off US 97 onto Franklin Boulevard, following the signs for Cascade Lakes/Mount Bachelor Ski Area; the route rounds Drake Park. In 1.6 miles, turn left onto 14th, which becomes Century Drive/Cascade Lakes Highway. In another 24.3 miles, turn right off Cascade Lakes Highway for the Green Lakes Trailhead parking area.

The Soda Creek Trail leaves from the trailhead to the right (east); there's a mileage sign for Todd Lake and Broken Top trails. Touring an open lodgepole pine forest, the route shows a wandering character as it enters the wilderness. Broken Top and South Sister rise above the treetops, but better views await.

At 1.5 miles, the route crosses the Crater Creek footbridge and a boardwalk at the head of a sweeping grass meadow. It then enters a dark, full forest of mountain hemlock and fir and begins to climb, crossing over side creeks. Small meadows with lupine, thistle, aster, and false hellebore interrupt the forest stands.

The trail next travels the ridge above Soda Creek. The upper meadows offer views of Sparks Lake and Talapus and Katsuk buttes. The scarlet skyrockets attract hummingbirds.

Where the trail crosses over the ridge (3.1 miles), Devils Hill catches the eye. Ahead rises South Sister, only to be dethroned by Broken Top raising its tilted, craggy crown.

Soon, wooden posts point the way through an arid, bunchgrass meadow to the trail junction at 3.8 miles. Go left for the loop. Over-the-shoulder views find Mount Bachelor.

The loop continues following the wooden posts along the low, rolling, exposed meadow slopes. Views sweep up and into the blown-out crater of Broken Top.

At the 4.6-mile trail junction, continue straight ahead. The route travels a transition zone between dry meadow and high-elevation forest. As the trail contours the slope, South Sister and Mount Bachelor engage the eye. At 6 miles, the trail offers a glimpse at North Sister and overlooks the studded lava flow from South Sister; Mount Bachelor slips from sight.

A stone-step creek crossing at 7.2 miles signals the approach to Green Lakes Basin. Ahead, a path leads downhill to the first small lake cradled between Broken Top and South Sister. Numerous paths web the lake area. Shaped like a painter's palette, this first blue lake occupies a bowl with low, rolling pumice ridges, mountain hemlock stands, and meadow shores. In late summer, frogs and toads enliven its banks.

At 7.6 miles, the route crosses the rise to the north separating this lake from the main lake of the basin. The larger lake appears cloudy and

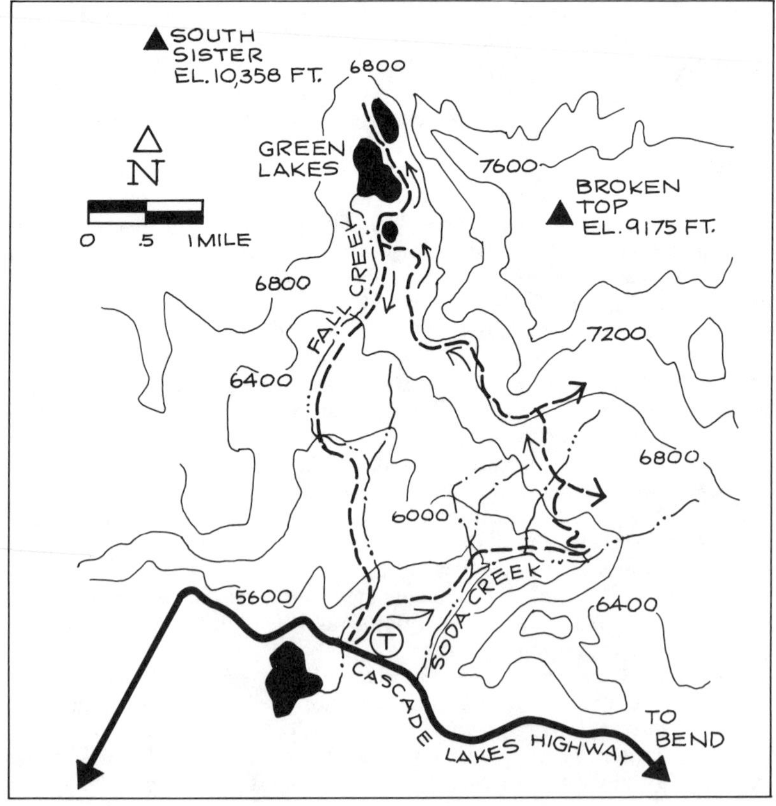

South Sister, Green Lakes Basin

green. The primary trail rounds the steep, forested slope of Broken Top Ridge, staying well above the shore; campers' paths travel closer to the water.

A third small lake lies still farther north, offering yet another look at the South Sister–Broken Top basin. Forgoing a trip to it, return to the first lake rounding its west shore to reach the Green Lakes Trail junction at 8.2 miles.

The Green Lakes Trail leads away from the lake bowl, bearing right. Following this popular trail to close the loop, one may expect to encounter a steady flow of hikers and horseback riders.

The trail tours a mountain hemlock forest alongside cloudy Fall Creek with the lava flow of South Sister rising to the west. A low-grade obsidian dots the flow. By 8.5 miles, some side creeks require stone-step crossings. Where Fall Creek drops sharply, the trail tours a fuller forest.

At 10.2 miles, the route crosses a Fall Creek footbridge followed by a second creek crossing. Here, the trail becomes lane-like. Past the Moraine Lake Trail junction at 10.6 miles, Fall Creek Canyon grows more defined. Its series of roaring cascades, chutes, and broad falls calls hikers to canyon overlooks. With the final Fall Creek bridge crossing, the loop closes at the Green Lakes Trailhead parking area at 12.8 miles.

46 WALDO LAKE–SHORELINE LOOP

Distance: 21-mile circuit
Elevation change: 300 feet
Difficulty: Strenuous
Season: Summer through fall
Map: USFS Waldo Lake Wilderness and Recreation Area, Willamette
For information: Oakridge Ranger District

In this central Cascade region, some 12,000 years ago, a glacial cap gouged out Waldo Lake along with hundreds of potholes and other lake depressions. With no permanent inlet, 10-square-mile Waldo Lake defies plant growth, making it one of the four clearest lakes in the world. Crater Lake, Lake Tahoe in the Sierra Nevada, and Lake Baikal in Siberia complete the list. With rocky spits, islands, and bays, Waldo Lake is a scenic water body to view and to tour with numerous retreats for private reflection. Cross-lake vistas include Charlton Butte, The Twins, Three Sisters, Waldo Mountain, Mount Fuji, and Diamond Peak.

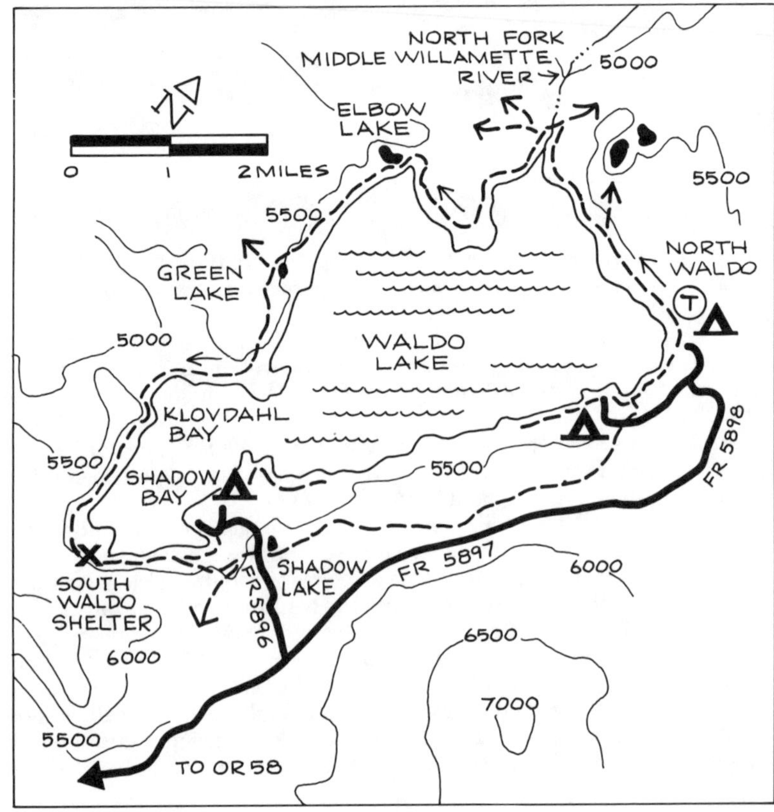

View along Waldo Lake

The 21-mile Waldo Lake Trail encircles this prized water body often traveling inland through forest. With its east-shore segment completely removed from Waldo Lake, the neighboring Shoreline Trail offers the preferred signature on the loop, capping the journey with lakeside enjoyment.

Much of the Waldo Lake Trail serves as a wilderness boundary; numerous trails branch from it entering Waldo Lake Wilderness. Early-season hikers must contend with mosquitos, which thrive in meltwater ponds. August ushers in the gentle days of touring.

From Oakridge, travel 23 miles southeast on OR 58 and turn left onto FR 5897 at the Waldo Lake sign. Continue north on FRs 5897 and 5898 for 12.7 miles, following the signs to North Waldo Campground. The trailhead lies in the upper parking lot of its day use.

Rounding the lake in a counterclockwise direction, the Waldo Lake Trail travels an inland route through a forest of true fir, mountain hemlock, and white pine. The trail bypasses a series of small ponds with lily pads and open, shallow water in its first mile.

At 1.6 miles is the Rigdon Lakes Trail junction. Here, the lake circuit continues straight rising and dipping with the basin terrain en route to the North Fork Middle Willamette River. In 0.5 mile, the trail skirts a large pond. Just beyond, a Waldo Lake detour applauds the indigo waters over which ospreys and gulls soar. At 3.4 miles, the trail reaches the North Fork Middle Willamette River. Upstream, at its lake headwaters, are a gauging station, levee, beach, and primitive boat-to camp.

The loop then continues through similar forest with a true huckleberry–bear grass understory. The trail grows less root- and rock-bound, but narrower. Along this end of the lake, the trail travels close enough to tag the shore for views and easy access.

Approaching the peninsula at the northwest end of the lake, the trail crosses an open talus slope dotted by bear grass and mountain ash. The slope drops away steeply some 30 to 50 feet to the lake.

At 5.9 miles lies Elbow Lake, a good-sized, shallow lake with a crook. The trail travels along and above the lake, bypassing a trail junction and a lily pond. Moist meadow patches interrupt the rolling forest tour.

Going another 2 miles finds the junction for Green Lake, a larger shallow water located 200 yards downhill. South of the Green Lake area, the trail grows more rugged, with some steep pitches and descents as it rolls through forest removed from Waldo Lake. Small meadows and ponds lie along the route.

At 10.4 miles, the trail reaches a junction above Klovdahl Bay. Detouring downhill from the lake circuit finds Klovdahl Camp and Headgate, named for the civil engineer who led a 1908 effort to divert the Waldo Lake waters for irrigation and power projects. The legacy of the failed project is visible from the side trail.

By 12 miles, the loop trail eases and again draws nearer the shore. In a half mile, it arrives at meadow-surrounded South Shelter, a typical USFS open-front overnight structure looking out toward the lake.

Beyond a trailhead register at 14.1 miles, lies a junction: To the left, a completed portion of the Shoreline Trail enters Shadow Bay Campground. To the right begins a long, forested route traveling inland from the east shore en route to North Waldo Campground.

The Shoreline Trail, which will tie Shadow Bay and North Waldo campgrounds, offers the preferred return for the lake circuit. It visits rocky coves and points and small sandy beaches and holds fine lake views. The USFS projects a 1993 completion date.

Meanwhile, follow the Waldo Lake Trail uphill from the 14.1-mile junction. It bypasses meadows and vernal and year-round ponds, tags the Betty Lake Trail junction, and crosses the Shadow Bay Campground Road at 15 miles. Just ahead, the route skirts above Shadow Lake, the lone attraction of this segment. In 4 miles, the trail crosses Islet Campground Road to enter Islet Campground at 19.5 miles. It's a comfortable, rolling tour free from obstruction for quick passage.

From Islet Campground, head north on a completed segment of the Shoreline Trail to sign off the tour with images of Waldo Lake. The loop closes at North Waldo Day Use at 21 miles.

47 MAIDEN PEAK TRAIL

Distance: 11 miles round trip
Elevation change: 3,000 feet
Difficulty: Strenuous
Season: Summer through fall
Map: USFS Waldo Lake Wilderness and Recreation Area, Willamette
For information: Oakridge Ranger District

This trail climbs to the summit of Maiden Peak (elevation 7,818 feet), halting at the site of a former lookout. The first 90 percent of the hike tours an undisturbed forest; the final 10 percent holds the vistas and introduces the volcanic nature of the peak.

Mountain hemlock, high-elevation firs, and lodgepole, white, and whitebark pines shade the path. Only subtle changes in the forest mix vary the tour. For the most part, it's a relaxing hike wrapped in a shroud of familiar sameness, but the steepness of the upper mountain reaches dispels the trail's meditative quality.

The summit unfolds a grand panorama overlooking Diamond Peak to the southwest with Odell and Crescent lakes and Mounts Thielsen and Scott to the south. Northward lie the reservoirs of the Cascade Lakes Area; the Three Sisters; Broken Top; Mounts Bachelor, Washington, and Jefferson; and Waldo, Betty, and Bobby lakes.

From Oakridge, travel 26 miles southeast on OR 58. There turn left at the sign for Gold Lake. Go 1.6 miles on gravel FR 500 to reach the trailhead parking turnout on the left, the trail on the right. Blue cross-country ski signs and trailhead markers indicate the Maiden Peak Trail.

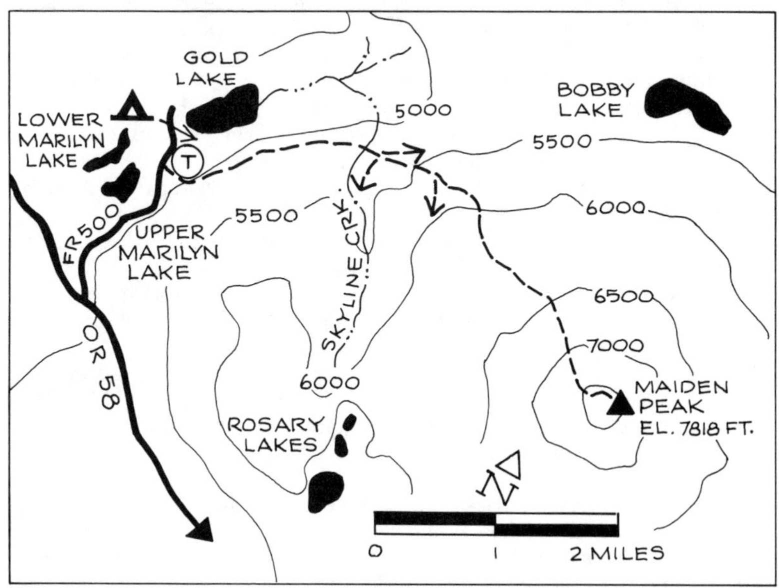

The hike begins amid mountain hemlocks and lodgepole pines. Dangling yellow-green lichens weight the branches. For the first 0.1 mile, the trail angles up the slope above FR 500. Topping a rise, it then curves away touring a deeper forest with many firs. The floor displays a hit-and-miss ground cover of lupine, true and dwarf huckleberry, and kinnikinnick.

Trailside mileage markers aid hikers in keeping tabs on their progress. Higher on the trees, the blue-diamond ski markers hint at the winter snow level. The rusted communication wire that strung to the one-time lookout now lies silent along much of the trail.

The first couple of miles of the hike show a minimal grade with the miles toppling quickly. At 1.75 miles, the trail arrives at Skyline Creek. Side-by-side logs allow a dry crossing of this year-round waterway. Currant and huckleberry bushes crowd its banks.

Soon after, the trail reaches the primitive Wait Here Camp and a three-way trail junction: To the left is a connector trail to the Pacific Crest Trail (PCT); to the right lies the Maiden Lake Trail, which offers a possible loop option; and straight ahead past the camp continues the Maiden Peak Trail.

The trail climbs steadily through a tall forest of mountain hemlock and high-elevation firs to the 2.3-mile trail junction. Here, the Maiden Peak Trail crosses over the PCT. Following the PCT to the right finds Rosary Lake; to the left finds Bobby Lake.

Leaving the junction, the trail grade eases. Dwarf huckleberry remains as the sole floor covering. Beyond the 3-mile marker, boulder outcrops and ridges spot the forest, which is now mostly mountain hemlock.

After 4 miles, the trail undergoes a character change showing a steep uphill intensity, but it retains its good earthen bed free from obstruction. Ahead, tree blazes and a few cairns help indicate the path. Smaller hemlocks and whitebark pines claim the upper mountain reaches; barren sandy flats interrupt the forest.

At 5.1 miles, the trail offers the first open view of the hike looking south at Odell and Crescent lakes, Redtop and Lakeview mountains, Diamond Peak, and Mounts Thielsen and Scott. Here, too, the trail affords the first look at the summit destination. The trail grows rockier, sandier, and more open, traveling amid small, scattered whitebark pines.

In another 0.2 mile, the trail is opposite a small crater bowl. Crossing to its other side finds a North Cascade vista, but the trail affords similar views ahead, showcasing the Three Sisters, Bachelor, Broken Top, and Mounts Washington and Jefferson, along with Davis, Wickiup, and Crane Prairie reservoirs and Waldo and Bobby lakes.

Looking down the north face of Maiden Peak finds some rugged, crusty red-black volcanic pillars with craggy fingers. The north side of Maiden Peak is more blown out. Cinders cap the mountain. At 5.5 miles, the trail tags the Maiden Peak summit for a 360-degree view of the key Central Cascade features.

For the return trek, retrace your steps. Or add a loop, descending the south flank of Maiden Peak to the Maiden Lake Trail and following it west and north to return to the original hike near Wait Here Camp, for a 15-mile round-trip tour returning to FR 500.

48 HARDESTY MOUNTAIN LOOP HIKE

Distance: 14.5 miles round trip (with summit detour)
Elevation change: 3,300 feet
Difficulty: Strenuous
Season: Spring through fall
Map: USGS Mount June, Westfir West; USFS Willamette
For information: Lowell Ranger District

Built in 1910, the Hardesty Trail is now more noted for its old-growth forest than for its vista. Trees have nearly eclipsed the site of the former lookout. All that remains is a strained view to the north toward Lookout Point Reservoir.

This circuit ties together the Hardesty, Eula Ridge, and South Willamette trails often traveling through the wonder and bounty of ancient forest. Stout Douglas firs and western hemlocks tower above the trail. In places where the rhododendrons are well entrenched, springtime hikers find a grand floral display of the pink pom-pom blooms. The steep Eula Ridge Trail quickly marches hikers down from the mountaintop.

From Eugene, go east on OR 58 for 20.8 miles to reach the Hardesty Trailhead on the right-hand side of the road east of Goodman Creek.

The trail begins touring a full forest with a thick vine maple midstory to the 0.2-mile junction with the Goodman Trail. Go straight on the Hardesty Trail for a steady climb to the summit.

The understory shows a chaos of greenery, while a few cedar and snags intersperse the old-growth fir and hemlock canopy. Rough-skinned newts, snails, and slugs slowly move amid the undergrowth and across the trail. A clearcut to the east showers light on the setting.

At the loop junction (0.7 mile), the South Willamette Trail branches left, while the Hardesty Trail heads uphill. For a counterclockwise loop, stay on the Hardesty Trail.

As it rounds an older cut and crosses FR 515 at 1 mile, shrubby vegetation at times pushes into the path. Where it returns to a full forest, bigleaf maple, chinquapin, rhododendron, and an occasional dogwood add richness. Oregon grape abounds in the forest tapestry.

At 1.5 miles, the trail enters a set of short switchbacks and travels the ridge meeting FR 5835 at 2 miles. Follow it right for 0.2 mile to resume the hike, soon returning to the full forest of the ridge. Grouse sound from far-off perches.

At 3 miles, the trail leaves the ridge rounding the slope. Ahead is an abrupt transition between the full forest and a dense, choked forest of smaller-diameter cedar and hemlock.

A few rock outcrops and mossy green cliffs mark the next trail stretch. Before long, the trail returns to the ridge taking a couple of switchbacks to reach the Eula Ridge Trail Junction at 4.7 miles. The circuit follows Eula Ridge downhill to the left, but first stay on the Hardesty Trail to reach the summit (elevation 4,273 feet).

At 4.9 miles, the Hardesty Trail bears left to claim the mountaintop.

The rock base and low support columns remain from the former lookout. Deciduous bushes and evergreens encroach on the site allowing only a limited view to the north. Thimbleberry, Oregon iris, and ferns sprout between the rocks. Despite the lack of a view, the site proves a pleasant picnic stop.

To continue the loop, return to the Eula Ridge Trail (5.3 miles) and follow it downhill. This less-traveled route lacks a formal tread and often mirrors the steepness of its slope for a no-nonsense descent. A wonderful forest enfolds the trail, encouraging "breathers" even when the trail does not. Snags pierce the canopy, and logs lace the floor. Here, the hemlocks dominate more than on Hardesty Ridge, creating a darker forest setting.

By 6.3 miles, the trail is descending the backbone of the ridge. Oxalis embroiders the sides of the thin brown trail as it becomes more rolling. Through openings in the now drier, madrone-punctuated forest, hikers make out the shape of Hardesty Mountain.

At 7 miles, the hiker finds a more formalized trail with a cut tread and switchbacks, which, by comparison, almost seem tedious in their slow, downhill progression. Bigleaf maples rejoin the mix.

The trail crosses over FR 5840.529, followed soon after by the crossing

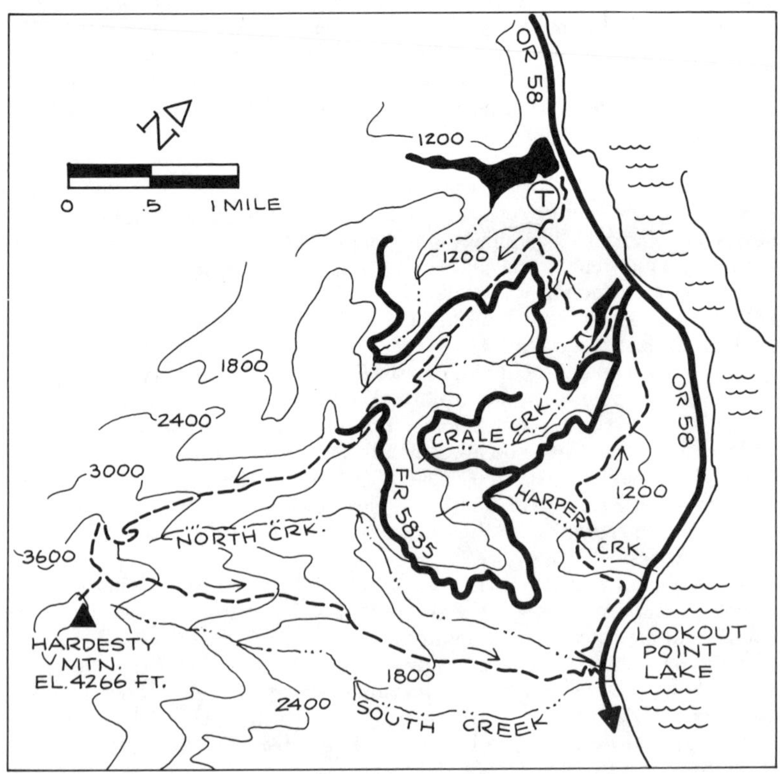

Newt

of overgrown FR 528. The trail then switchbacks downhill toward the South Willamette Trail Junction at 8.8 miles. Noise from OR 58 rises up the hillside.

At the junction, go left on the South Willamette Trail to close the loop. The rolling, westbound trail tours a forest corridor parallel to OR 58. Second-growth forest, ancient forest, and cuts alternately command the stage. OR 58's presence is variously noted depending on the width of corridor and the forestation. Often, the tour is surprisingly lush and pleasant.

Past the Harper Creek footbridge, the trail skirts a cut site traveling through its thick shrubby border. At 11.7 miles, the route crosses over an old two-track for a comfortable forest tour to reach Crale Creek Road, FR 5835, at 12.4 miles.

Across the road, the trail resumes with the Crale Creek log-bridge crossing. It again alternately tours forest and cut to reach the Hardesty Trail at 13.8 miles. Go right to end the hike in another 0.7 mile.

49 LARISON CREEK TRAIL

Distance: 6.3 miles one way
Elevation change: 1,400 feet
Difficulty: Moderate
Season: Spring through fall, with the lower 4 miles open year round
Map: USGS Oak Ridge, Holland Point; USFS Willamette
For information: Rigdon Ranger District

This trail, closed to motorized travel, tours an isolated arm of Hills Creek Reservoir and the upstream waters of Larison Creek. Along the way, it unveils three distinct forest faces: the disturbed forest along the reservoir, a rich middle stretch of ancient forest, and a clearcut site along the final leg to the upper trailhead. It is the old-growth tour that recommends this trail, along with the scenic upstream waters of stair-stepping Larison Creek.

Thick mosses drape the old-growth gallery. An alder-shrub tangle often houses the lower creek, defying access. Varied thrush, woodpeckers, and newts are among the wildlife discoveries.

At the east end of Oakridge, turn south off OR 58 onto Kitson Springs County Road, heading toward Hills Creek Dam. In 0.5 mile, turn right onto FR 21 to round the west side of the reservoir. Going another 3.4 miles finds the lower trailhead parking area on the right.

Madrone and fir frame the trail as it travels above the Larison Creek Arm of Hills Creek Reservoir. The added light from the reservoir introduces the presence of rhododendron and chinquapin. Sword fern, salal, and Oregon grape spot the floor. Where the trail dips into a narrow side canyon and crosses a gurgling creek (0.5 mile), mosses grow in abundance, and sword ferns cascade down the hillside.

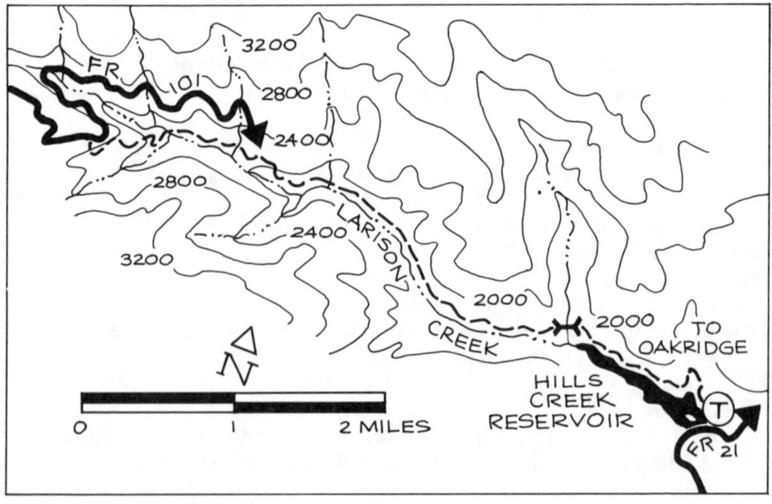

Footbridge over side creek

On the steep, thin-soiled slope of the reservoir, hemlocks join the fir. Low waters reveal the tree stumps dotting the reservoir's bed and terraced banks. The openness of the trail affords up-canyon views.

At 1.1 miles, the trail enters a scenic forest stand with many hemlocks. On either side of the log footbridge at 1.5 miles, hikers find short spurs leading to flat, comfortable camp spots amid the multistory forest. A pit toilet serves hikers and overnighters.

Cattails crowd the end of the reservoir, as the hike begins following the upstream waters of the creek proper. Almost immediately the trail is immersed in green old-growth splendor. Cedars line the creek flat; ancient fir and hemlock shade the low bench above it. A thick, spongy moss carpets the ground and logs, while snags, vine maple, and Pacific yew accent the forest. The trail remains of good grade and width with a rolling character.

At 1.9 miles and at 3.2 miles, the trail briefly pulls out of the old growth, offering looks at Larison Creek, a 15-foot-wide watercourse spilling over a gravel floor. The creek runs cloudy, silted from upstream cuts. Small deciduous trees overhang its bank; bigleaf maples shade the rocky flats alongside it.

Eventually, the dense forest of old-growth towers yields to a younger, less diverse stand. At 3.5 miles, the trail passes beneath the trunk of a tumbled, old colossus, marking the start of a climb.

Salal now crowds the path. The rush of the creek signals its presence deep in the canyon. A few sugar pine dot the forest with their long, oversized cones. The rhododendrons are again prominent.

At 3.9 miles, the trail tops the rise. Here, mosses claim the less-trodden path. With a rolling dip, the trail briefly crosses a clearcut and tours a disturbed-forest just below a cut. In the off-season, wind-fallen trees clog the trail where the cuts have left the standing forest vulnerable.

By 4.6 miles, the trail is back at the creek flat amid the rich forest. Here, Larison Creek presents a finer face, with clearer water, mossy rocks and banks, and overhanging evergreens. The scenic waters skip over small rock ledges, creating pools and cascades.

At 5 miles, the trail requires the crossing of one of the headwater forks, via a log or wading. Up ahead, the trail affords views of a second headwater fork cascading down a steep, pinched, green canyon. The forest-shaded trail then switchbacks up slope, overlooking the canyon of the first headwater fork.

At 5.6 miles, the trail arrives at a 1990 clearcut slope, which it criss-crosses uphill. After 0.4 mile, the trail hugs the cut's border, passing amid small fir, salal, bracken fern, and woody shrubs. At 6.3 miles, it ends at FR 2102.101; a brown hiker sign marks the trailhead on this good single-lane gravel road.

For round-trip hikers, though, the headwater-forks area proves the better turnaround destination.

50 TIMPANOGAS AREA LAKE TRAILS

Distance: 9.5 miles round trip (total distance)
Elevation change: 700 feet (maximum)
Difficulty: Moderate
Season: Summer through fall
Map: USFS Willamette, Diamond Peak Wilderness
For information: Rigdon Ranger District

Mile-high Timpanogas Lake is the hub to this system of fine, short, lake-destination hikes. Meadow, forest, and rugged slope border this deep, blue water. Smaller Lower Timpanogas Lake rests next door.

During an area stay, hikers can easily combine three of these hikes, beginning with the Timpanogas Lake Trail, which encircles the host lake. Other trails venture out to June Lake, cradled in a peaceful, forested basin, and Indigo Lake, perhaps the star of this line-up. Its incredible turquoise waters shine at the base of rugged Sawtooth Mountain.

Unfortunately, from early to mid-summer, hoards of visitor-repelling mosquitos appear. Even then, the beauty of the lakes can sometimes win out over the aggravation of spray and netting.

From OR 58 east of Oakridge, turn south onto Kitson Springs County

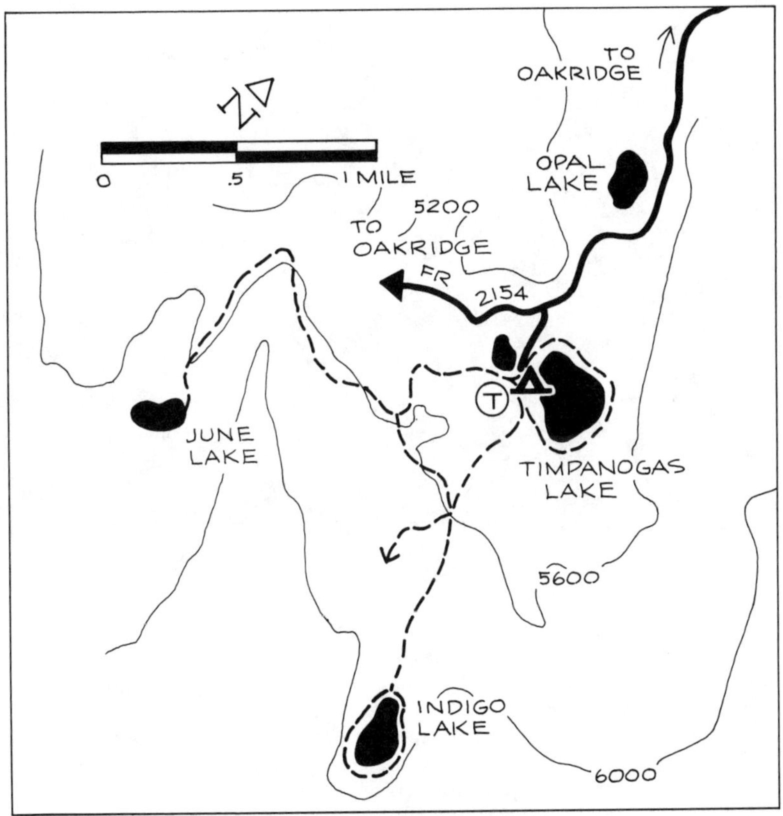

Road. At the junction in 0.5 mile, bear right onto FR 21, staying on it for some 32 miles. At the FR 21–FR 2154 junction, go left on FR 2154. At the junction in 6.2 miles, turn right for Timpanogas Lake. After going another 2.4 miles, turn left onto FR 2154.399 to enter Timpanogas Lake Campground, reaching the trailheads in 0.3 mile. It's a paved and good gravel route.

Timpanogas Lake Trail: This 1-mile loop starts from the campground touring the lakeshore. It offers views of Sawtooth Mountain and the forested ridges above Timpanogas Lake. The overhead canopy parades Pacific silver fir, pine, and spruce; the understory mat consists of dwarf and true huckleberry, vanilla leaf, bunchberry, and prince's pine.

The rockier areas sport purple penstemon, while the marshy areas sport false hellebore and shooting stars. Unfortunately, the peak wildflower season coincides with the peak mosquito season.

On the east and southeast shores, hikers encounter inlets and marshy reaches, but usually there are adequate numbers of fallen logs and patches of high ground to negotiate a dry loop.

June Lake Trail: Under escort of mosquitos, we logged this trail in at 2 miles, the USFS lists it at 3 miles, and likely the truth falls somewhere

Timpanogas Lake and Sawtooth Mountain

in between. The trail has an elevation change of 400 feet.

From the end of the trailhead turnout above Lower Timpanogas Lake, this hike follows a closed road above the lake. The footpath begins at 0.1 mile with an uphill spurt.

Touring a mid-elevation fir forest with ground-hugging true and dwarf huckleberry, the trail soon passes above a pond. As the path climbs and contours the slope, lodgepole and white pines dominate a more open forest above an ashy floor dotted by white lupine.

A small, wet meadow drainage precedes the 0.7 mile junction for the June Lake–Indigo Lake Tie, which branches left, offering an opportunity to link these two hikes. For the June Lake Trail, continue straight.

Smaller fir, mountain hemlock, and white pine next claim the rolling trail. Dry meadow patches intersperse the stands, while openings in the tree cover afford brief, limited looks at Hills Peak and Mount Thielsen.

At 2 miles, the trail reaches medium-sized June Lake, nestled below the forested west and northwest ridges of Sawtooth Mountain. Kinnikinnick and heather dot the shore; a few grasses invade the shallow waters. When ready to surrender this setting, return as you came.

Indigo Lake Trail: This 1.9-mile trail has an elevation change of 700 feet. It, too, leaves from the trailhead turnout above Lower Timpanogas Lake or may be reached via the 0.8-mile June Lake–Indigo Lake Tie.

The trail travels through a forest of Pacific silver fir and Engelmann spruce with an understory of huckleberry and heather. At 0.75 mile, the trail arrives at a junction: The path ahead continues the Indigo Lake hike, the center fork leads to Sawtooth Mountain in 3.5 miles, and the right fork is the tie to the June Lake Trail.

From the junction, the Indigo Lake Trail follows the outlet creek upstream. Where it leaves the creek, the trail laces through forest, stringing together small meadows and views of Sawtooth Mountain.

Rugged Sawtooth Mountain (elevation 7,302 feet), with its scree slopes and vertical broken cliffs, looms above the Indigo Lake setting. A 0.7-mile trail rings the blue brilliance, touring a mixed conifer forest and crossing the scree slope. Pikas sound at hikers who invade the rocky complex. The water is deepest below the scree slope, offering a hole for swimming or fishing. A couple of primitive campsites dot the forested lakeshore. The return is as you came.

51 NORTH UMPQUA TRAIL

Distance: 77.5 miles one way
Elevation change: 5,400 feet
Difficulty: Strenuous
Season: Spring through fall (lower parts, year round)
Map: USFS Umpqua; USFS/BLM North Umpqua Trail brochure
For information: Diamond Lake and North Umpqua ranger districts, Roseburg District BLM

This long-distance river-companion trail has its start below the Cascade Crest at Maidu Lake. Its roller-coaster route travels forested slope and rocky shore pursuing the North Umpqua River downstream to Swiftwater, a Douglas County Park. En route, the trail journeys into side canyons, visits ancient and second-growth forests, bypasses scenic cliffs and falls, and overlooks the hypnotic, blue-green host waters.

Early Indians fished and camped along this river and conducted religious ceremonies atop its ridges.

While most hikers do not attempt the full tour, the given reason is one of time, not offering. The trail's many access points allow for day hikes and shorter backpacks. Side trails invite further exploration, and camp areas mark the route. The trail's scenic and historic bounty draws visitors back again and again.

Hikers find access to the trail at points off OR 138. The easternmost is at Bradley Creek Trailhead: East of the Lemolo Lake area, turn north off OR 138 onto FR 60; then turn east off FR 60 onto FR 6000.958. The westernmost is at Swiftwater County Park, south off OR 138 east of Idleyld Park.

East of the Cascade Crest, hikers may access Maidu Lake via the Miller Lake Trail (See Hike 53).

From Maidu Lake, a remote trail segment journeys downstream through the Mount Thielsen Wilderness Area, bypassing Lake Lucille in the early miles. The trail tours a semi-open lodgepole pine forest and crosses meadows as it travels along the headwaters—a creek-sized clear water. Hikers often send elk thundering into the forest; beaver signs mark the waterway.

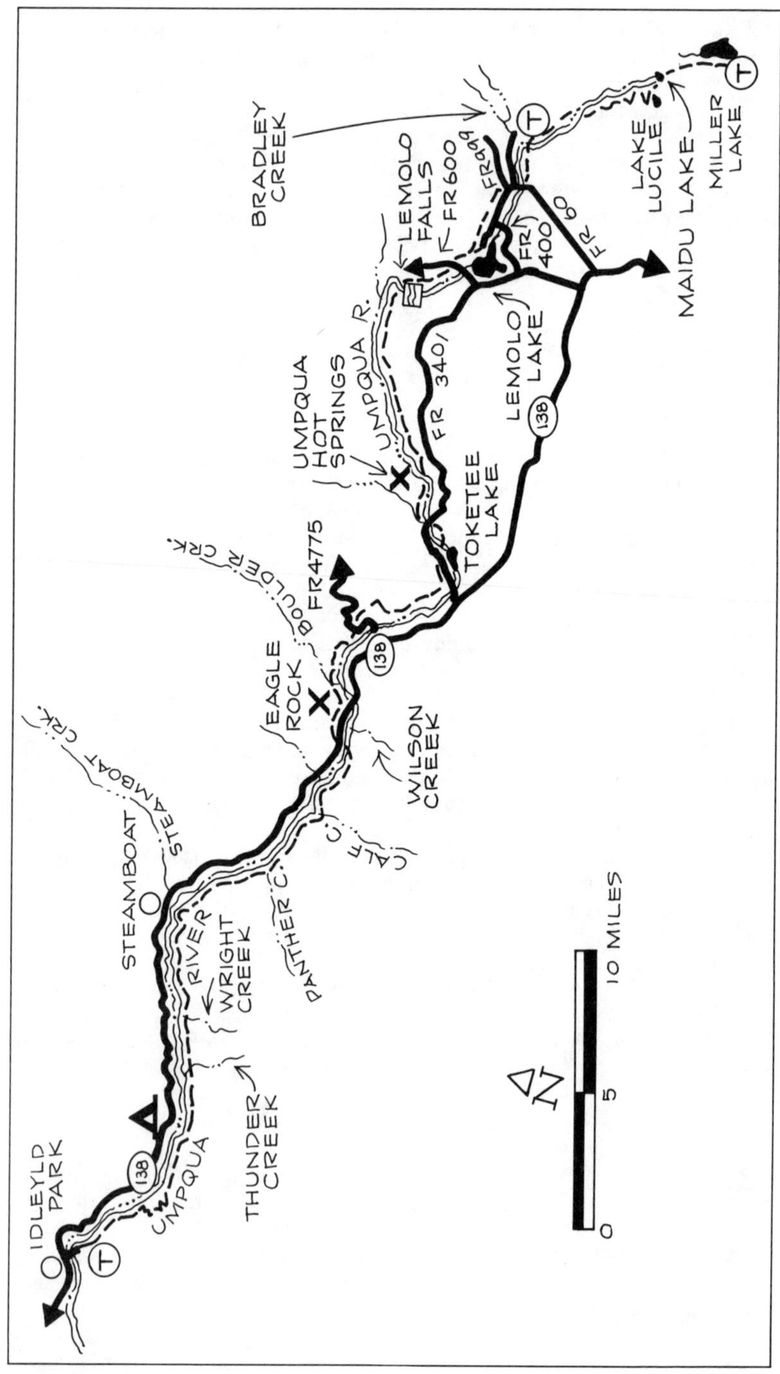
IDLEYLD PARK
138
UMPQUA
RIVER
THUNDER CREEK
WRIGHT CREEK
STEAMBOAT
STEAMBOAT CRK.
PANTHER C.
CALF C.
WILSON CREEK
EAGLE ROCK
BOULDER CRK.
FR4775
TOKETEE LAKE
UMPQUA HOT SPRINGS
UMPQUA R.
FR 3401
LEMOLO LAKE
LEMOLO FALLS
FR600
FR999
FR 400
FR 60
BRADLEY CREEK
MAIDU LAKE
LAKE LUCILE
MILLER LAKE
N
0
5
10 MILES

North Umpqua River

The route passes the Bradley Creek Trailhead spur at 10.1 miles and continues downstream. Arriving at FR 60, it heads north to the junction of FRs 60 and 999. There, the trail turns west touring a similar forest with dwarf huckleberry and iris, as it parallels the road on the north side of Lemolo Lake.

At 16.4 miles, the trail crosses a canal as it heads toward Lemolo Falls (18.2 miles)—the most popular single attraction along the route. The next 15 miles hold some of the trail's finest, most remote offerings. Contouring the wildflower-dotted open forest of the north slope, the trail overlooks a tumbling, reduced river segment marked by swirling pools, canyon bowls with 5- to 10-foot cascades, and the impressive 169-foot Lemolo Falls chute, framed by sheer cliffs.

Beyond the falls, the trail continues a high-road tour along the old-growth-forested slope bypassing rock outcrops and cliffs. It then switchbacks downhill to a bridge crossing at 19 miles. A newer trail leg now leads the way staying closer to the river. At 19.3 miles, cross-river views find the landslide that broadened and slowed the upstream waters.

By 25 miles, scenic side creeks slice to the river. Weeping Rocks and a line-up of falls—Coffeepot, Cedar Creek, Teardrop, and Surprise—engage hikers. From the flat below Teardrop Falls, cross-river views find the mineral-streaked cliff beneath Umpqua Hot Springs.

Reaching FR 3401, go right. From the hot springs parking area, descend and cross the bridge. The river trail continues left (downstream); the hot springs trail climbs steeply to the right for 0.3 mile reaching the open-air, lean-to–covered, small, steamy pool.

The steep canyon slope now features the classic Douglas fir–western hemlock forest characteristic of the 2,500-foot elevation. The route is well above the river. Downstream from Toketee Lake (33 miles), more cut areas and utility corridors intrude on the route.

Where the trail briefly meets and tours the southern boundary of Boulder Creek Wilderness (38 miles), it follows the Jessie Wright Trail across the Boulder Creek footbridge for an old-growth shoreline tour close to the river and to OR 138. At an unnamed creek west of Eagle Creek, the route climbs, offering limited views of Eagle Rock.

At the upcoming junction, the river trail descends steeply to the left traveling a path and old road to reach OR 138 opposite Wilson Creek (44 miles). A plaque notes the early-day homesteaders—the Wrights.

To resume the trail, cross Marsters Bridge to the south shore and follow the gravel road downstream for 600 feet; care is needed on the bridge due to logging truck traffic. For the next 33.5 miles, the trail rolls along the semi-open, forested south canyon wall, often opposite OR 138. River access is limited.

At 56.3 miles, a 5.5-mile national recreation trail segment leaves near Mott Bridge traveling a low-level route along the river bank with nearly continuous views of the still waters, rapids, and bends. The trail passes moss-etched cliffs, white-bubbling side creeks, and the site of one of Zane Grey's fishing camps.

From Wright Creek at 61.8 miles, the trail again travels the "high road" through a mid-sized forest to arrive at a side canyon housing the spectacular, quick-dropping Thunder Creek (64.1 miles).

The trail continues its rolling canyonside tour with occasional river overlooks. The deeper forest filters out the presence of OR 138. Nearing Bob Creek, the trail climbs to round the north shoulder of Bob Butte. It then returns to character passing through stands of old- and second-growth Douglas fir, sugar pine, and maple to end at Swiftwater Park.

52 YELLOW JACKET GLADE LOOP TRAIL

Distance: 7.1-mile loop, includes Flat Rock spur
Elevation change: 900 feet
Difficulty: Moderate
Season: Late spring through fall
Map: USGS Quartz Mountain; USFS Umpqua
For information: North Umpqua Ranger District

Alternating between forest and meadow, this trail visits some magnificent old-growth Shasta red fir stands. While a definite tour plus, the old-growth stands also magnify the tour minuses—the many encroaching and neighboring cuts tagged and seen along the route.

In the meadows and glades, hikers find a wildflower bonanza with shooting star, American globeflower, camas, arrowhead butterweed, giant red paintbrush, lupine, cow parsnip, and wandering daisy. The more remote meadow patches attract area deer.

Hemlock Lake is a small, earthen-dammed, forest-rimmed reservoir; it is but briefly visited at the end of a counterclockwise tour. While the area trails are designated for foot, horse, mountain bicycle, and trail motorcycle traffic, they remain neatly narrow with full vegetation at their sides.

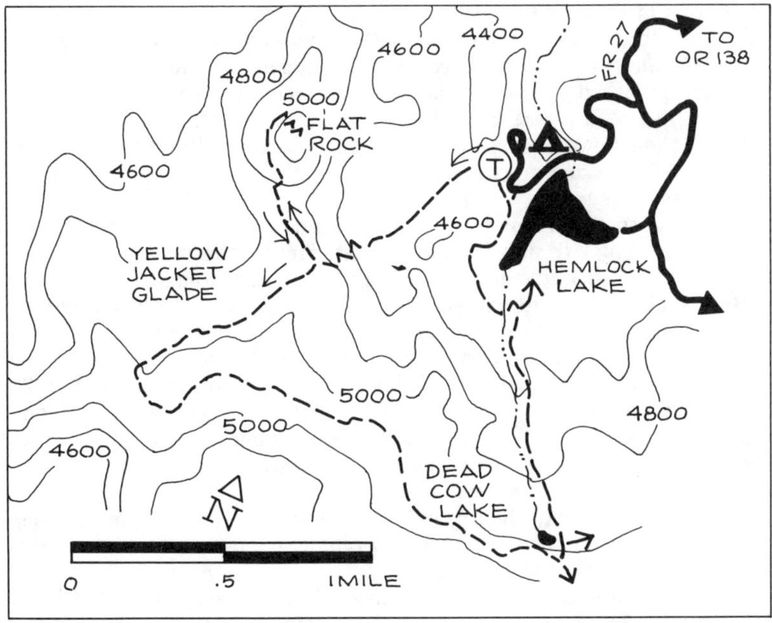

From Roseburg, go 16.1 miles east on OR 138 and turn south at Glide onto Little River Road, County 17/FR 27. Stay on FR 27 following the signs to Hemlock Lake. At the junction in 28.9 miles (the sign is missing), turn right. Go another 0.7 mile on FR 27 and again turn right onto FR 2700.495 to reach Hemlock Lake Campground and the trailhead in 0.7 mile.

A counterclockwise tour of this well-signed loop begins directly behind the campground entrance signboard. Beautiful old-growth lichen-showered Shasta red firs and towering white pines frame the trail as it passes between the camp and a large meadow. Bride's bonnet, false Solomon's seal, wood violet, and vanilla leaf contribute the rich vegetation mesh of the forest.

The loop then travels a meadow boardwalk, passes through an old-growth stand, and enters a second meadow with a view of cliff-faced Flat Rock. Early-season hikers may encounter some marshy meadow areas.

At 0.5 mile, the trail begins to climb. Where the forest is more open, vine maples flourish. Meadow openings offer new perspectives on Flat Rock.

The trail to this mountain branches right at 1 mile; the loop bears left. The side trip to Flat Rock follows a little-tracked trail across a moist meadow to round and climb the forested slope. At 1.8 miles, it claims the mostly forested former lookout site (elevation 5,310 feet). Limited views feature the Little River drainage, Hemlock Lake, a meadow, and near and far Cascade peaks. Morning hikers often discover a heavy fog in the valley.

The most interesting discovery rests in the summit treetops—the remnants of a bird's-nest fire-lookout platform along with its stilt supports. The tops of the trees cut when the platform was put in place have now regrown. Return as you came to resume the loop at 2.6 miles.

Heading toward Yellow Jacket Glade, the loop tour continues through an ancient true fir forest. Fawn lilies and trillium dot the higher meadow patches; their flowers peak in late June. At 3.3 miles, the trail arrives at Yellow Jacket Glade, a grassy meadow swath with a thick tree border and alders at its foot.

The trail then passes through forest and slowly climbs topping an open, grassy ridge from a former harvest. The southern view features a tapestry of forests and cuts in the South Umpqua drainage.

By 3.8 miles, the trail travels an old skid road for an easy rolling tour bypassing several large stumps. The new forest is open with trees only 3 to 15 feet tall. Bleeding heart, currant, and vanilla leaf weave amid the grasses. Cross-harvest views find the forested side of Flat Rock. In 0.25 mile, the trail dips into an uncut forest. At the stump with the diamond markers, go left for the loop; a footpath soon resumes the journey. Where the trail climbs along a ridge, a sign to the right at 4.6 miles indicates it has reached the Umpqua Divide.

As the trail descends, bear grass enters the mix. At 5.1 miles, the loop reaches an open saddle near a logging road and crosses over a small rise in the cut area before returning to forest.

At the junction ahead, the loop curves left to reach spring-fed Dead Cow Lake at 5.6 miles. This is a small, shallow frog pond secluded in the trees. A wonderful croaking chorus sometimes erupts from shore. A meadow tongue extending from the lake is host to American globeflower.

From the lake area, the trail to Snowbird Shelter branches right; the loop continues ahead. The forest descent follows alongside a narrow spring-fed drainage. Douglas firs join the forest ranks. At the 6.4-mile junction, the loop continues left; to the right lies the Hemlock Lake boat ramp.

The route now crosses a footbridge to skirt the meadow-shrub clearing at the end of Hemlock Lake. The lake rim shows mostly young, replanted fir with a richer forest on the low hillsides. At 6.9 miles, the loop trail reenters a full forest above the lake to return to the campground at 7.1 miles.

53 MILLER LAKE TRAIL

Distance: 4.25-mile loop
Elevation change: Minimal
Difficulty: Easy
Season: Summer through fall
Map: USFS Winema
For information: Chemult Ranger District

This circuit hugs the shore of Miller Lake, a large, natural mountain lake (elevation 5,600 feet) situated in a forest pocket just below the Cascade Crest. The rolling tour passes through mixed and lodgepole pine forests and crosses moist meadow drainages, offering splendid lake views with cross-lake views of Mount Thielsen, Red Cone, and Sawtooth Ridge. The lake tour also holds convenient access to the neighboring Mount Thielsen Wilderness Area.

Digit Point Campground offers hikers a comfortable base for their exploration; the facility is open from mid-June through September.

On US 97, go 1 mile north of Chemult and turn west onto improved FR 9772. Trailheads are found at the Digit Point boat launch and day-use swimming area in about 12 miles.

A counterclockwise lake tour heads southeast from the boat launch loop. The wide pumice trail normally travels just above the lake through a semi-open forest of fir, mountain hemlock, spruce, and mixed pine. Dwarf huckleberry spots the otherwise open needlemat floor. In places, the denuded skeletons of the fallen lodgepole pines weave a mat.

Along the early part of the loop, the forest road sometimes crowds the trail. Beyond Gideon Creek, picnic tables dot an open bench, where one finds easy lake access to an anchored floating dock. The view from shore features Digit Point and the blue expanse.

At 0.9 mile, the trail travels atop the 20-foot-high sandy cliffs that drop steeply to the lake. Trees cling tenuously to the eroding edge. Bald eagles often roost in the snags overhead.

Soon, the trail passes through the meadow drainage of meandering Miller Creek, the lake outlet. Beetle-killed lodgepole pines line the meadow; the pencil-point stumps from beaver activity mark the bench

Miller Lake

above it. The trails branching to the right lead to FR 9772; stay left for the circuit.

By 1.5 miles, the lake trail begins offering tree-filtered views of Sawtooth Ridge, Red Cone, and Mount Thielsen. Along the north shore, the forest features a few larger trees and a richer understory with prince's pine, sticky laurel, fern, and chinquapin.

A few areas along shore are adequately open to allow angling, but the lake is better suited for boat fishing. Mergansers claim the small, quiet cove waters. Inlet creeks now fragment the trail.

At 3.6 miles, the Skyline Trail (Maidu Lake Trail) heads northwest alongside Evening Creek to reach Maidu Lake in 3.25 miles. This detour proves a nice extension for hikers seeking an all-day outing. Upon entering Mount Thielsen Wilderness, the route climbs the forested slope above Miller Lake, offering lake overlooks. It then crosses the Cascade Crest and descends to Maidu Lake, a mid-sized mountain lake rimmed by low forested slopes. Gray jays, Clark's nutcrackers, ducks, and shorebirds engage visitors along the 0.75-mile trail encircling the lake.

Forgoing the Maidu Lake detour, the Miller Lake circuit crosses a grassy flat, touring close to the lapping lake waters. It then resumes its slope-wrapping, forested course tagging more inlet drainages to arrive at the day-use picnic and swim area (4.1 miles). Where the trail splits, either path leads to the day use.

From the day use, continue rounding the shore, passing below the campground to return to the boat launch.

54 MOUNT BAILEY NATIONAL RECREATION TRAIL

Distance: 10 miles round trip
Elevation change: 3,200 feet
Difficulty: Strenuous
Season: Summer through fall
Map: USGS Diamond Lake; USFS Umpqua
For information: Diamond Lake Ranger District

This trail climbs to the bald summit of Mount Bailey (elevation 8,363 feet) for a wonderful Diamond Lake–Crater Lake Country vista. The Cascade lineup features Mounts McLoughlin, Scott, and Thielsen, Diamond Peak, and the Three Sisters. Strong winds frequently buffet the summit, bringing a wild excitement to the lofty post.

According to legend, the Klamath Indian medicine men would visit the mountaintop when seeking a communion with the upper world. This site holds a similar spirit-lifting invigoration for the modern-day seeker.

To access Diamond Lake's south shore, from the OR 138–OR 230 junction north of Crater Lake, turn west onto OR 230, followed by a quick right onto East Shore Road. Go 0.7 mile on East Shore Road and turn left on FR 4795, heading west along the lake's south shore. In 1.6 miles, turn left onto Bailey Road, FR 4795.300, a dirt road. The Bailey Mountain Trailhead is on the right in 0.4 mile, opposite the Silent Creek Trailhead.

The trail crosses a small drainage—at times, active with frogs—to ascend through an open lodgepole pine forest. Silver logs weave a tangled maze across the floor. Prince's pine and manzanita supply the feeble

Mount Bailey summit ridge

touches of green. A few climbing bursts mark the otherwise rolling ascent. Blue-diamond markers indicate the route's winter use as a nordic ski trail.

At 0.75 mile, a break in the tree cover offers a brief view to the south. As the trail rounds Hemlock Butte, the forest becomes more mixed with a taller, fuller canopy offering more shade. Mountain hemlock, Shasta red fir, and white and lodgepole pines unite above a patchy floor of huckleberry and kinnikinnick.

From the bend at 1.5 miles, the trail travels a forested flat for 0.5 mile to reach FR 380, a high-clearance vehicle road. (For a shorter hike option, go south from the Diamond Lake Area on OR 230 and follow FRs 3703, 300, and 380 northwest to this trailhead.)

From FR 380, the trail climbs advancing in a similar manner, sometimes dusty from summer foot traffic. Wonderful big trees claim the slope. In late summer, squirrels busy themselves aloft knocking cones to the forest floor. Hummingbirds buzz past the hiker. By 2.9 miles, the forest floor becomes rockier with purple penstemon growing amid the outcrops. The trees are notably shorter in stature, and whitebark pines enter the mix. Ahead, the climb intensifies. Gaps in the tree cover afford early looks at Diamond Lake, its meadowy south shore, Sawtooth Ridge, and Mount Thielsen.

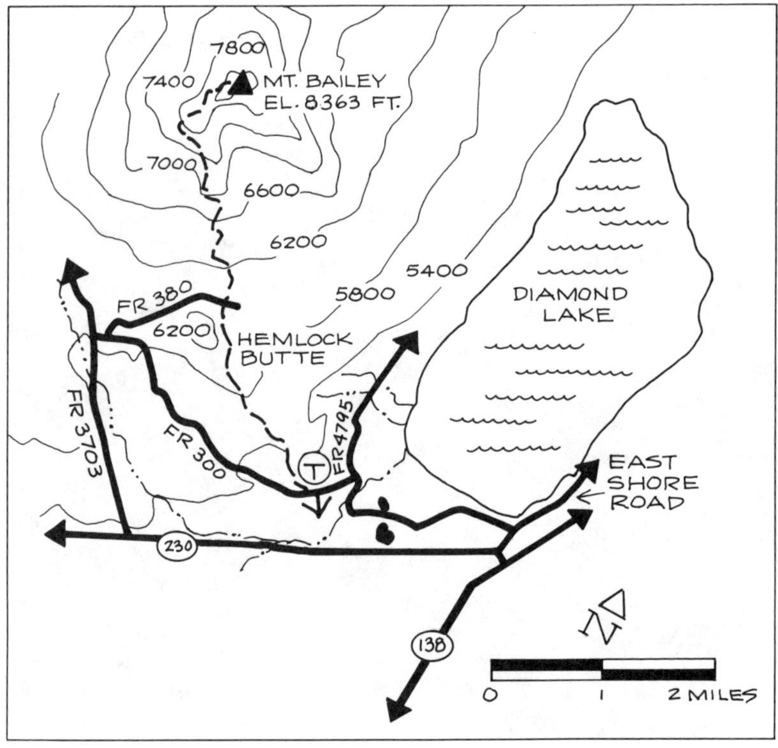

Where the trail tops a ridge at 3.4 miles, a detour to the right finds an open view of the Diamond Lake area along with a look at the rounded summit of Bailey, its avalanche bowl, red-streaked scree, and volcanic cliffs.

The trail then wraps around the slope, tags a Mount McLoughlin vista, and again swings back toward the ridge. The route grows more exposed with an open scatter of small mountain hemlocks and firs.

By 4.1 miles, the trail tours the open lava-rock slope with views to the south and east featuring the rim skyline and Desert Ridge of Crater Lake National Park along with Mount McLoughlin. Western anemone and other alpine wildflowers dot the slope.

In another 0.25 mile, the trail rounds a small crater bowl. Here, black cinders form the trail; the view remains open. This perfectly round crater measures some 50 to 100 feet deep and perhaps some 100 yards in diameter. It often cradles snow well into summer.

The trail arrives atop a secondary summit knob at 4.7 miles. This post offers a nearly full 360-degree view save for an area to the north blocked by the primary summit. Among the best views are those of the avalanche chute and the summit's craggy ridge and saddle. A forested expanse spreads outward from the mountain. For many, this site marks the tour's end.

For the more experienced hikers though, the primary summit awaits. The route heads down the saddle and rounds the bottom of the ragged cliff ridge just ahead. It then climbs along the cliff base for a difficult, sliding tour. After contouring the steep west flank via a narrow, secondary footpath, the trail again tops the ridge at 4.9 miles. Be careful when steadying yourself with the sharp volcanic rock.

Once atop the ridge, a good path leads to the main summit and the former lookout site, completing the 360-degree panorama with views of Diamond Peak and the Three Sisters. At times, the wind carries small cinder bits which sting, chasing hikers from their victory post.

55 FISH LAKE LOOP

Distance: 10 miles round trip
Elevation change: 1,100 feet
Difficulty: Moderate
Season: Spring through fall
Map: USFS Rogue-Umpqua Divide, Boulder Creek and Mount Thielsen Wildernesses
For information: Tiller Ranger District
Rogue–Umpqua Divide Wilderness Area

This hike explores a rich and varied old-growth forest and strings together three lakes of the Rogue–Umpqua Divide: Fish, Cliff, and Buckeye. Multiple trails access Fish Lake and its circuitous route, located on the west side of this 33,000-acre wilderness. The Beaver Swamp Trail offers one of the shorter routes of modest ease.

Each of the lakes presents a unique character. Highrock Mountain, Grasshopper Mountain, and Rocky Ridge are skyline features briefly spotlighted along the tour.

From I-5, take the Canyonville exit and head toward Crater Lake. In Canyonville, the route heads left on 3rd Street, which becomes County 1; stay on it to Tiller (22.3 miles). In Tiller, go left on South Umpqua Road, County 46/FR 28. In 23.1 miles, bear right onto FR 2823. Go 2.3 miles and again bear right, this time onto FR 2830. Pavement ends. In 1.6 miles at the junction of FRs 2830 and 2840, go left on FR 2840 to reach the Beaver Swamp Trailhead in another 4.9 miles. The Beaver Swamp Trail to Fish Lake heads right.

Entering the wilderness, the hike descends through a forest of big-diameter old-growth trees. Vanilla leaf, Oregon grape, pathfinder, and prince's pine decorate the floor. The large ponderosa and sugar pines, madrone, chinquapin, and occasional cedar add texture; the firs bring a multistory effect. In autumn, a rustling mat of yellow-brown leaves tops the trail.

At 0.9 mile, the trail enters a burn area resulting from a natural fire; it affords an interesting glimpse at plant succession. While the fire snapped life from the smaller trees, the ancients survived little touched,

Fish Lake

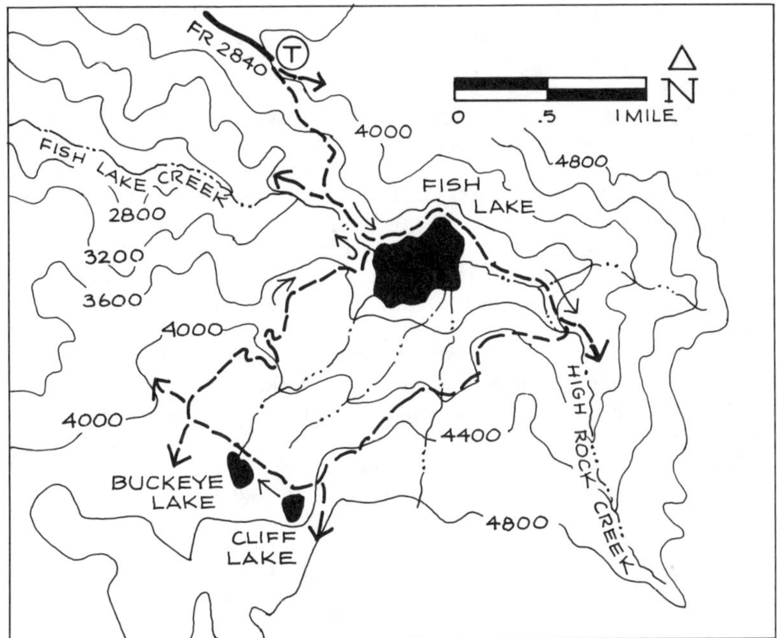

and the ground cover is vital and new. At a drainage, rhododendrons burst with life.

At 1.4 miles lies a T-junction: to the right finds Beaver Swamp; to the left lies Fish Lake and the loop. The upstream trail contours the canyon slope above Fish Lake Creek. Moss-decked boulders frame the water, as cedar, maples, and fir fill the canyon.

At 1.7 miles, the trail arrives at Fish Lake and the loop junction. The Indian Trail crosses the outlet waters via the log jumble to the right. A clockwise loop contours the lake slope ahead, traveling some 10 feet above the water.

Fish Lake is a large, rounded, forest-rimmed lake with an inlet meadow. Highrock Mountain rises to the south, Rocky Ridge rises to the east. Small chinquapin, hazel, salal, and rhododendron add to the shoreline. Kingfishers often patrol the waters.

At 1.9 miles, the slope eases creating a nice camp flat along shore. Other camps dot the next 0.5 mile.

At 2.1 miles, the trail tours an ancient forest grove, which is magical with its great number of enormous firs and cedars—an exceptional grouping. Horsetail reeds abound. Beyond it, the trail skirts the inlet meadow leaving Fish Lake.

At 2.5 miles, the primary route bears left at the "trail" marker. The tour now travels the Highrock Creek Canyon, a rich, shadowy, old-growth haven with big fir, western hemlock, maples, and Pacific yew. A low-elevation Cascade flora showers the mossy floor.

At the 3-mile junction, the loop heads right toward Buckeye Lake, ascending from the canyon and rounding the slope well above Fish Lake. Drainages slice through the fir–hemlock forest, and more light penetrates. The trail climbs at a steady rate.

From the 5.1-mile junction, the Grasshopper Mountain Trail continues uphill; the trail to Cliff and Buckeye lakes bears right. Again, the big trees appear.

At 5.3 miles, the loop arrives at Cliff Lake situated below the rock rim of Grasshopper Mountain. This scenic, small lake supports a heavily vegetated bottom and a moist shoreline with thick grasses and horsetail reeds. As the trail rounds the lake, it squeezes through a jungle of the waist-high reeds to reach a spur leading to a primitive lakeshore campsite.

The loop continues straight ahead touring a similar mixed forest with mossy rock outcrops—some massive, others pillar-like, but all interesting. The rolling trail arrives at Buckeye Lake at 5.7 miles, passing beneath an impressive, old sugar pine.

Rimmed by a rock outcrop-punctuated forest, Buckeye is larger and deeper than Cliff Lake. Marshy patches with cattails and grasses mark its shoreline. Beaver dams line its outlet arm.

Past the outlet bridge, a spur heads left to a campsite along this lake; the loop continues ahead. It again goes straight at the 6.25-mile junction. In late August, the trail seemingly moves with dozens of newly hatched toads jumping every which way.

At the 6.4-mile junction, the loop swings right following the Indian Trail back to Fish Lake. This route is for hikers only; it's narrower and more rugged. Where the trail takes a sharp turn at a drainage in 0.5 mile, its grade temporarily becomes knee-taxing and steep. At 8.3 miles, the loop closes with a log-jumble crossing at the Fish Lake outlet. After a short, steep uphill scramble, head left on the trail retracing the route to the Beaver Swamp Trailhead.

56 COW CREEK NATIONAL RECREATION TRAIL

Distance: 12.4 miles round trip
Elevation change: 2,000 feet
Difficulty: Moderate
Season: Spring through fall
Map: USGS Richter Mountain, Cleveland Ridge; USFS Umpqua
For information: Tiller Ranger District

An ancient forest setting of magnificent sky-scratching evergreens, thick trunks, rushing ground cover, jagged snags, and the rippling South Fork Cow Creek won this route national recreation trail distinction in 1981. According to the National Trails System Act of 1968, such trails possess outstanding recreational merit and offer convenient access to this country's open-air, outdoor treasury. The trail, open to foot, horse, and mountain bike traffic, receives annual maintenance.

A blanket of tranquillity wraps the route. In springtime, prince's pine, bride's bonnet, and bunchberry join the rhododendron and dogwood in floral celebration. Pileated woodpeckers, Steller's jays, grouse, and squirrels can be seen.

Taking exit 88 off I-5 at Azalea, travel east 19 miles on Cow Creek Road (County 36), reaching the junction of FRs 32 and 3232. There, turn right onto FR 3232. The trailhead is on the right just past the East Fork Cow Creek bridge, in less than a mile.

Passing through an open, alder-riparian corridor, the trail briefly parallels the East Fork Cow Creek downstream, before entering the South Fork drainage. Here, an old-growth Douglas fir forest claims the canyon; rhododendron and vine maple form the midstory. Across the for-

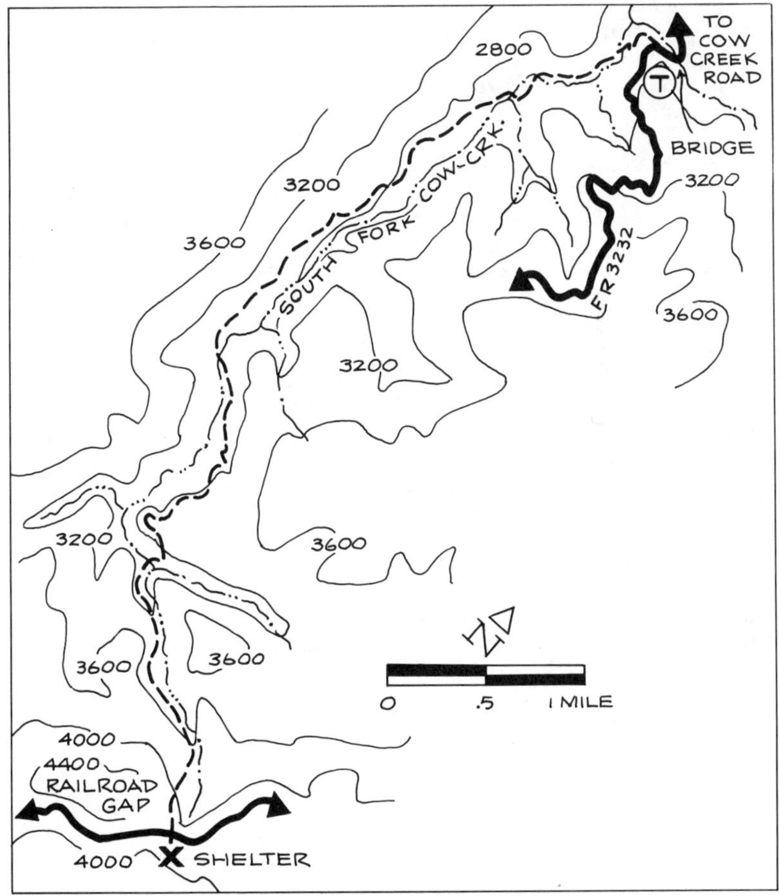

est floor, sword fern, salal, Oregon grape, and vanilla leaf puncture the mossy mat.

At 0.6 mile, the trail crosses the South Fork Cow Creek for the first time—the most difficult crossing of the trek. During high water, a fording is necessary. In autumn, a stone-hop crossing is possible for the surefooted; beware, the flat, rounded stones have a slippery finish, particularly when paired with wet-soled boots.

The gently graded trail now travels the canyon bottom, never straying far from the murmuring creek. In spring and fall, the vine maples add a signature of color to the forest of fir, hemlock, yew, and cedar. Stout, eye-teasing old-growth firs hug the path.

Where light gains admittance, concentrations of dogwood can be found, as well as bigleaf maple. Across the forest floor and in decaying stumps, a variety of mushrooms offer a study in shape, texture, color, and size. The creek canyon long holds the morning chill.

At 1.1 mile and again at 1.2 mile, the trail crosses the creek. Here, as elsewhere along the route, fallen trees provide a dry alternative to fording, but the bare-bark areas on these natural "bridges" can pose slippery footing when wet. Alder and waterleaf line the creek.

Soon, the trail draws away from the creek and begins a modest climb leaving behind the big-diameter trees, but still touring an old-growth habitat. It bypasses a swampy flat, and wraps around the west slope, traveling well above the water. By 2.7 miles, the trail is again alongside the creek, passing through a marshy section, pungent with skunk cabbage and thick with bracken and maidenhair fern, salal, and salmonberry.

At 3.2 miles, just before the creek crossing, the trail bypasses a small camp/picnic area, with stump-carved stools and a rock-and-brick firepit. For a shorter hike, this site proves a nice turnaround destination.

Upon crossing the creek, the trail traces the slope just below an old cut, brushed by the 1987 Angel fire, which jumped Cow Creek. Fire-scorched trees stand trailside. Leaving the disturbed area, the trail climbs more steeply, traveling through an open forest with rhododendron, madrone, chinquapin, and small fir.

With one more creek crossing, the trail bids farewell to the South Fork Cow Creek, streaking up the slope toward Railroad Gap (elevation 4,567 feet). A mixed chinquapin-evergreen forest shades its course. Large-diameter trees crowd the trail upon its approach to the gap.

At Railroad Gap (6.2 miles), one discovers a shelter with a picnic table and firepit. The small footpath leaving the shelter, paralleling the secondary road, leads to an open-air pit toilet. The shelter is a remnant from the glory days of trail travel. It served as a rest stop along a more extensive trail of the old system.

Return as you came.

57 MOUNT SCOTT TRAIL

Distance: 5 miles round trip
Elevation change: 1,300 feet
Difficulty: Moderate
Season: Summer through early fall
Map: USGS Crater Lake National Park; Crater Lake National Park map and guide brochure
For information: Crater Lake National Park

This trail climbs to a fire lookout perched on Mount Scott, the highest peak in Crater Lake National Park (elevation 8,926 feet). Mount Scott is the earliest-formed of the overlapping volcanic cones that constituted Mount Mazama, the ancient volcano which collapsed some 6,800 years ago and ultimately created Crater Lake, the deepest lake in the United States.

Views encompass the large caldera lake, its immediate neighborhood, the Klamath Basin, and a volcano lineup that includes Three Sisters, Diamond Peak, Mounts Thielsen and McLoughlin, and California's Mount Shasta. As the trail wraps around and switchbacks up the peak, it travels through open forest and across rocky terrain. Alpine flora dot the upper mountain reaches with white, yellow, red, and purple. Common wildlife spied along the trail are deer, marmots, and Clark's nutcrackers.

Situated along the Pacific Flyway, Mount Scott offers a fine post for viewing the fall migration of raptors and waterfowl to the wildlife areas of the Klamath–Tule Basin at the Oregon–California border.

Crater Lake National Park has entrances on OR 62 and OR 138; the south entrance on OR 62 lies 54 miles northwest of Klamath Falls. The nominal gate entry fee gives visitors seven-day park access. The Mount Scott Trailhead is found on the east side of the park's Rim Drive. It's

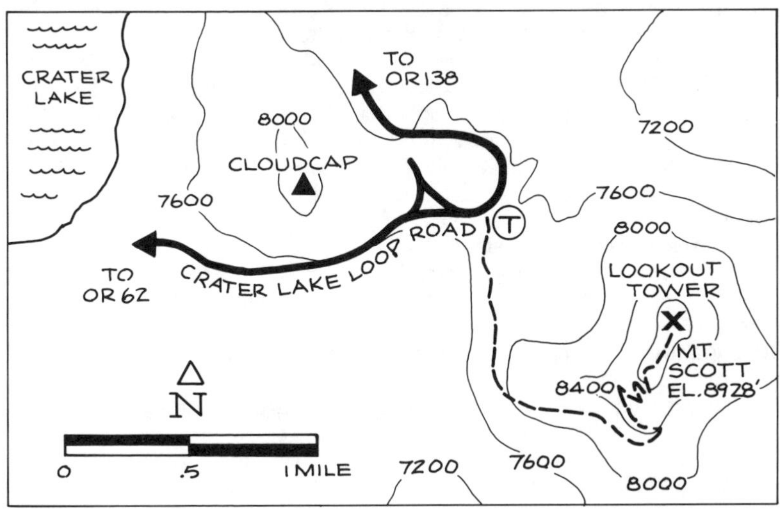

Crater Lake

well-marked and has pull-in parking. Park trail rules apply: foot traffic only; no pets.

Following an old two-track, the trail travels the whitebark pine- and mountain hemlock-forested rim along a glacier-chiseled bowl at Mount Scott's base. The area sports a mottled floor of dry grasses and low-growing annuals. The face of Mount Scott is sheer, rugged, and imposing; snow patches linger into summer.

As the trail ducks into the open forest at the foot of the steep, rocky western slope, the two-track narrows to a wide path. With much of the trail sunny and exposed, carry plenty of water.

By 0.6 mile, hikers gain early western views of Crater Lake's south end with Wizard Island, The Watchman, and Hillman and Garfield peaks. Cloudcap (elevation 8,065 feet), rising up on the crater rim in front of Scott, succeeds in blocking the remainder of the lake from view.

In another 0.1 mile, the view broadens to include the Klamath Basin and Mount McLoughlin. The trail is steady climbing with a well-groomed bed; although under heavy foot traffic, it can become dusty. The slope's spare ground cover features kinnikinnick and paintbrush.

After 1 mile, the trail wraps onto the south face of Scott unfolding a 120-degree view featuring much of the Winema National Forest, the Sand Creek drainage, more of the Klamath Basin, and Mount McLoughlin. The trees now show a scattered growth pattern; the slope is less rocky and more pumiceous.

Looking back to the west at 1.3 miles captures a fine view of Crater Lake, its rim, and Wizard Island. Soon, hikers spy Mount Shasta's showy crown rising to the south. Occasional clearcuts patchwork the basin outside the park boundary.

In another 0.5 mile, a ridge outcrop off a trail switchback overlooks the bowl where the trail began. Here, the view to the north looks across the crater rim toward Mounts Bailey and Thielsen and the Diamond Lake Area, with Three Sisters to the northeast. The next switchback holds an encore view.

Amid the rocks, the woolly headed western anemone, Indian paintbrush, phlox, lupine, yellow composites, and purple rock penstemon lend a dash of color. The end of July to early August marks the peak bloom time.

By 2.25 miles the trail tags the summit ridge of Mount Scott, touring just below its rocky spine. Chill winds often suggest a layering-on of clothes.

Ahead lies the lookout tower, where all the views come together in a grand 360-degree spectacle. The park's Pumice Desert offers a striking contrast to the surrounding forest expanse. The looking-glass face of Crater Lake reflects the red, gray, and buff cliffs of the caldera rim. The lake is fully visible in its indescribable blue splendor.

When quenched of the view or chased down by the clouds, return as you came to the trailhead.

58 UNION CREEK RECREATION TRAIL

Distance: 4.5 miles one way
Elevation change: 400 feet
Difficulty: Moderate
Season: Spring through fall
Map: USGS Union Creek; USFS Rogue River
For information: Prospect Ranger District

Located within the prized Upper Rogue–Crater Lake–Diamond Lake recreation complex, this trail is both a showcase for and a gateway to some of this region's most notable offerings: its premier hiking trails and fishing waters and its old-growth galleries. The trail's comfortable grade recommends it for the entire family.

Unlike many creek trails that travel the canyon wall putting forest and distance between hiker and water, this trail tours the forested valley bottom right alongside clear-bubbling Union Creek.

The creek is named for Union Peak in Crater Lake National Park; its headwaters lie due west of the peak just outside the park boundary. Diverse ancient forest and riparian habitat enclose the trail.

The lower trailhead is found at the small community of Union Creek on the east side of OR 62, along the creek's south bank; Union Creek Resort, on the National Register of Historic Places, occupies the northeast bank. Trailhead parking lies on the west side of OR 62, just south of the trailhead.

For the upstream trailhead, from the OR 62–OR 230 junction, go a couple of miles east and turn south (right) onto single-lane FR 6200.600; a trail sign marks the turn. Another sign then points the way onto FR 610, where the trailhead is located on the right soon after turning onto the road; parking lies just beyond. With the trailhead less than a mile from the main highway, the route easily lends itself to shuttle hiking.

Beginning from the community of Union Creek, an upstream journey quickly crosses a log footbridge to the north bank, where it will remain for the rest of the tour. Middle-aged forest and an alder–dogwood woodland alternately frame the path as it leaves the area of the rustic resort.

At 0.5 mile, the trail crosses an old dirt road after touring a small disturbed area. The creek here holds a fine deep pool that begs for the kicking-off of boots and the cooling of ankles, especially on the return leg of a round-trip journey.

Beyond the road, the trail enters the enchantment of the ancient forest graced by sparkling Union Creek. The rich understory collage presents bride's bonnet, prince's pine, huckleberry, June-flowering dogwood, twin and star flowers, wild rose, and bunchberry, among others, united in various numbers and patterns.

At 1.5 miles, the route passes through a hiker gate. Along the way, there are many places to sit alongside the creek or drop a fishing line into the water. The deep pools and shadowy recesses hide challengers ready to test the angler's prowess. As the blue diamond markers would suggest, in winter, the trail doubles as a cross-country ski route.

Union Creek

The pencil-point stumps and piled shavings of past and more recent beaver activity dot the shore. Where the trail drifts briefly away from the creek, more white pines and some large Pacific yews join the ranks of the ancient Douglas and grand fir and western hemlock. At 3.25 miles, the trail passes a scenic multi-angled, multi-tiered cascade on a bend of Union Creek.

The trunks of some trailside giants reveal the scorching of fires over time. The eyes are forever kept busy tracing the many trunks skyward.

At 4.2 miles, the trail offers a closing look at Union Creek before climbing the slope to the trailhead on FR 610. Upstream, a cascade launches the tumbling, churning water that squeezes through the narrow, moss-decked gorge alongside the trail. Round-trip hikers may wish to turn around here versus climbing the forested slope to the FR 610 trailhead.

For additional exploration, back at the community of Union Creek, hikers can cross to the west side of OR 62 and follow Union Creek downstream through Union Creek Campground to the confluence with the Rogue River.

There, they will find two hiking options along the Rogue Gorge Trail: Hiking it to the south leads to Natural Bridge in 2.5 miles—a geologic oddity where a lava tube swallows the river whole only to release it 200 feet downstream. Hiking it to the north finds the Rogue Gorge Viewpoint in 1 mile, another geologic eye-teaser featuring the powerful matchup of steep, rugged basalt and bubble-churning water.

Both vista sites have roadside access off OR 62, for those hikers with limited time.

59 CHERRY CREEK–SKY LAKES BASIN LOOP HIKE

Distance: 25 miles round trip
Elevation change: 2,200 feet
Difficulty: Strenuous
Season: Summer through fall
Map: USFS Sky Lakes Wilderness
For information: Klamath Ranger District

Volcanic and glacial forces shaped the terrain of the Sky Lakes Wilderness Area. This hike incorporates a national recreation trail, a good length of the Pacific Crest Trail (PCT), and a fine lake-wilderness tour. The region features elevation-diverse forests, multiple lakes, an impressive cliff ridge above Margurette Lake, and some small wildflower meadows. The mostly forested route allows but a few prized vistas. They include lake overlooks, Luther Mountain, Cherry Peak, Pelican Butte, Brown Mountain, and Mounts McLoughlin and Shasta.

The many meltwater ponds of this wilderness give rise to a vital, hungry mosquito population. Early season hikers should carry netting and repellent.

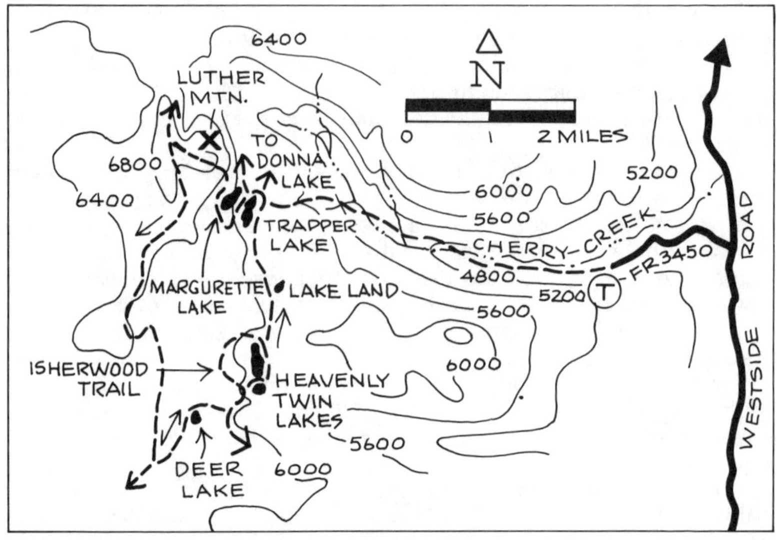

From Klamath Falls, go 25 miles northwest on OR 140 west to reach Westside Road and follow it north for another 10.6 miles. There, turn left onto FR 3450 at the sign for Cherry Creek Trail and go another 1.7 miles to reach the trailhead parking area.

Traveling above the Cherry Creek drainage, this well-designed trail passes through a grand fir forest with a shrub floor to enter the wilderness at 0.75 mile. Going another mile finds the footbridge crossing of Cherry Creek and a second crossing of a side water with a beaver dam downstream. In the meadows, grasses, lupine, and dwarf huckleberry mat the floor.

The trail passes through a mature, mixed forest and crosses raised walkways over moist meadow strips to arrive at a rock and log crossing of Cherry Creek at 3.25 miles. After a side creek crossing begins the forested uphill haul. By 5 miles, Shasta red fir and mountain hemlock command the skyline. True and dwarf huckleberry patch the floor.

Bypassing a pond, the trail tops out reaching the Sky Lakes Basin Loop near Trapper Lake, a big, forest-rimmed, high lake below rocky-topped Luther Mountain. Small campsites rest in the forest away from the lake.

A right begins a counterclockwise basin tour rounding the shore of Trapper Lake. At the 6.1-mile junction lies a side loop to Donna Lake; the primary circuit continues straight still rounding and climbing above Trapper Lake. In a short while, the trail approaches Margurette Lake, a long, deep lake at the foot of Luther Mountain Ridge. Margurette is the prized lake in this part of the Sky Lakes system.

Traveling the Divide Trail, the loop rounds a rise to the next lake basin at 6.7 miles. Skirting the shore of this shallow unnamed body, the trail reaches the foot of Luther Ridge. A slow, comfortable climb follows, utilizing long contours and switchbacks.

By 7.8 miles, the trail tags the rockier reaches of the ridge overlooking the Cherry Creek drainage and the Upper Klamath Lakes area with Pelican Butte. Where the trail tours the rim, it affords a grand lakes basin panorama. A small, deep pond beside the trail at 8.5 miles provides the last good chance to top the water jugs for a while; as always be sure to treat the water. Talus crossings now mark the route.

Trapper Lake

The view expands to include Mount McLoughlin, Brown Mountain, and California's Mount Shasta. Ahead, the trail contours a mostly open slope to reach the 9.3-mile trail junction where the loop follows the PCT left toward Island Lake.

The southbound trail rounds the rocky east slope below the ridge broadening the Upper Klamath vista. Small hemlocks and firs offer shady breaks. The talus ends at 10 miles as the ridgeline dips to the trail.

The tour now follows the open-forested ridge crisscrossing the crest before descending the west side. Some dry meadow patches interrupt the otherwise full forest. At 12.2 miles, a 300-foot side path branches right to an overlook of the expansive, forested South Fork Rogue River drainage.

The trail again climbs to cross over the crest at 12.5 miles. An open rocky slope affords vistas before the trail descends the forest-shaded slope to arrive at a small meadow. Deer graze the remote meadow patches.

At 14.6 miles lies the PCT–Sky Lakes Trail junction. The loop continues left reaching Deer Lake at 15.2 miles. Deer Lake is a mid-sized, forest-rimmed, round, shallow lake. Berry bushes hug its shore.

Beyond it, Cold Spring Trail enters from the right; the loop bears left traveling a boulder-studded terrain as it rolls toward the Isherwood Trail junction (16 miles). Here, the primary basin loop continues straight; the Isherwood Trail heads left, adding 0.5 mile to the distance and four more lakes to the trip.

The Sky Lakes Trail continues the primary basin loop soon crossing the narrow land strip separating the Heavenly Twin Lakes—two large lakes with attractive, irregular shorelines and shallow waters where grasses invade. Luther Mountain overlooks the northern lake. At 16.7 miles, the Isherwood Trail rejoins the Sky Lakes Trail. Between the two Isherwood Trail junctions, prime huckleberry patches line the main loop. An open tour through lodgepole pines follows.

Off the trail at 17.6 miles is the oval water of Lake Land. Ahead, the rolling trail skirts a couple of mirror ponds with floating lily pads and meadow shores to round the east shore of Trapper Lake. After crossing the outlet, the loop closes at 19 miles. A right on the Cherry Creek trail ends the hike at 25 miles.

60 MOUNT McLOUGHLIN TRAIL

Distance: 11.5 miles round trip
Elevation change: 3,900 feet
Difficulty: Strenuous
Season: Summer through fall

Map: USFS Sky Lakes Wilderness
For information: Klamath Ranger District

This popular hike climbs to the summit of southern Oregon's premier peak Mount McLoughlin (elevation 9,495 feet) for a top-of-the-world panorama spanning parts of two states: Oregon and California. Of all the Or-

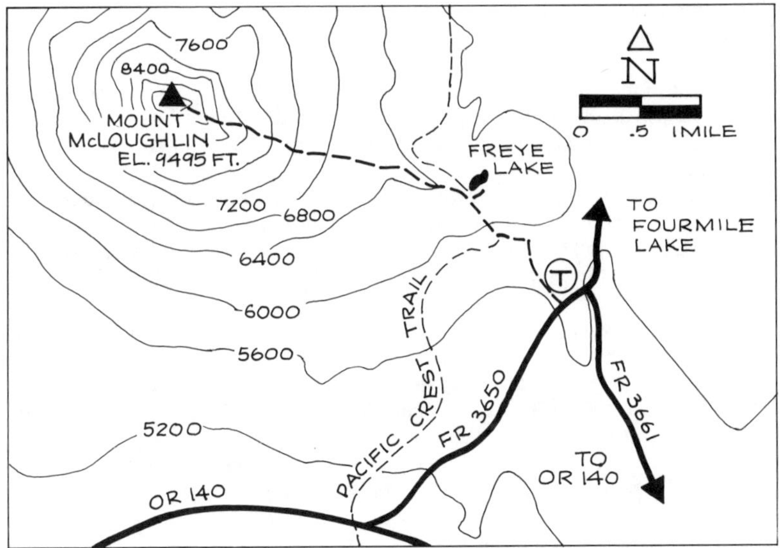

egon volcano peaks, this one is the easiest to conquer. The route passes through old-growth forest and a boulder-studded open forest before breaking out above timberline to scale the rugged, rocky, exposed upper slope. The rock foundation of a former lookout tops the mountain.

Mount McLoughlin, a composite volcano, sports a crown of cinders and volcanic rock and debris from its most recent eruptions some 12,000 years ago. Ice Age glaciers excavated great amounts of rock from the northeast face. An overlook of this glacier-chiseled face paired with a grand view of the mountaintop at 4.5 miles marks an alternative ending site for the hike.

To tackle this mountain, wear sturdy boots and carry a good supply of water. Morning hikes tend to offer more comfortable temperatures and crisper views, while avoiding the threat of afternoon thunderstorms.

Due to the hike's popularity, hikers must show added responsibility for the care and protection of the mountain and its wilderness integrity: Schedule midweek or fall visits, carry away good memories so you can reduce frequency of your visits, keep your party size small (well under the eight maximum), and do not cave in to the temptation of paint-blazing or otherwise marking the rocky route of the upper trail. If you feel uneasy without the security of a trail, select another hike.

From OR 140 near Lake of the Woods, turn north onto gravel FR 3661, heading toward Fourmile Lake. Go 2.8 miles and turn left onto FR 3650 to reach the large trailhead parking area on the right in another 0.2 mile.

A wide trail launches the hike crossing the Cascade Canal footbridge to enter the wilderness. The route passes through forest of mountain hemlock, grand fir, and white pine and crosses bracken fern and wildflower meadows. Scarlet skyrockets abound in late July. At 1 mile is the Mount McLoughlin–Pacific Crest Trail (PCT) junction. For the summit route, go right.

The hike now follows the PCT north. At 1.2 miles, the spur to the right leads to Freye Lake just over the rise in 0.25 mile. Freye Lake is a small, shallow lake buzzed by dragonflies. The lake approach offers a quick look at Mount McLoughlin.

At 1.4 miles, the summit route branches left off the PCT. Lichens encrust many of the large fir hinting at a snowline some 8 to 10 feet high. Downed sticks and branches litter the floor; kinnikinnick and prince's pine supply the few touches of green. Soon, Shasta red fir is dominant.

The draw at 2.4 miles signals a trail character change from a forest tour to a progressively rugged, steep climb. The route ahead features more sunny openings with chinquapin and sticky laurel.

In another mile, the intensity of the climb again increases as the trail tours a boulder-studded, semi-open forest of mountain hemlock and whitebark pine. At times, the trail grows dusty or gravelly or sports large boulders to step around or over. Red dot markers presently guide the way. These are an act of vandalism that will be removed or allowed to fade with time.

Former lookout, Mount McLoughlin

Forest gaps offer snapshot views; better views await above tree line. The common passersby include hummingbirds and Clark's nutcrackers.

At 4.5 miles, the trail tops a ridge for a bold look at the glacier-planed northeast face of the volcano with its jagged crags, snowfields, and moraines (mounds of moved earth) marking the bottoms of ancient glaciers. Here, too, hikers find an impressive first view of the summit crown, along with a 180-degree panorama featuring California's Mount Shasta, the Cascade Crest stretching north, the nearby lakes, and Upper Klamath Lake.

The view suggests hikers linger a while and catch their breath. For many, this site also suggests a fine turnaround point. Although the summit builds upon the view, this bold confrontation with the mountaintop is truly the most striking view of the tour.

A much rougher, make-your-way rock scramble to the top follows. As you leave the regular footpath, climb staying along the east ridge to avoid the more difficult slope ahead. A few whitebark pines and purple penstemon dot the rocky terrain. The occasional cairn or footprints of earlier travelers may assist in the route selection, but hugging the ridgeline remains key.

At 5.25 miles, the route again overlooks the glacier-gouged bowl with its spired, pink and gray volcanic palisades. After tracing the bowl's rim, the trail begins its final, steep 0.25-mile assault on the summit. Loose gravel and rocks sometimes foul footing.

The top has two vista posts separated by the former lookout. Together they build a 360-degree panorama. Views stretch south to Mount Shasta and the Klamath–Tule Basin and north to the far-distant Three Sisters. The view to the west overlooks the Rogue River drainage; to the east, it spans the Upper Klamath–Agency lakes area.

Return as you came again hugging the east ridge to avoid losing or complicating your way. Every summer hikers get lost on their descent, so keep frequent tabs on the ridge.

61 VARNEY CREEK–MOUNTAIN LAKES LOOP HIKE

Distance: 17 miles round trip
Elevation change: 2,000 feet
Difficulty: Strenuous
Season: Summer through fall
Map: USFS Mountain Lakes Wilderness
For information: Klamath Ranger District

Mountain Lakes Wilderness Area

This hike travels up a gentle creek drainage to string through broad basins and along ridges tagging the shores of several small lakes and the wilderness's star lake attraction—Lake Harriette. Varied forests, dry, wildflower meadows, and peak vistas mark the route.

A collapsed ancient composite volcano houses this wilderness tour. Over time, glaciation, running water, wind, and weathering have smoothed its caldera rim. Today, numerous small tarns and ponds speckle its bowl. The glacial rupturing of the rim defied the creation of a single great caldera lake, such as Crater Lake to the north. The snowmelt pools support a thriving mosquito population, discouraging to early-season hikers.

Entering from Klamath Falls, go 21 miles northwest on OR 140 west. Entering from the north, from the OR 140–Westside Road Junction, go east on OR 140 for 4 miles. At the sign for Varney Creek Trailhead, turn west onto gravel FR 3637. In 1.7 miles, turn left onto FR 3664. The trailhead is on the right in 1.9 miles; parking lies just beyond, at the road's end.

Varney Creek echoes up from its drainage, as this comfortably graded trail passes through a fir and ponderosa pine forest with patchy kinnikinnick, manzanita, and sticky laurel. At 1 mile, the trail enters the wilderness. Pikas pipe from a talus slope.

Ahead, the route crosses Varney Creek via a log boardwalk. The trail then alternates between open stands of lodgepole pine and fir and dry meadow slopes with wild rose, currant, lupine, lily, and fireweed.

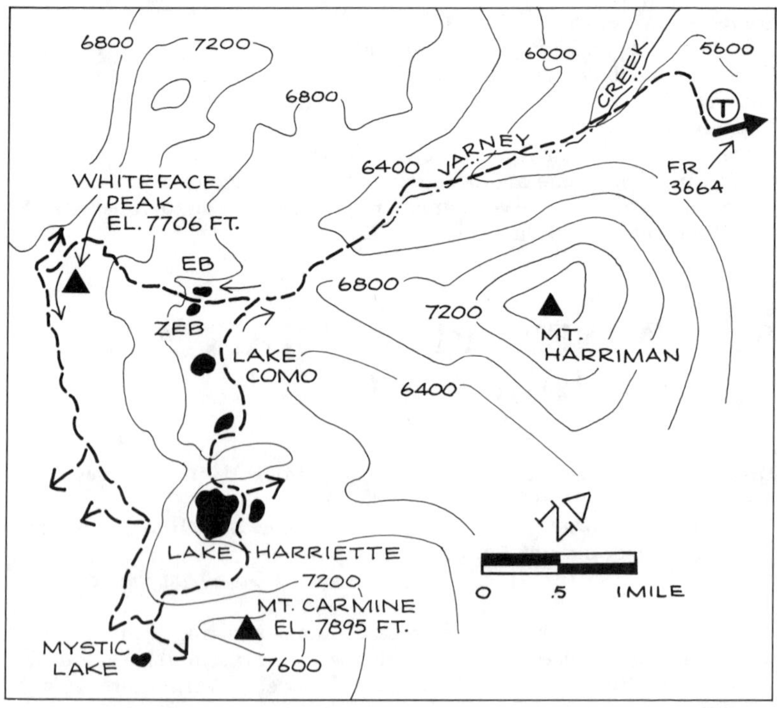

Mount Harriman commands the early view. By 3 miles, the trail affords up-canyon looks at the semi-bald ridge of Greylock Mountain. A high-elevation forest now frames the route. Dwarf huckleberry spots the floor. At 3.75 miles, the trail tops out; at 4 miles it meets the Mountain Lakes Loop Trail.

A right begins a counterclockwise tour quickly arriving at the shallow twins, Eb and Zeb lakes. Shasta red fir and mountain hemlock crowd the basin. Whiteface Peak overlooks Zeb Lake; its unnamed, equal-height side peak rises above Eb. Dragonflies abound at the lakes.

The trail then mounts the forest–talus saddle between Whiteface Peak and its counterpart. Atop the saddle at 5.2 miles, northeastern views feature the Varney Creek drainage, the Klamath Lakes Area, and the nearby wilderness peaks. A pocket grove of mountain hemlocks all with multiple trunks catches the eye.

Across the saddle, the opposite slope shows a more mixed forest; gaps in the tree cover reveal Mount McLoughlin, Brown Mountain, and the Lake of the Woods. At 5.6 miles is an open saddle and trail junction. Go downhill to the left for the loop. The spare slope gives way to a mountain hemlock–white pine forest.

The trail levels approaching the 6.6-mile junction, where the loop again heads left. Straight is Clover Basin. Keep an eye out for this junction marked only by a splintered sign. The loop trail now rolls passing through forest and crossing the tongues of talus slopes.

At 7.3 miles, the trail swings left and begins climbing along a tree-blazed route. In places, it grows faint. At 7.8 miles is another easily missed junction, no markers. Here, the blazed Clover Basin Loop arrives on the right; the Mountain Lakes Loop curves left.

Ahead, the Mountain Lakes Loop tops the ridge overlooking Lake Harriette and Mount Carmine. It then heads right dipping just below the ridge only to again top it in another 0.5 mile.

At the 8.7-mile junction, continuing along the ridge to the right leads to the Aspen Butte summit (elevation 8,208 feet) for a vista detour; the lakes loop crosses over the ridge descending and rounding the steep forested slope above Mystic Lake. Views feature Paragon and Mystic lakes and Aspen Butte's cliff and talus face. Bleeding hearts accent the rocky areas of the slope.

Where the trail tags the 9.3-mile junction, a right leads to South Pass Lake, a large, remote wilderness lake; a left continues the loop to Lake Harriette with a long, forest-shaded descent.

As the loop trail bypasses the talus base of Mount Carmine, boulders dot the open forest. At 10.7 miles, the trail flattens, skirting a couple of green ponds with still-water reflections. It then finds Lake Harriette, the pride of the wilderness—shining beautiful, deep, and blue.

Lake Harriette is the most popular day and overnight destination in the Mountain Lakes Wilderness Area, yet its shore remains wild and its water pristine. Crisp reflections of the forest rim interrupted by the tongues of white talus lapping to the lake's splashline engage and relax visitors. Fish-launched expanding ripple-rings further add to the lake's tranquillity. The forested shore adequately isolates visitor parties, ensuring a private enjoyment of the lake and its setting.

As the trail rounds Lake Harriette, at the 11.1-mile junction, the loop bears left; to the right lies Hemlock Basin. The loop then climbs away from the lake.

It crosses a saddle for a rocky, dusty descent through mixed forest to reach the Lake Como Basin at 12.6 miles. This mid-sized lake below Whiteface Peak is deeper than Eb and Zeb and supports trout. Ospreys sometimes fish this water. The loop closes at 13 miles; retrace the Varney Creek Trail to end the hike.

62 PACIFIC CREST NATIONAL SCENIC TRAIL

Distance: 424 miles one way
Elevation change: 7,200 feet, with an average elevation of 5,120 feet
Difficulty: Strenuous, with samplings of all difficulty levels
Season: Summer through fall (for hiking entire route)
Map: USFS Pacific Crest Trail: Oregon portion (3 maps)
For information: Pacific Northwest Regional Office

First proposed in the 1930s, the Pacific Crest Trail (PCT) is one of two national scenic trails named under the National Trails System Act of 1968; the other is the Appalachian Trail. By description, these trails possess outstanding scenic, historic, natural, or cultural value and are long-distance, journeying into the hinterlands. The year 1987 marked the completion of the Oregon portion of this 2,600-mile hiker filament, which travels the Sierra Nevada, Siskiyou, and Cascade crestlines from Mexico to Canada.

In Oregon, the trail passes through bureau lands, national forests, wilderness areas, scenic areas, and Oregon's only national park, with brief stretches across private lands. The Oregon portion incorporates segments of the 1920s-built Oregon Skyline Trail, which linked Mount Hood and Crater Lake.

The premier hiking route boasts a well-designed, -constructed, and -maintained trailbed suitable for foot/horse traffic. Management and construction considerations have placed the PCT to avoid steepness, generally rounding versus mounting ridges. It bypasses wet areas where passage is difficult and the damage potential to natural areas is great. Likewise, it skirts areas of heavy use (lakes, vistas, and other drawing-card destinations) to minimize hiker influence to the crest's pristine treasures.

Mount Hood above Zigzag Canyon

Despite its responsible routing, the trail still reveals many of the state's wild and natural offerings. And for times when the call to "come see" is too great to ignore, the vast network of interconnecting trails invites side trips.

Large, formal, marked parking areas on the passes of the east-west routes crossing the Cascades provide convenient access to the PCT. The trailheads for the PCT-tie trails also serve this long-distance route.

From California, the trail enters Oregon east of the Applegate River and southwest of Mount Ashland, passing over Observation Gap. The trail leaves the state for Washington via the Bridge of the Gods, crossing the Columbia River near Cascade Locks.

The southern Cascades hold the PCT's highest Oregon point—the pass between Devils and Lee peaks in the Seven Lakes Basin of the Sky Lakes Wilderness Area. The Columbia Gorge houses the low point, where the PCT approaches sea level at the Bridge of the Gods crossing.

As the trail travels Oregon's rolling ridges, the typical forest setting features some combination of mountain hemlock, true fir, and lodgepole and whitebark pines. The PCT offers only glimpses of the state's rich forest diversity, which includes magnificent ponderosa pine and ancient Douglas fir–western hemlock forests.

Lake-bound basins; wet, prairie, and alpine meadows; arid expanses; and lava lands, along with some harvest and clearcut sites interrupt the forest stretches. Along the way, hikers find grand wildflower displays, with peak blooms in late summer. Bear grass and huckleberry bushes often reclaim the cut areas.

Volcano vistas punctuate the journey and mark northbound (or southbound) progress through the state. Vistas along the Oregon segment of the PCT span from California's Mount Shasta to Washington's Mount Rainier, with Oregon's all-star lineup in between.

The Timberline Trail component of the PCT (see Hike 26) offers upclose looks at Oregon's own Mount Hood (elevation 11,235 feet), with its glaciers, deep-chiseled canyons, and lahar (a ridge of rock and debris deposited by a mud flow).

The PCT touches upon early Oregon history, as it follows or parallels segments of Indian trails and pioneer and military wagon routes. The countryside holds stories of early-day prospecting and logging. The navigational landmarks used by early settlers serve the contemporary traveler as well.

For many users, the PCT's primary attraction is that of a gateway for day hikes and short backpacks. The PCT easily facilitates loops with neighboring trails.

For PCT samplings, see Hikes 25, 26, 59, and 60, or contact the appropriate managing agency or agencies for information about PCT tours of your choosing. Entire books have been devoted to this premier trail; consult your local library or bookstore for these.

63 McCALL POINT TRAIL

Distance: 3 miles round trip
Elevation change: 1,000 feet
Difficulty: Moderate
Season: Spring through fall
Map: None
For information: State Parks, Portland Regional Office
Mayer State Park

There's nothing like the stiff wind of the Columbia River Gorge to blow away the cobwebs of civilization, and here, at the center of the gorge awaits a springtime bonanza. The bloom calendar runs from mid-March to early June—the favored time to tour the trail.

The microclimates found along the trail and across the road at the 231-acre Tom McCall Nature Conservancy Preserve introduce tremendous wildflower variety with rare and endangered plant species. Together, the native grasslands, mounds, swales, rocky rims, and Oregon oak woodlands support a wildflower showcase that includes widow grass, Columbia and Suksdorf desert parsley, yellow bell, lupine, stork's bill, balsamroot, goldfield, and more.

Hand lenses and a good wildflower field guide, such as Russ Jolley's *A Comprehensive Field Guide: Wildflowers of the Columbia Gorge* (Oregon Historical Society, 1988), add to the appreciation.

The trail begins from Rowena Crest nearly 750 feet above the Columbia River and climbs to McCall Point, elevation 1,722 feet. En route to

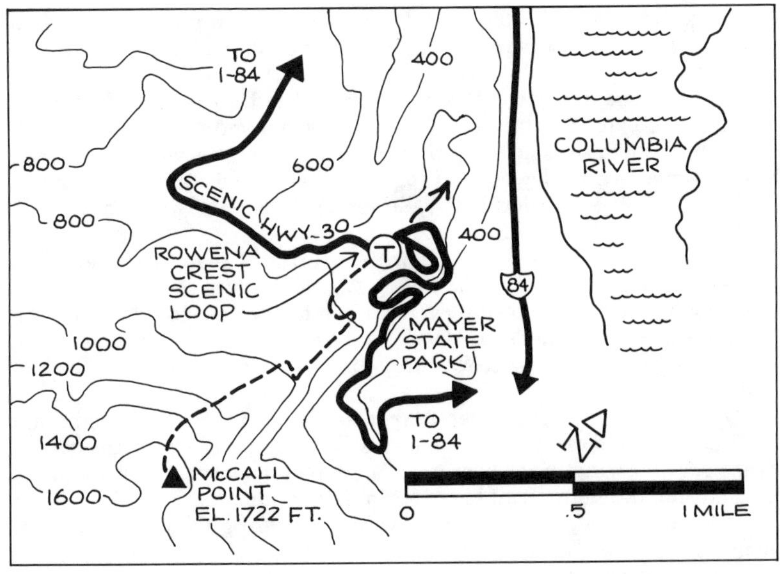

Columbia Gorge vista

the summit, the narrow path wriggles up and across the multi-level benches of the steppe plateau, passing through grassland and Oregon oak woodland, while offering river overviews. From the grass-topped summit, the snowy crowns of Mounts Adams and Hood vie for the hiker's attention.

The trail is dry and can be hot, so carry plenty of water. With much of the area having preserve status, stay on the trail and do not disturb the vegetation.

The trailhead lies about 10 miles west of The Dalles. From I-84 westbound, take exit 76 for the scenic loop, Rowena, and Mayer State Park. After crossing to the south side of the freeway, continue west 2.8 miles to the Rowena Crest Viewpoint. From I-84 eastbound, take the Mosier–Rowena exit 69, and follow US 30, Rowena Loop Scenic Drive, east for 6.4 miles to the crest viewpoint.

On the native grass bench above the entrance road, a wooden sign marks the start of the trail. Its grassy footpath leaves the viewpoint circle traveling along the abrupt edge of the plateau. Overlooks feature the winding Rowena Loop Scenic Drive and the Columbia River upstream; cross-gorge views find Lyle, Washington. McCall Point rises overhead on the rim.

By early March, the pinkish-purple heads of the widow grass herald the approach of spring. Before long, the footpath merges with an old two-track slowly arcing to the base of the next plateau level. Below its moss-decked rim, the Point Trail bears left at 0.25 mile.

In a short distance, the footpath resumes passing through a grove of small oaks. Ahead lies a sign reminding hikers of the crest's preserve status and warning of the presence of ticks, snakes, and poison oak.

The grade steepens where the trail again climbs along the plateau edge. The growth-stunting impact of the wind on the trees is readily apparent. Hawks soar at eye level; deer tracks weave along the trail.

As the trail ascends, a full-volcano view of Mount Adams slowly emerges. Downstream views across the plateau find a few clustered oaks, single ponderosa pines, and an occasional vernal pool dotting pattern to the open, semi-arid grassland. The river well below is hidden from view.

At 0.7 mile, the trail passes beneath a utility pole. From there, the route briefly hugs the edge of the plateau before entering a series of short switchbacks advancing up the slope through another grove of low-growing, often bush-sized white oaks. Oregon grape, ocean spray, and poison oak spill beneath the trunks. Stairs recessed into the slope aid the climb; the trail is slippery when wet.

After tagging a nice westward-looking view at 1.25 miles, the trail makes another climb through the oaks drawing out onto an open grassland slope for the final assault on the summit.

Grass-topped McCall Point offers views to the north and west which include Mount Adams and Mount Hood, along with scenic downstream Columbia River views but only token upstream views. Footpaths travel the summit point offering different vantages on the Columbia River stage. Mount Hood is best viewed and photographed in the morning hours when hikers have the sun to their back.

The return is as you came.

64 IRRIGON WILDLIFE AREA HIKING

Distance: 6.5 miles or 12 miles round trip
Elevation change: Minimal
Difficulty: Moderate
Season: Spring through fall
Map: None
For information: Oregon Department of Fish and Wildlife

This 980-acre wildlife area occupying the Lake Umatilla shore on the Columbia River features pond, arid grassland, abandoned field, and riparian habitats. False indigo, Russian olive, cottonwood, white poplar, and willow trees overhang the shore and ponds.

Some 44 ponds dot the 8-mile-long corridor. They exhibit a varying character: some overtaken by cattails, some marshy, and some sporting open water. At the ponds, beaver signs abound, painted turtles sun on the logs, and red-winged blackbirds animate the brush.

Dependent on lake levels, the shoreline may welcome additional exploration. Low-hanging willows or pinched sections of beach sometimes dictate inland detours. Open clam shells and the tracks from nighttime raiders mark the sands, while gulls and terns cut the sky.

Fall waterfowl migrations swell the area's birdlife numbers. The mild climate of this and neighboring river wildlife areas makes them a chief wintering ground. Bald eagles, feeding on the sick and injured birds, also add to the ranks.

To reach the wildlife area, take the US 730 exit north off I-84 east of Boardman. The west access is found at the northeast end of Irrigon. In Irrigon, take 10th Street north toward Irrigon Park and turn right onto Washington. At the end of the ball field, go left on the gravel road to reach a riverside picnic area and the trailhead.

The east access occupies the west bank of the Umatilla River mouth at Umatilla. Additional accesses rest in between these two off US 730; look for the triangular wildlife area signs.

A network of interlocking, well-tracked paths explore this area. Despite the number of choices, one has little worry about going astray in this 0.25-mile-wide, east–west corridor bound by the river to the north and US 730 to the south. Hiking from the Irrigon Trailhead holds the finer, wilder tour.

Journeying east from the Irrigon access, hikers find a cattail reed pond just south of the main trampled footpath. Sage, rabbitbrush, bitterbrush, and grasses spread between the river and ponds. With prickly pear cactus dotting the arid expanse, beware footing. Ticks are a springtime concern.

At the first fork, bear right staying inland from the river to find the most consistent east-bound route through the wildlife land. No single correct trail presents itself, but hikers can easily travel via tried routes. This footpath passes atop a low ridge; loose sands work the legs.

At 0.3 mile, the ridge dips to travel beside a tree-enclosed pond. In 1991, a fire swept this portion of the wildlife area; hikers will discover the natural renewal cycle in progress. In another 0.5 mile, the trail bids farewell to the burn, as it skirts a long pond to the south. Thistle, fiddlenecks, balsamroot, desert parsley, and other wildflowers and flowering brush sprinkle color to the sage–grassland.

Throughout the tour, isolated sections of river beach suggest detours north. Views into Washington find open shores and distant rolling hills. Where the trail travels a bench above shore at 0.9 mile, it rounds an enticing half-moon beach. The oft-persistent Gorge winds launch whitecaps on the river and bring a welcomed cooling to the open trek.

By 1.6 miles, the trail is passing alongside a cutoff portion of the river lake. At the drainage in another 0.1 mile, hiking south to the next set of ridges finds an easier route east through a less congested sageland. By 2 miles, the paths are less defined, but staying on the low ridges continues to provide fairly easy walking, even when selecting your own routes.

As the hike approaches the fenced TriCity facility at 3.25 miles, the footpaths are again well established. Hiker gates access the wildlife area on either side of the facility. Hikers may turn around here, or continue east via the beach strand or the inland path.

The inland path tours a portion of the wildlife area featuring grasslands punctuated by low, lichen-etched basalt outcrops; it shows fewer rises and no ponds. The path remains in good shape for 0.5 mile, where a grassy jeep trail replaces it.

Arriving at a Russian olive grove, travel the clearing to its center and

Cattail pond

look right. A semi-hidden path leaves the grove beyond a small island of basalt; follow it. A few feet ahead the sandy path resumes in sageland. Jackrabbits bound away upon hiker approach.

At 4.2 miles, the trail arrives at a large, open-water bay; cattails crowd the isolated east end. By 5 miles, civilization begins to encroach on the tour, as residences crowd the corridor. A rolling path over the shore's vegetated dunes now leads the way.

The pump station at 6 miles marks the suggested turnaround point. Farther east the corridor continues to narrow, with the residences becoming more apparent and the route less passable.

65 TROUT CREEK TRAIL

Distance: 7.75 miles one way
Elevation change: 100 feet
Difficulty: Moderate
Season: Year round
Map: USGS Gateway, Eagle Butte
For information: Prineville District BLM

The Deschutes Wild and Scenic River is the focal point of this arid river-canyon tour. The trail follows a former railroad grade with sections of footpath dipping to shore for more intimate river views.

The route alternately travels below steep, rounded, golden-colored sage and grassland slopes and dark basalt or red rock rims with rocky

Bicyclists tour along the Deschutes River.

skirts spilling to the river bench. Nearly continuous river views of mesmerizing black pools, swirling green waters, and white pulsing riffles recommend the journey. Ducks, herons, geese, magpies, red-winged blackbirds, deer, and beavers are among the wildlife sightings.

The grassy flats along shore suggest a camp or just a prolonged visit. Willows and white alders line much of the river; junipers dot the canyon slopes. Several flats have pit toilets for hiker, camper, and river-user convenience.

Mecca Flat, the upstream terminus, borders a wide stretch of the Deschutes where the river canyon opens up. The flat was the one-time site of a post office and a station along the Oregon Trunk rail line. It also marks the river-crossing site for the historic Madras–Warm Springs Agency wagon road.

To reach the Trout Creek Trailhead, from the US 97–US 26 junction at Madras, go north on US 97 for 2.4 miles and turn left toward Gateway on Cora Lane/Clark Drive. In 3.9 miles, as the main road bears right, veer left for Trout Creek Recreation Site; there's a small sign at the junction.

At Gateway in 4 miles, go right on gravel Clemens Drive toward the Deschutes River–Trout Creek. Where the road dips toward the river in another 4.2 miles, go left (upstream) to reach the campground in 0.3 mile, the trailhead in 0.7 mile.

To reach the Mecca Flat Trailhead, from the US 97–US 26 junction in Madras, go west on US 26 for 11.9 miles and turn right just before the

Deschutes River bridge to find a four-way dirt-road junction. Take the upper-middle fork along a public easement and the bumpy former railroad grade to reach the trailhead in 1.6 miles (high-clearance vehicles are recommended).

An upstream tour from Trout Creek Recreation Site passes between two birdhouse-topped posts, crosses a cattle guard, and rounds a gate to follow the former railroad grade. A low bordering ridge semi-blocks the early river view. Over-the-shoulder looks find a couple of large, red buttes and the open downstream canyon.

At 0.75 mile, a wooden bench overlooks the river. Beyond it, the route tours a sunken grade where a high bank blocks the cross-canyon view. In spring, wildflowers dot color to the bunchgrass. Sagebrush, an occasional bitterbrush, and juniper frame the corridor. Beware of ticks in this arid terrain.

The first of many side paths branches to the river at 1.2 miles. Although the old rail line travels within 100 feet of Deschutes, in places its steep embankment discourages river access.

In another mile, the trail again passes through a sunken, narrow corridor enclosed by towering, dark basalt cliffs. Just upstream, a picturesque side canyon angles to the southeast; yellow lichens etch its rim.

At 2.5 miles is the first of a pair of hiker gates, where the trail crosses a broad river bench. Along the river, there are small islands with hummocky yellow-gold grasses; low white alders top the larger ones. Upcanyon views unfold with each bend.

At 3.4 miles, hikers find a juniper-shaded wooden bench, which invites a stop, particularly on hot summer days. A stubborn gate lies at 5.2 miles; be sure to resecure it upon passing. Side trails again dip to the river. Where the river briefly narrows, its rush is amplified.

At times, tall sage measuring 6 to 8 feet high nudge the corridor. Where the weeds begin to push up through the railroad grade at 5.8 miles, the hiker route leaves the grade via the footpath descending the bank to the river. A Bureau of Land Management (BLM) "Trail Boundary" sign marks the site.

The path briefly rolls along a rocky slope with some head-brushing branches to reach a hiker gate at 6 miles. Here, the route travels a public right-of-way across private property. Stay along the river edge bypassing the residence. Pass quickly and quietly, respecting owner privacy, and obey the posted signs.

The trail next travels along a windbreak of trees, rounds a fence, and leaves the easement via a fence stepover at 6.8 miles. Soon, deep canyons punctuate the Warm Springs Reservation side of the river.

Where the trail emerges from a willow thicket, it strays from the base of the old rail line to follow a two-track along the grassy, sometimes brushy river flat to reach the Mecca Flat Trailhead and its undeveloped camping area—the end of the one-way tour.

Management plans call for improved access roads, the addition of signs, a reduction of gates, and other trail enhancements beginning in 1992, which should make this relatively new trail all the more inviting.

66 BLUE BASIN TOUR

Distance: 4 miles round trip
Elevation change: 700 feet
Difficulty: Easy to moderate
Season: Year round (when trails are dry)
Map: John Day Fossil Beds National Monument brochure
For information: John Day Fossil Beds National Monument

John Day Fossil Beds National Monument consists of three geographically separated units, featuring rainbow-colored hillsides, dramatic cliffs, and fossils dating back 50 million years. This particular tour visits the eroded, blue-gray amphitheater dubbed "Blue Basin," located in the Sheep Rock Unit.

Nearby flows the main stem of the John Day River, grassy fields intersperse the sage–juniper–bunchgrass expanse, and badlands spread beneath the desert sky. The wail of coyotes and the cheerful notes of the meadowlark blend in an awkward morning harmony. Squawking "V"s of Canada geese pass overhead.

Two interlocking trails explore this geologic gallery and tomb of history: The 3-mile Overlook Loop Trail skirts the outer bowl and mounts a ridge offering prized looks into the basin and across the John Day Country. The shorter Island in Time Trail probes the basin interior, visiting sites with replica fossils and storyboard explanations.

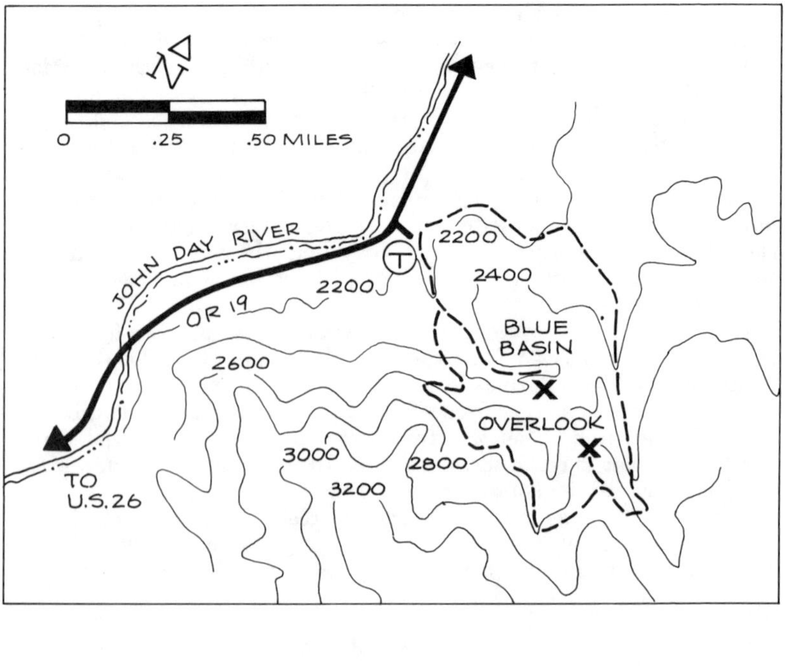

Blue Basin overlook

The Overlook Trail is steep in places and slippery when wet. When touring this sensitive landscape, keep to the trails; off-trail hiking is prohibited. The edges of day promise more comfortable temperatures for summer discovery. As these trails are open—save for the few juniper-shaded benches—carry water.

From US 26, 6.7 miles west of Dayville, turn north onto OR 19 to reach the Visitor Center in 2 miles, the Blue Basin Trailhead in 5 miles. The visitor center is open daily, mid-March through October.

Passing through the turnstile, the hiker finds an immediate junction near the display: A right enters the basin; a left finds the Overlook Loop. Go left for a clockwise basin tour.

The initially wide, gravel trail travels the foot of a sage slope above a field, offering looks at the John Day Valley and the eroded, arid hillsides to the north and west. Burrows ripple the sage floor. At 0.2 mile, the trail curves serving up the first view of the volcanic-ash outcrop known as Blue Basin.

Soon, an earthen path continues the journey, as the trail bypasses a more extensive ridge of the eroded formation isolated by a juniper-dotted drainage cut. Deer track abound. The countryside reveals other pockets of the time-exposed ash-clay beds.

At 0.7 mile, the trail crosses over the drainage and climbs traveling through a similar shrub complex below a wall of light-colored ash. Nearing the end of the exposed cliffs, the trail climbs more quickly advancing via boardwalks.

At 1.2 miles is a juniper-shaded bench where the trail leaves the drainage. Ahead, hikers gain views of the serial red ash beds to the northeast.

Atop the ridge, the trail arrives at a viewpoint junction (1.5 miles). Here, a short detour from the loop finds a grand overlook of the Blue Basin's fluted walls, the main stem of the John Day River, and the surrounding multicolored badlands and terraced ridges.

From the junction, the loop quickly descends stitching together more exciting basin views peering down a drainage into the amphitheater bowl. A stairstep crossing of a fence signals the start of a right-of-way across private property; stay on the trail and use your best hiker manners to ensure the privilege continues. With a second stairstep crossing at 2 miles, the trail leaves private land. Springtime decorates the ridge with yellow bells, shooting stars, and phlox.

The trail next contours the slope. Where it approaches the red rock rim, the route switchbacks downhill to meet the Island in Time Trail.

Turning right at the foot of the hill (3 miles), the tour continues upstream crisscrossing the basin drainage with its puddles of blue-green water and bluish mud. Trailside exhibits describe the badlands, which measure 0.5 mile thick, their geology, and the fossils dating back 25 million years. Weathering over time continues to unfold the tale long held secret by the volcanic ash. Shadows animate the basin.

The nature trail halts at the heart of the basin (3.4 miles), presenting an imposing and impressive view. When ready to leave the bowl, backtrack along the nature trail to reach the trailhead in 0.6 mile, concluding the basin tour.

67 SMITH ROCK LOOP TRAIL

Distance: 5.25 miles round trip
Elevation change: 900 feet
Difficulty: Strenuous
Season: Year round

Map: State Park flier
For information: State Parks, Bend Regional Office
Smith Rock State Park

At this 640-acre high desert park, the scenic waters of the Crooked River sleepily curl around the base of the park's central feature—a group of burnt-orange rhyolite-ash spires collectively dubbed Smith Rock. The tour offers canyon-floor views of the crags and fissures and such features as Red Wall, The Monument, Little Three Fingered Jack, and Monkey Face. Where the trail tours the ridgetop, deep-canyon, juniper flat, and Cascade Crest vistas greet the hiker. The tallest peak, Smith Summit, rises some 800 feet above the Crooked River. Dark basalt cliffs enclose the upstream canyon.

Discoveries along the loop include the few eagles' nests perched on the high rock ledges, the colorfully attired climbers scaling the vertical rock, and the crown-circling pigeons and swallows. Geese pairs nest along the quiet river bends.

A counterclockwise circuit travels the river bank upstream, switchbacks between canyon walls, and tours the ridgetop, exploring the rock from all perspectives. Where the loop descends from the ridge to the river-canyon floor finds a troublesome 3- to 4-foot drop.

From US 97 at Terrebonne (north of Redmond), turn east onto Smith Rock Way. Park signs mark the road junctions, as the route travels the county roads north and east to reach the park in about 3.1 miles.

From the park picnic area, the trail descends 200 yards to a canyon vista and another 0.25 mile (or 0.4 mile via the closed road) to the footbridge. For the loop, cross the bridge and head upstream toward Staender Ridge. A side trail climbs to Red Wall; all along the circuit, spurs branch to climber routes.

The narrow dirt path travels along the sagebrush–rabbitbrush–juniper shore, punctuated by a few stout old-growth ponderosa pines. Boulders dot the river bed; the river melody tranquilizes. Magpies, dippers, and kingfishers divert the eyes from the towering rock.

After passing below Red Wall, the loop rounds a bend, offering views of Staender Ridge with its sheer cliffs, rugged skyline, and nearly vertical drainage fissures. At 0.8 mile, the nests of large raptors come into view; binoculars are needed to spy any occupants.

Ahead, the trail climbs away from the river. Junipers offer patchy shade. Upon crossing a scree slope, a serious uphill spurt follows the small drainage isolating the Smith Rock–volcanics from a basalt rim.

At 1.25 mile, the trail meets a dirt road at the Crooked River Canal. It

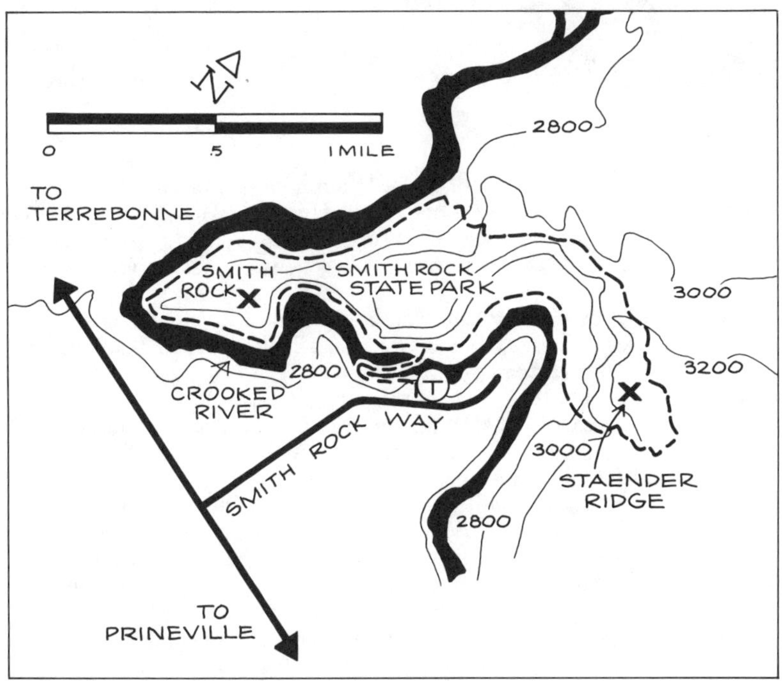

Smith Rock and Crooked River

traces the road uphill for about 40 feet then breaks into a steep, snaking climb on the open bunchgrass slope marked by boulders and volcanic outcrops. Over-the-shoulder views feature the canyon rim and nearby ranchland. The trail grows thinner and less defined, but remains easy to follow.

Before long, it passes between two rock outcrops, offering an open view to the southwest. The skyline shows Black Butte, Mount Washington, Belknap and Black craters, and the Three Sisters.

Heading up and to the left, the trail crosses to the other side of Smith Rock, passes beneath an overhang, and travels across a steep outcrop before topping the ridge. Views pan the juniper–sage valley of Sherwood Canyon. Mount Jefferson looms to the west.

After crossing a jeep road, the trail follows the ridge to the left and drops steeply; beware the loose, crumbly rock. Windows created by the deep drainage fractures offer outward views. As the trail rises and dips with the ridge, still more canyon-crest panoramas await with Crooked River views down either side of Smith Rock.

Amid the large boulders at 2.5 miles is another steep, downhill segment. The view includes a hammer-like pillar located just upstream. Beware the loose rock and use care when lowering yourself down the 3- to

4-foot rock outcrop. The descent now follows a sage and bunchgrass slope to the river at 2.8 miles.

Bypassing a house-sized boulder, the trail travels upstream along the river offering additional views of the 400-foot hammer rock, gradually revealing the ape-like profile which won it the name "Monkey Face." Low waters reveal den holes of beaver, otter, and muskrat.

By 3.2 miles, the trail is following the oxbow bend of the river, and at 4.5 miles, it skirts below Asterisk Pass, entering the area where the most popular climbs are found. Beyond this area lies a more fractured cliff not used by climbers. Several ponderosa pines shade the final way to the footbridge and the loop's close. An uphill climb returns to the parking area.

68 DRY RIVER CANYON HIKE

Distance: 5 miles round trip
Elevation change: Minimal
Difficulty: Easy
Season: Year round
Map: None
For information: Prineville District BLM

Where most hikes celebrate the wide, open spaces, this one celebrates the intimacy and vitality of the narrow, enclosed spaces of the great outdoors. This central Oregon lava bed canyon was eliminated from Bureau of Land Management (BLM) wilderness study consideration because the reviewers felt the canyon flow of traffic would prevent solitude. Hikers, however, soon discover that the canyon location, far from the madding crowds, adequately screens hiker numbers, ensuring a wild adventure with ample peace and solitude, despite the narrow corridor.

The aptly dubbed Dry River is but a wash recording the course of an ancient river that drained an Ice Age lake located east of here in what is today the High Desert of Millican Country. Its course ran some 50 miles. Here, the river parted Horse Ridge.

Basalt canyon walls frame the ancient river. A sagebrush and juniper grassland vegetates much of the canyon floor. The dry river bed and well-tracked animal paths form the hiker route.

To reach Dry Canyon, travel 21 miles east of Bend on US 20, or go 2 miles west from US 20's marked Dry Canyon Viewpoint. There, turn north on an unmarked dirt road leading into an old gravel quarry site.

At the quarry, drive across its center via the good two-track and head east into the juniper grove. The route roughly parallels US 20. In 0.6 mile, the road halts at an informal camp at the canyon mouth—the starting point for this hike.

The hike enters the mouth of the canyon following the boulder-blocked, closed jeep trail generally east for 0.25 mile. The route passes between low, basalt-boulder walls; sagebrush, juniper, and arid-wash trees frame its sides. As the canyon is often sun-baked, carry plenty of water.

Dry River Canyon

After 0.25 mile, the canyon floor becomes more rock littered, as some large boulders have tumbled from the cliffs. The now-narrow path snakes among and between the rocks and the shade-throwing junipers drawing deeper into the true canyon. Loose sands work the leg muscles.

Although the route is informal, it is fairly well-trodden and easy to follow. Deer, mice, and rabbit tracks blend with the boot prints of hikers.

High, steep cliffs soon define the canyon gorge. Junipers punctuate the north-facing wall; boulders shape the south-facing wall. Although both sides are steep, they remain mountable for overlooks.

The canyon successfully insulates hikers from the presence of US 20, which parallels the top of the south canyon rim. A desert remoteness prevails.

By 0.7 mile, the basalt rims of the clifftops give way to rock outcrops, creating a more irregular skyline. Fiddlenecks, bitterbrush, sweet clover, mariposa lily, yarrow, and squaw currant contribute to the arid landscape, lending quiet splashes of springtime color.

The canyon undergoes various changes as the tour continues. At times, the canyon walls dip lower or become more pinched or gaping. The passage of the sun and the clouds alters the look and the mood of the canyon with a play of shadow and light.

At 1.4 miles, trees, shrubs, and boulders congest the canyon floor. Here, hikers must choose the way of least obstruction. A path again presents itself.

Raptors and vultures soar across the canyon briefly shadowing the floor. The overhead cliffs are a vital nesting site for area birds of prey. Icings of guano reveal the preferred ledges and hollows for roosts and nests. In places, hikers may discover small piles of tiny bleached bones indicating where birds of prey have taken their meals.

After 1.75 miles, a canyon path no longer exists, but hikers can continue weaving their way amid the canyon treecover and boulders to explore another 0.75 mile farther. Near the east end of the canyon, traffic noise from US 20 bounces off the rock walls intruding on solitude.

Before the canyon opens up, it's time to turn around and return as you came to avoid trespassing. Private property occupies the eastern 0.25 mile of the canyon; to continue any farther would require special permission from the owner. New canyon perspectives await as you return west.

69 DESCHUTES RIVER TRAIL

Distance: 8.5 miles one way
Elevation change: 300 feet
Difficulty: Moderate
Season: Spring through fall
Map: USFS Deschutes
For information: Bend Ranger District

The Deschutes Wild and Scenic River is both a national and state treasured waterway. This companion trail offers prized overlooks of falls, rapids, and sleepy bends. The route visits historic and present-day campsites, bypasses wetland ponds and mature ponderosa pines, tours scenic aspen groves, crosses thick grass meadows, and tops a crusty lava flow. The crowns of area volcanos sometimes rise above the setting. Ducks, geese, herons, and kingfishers accompany the traveler.

The volcanic activity of nearby Lava Butte some 6,200 years ago shaped the Deschutes River channel, both damming and narrowing the river. The dams created quiet upstream waters; the narrows shaped the rapids. Multiple footpaths or jeep tracks at times confuse the hiker route, but as long as the selected path follows the river course you cannot go far wrong.

For the upper trailhead, from Bend, go 12 miles south on US 97 and turn right for Lava Lands Visitor Center. Follow the route indicated toward Benham Falls arriving at the picnic area and trailhead in 5 miles. The lower trailhead at Meadow Recreation Site lies about 7 miles southwest of Bend off Cascade Lakes Highway.

From Benham Falls Picnic Area, the hike heads downstream to cross the footbridge built on the pilings of a 1920s logging-railroad bridge. The trail then follows the open corridor of the old railway grade and a semi-shaded path to reach the falls vista (0.8 mile). Here, Benham Falls, actually a large river cascade, cuts through an old lava dome. Dippers fly into the churning green–white water.

From the viewpoint, the trail continues downstream, narrow and meandering, rolling with the terrain and hugging the river course. Pines with a few fir, manzanita, bitterbrush, and bunchgrass frame the route. A lava flow, black and stark, shapes the opposite shore.

At the 1.6-mile trail fork, follow the wider path away from the river to tour an evergreen–aspen flat. Ahead, the trail bears right, skirting a wetland field with ponds. Songbirds, garter snakes, and waterfowl enliven the setting.

At 2 miles, the trail crosses a grassy river bench. Scent mounds and anchored, submerged aspen limbs hint at a presence of beaver. The river here is wide and smooth-flowing with a few hummocky islands.

From Slough Camp, the trail follows the two-track downstream from the boat launch to round a seasonal pond or mud hole ringed by cattails. Midway around the wetland, a footpath replaces the track. In 0.5 mile,

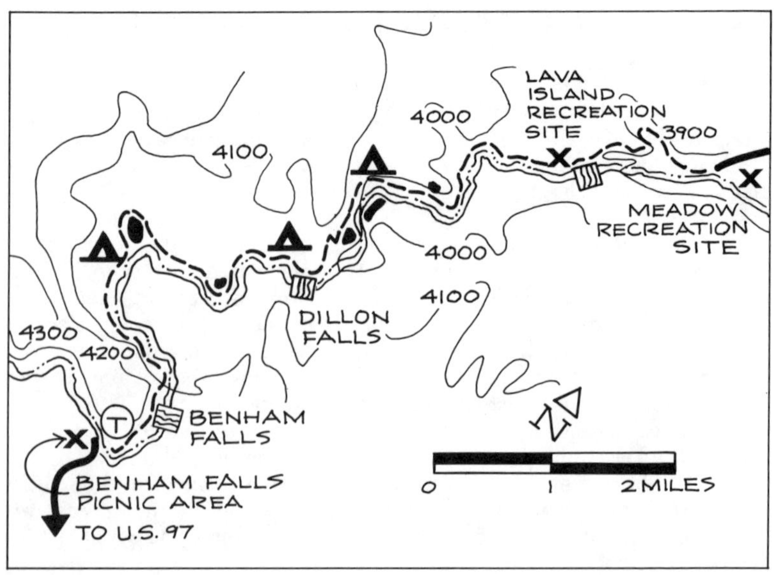

Dillon Falls

the trail again nears the river, but the tight forest of lodgepole and ponderosa pines denies views.

A gateway of two silvered poles soon points hikers around another pond. The path then travels atop a riverside levee at the meadow's edge. Looks upstream find Lava Butte. In the spring, geese pairs noisily fend off nest area intruders.

At 3.8 miles, the trail arrives at the boat take-out above Dillon Falls. After crossing through the primitive camp, hikers find the lava flow now extends to the west shore, creating a narrow river gorge. At 4.25 miles, side paths lead to an overlook of Dillon Falls, where the river surges over an old fault scarp.

The primary trail now travels away from the river touring a dry-shrub, open-forest complex. The bluff sometimes affords river views. Ahead, the trail quickly descends a fully forested slope. Approaching the meadow bottom, keep an alert eye; the river trail branches left staying in the forest. A meadow detour finds a riverside camp with a nice upstream view.

At 5.2 miles, the trail travels an aspen corridor leading to Aspen Camp, a scenic riverside location shaded by second-growth ponderosa pines. In another half mile, the trail arrives at a grassy river bench rounding yet another pond. At the river access at 6.4 miles, iron stakes mark the hiker/horse trail.

Just ahead, the trail presents a great look at Big Eddy with its bending course, deep pools, and fast water. Here the signatures of the lava flow and river merge for a first-rate spectacle. Above the river, the trail briefly merges with the closed road of the bicycle trail, before dipping back toward shore.

Nearing Lava Island Recreation Site, the primary route stays low. Mature ponderosa pines and juniper line this segment. At 7.6 miles are the parking area and restrooms. The trail continues past the interpretive sign.

Downstream, a log bench overlooks the lava island. At 7.75 miles is the large boulder outcropping with an overhang shelter. Archaeologists believe this shelter intermittently served Native American hunting parties over the past 7,000 years. The trail next rounds the slope above the river channel passing beneath a rock ledge. Houses dot the opposite slope.

Ahead, the trail dips to cross the end of a spillover pond below the Inn of the Seventh Mountain. It then curves right following a well-defined path along the slope overlooking the tongue of the flow and the returning river. Mature ponderosa pines dot the arid slope. The trail halts at Meadow Recreation Site, a scenic grassy flat along a quiet river passage.

70 PETER SKENE OGDEN–PAULINA LAKE HIKE

Distance: 15.5-mile one-way trip
Elevation change: 2,100 feet
Difficulty: Strenuous
Season: Late spring through fall
Map: USFS Deschutes
For information: Fort Rock Ranger District
Newberry National Volcanic Monument

Peter Skene Ogden National Recreation Trail (NRT) begins this hike, following Paulina Creek upstream passing through open pine–fir forests and bypassing scenic cascades and waterfalls, including Paulina Falls. Capping off the journey, a 7-mile hiker-only loop explores the shore of the creek's headwater, Paulina Lake—the larger and deeper of the two

Paulina Falls

Newberry Crater lakes; East Lake is the other. The combined tour reveals the volcanic origins of this region, traveling surfaces of ash and pumice, cinder, lava, and obsidian.

The split-drop, 100-foot Paulina Falls spills into a canyon of reddish-brown volcanic cliffs, while the cobalt-azure waters of Paulina Lake shine up beautiful and deep from the crater bowl. The lake circuit offers looks at craggy Paulina Peak (elevation 7,985 feet), the highest remnant on the crater rim. Osprey and eagle soar over the high lake.

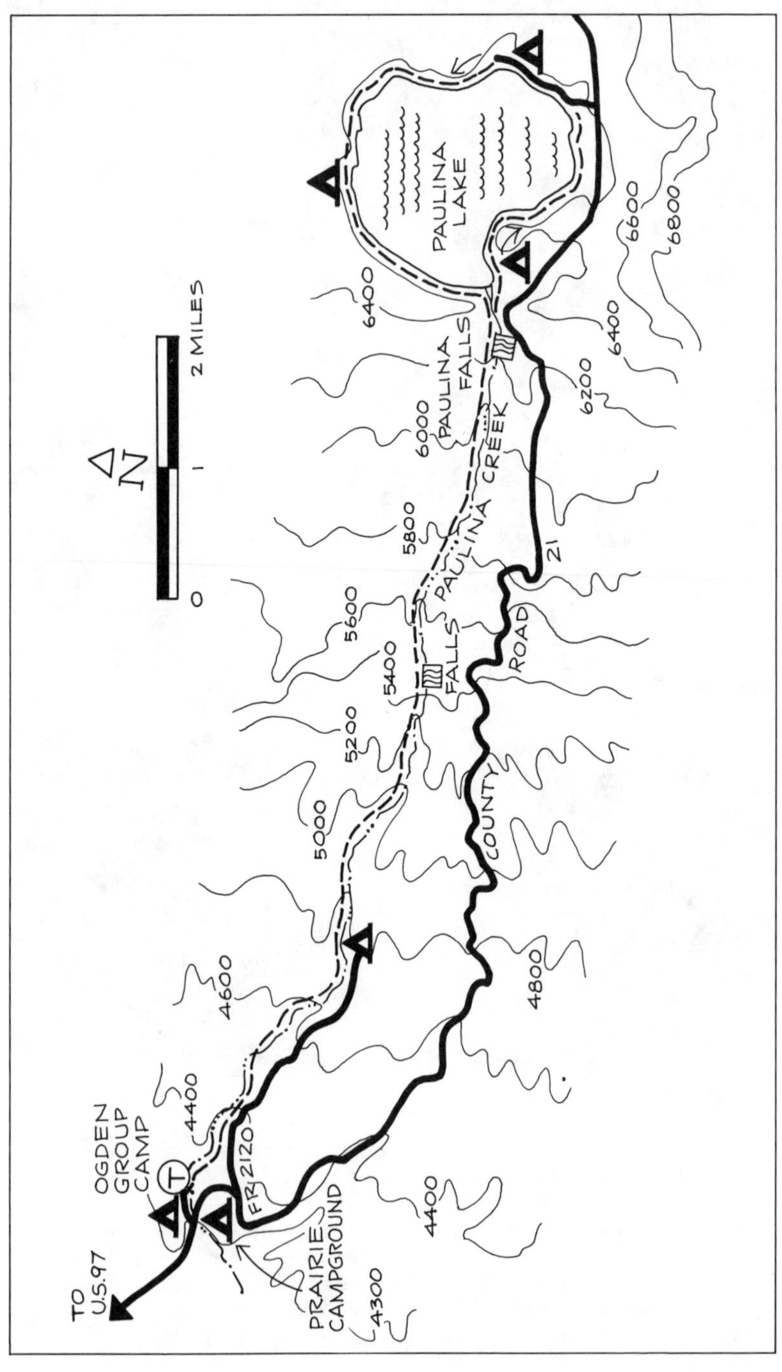
TO U.S.97
OGDEN GROUP CAMP
T
PRAIRIE CAMPGROUND
FR 2120
COUNTY ROAD 21
FALLS
PAULINA CREEK
PAULINA FALLS
PAULINA LAKE
N
0
1
2 MILES
4300
4400
4400
4600
4800
5000
5200
5400
5600
5800
6000
6200
6400
6400
6600
6800

Newberry, a broad shield volcano, and much of its outlying neighborhood received national monument designation in 1990. In 1826, Peter Skene Ogden and his company were the first whites to visit the crater.

From Bend, go 22 miles south on US 97 and turn left onto County 21/FR 21 for Newberry National Volcanic Monument. In another 3.3 miles, turn left for Ogden Group Camp and follow the marked spur to reach the trailhead alongside Paulina Creek in about 0.2 mile.

With a Paulina Creek fording or log crossing, the hike travels upstream along the gravelly shore soon crossing over a low ridge. Horseshoe markers indicate the often dusty route. Open and tree-filtered views feature the lower creek with its alternating slow stretches and skipping cascades. A couple of nice aspen stands mark the meadowy shore. At 0.4 mile, the trail crosses an old jeep road.

After squeezing through a rock barrier at 0.75 mile, the NRT bears left to follow a closed jeep road for 0.2 mile, reaching a footbridge crossing. The trail now shows a steady uphill progress. A few manzanita, lupine, bitterbrush, and grasses supply touches of green beneath a canopy of lodgepole and ponderosa pines.

At 2.5 miles, the trail offers a tree-limited view of a 20-foot falls, where a gorge-narrowed Paulina Creek spills over a brownish green cliff. The opposite shore holds the preferred vista. Ahead, the trail rounds above McKay Crossing Campground and continues upstream.

Where the trail follows an old manufactured grade, the forest corridor between the trail and the creek grows both fuller and wider with a few fir joining the mix. Before long, the creek canyon gains more definition, featuring numerous falls and cascades.

At 4.6 miles, the trail overlooks a 15-foot watery veil spilling to a circular blue pool, all enfolded in a scenic rock bowl. Just upstream finds another beauty where the creek course splits into three bubbling 30-foot falls spread across a 70-foot-wide terrace.

At 5.3 miles, the Peter Skene Ogden Trail continues straight; a horse trail descends to a bridge. Soon, beautiful red-trunked ponderosa pines line the canyon. Bypassing a stepped, funnel-shaped falls at 6 miles, the trail bears left following a jeep trail a few feet. The path then resumes to the right.

Afterwards, the trail drifts slightly away from the creek canyon. At 7 miles, hikers gain a quick view of the creek, its cliff and boulder confine, and the forested canyon walls. The upper canyon is more rugged and narrow. Much of the tour is now characterized by a tight lodgepole pine forest, huge snags, and some unusually big firs for this locale.

At 8.25 miles, the trail offers a Paulina Falls vista. While this shore delivers the best angle for viewing the southern fork of the falls, it only hints at the northern fork. A wire mesh fence lines the vista.

The NRT now follows the churning, cascading creek upstream, ending at the headwater, Paulina Lake (8.5 miles). Here begins the lake circuit, which visits both natural shoreline and developed and primitive camp areas.

From the outlet, a counterclockwise tour skirts the shore along Paulina Lake Day Use and Campground. Ahead lie a mixed-forest setting and a more rocky shore. Past the group camp, the trail travels a black coarse-sand beach. Meadow, beach, and forest stretches follow as the route bypasses summer homes and the Little Crater Day Use and Campground. The lake reflects the forested crater rim.

On the east shore, jagged lava tongues jut into the lake, creating ideal posts for lake viewing and angling. Craggy Paulina Peak overlooks the setting. At 12.2 miles, the trail travels the base of an obsidian flow, a ridge of shiny black volcanic glass—the material prized by early Native Americans for shaping tools and weapons.

Where the trail climbs the red cinder slope (12.9 miles), the view features the lake, Paulina Peak, a lava flow, and Little Crater. Semi-open slopes of manzanita and juniper next claim the route.

At 13.75 miles, the trail arrives at a coarse gravelly beach near North Cove Campground. A mixed forest frames the next 1.5 miles. Past the small lake resort, the loop closes at 15.5 miles.

71 THE DOME TRAIL

Distance: 1.5 miles round trip
Elevation change: 200 feet
Difficulty: Easy
Season: Late spring through fall
Map: USGS East Lake; USFS Deschutes
For information: Fort Rock Ranger District
Newberry National Volcanic Monument

With the signing of the monument bill on November 5, 1990, Central Oregon's backyard playground, Newberry Crater, quietly crossed the threshold from local attraction to one of national standing. At the southeast corner of the monument, this hike claims the horseshoe-shaped summit of the Dome (elevation 7,150 feet) for an overlook of some of the rugged lands that comprise Newberry National Volcanic Monument and its neighborhood.

Cinder and obsidian cones and buttes, the ancient caldera, lava flows, and a glimpse of one of the crater lakes create an intriguing field of view. Fort Rock and the surrounding pine forests fading into the high desert expanse complete the panorama. The sweeping views east and south prove especially rewarding.

Newberry Crater, measuring some 25 miles across its base, is the largest Ice Age volcano east of the Cascade Crest. Most of the volcanic activity quieted here some 2,000 years ago.

From Bend, travel south on US 97 for 22 miles, turning left onto County 21/FR 21, south of the La Pine State Park exit. Stay on this road for some 21 miles to find the marked trailhead on the right-hand side of FR 21, just past the FR 21–FR 2127 junction.

The trail climbs through an open forest of lodgepole pines above a barren floor of light-colored pumice. Along the way, hikers should take the

View from the Dome summit

time to examine the rock closely; it proves an interesting study even for those familiar with its qualities.

Pumice is a gas bubble-filled volcanic glass that's so lightweight for its size that it usually floats. During the various Newberry Volcano eruptions, pumice spewed out over the area. The most prominent deposits originated from the same vent source that created the Big Obsidian Flow to the west.

In places along the east rim of the crater, the pumice layer measures some 10 feet thick.

At 0.3 mile, the trail tags the top of the Dome. The horseshoe-shaped plateau invites a summit stroll, overlooking the region of cinder cones and buttes to the south. Fort Rock, a natural, crescent-shaped rock fortress, stands out on the open, high plain. To the north, a limited look at the East Lake–Central Pumice Cone area of Newberry Crater contributes to the view.

Dwarf plants push up between the volcanic soils of the summit. In July, hikers find accents of purple, red, yellow, pink, and white dotting the whitish-gray rock. Lupine, Indian paintbrush, blue-eyed Marys, phlox, and western yarrow contribute to the floral display. Some species are so minute, hikers must surrender to their hands and knees to spy them.

Winds lash the top, influencing plant growth and the pattern of vegetation. From the end of the horseshoe, the trail overlooks Sand Butte, the small butte with a crater, just south of the Dome.

When exploring the Dome, keep to the trail and the rim top, as the pumice slopes scar easily. When ready, return as you came.

If this hike piqued your interest, you may wish to sample some of the 21-mile Newberry Crater Rim Trail, which is easily accessed off FR 21 near East Lake.

72 FREMONT NATIONAL RECREATION TRAIL

Distance: 7.6 miles round trip (longer depending on final management plan; prior to trip, call district)
Elevation change: 800 feet
Difficulty: Moderate to difficult
Season: Late spring through fall

Map: USFS Fremont, Winema
For information: Silver Lake Ranger District
Yamsay Mountain Recreation Area

This trail travels across a northwest portion of the Fremont National Forest to claim the summit of Yamsay Mountain (elevation 8,196 feet), located in next-door Winema National Forest. Yamsay Mountain is an exciting crater destination. From a distance, it gives little clue to its eruptive history.

En route to the summit, the trail tours a forest of mixed pines and mountain hemlock, moist and dry meadows, and the crater rim. The 360-degree summit vista sweeps the crater bowl, the Cascade volcano chain from Three Sisters in the north to California's Mount Shasta in the south, Fort Rock, Hager Mountain, the rim country of Fremont National Forest, and the High Desert expanse, including Newberry Crater.

Yamsay Mountain figured prominently in Klamath Indian mythology—their supreme being resided here. In their language, the mountain's name refers to the north wind.

From Silver Lake, take OR 31 north for 0.8 mile and turn left onto County 4-11/FR 27, at the sign for Silver Creek Marsh Campground/Thompson Reservoir. In 8.7 miles, turn right onto FR 2804. Go another 2.5 miles and turn left onto FR 7645. Stay on FR 7645. At the T-junction in 5.4 miles, go right remaining on FR 7645. In 1.8 miles, turn left onto FR 024.

Presently, staying on FR 024, a high-clearance vehicle road, finds the trailhead for the 3.8-mile National Recreation Trail (NRT) in 5.9 miles. But the final plans for the recreation area are incomplete, and the decision whether FR 024 will remain open to motor vehicle travel is pending.

Should FR 024 be closed to vehicles, the resulting hike would add about 9 miles to the total round trip distance, depending on which of the considered closure sites is ultimately selected.

Even with such added road miles, the destination is rewarding. FR 024 proves a pleasant, narrow, forest-shaded corridor with a comfortable grade and walking bed allowing for a quick hike to the NRT. The route passes through a semi-open lodgepole pine forest, a full, mixed forest, and a replanted harvest site. Lupine, currant, and kinnikinnick dress the floor. Huge boulders frame the road at one of the proposed closures.

At the junction in 4.6 miles (mileage measured from FR 7645), FR 024 bears right; in another 0.3 mile, it again bears right. At 5.5 miles, FR 024 skirts a lush grass–false hellebore meadow. Beyond lies Antler Spring

Camp. Uphill from the camp on the right-hand side of the road, hikers find the NRT (5.9 miles); a hiker/horse symbol marks the trailhead.

The 3.8-mile NRT begins in a open-canopied forest of lodgepole and whitebark pines. The forest floor is log-strewn and absent of vegetation. Little hint is given that hikers are about to climb a mountain—both terrain and path appear flat.

By 0.5 mile (mileages now shown are for the NRT only), mountain hemlocks share the stage with the pines, offering welcomed shade. A slow climb follows. Ahead, forest gaps afford looks to the north-northwest of the Three Sisters and the Fort Rock area.

The trail offers its first look at Yamsay Mountain at 1.1 miles. Soon, the rolling trail bypasses small meadow patches. Elk tracks commonly spot the trail. In summer, the animals feed on the higher mountain slopes. At 2 miles, the trail passes a large, moist meadow threaded by intermittent creeks. Buttercups, Lewis monkey flowers, shooting stars, bog orchids, American globeflowers, and elephant-heads put on a spring–summer show.

The trail then crosses over a creek at the upper meadow to climb the dry, pine-forested slope. At 2.5 miles, it switchbacks uphill to reach the crater rim.

Stepping off the trail at 2.7 miles, hikers gain their first Yamsay Mountain–crater bowl vista. A rich drainage-laced meadow spills across the crater bottom, while mountain hemlocks and mixed pines march up the bowl's steep sides.

Sharp, ragged volcanic rock shapes the rim. The north opening indicates where the volcano blew out. Cross-crater views find the Cascade lineup of Mounts Thielsen, Bailey, and Scott.

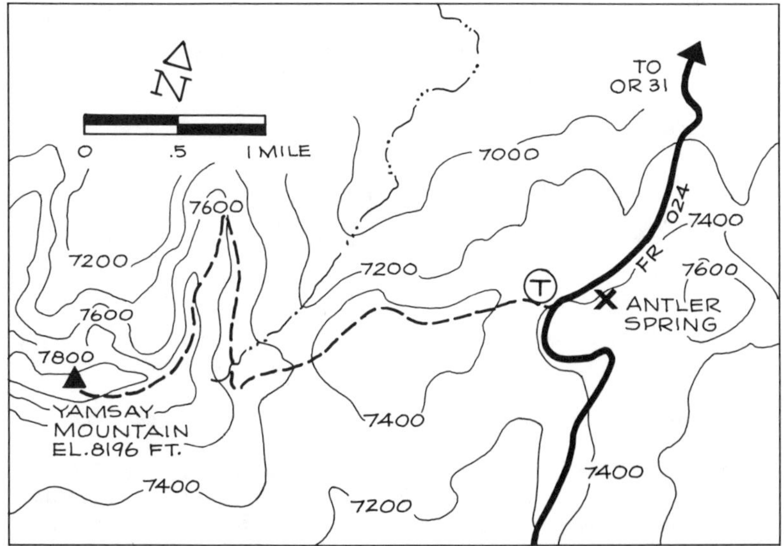

Yamsay Mountain summit view

Passing through a tilted rock, the trail continues rounding the crater traveling along or just below the rim. The route adds new perspectives on the crater bowl and views of the Three Sisters, Fort Rock, and the High Desert. A dry lupine meadow floor spreads beneath the pines of upper Yamsay.

At 3.5 miles, the pumiceous trail makes its final climb offering views to the south-southeast. The trail tags the summit at the site of a former lookout, where a grand 360-degree vista pulls together the celebrated landmarks and a superb look into the crater bowl at the meadow headwaters of Jackson Creek. Golden eagles sometimes soar below the lofty post; Clark's nutcrackers chide rim visitors.

From the rocky summit, a closed jeep road descends into Winema National Forest. Future plans call for the NRT's incorporation into the Desert–Crest Intertie linking the Desert and Pacific Crest trails. Meanwhile, return as you came.

73 BLUE LAKE TRAIL TO NOTCH HIKE

Distance: 14.5 miles round trip
Elevation change: 1,800 feet
Difficulty: Moderate
Season: Late spring through fall
Map: USFS Fremont
For information: Bly Ranger District
Gearhart Mountain Wilderness Area

Journeying to the heart of this 22,800-acre south-central Oregon wilderness, this hike visits the key features of Gearhart Mountain and Blue Lake. Gearhart Mountain, a remnant shield volcano (elevation 8,364 feet), towers above a neighborhood of Ice Age–carved valleys and

View from the Notch

cirques. Mixed pine–fir forests and aspen–wildflower meadows spill outward from the mountain. Blue Lake, a deep, circular lake situated below a side ridge of Gearhart Mountain, extends an invitation to serenity. Wild onions abound along its southwest shore.

The Notch and a rise above it hold the vistas of the hike. The stand-out view is that of the rugged, vertical north wall of Gearhart Mountain's summit rock, rising some 250 feet above the Notch. The ridge, the cliff bowl of the volcano, the Dairy Creek drainage, and distant Abert Rim contribute to the view. Identifiable from afar, the Notch is what sets

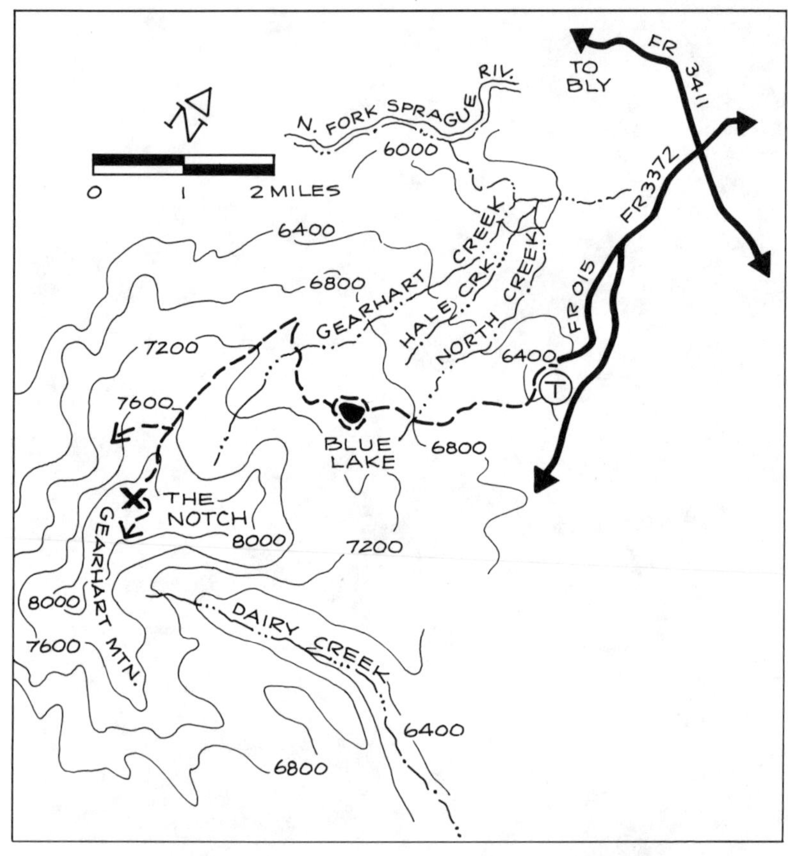

Gearhart apart from the other rim features of Fremont National Forest.

From OR 140 1.4 miles southeast of Bly, turn north at the sign for Gearhart Mountain Wilderness. Go 5.2 miles on the county road. Where it enters a 90-degree turn, leave the pavement, going straight on the red dirt road. This is FR 3411; it has no sign. Stay on FR 3411 following it northeast for 17.4 miles. There turn right onto FR 3372. In 1.9 miles, at the sign for Blue Lake Trail, Gearhart Wilderness, turn right onto FR 3372.015. A large trailhead parking area, primitive camp, and pit toilet are in 1.2 miles. The entire route is via good, improved forest road passable for conventional vehicles.

The hike begins above the meadow of the Upper North Fork Sprague River, entering the wilderness at 0.2 mile. The lodgepole pine forest shows an uncommon meadow floor and some huge trees. The brown ribbon of the narrow earthen trail weaves through the forest green.

Sunrise hikers often spy deer or elk in the meadow. One of the largest elk herds within Fremont National Forest ranges the Gearhart Mountain Wilderness; it numbers some thirty to forty animals.

The trail crosses over a small creek at 0.6 mile. It then progresses with a slow rise marked by a few brief, steeply climbing spurts. Firs enter the mix, and the forest floor shows the traditional spare cover of a high-elevation forest. Bright yellow-green lichens cluster on the trunks and dead limbs. Snags dot the forest.

At 1.4 miles, the trail crosses over a usually dry meadow drainage lined by aspen. Beyond lies a thick stand of lodgepole pines punctuated by a few grand old ponderosa pines. A scenic lupine–false hellebore meadow with aspens for shade next claims the trail. Aster, columbine, and other wildflowers divide the tall lupine.

The trail makes a sharp climb at 2.4 miles only to resume its meandering. A tight stand of lodgepole pines announces the approach to the lake at 3 miles.

A 0.9-mile trail encircles Blue Lake, a large lake below an extension arm of Gearhart Mountain. Lodgepole pines ring the lake. Set back from the lake are the forested campsites. The still morning waters reflect the side ridge and the forest shore. Ospreys soar over the lake.

A left on the loop travels the south shore to the 3.4-mile junction with Gearhart Trail. A north-shore tour awaits for the return trek. Near the junction, the aroma of wild onions rides the crisp morning air.

Follow the Gearhart Trail to the left to continue the hike to the Notch. The trail alternates between pine forest and meadow patches, crossing the dry drainage of Gearhart Creek at 4.25 miles. Soon after, the trail begins to climb, touring the gentle, uphill curvature of the Gearhart Mountain ridge. The trail enjoys patchy shade much of the way; subtle forest changes hold hiker interest.

At 6.1 miles, as the trail bypasses a rock outcrop, the intensity of the climb increases. The lone star of the forest is now the lodgepole pine. By 6.6 miles, the trail travels close to the ridge drop-off. Gaps in the forest offer limited views northeast of Winter Ridge, Lee Thomas Meadow, Gearhart Marsh, and the extension of Gearhart Mountain.

Going another 0.8 mile finds the junction for the Boulder Spring Trail, which descends to the right. Before the junction, the forest opens up. Beyond it, Gearhart Trail levels out, touring the west slope just below the ridge. At 7.25 miles, the trail reaches the Notch saddle with a vista of Gearhart Mountain's steep, rugged rock summit.

Deep cracks, fissures, and ledges mark the chiseled north face of Gearhart, which defies conquer. Green lichen, wind-shaped pines, and snags touch color to the gray-black rock.

A 0.1-mile off-trail scramble from the Notch up the small rise to its north finds an outcrop with a better vantage on Gearhart's summit rock, the cliff bowl, the dips and saddles in Gearhart Ridge, the Dairy Creek drainage, and Abert Rim in the eastern distance. Staying just west of the ridge finds the route of least rocks to the outcrop post.

The Gearhart Trail continues, descending from the Notch, working its way south through the wilderness for another 5 miles to reach the southern terminus, Lookout Rock Trailhead. Extend your tour, or return as you came.

Campbell Lake and Hart Mountain

74 WARNER LAKES TRAIL

Distance: 4.5 miles round trip
Elevation change: Minimal
Difficulty: Easy
Season: Year round
Map: BLM Warner Wetlands
For information: Lakeview District BLM

This trail samples the offering of Warner Wetlands, a Bureau of Land Management (BLM)–designated Area of Critical Environmental Concern. The area, a stopover and wintering site on the Pacific Flyway and vital nesting ground, is critical to bird populations. The major lakes, hundreds of shallow potholes, playas, marshes of bulrush and cattail, dunes, arid scrubland, short-grass meadow, and irrigated lands create a rich habitat diversity. The closed lake-basin system is the home of the endangered Warner sucker.

The Warner Basin also holds significant cultural value, cradling Native American artifacts and remains recording some 10,000 years of oc-

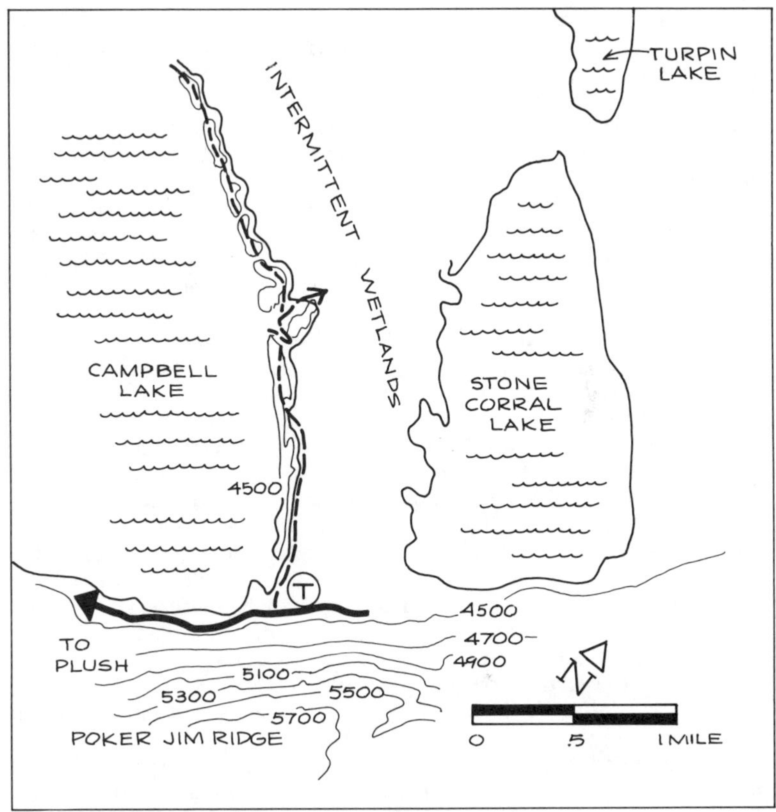

cupation. Strict laws protect the sites and the artifacts they hold from collection and/or disturbance.

The recreational potential of this land is only now being tapped. BLM plans call for the creation of formal hiking and canoe trails and a camp facility. The delay in the hiking-trail construction is due to a concern that the final trail blend with the habitat, serve users, and withstand the environmental changes that do occur: the cyclical changes in lake basin water levels and the muds resulting from the freeze-thaw conditions.

Meanwhile, an abandoned jeep track invites the visitor to walk amid the lakes and discover the wildlife and area geology and history. This particular tour passes between Campbell Lake and the serial ponds of Stone Corral Lake. The bold western escarpment of Poker Jim Ridge and Hart Mountain rises above the basin.

Canada geese, herons, sandhill cranes, egrets, white pelicans, ibis, avocets, and cinnamon teals keep the binoculars moving. Antelope, mule deer, and coyotes range the brush.

From OR 140 at Adel, take County 3-10 north for 17.3 miles to Plush. From Plush, go another 0.8 mile north and turn right onto County Road

3-12 at the sign for Hart Mountain/Frenchglen (a paved and gravel route). In 16.6 miles, opposite the sign for Hart Mountain National Antelope Refuge, go left toward Campbell Lake for the main entrance to Warner Lakes; it's a high-clearance-vehicle, dry-weather access.

The closed jeep trail for the hike begins on the left in 2.1 miles, just past Campbell Lake. Hikers may opt to walk this 2.1-mile distance; the route is pleasant touring alongside Campbell Lake.

The designated hike begins traveling the abandoned jeep trail northwest along the broad, flat interlake area between Campbell Lake and the serial ponds of Stone Corral Lake. Greasewood, saltbrush, sagebrush, wild rye, and other grasses attire the dry upland expanse. Jackrabbits bound through the brush.

Spring–summer visitors may find a healthy mosquito population—the insect food of the winged inhabitants, but the opportunity for superior wildlife sightings usually outweighs the nuisance. In fall, thousands of tundra swans stop over on their migratory track south.

A few smaller jeep trails branch from the main artery offering additional routes to investigate. Soon a 15-foot-high ridge blocks Campbell Lake from view. In this terrain, the ridge proves a major land feature.

By 0.75 mile, the trail is passing through an area of brushy scrub. At 0.9 mile, it tops a rise. Basin overlooks feature the open-water bodies linked by a maze of channels, cutting the landscape into jigsaw pieces. Foxtail barley seas claim the dry lakebeds. The floor of the rise shows a cracked hardpan, absent of grasses. Burrows riddle the roadbed.

Coyote wails, meadowlark songs, and cattle moos sound a discordant harmony. Geese string overhead in honking flight. Breaking the open expanse are Rabbit Hills to the southwest, Juniper Mountain to the northwest.

At 1.3 miles is a T-junction: To the left is the Campbell Lake shore (0.1 mile); to the right continues the main tour. At 1.4 miles, the hike continues to the left, ascending the ridge above Campbell Lake. The jeep trail straight ahead quickly ends at a pothole basin.

At 2 miles, the trail overlooks a watery arm of Turpin Lake. The jeep trail becomes more overgrown, but remains easy to follow. By 2.25 miles, the hike concludes with a grand expansive look at Campbell Lake, its basin, towering Hart Mountain, and the distant Rabbit and Coyote hills. When the lake is full and the conditions of light and weather are ideal, a superb reflection of Hart Mountain caps the view.

When water levels allow it, an alternative to backtracking along the jeep trail is to descend the 20- to 25-foot ridge and follow the Campbell Lake shore back to the wetlands entrance road. Both ways are shadeless. Cracked muds and loose sands characterize the shore. In places it's heavily overgrown with such vegetations as saltgrass, foxtail barley, and borax weed. Discoveries may include obsidian shards and broken scrapers and arrowheads. Look, photograph, but do not remove these protected artifacts.

Shell fragments and animal tracks are other shoreline discoveries. As burrowing bees sometimes nest along soft sands of shore, beware when touring.

With hot summer temperatures, early morning and evening tours prove more comfortable. Carry water.

75 ROCK CREEK HIKE

Distance: 4 miles round trip
Elevation change: 400 feet
Difficulty: Easy
Season: Late spring through fall
Map: USGS Warner Peak
For information: Hart Mountain National Antelope Refuge

Established in 1936, this refuge serves as a fair-weather range for the remnant antelope herds that winter in Catlow Valley, east of here, or some 35 miles away on the Charles Sheldon Antelope Range in northwest Nevada. The refuge receives its name for its massive fault-block feature, Hart Mountain.

No formal trails explore this 275,000-acre high-desert refuge, but deserted cattle trails along Rock Creek serve as a convenient guide for an informal canyon tour. Rock Creek's headwater springs dot the east flank of Hart Mountain. This upstream hike halts in a basin at the foot of Hart Mountain's highest feature, Warner Peak (elevation 8,065 feet).

Coyotes, rabbits, and mule deer number among the possible wildlife sightings. Antelope groups may be seen crossing the arid slopes en route to the preferred lower-country range. Red-winged blackbirds, grackles, and woodpeckers keep the birdwatchers busy.

Obsidian shards and broken arrowheads and scrapers scatter much of the refuge land. The wildlife bounty of this area and neighboring Warner Lakes to the west attracted early Native American hunting parties. Look, but do not disturb the artifacts. All are protected under the Antiquities Act.

Backpackers planning to camp in the canyon will need to secure a free special-use permit from the headquarters or the Lakeview refuge office. For other public-use regulations and information, secure a refuge brochure at the headquarters' visitor room.

The hike, which both begins and ends at the primitive refuge campground, has an added attraction: Centerpiece to the camp is a hot springs bathhouse featuring a 5-foot-deep, steamy pool in an open-sky structure, welcoming hikers to cap the outing with a relaxing soak.

To reach the refuge, from OR 140 at Adel, take County 3-10 north for 17.3 miles to Plush. From there, go another 0.8 mile north and turn right onto County Road 3-12 at the sign for Hart Mountain/Frenchglen; keep an eye out for the turn, as the sign is in poor shape. Go 23 miles to reach the refuge headquarters. The camp area lies another 4 miles beyond; follow the signs. This paved and good gravel route is part of the Lakeview to Steens National Back Country Byway.

This upstream hike leaves the end of the camp road following a well-tracked footpath along the east bank of Rock Creek. Juniper, aspen, and

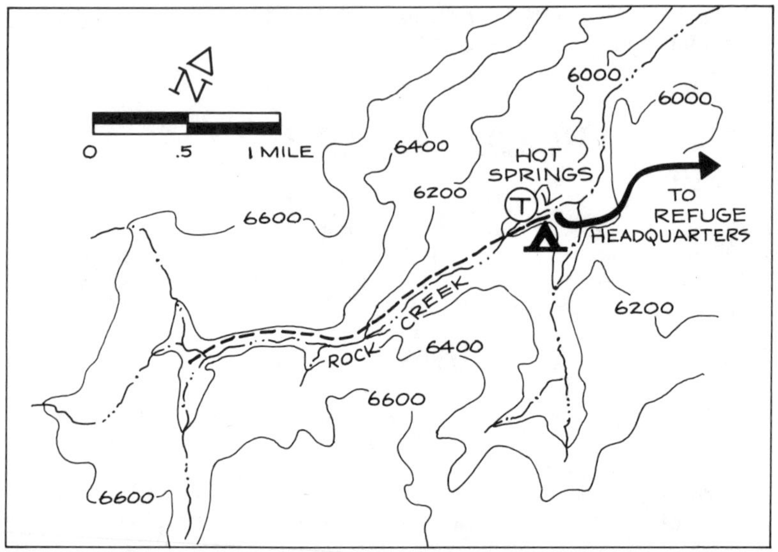

willow shade the route. Rodent holes riddle the slope.

In 0.1 mile, there's a barbed-wire fence; the unanchored top wire allows for an easy step over. Up ahead, the hike requires a creek crossing to the west bank. The fording site lies just below a beaver pond. Several beaver-enhancements mark the 2.5- to 3-foot-wide creek, reserving water well into the summer for fish and wildlife.

Hart Mountain rises to the west. The arid dividing ridge between Bond and Rock creeks rises to the east. Ahead, the sage foothills steal Hart Mountain from view.

Following the deserted cow trails along the base of the sage slope avoids the downfalls, branches, and wet meadow stretches that tend to line the creek. With the absence of cows on the refuge and the few hiker numbers seen here, these paths will eventually grow faint. Refuge plans, however, call for the route's signing.

Gooseberry, snowbrush, and chokecherry intermix with the grasses and sagebrush. It's a hot, open tour, but the aspens below offer shady escapes.

Deeper in the canyon, mountain mahogany claims the eastern ridgetop. Balsamroot, desert parsley, Indian paintbrush, phlox, and lupine dot spring color to the rocky terrain. Mule deer migrating to or from the creek are often seen.

By 1.2 miles, the canyon gap reveals Warner Peak to the southwest, identifiable by the microwave tower at its summit and sometimes by the snow it retains longer than its neighbors.

Just ahead, the canyon splits. Continuing along the path that travels up the main stem finds a more pinched canyon with a rugged western flavor. Rock outcrops punctuate the canyon walls. Willows begin replacing the aspen alongside the creek.

At 2 miles, the canyon opens up to a peaceful mountain basin at the foot of Warner Peak. The crooked, narrow ribbon of Rock Creek parts the rich basin grassland. Small trout ripple the water. Sagebrush marches up the canyon sides, while aspens crowd the headwater springs high on the slope.

Hikers should beware the sage–grassland habitat in the canyon does present a springtime tick problem. When traveling in this terrain, be alert for snakes.

Return as you came.

76 BIG INDIAN GORGE HIKE

Distance: 15.5 miles round trip (to headwall vista)
Elevation change: 1,600 feet
Difficulty: Moderate
Season: Summer through fall
Map: Desert Trail Association's Desert Trail Guide: Steens Mountain to Page Springs; BLM Steens Mountain Recreation Land
For information: Burns District BLM

This hike explores a wilderness study area via an abandoned jeep track and informal trail. It travels up one of the deep-gouged canyons of Steens Mountain, a 30-mile-long fault block feature rising a vertical mile above the Alvord Desert floor. A valley glacier originating near the summit (elevation 9,773 feet) carved out Big Indian Gorge's headwall cirque. Springs and snowmelt feed the creek.

The canyon enfolds the sage, juniper, and aspen vegetation belts. Lupine, geranium, columbine, monkeyflower, buttercup, and paintbrush lend their floral signatures to the meadow tapestry of the canyon floor. Blooms peak in July and August.

Historically, Big Indian Gorge was a popular Native American summer-gathering ground. Great numbers came for fishing, hunting, and sport. Among the amusements were gambling and pony racing; the bottom of Big Indian Gorge was their race track.

From the junction of OR 78 and OR 205, just east of Burns, go south on OR 205. In 66 miles, turn left onto Steens Mountain Loop Road (south entrance), toward Upper Blitzen River. At 16.1 miles is Blitzen Crossing. Go another 2.2 miles, turning right on the jeep track indicated "Big Indian Canyon Road."

This rough, narrow, high-clearance/4-wheel-drive-vehicle road is closed to motor travel 2.2 miles ahead. Due to its condition though, it's best to park at the flat areas to the side of the road within the first 0.1 mile and hike the distance to the wilderness study area.

Despite following an old jeep track, the hike retains a rugged, wild flavor. The tour begins juniper-shaded, then grows more open passing at the edge of a vast sage–grassland expanse. Sounds of the creek announce the approach to the canyon mouth. Deer tracks dot the dusty, rock-studded route.

At 2.2 miles, the hiker reaches the road closure and the Big Indian Creek fording site. Cottonwoods, alders, and juniper shade this good-sized creek flowing through an arid canyon setting. Mountain bikes, as well as other vehicles, are prohibited beyond this point.

A footpath leads to the Little Indian Creek fording just ahead. The coyote's cry and the coo of the mourning dove ride the morning breeze.

In the canyon, the vegetation is more varied with sage, juniper, mountain mahogany, currant, rabbitbrush, sticky laurel, chokecherry, and wild rye. At 2.4 miles, the route passes through a gate in an old rail fence.

Well-healed with plants, the jeep track is now more a true trail. The rounded bottom of the glacier-carved gorge offers a mostly flat tour.

At 2.7 miles, the trail bypasses an old, weathered, juniper-log cabin, with sagging sides and no roof. Be careful not to disturb the cultural resources of the gorge. Knee- to waist-high grasses brush against the hiker. The seeds of foxtail barley and other species are the demons of fall; ticks are a concern in early summer. At 3 miles, a corridor of small aspens ushers hikers to a nice camp flat and the next fording.

The often-open, sunny trail now travels below the north wall just away from Big Indian Creek, but within a reasonable distance for obtaining water. Yellow-green lichen etch the dark, vertically layered volcanic-rock cliffs. Sage slopes part the rocky rims.

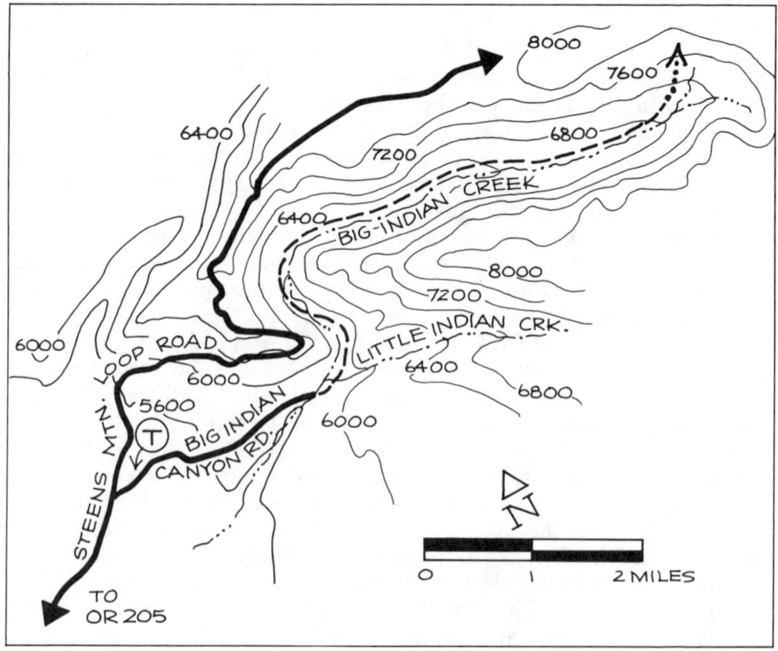

Big Indian Creek

Springs dot the route, often lined by aspen and seasonally announced by colorful wildflowers. Where the trail enters a bend at 3.75 miles, hikers peer through the gaping "U" of the canyon at the head basin.

By 5 miles, the open trail passes through a meadow flat where willows separate the creek from the trail. Sage remains prevalent even in the moist meadow stretches. Aspens now climb the canyon walls. The rim becomes more rugged with free-standing pillars and a small window on the north wall.

After passing through a fence opening, the trail draws nearer the creek, a shallow, riffling water. At 6 miles, the jeep track fades as the hike approaches a large, creekside cottonwood grove—a nice destination. A thin falls graces the south canyon wall.

Upstream, a well-tracked footpath soon reveals itself several yards north of the creek. It strings along, alternately touring aspen groves and sage flats.

At 7.6 miles, the trail crosses over a small drainage originating on the north canyon wall. Here, one of the Desert Trail options charges steeply uphill to the north rim. The route is faint, but traceable with a few low cairns for guides. A good hike ending lies along it.

At 7.75 miles, the steep, rugged path finds a rocky viewpoint overlooking a water-slide cascade on a side creek. It also presents an open view of the headwall and cirque basin along with an impressive look at the large, rounded jut of the south canyon wall. Glistening snowmelt drainages streak the headwall, while a rich, green vegetation splashes up the cirque bowl.

Return as you came; the down-canyon hike offers new perspectives on the wilderness study area.

77 CRANE MOUNTAIN NATIONAL RECREATION TRAIL

Distance: 16 miles round trip (to vista near California-Oregon border)
Elevation change: 900 feet
Difficulty: Strenuous
Season: Late spring through fall
Map: USGS Crane Mountain; USFS Fremont
For information: Lakeview Ranger District

This hike dips and rolls along the Warner Mountain crest, passing through open meadows of sagebrush, balsamroot, and lupine and touring mixed pine–fir forests. Vistas along the way feature 30-mile-long Goose Lake, California's Mount Shasta, Crane Mountain, the North Warners, and Big Valley, with Steens and Hart mountains in the distance. Benefiting from an annual maintenance schedule and accessed by a high-clearance-vehicle route, this little-visited trail offers pleasant strolling and prized solitude within the largely undisturbed Crane Mountain Semi-primitive Area.

A short distance via road from the trailhead finds the former Crane Mountain lookout site (elevation 8,347 feet). It offers a good, single-site 360-degree view of this exciting neighborhood.

Summer thunder-and-lightning storms, here as elsewhere in the high mountains, should be respected and avoided. When staged in the distance though, they provide grand theater.

Go 12 miles northeast of Lakeview on OR 140 and turn south onto FR 3915 (South Warner Road), heading toward Willow Creek Campground. At the junctions (all well marked), stay on FR 3915; the route becomes gravel. In 10.5 miles, go straight on FR 4011 for the trailhead. In 3.3 miles, the route follows FR 4011.015, a narrow, rocky, 4-wheel-drive, high-clearance vehicle road.

Midway along FR 015 finds a brief trouble spot with a series of mogul-like potholes. The southbound trailhead is on the left-hand side of the road in 2.4 miles; the lookout lies at road's end in 2.6 miles. Trailhead parking is to the side of the road.

The rock-studded, comfortably graded trail journeys south through semi-open forest offering preview looks to the west-southwest and to the east through clearings. Over-the-shoulder looks feature the rocky escarpment of Crane Mountain's lookout point. Large lodgepole pines accent the early full-forest stretches. The open meadows offer broader views, but prove hot for summer trekking. The trail is dry, so carry plenty of water.

At 1 mile and 1.3 miles, the trail affords its finest looks east. The 180-degree vista sweeps Hart and Steens mountains, Big Valley, the patchy forests of nearby slopes, and the Warner Mountains stretching south. At 1.4 miles, the view switches to the western setting, featuring Goose Lake and Mount Shasta.

The mountain holds some of the finest balsamroot meadows in the

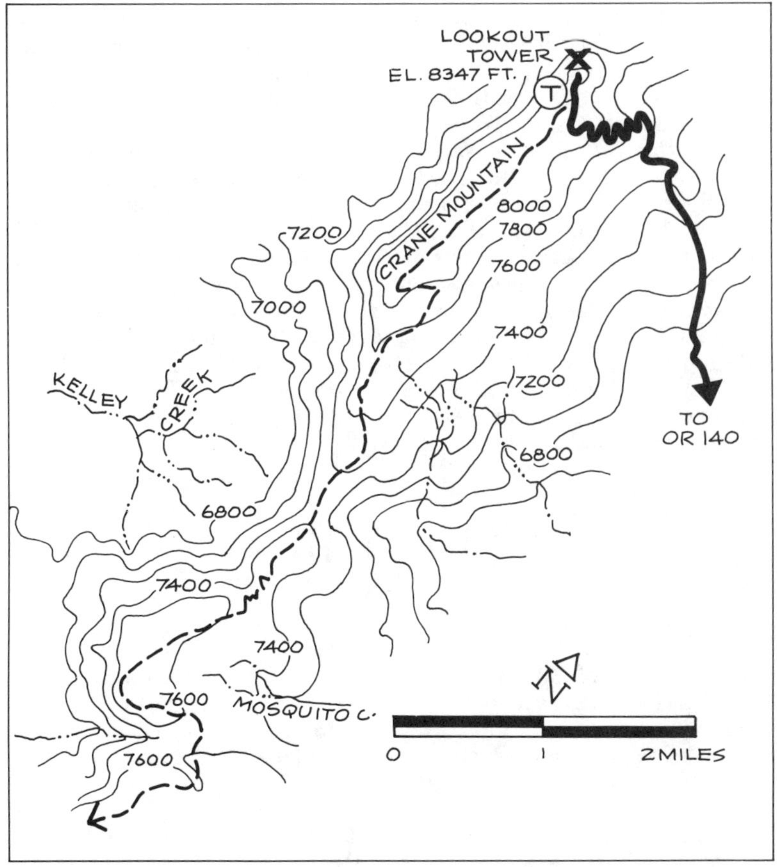

state, which unfold a yellow cheer in mid- to late July. In places, the meadow profusion masks the trail. When the kinnikinnick blooms, it attracts a swirling spectacle of hundreds of orange butterflies.

At 3.1 miles, the trail swings left, leaving the edge of the ridge with its open views of Goose Lake and Mount Shasta. Mountain mahogany, whitebark pine, sage, and balsamroot frame the path as it takes the turn. Western views return by 3.8 miles.

At 4.1 miles, the trail briefly forks; the path to the left holds the finer tour and more forgiving grade. At the junction ahead, stay right; a jeep trail travels to the left. Just beyond finds a campsite on the left with fire ring and makeshift table. After the first couple of rocky trail miles, the openness of the forest holds ample camping opportunity.

At 4.9 miles, the trail bottoms out near a spring. Aspens, a varied ground cover, and mosquitos hint at its presence. Soon, white pines join the forest mix. The alternating course continues with forested rises and descents and arid-meadow saddle crossings.

At 7 miles, the trail passes across a moist, false hellebore–meadow glade; look for the "106" trail sign on an opposite tree, indicating the crossing point. In 0.3 mile, stay right for the trail, soon passing over a seldom-used jeep track, as the National Recreation Trail (NRT) ascends to the California–Oregon border.

Where the trail tops the Warner Crest at 8 miles, venturing west 0.1 mile off-trail through a thin border of twisted whitebark and lodgepole pines finds a grand vista atop a bald spot on the ridge. Ahead, the long-distance trail begins its northern California tour.

From the ridge post, the view pans 180 degrees west. A pretty green lake rests in the drainage to the southwest, which feeds into Goose Lake. Lupine, sage, kinnikinnick, sticky laurel, low whitebarks, and mountain mahogany patch the open slope. Raptors glide below it.

Return as you came for an Oregon-only sampling of the Crane Mountain Trail. For those interested in more Oregon Warner Mountain touring, the trail has been extended to the north. Look for the sign on FR 015 as you head downhill.

78 DESERT TRAIL TO PUEBLO CREST

Distance: 7 miles round trip
Elevation change: 2,000 feet
Difficulty: Strenuous
Season: Late spring through fall
Map: Desert Trail Association's Desert Trail Guide, Pueblo Mountains, Oregon (necessary)
For information: Burns District BLM

This hike offers a sample of the adventure, the challenge, and the rugged wildness found along the extensive Desert Trail, which traverses the southeast corner of the state. The hiking is cross-country between cairns, which stand 3 to 4 feet high and are generally spaced from 0.1 to 0.3 mile apart. The Desert Trail Association's Guide includes a map, compass readings from point to point, and verbal descriptions to keep you on track. Binoculars aid in the search for cairns, though many markers are visible to the eye when panning the skyline.

There is no single direct line between the cairns, though game trails sometimes suggest an easier, tried route. The idea behind the trail was to retain as much as possible the naturalness of the area. Much of the trail falls within the Pueblo Mountain Wilderness Study Area, so low-impact recreation techniques should be exercised to preserve the land's wilderness integrity.

The springs are often far spread. Hikers touring the entire route should plan that a good amount of the carried weight will be water; treat trail sources. For this sampling, pack in the water that you will need and be generous. The desert is harsh, the terrain rugged, and the time and effort to accomplish the distance will be greater than normal.

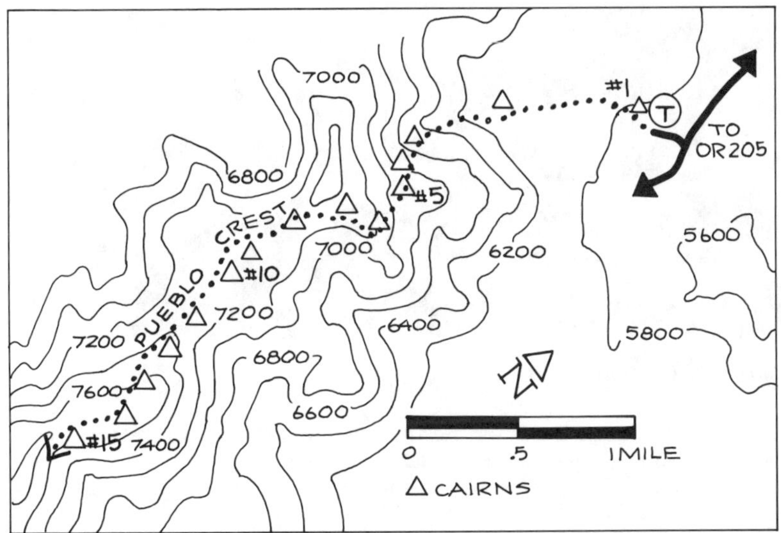

The remoteness of the trail affords great solitude. Often members of the hiking party offer the only human encounter. The sweeping, untouched expanses are humbling, even disquieting. Vistas feature chiseled desert mountains and arid plains; the fault-block geology shows in the landscape's many escarpment faces.

A high-clearance vehicle is required to reach the trailhead. From the junction of OR 78 and OR 205 east of Burns, go south 112 miles on OR 205 to Fields, where services are available. From Fields, continue south on OR 205 another 2.9 miles and turn right on the dirt road marked "Domingo Pass."

In 4.7 miles, the road forks around a ditch; stay left continuing to round the fenceline. In 1.2 miles, the route crosses over a small creek or spring. In another 0.9 mile, turn right onto the overgrown two-track heading west; pay attention to the odometer and keep a sharp eye. Wide areas for parking lie ahead at 0.2 mile and again at 0.4 mile. From the 0.4-mile turnout, hike 100 feet west along the overgrown track to find cairn #1 amid the sage on the right.

From cairn #1, the route journeys south to climb the mountain, reaching cairn #5 atop the saddle just east of the yellow lichen-etched cliffs. The cairns in between suggest a line of travel that crosses the sage flat, rounds to the left of the foothill rise, travels alongside a drainage, and climbs the steep, spare upper slope, skirting rock outcrops and passing through mountain mahogany to tag the saddle at 1.3 miles.

Sagebrush, rabbitbrush, miscellaneous grasses, lupine, paintbrush, and other flowering annuals carpet the flat and the lower slope. Chokecherries line the drainages, while buckwheat, bunchgrass, and mountain mahogany claim the upper mountain reaches.

Jackrabbits, hawks, and deer are the co-travelers. A raptor's large nest occupies a ledge below the lichen-etched cliffs to the west. Views feature

Cairn along Pueblo Crest

Ladycomb Peak and the desert north, east, and south. The terraced, treeless slopes of the expanse possess striking beauty.

From the saddle, the journey continues generally south to top the next saddle at 1.5 miles. Cairn #6 rises to the right; an old-time sheepherder cairn sits atop the cliffs to the left. It was well placed; hikers will find it a familiar skyline friend.

Where the route heads up the next rise, it locates the site of a natural arch housed in a bowl-cut rock (cairn #7). From there, the trail dips traveling a ridge to a saddle on the crest. Bold looks at the Pueblo Mountains engage the hiker.

The Desert Trail now crosses to the Pueblos's west slope, following a game trail just below the crestline. For the next half mile, such trails frequently ease the going. From the trail, the slope drops steeply away to a shadeless frontier spreading as far as the eye can see. At 2.1 miles, the route passes below a cliff wall, which sometimes shadows the trail, bringing welcomed coolness.

Western views grow to include the Rincon Valley, Catlow Rim, Lone and Square mountains, and a distant Hart Mountain with the plateaulands to the southwest.

On a rocky ridge above the 2.5-mile saddle sits cairn #12; it's best to skirt well below this cairn to the west, avoiding most of the rocks. The route then climbs sharply toward cairn #14 atop the crest, which has been long visible. A good game trail simplifies the final uphill; seek it out.

Cairn #14 marks both the end of this tour and the high elevation point for the Desert Trail in the Pueblos (elevation 7,750 feet). It holds excellent views of the rugged Pueblo front range, the jagged skyline to the southeast, Rincon Valley, and Catlow Rim. The view is nearly 360 degrees. Mounting a nearby rise completes the three-state picture of Oregon, California, and Nevada. Bitterroot dots an elegant white finery to the rocky crest in July; phlox, lupine, and buckwheat add color.

From here, hikers also can see the spring below on the east wall where the route will soon travel. Day hikers return as you came, utilizing lessons learned.

79 TWIN PILLARS TRAIL

Distance: 11 miles round trip
Elevation change: 1,500 feet
Difficulty: Strenuous
Season: Spring through fall
Map: USFS Ochoco
For information: Prineville Ranger District

This trail accesses the 17,400-acre Mill Creek Wilderness, applauding its meadows, the forest diversity, a wildflower showcase, the bubbling, clear waters of East Fork Mill Creek, and an exciting rock destination. Multiple creek crossings, some on makeshift footbridges, advance the first half of the journey; a steady climb often touring amid old-growth ponderosa pines characterizes the second half.

From the base of Twin Pillars, the panorama sweeps the rock towers and the wilderness expanse. Clear days add a peek at South Sister in the distant southwest.

From the junction of Main and Third in Prineville, travel 9.2 miles east on US 26. There, turn north on Mill Creek Road/FR 33 heading toward Wildcat Campground; a sign indicates the turn. Go another 10.4 miles to reach the campground via the paved and gravel route. The hike begins at the upstream end of the campground or at the day-use area.

The trail tours a slope of ponderosa pine and mixed firs, above the East Fork Mill Creek. As it draws deeper into the wilderness, it alternately tours forested slope and meadow floor, staying alongside the scenic 5- to 7-foot-wide waterway. At times, remnants of the old wagon road that led

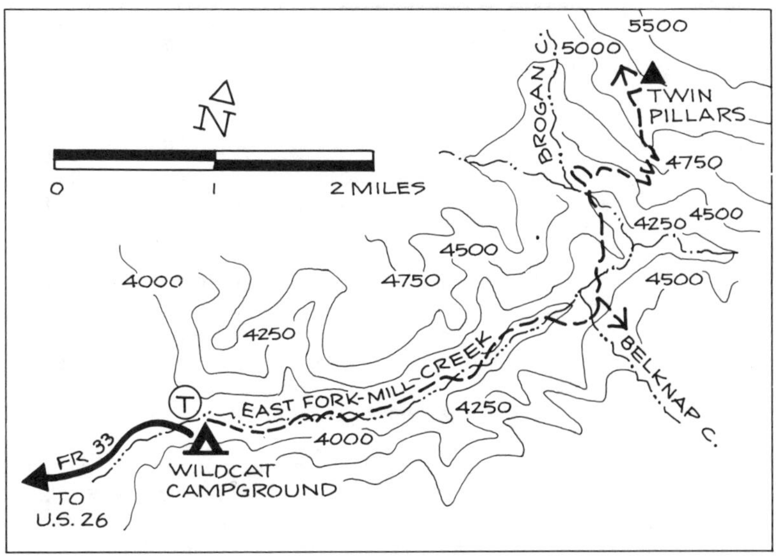

Twin Pillars

to the agate mines at Whistler Springs parallel the creek.

Shooting star, lupine, larkspur, buttercup, and dandelion color the meadow. Heart-leafed arnica and Jacob's ladder add spring accents to the forest. May through June, the wildflower show is at its finest.

The trail slips easily back and forth across the creek in a whimsical game of creek tag. Only a few gentle rises punctuate the first 1.5 miles. At 1.5 miles, the trail climbs, skirting a small gorge, before dipping to reach the Belknap Trail Junction (2.6 miles).

After the final creek crossing at 2.8 miles, the trail undergoes a character change with a fast, steep uphill charge. Don't let it be intimidating; the climb moderates from this initial show of intensity.

The first glimpse of the featured attraction comes at 3.5 miles, as the trail draws over the ridge saddle between Brogan and East Fork Mill creeks. The branches of a nearby ponderosa pine deny clear viewing, but the vista adequately answers one's curiosity about the Pillars. The saddle's grassy slope welcomes the unburdening of the pack for a lengthier appreciation.

The trail rounds the ponderosa pine-dotted slope, offering additional looks at the sturdy, imposing monolith rising above the treetops in the distance. The trail then descends into Brogan Creek Canyon.

At 3.7 miles is the rock-hop crossing of Brogan Creek, a narrow, little stream. This marks the last opportunity to top the water jugs for the final 1,000-foot elevation gain to the rocks. An infestation or disease has stolen many of the creek-area firs.

The trail briefly climbs a low ridge paralleling Brogan Creek upstream, before swinging a wide curve back toward the Pillars. A wonderful, open ponderosa pine forest houses this portion of the tour; many red-trunked ancients mark the forest. The trail climbs steadily.

By 4.3 miles, white firs begin filling in the midstory. Unfelt winds whistle through the treetops. A few arnica, waterleaf, yellow violets, and yarrow add delicate spring colors to the floor.

The trail now climbs via 0.1-mile-long switchbacks. At 4.9 miles, it levels, working its way toward the Pillars. A fuller, mixed forest frames the route, while a few Oregon grape dot an otherwise open, grassy floor.

At 5.25 miles, a sign posted on a trailside tree indicates the steep secondary route heading uphill to Twin Pillars; the primary trail continues straight to an upper trailhead.

The steep slope and loose rock and sand confound the climb to the base of Twin Pillars; exercise care especially when descending. Although this segment is less hospitable than that previously traveled, its shortness and rewarding vista excuse any faults. Juniper and mountain mahogany dot the hot, open slope.

From the rocky base of Twin Pillars, hikers gain a grand, neck-craning view of the tilted rock towers, as well as a fine wilderness panorama featuring the Brogan and East Fork Mill Creek drainages. Wildcat Mountain rises outside the wilderness's southwest boundary.

Green lichens paint the walls of the Twins; swallows circle their lofty crowns. Return as you came.

80 LOOKOUT MOUNTAIN TRAIL

Distance: 14 miles round trip
Elevation change: 3,000 feet
Difficulty: Strenuous
Season: Spring through fall
Map: USGS Lookout Mountain; USFS Ochoco
For information: Big Summit Ranger District

This trail climbs to the top of Lookout Mountain (elevation 7,000 feet) and the site of a former lookout for a grand overlook of the Ochoco neighborhood and the distant Cascade volcanos. The summit plateau affords 360-degree viewing and houses the largest alpine habitat in the entire Ochoco National Forest.

The trail tours the Lookout Mountain Management Area, a primitive-use area. Frequent habitat changes enfold the route. The trail passes through mixed and single-species forest stands, tours wet and dry meadows, rounds arid sagebrush slopes, and travels across a rocky plateau.

With these habitat changes comes a wonderful and varied wildflower show: balsamroot, iris, larkspur, false hellebore, fritillary, and yellow bells, among others. Commonly, hikers come upon meadow-grazing deer or elk.

From Prineville, travel east 15.3 miles on US 26 and bear right at the sign for the Ochoco Creek Ranger Station. Stay on the road (which becomes FR 22), traveling generally northeast, to arrive at the Ochoco Creek Campground in 8 miles. The trail begins at the campground's picnic/day-use area.

From the Ochoco Creek footbridge, the trail passes through a meadow and crosses FR 22 to begin its uphill odyssey. The good-quality trail tours a forest of ponderosa pine and white fir above a floor of grasses, arnica, and lupine. Cones collect against the logs.

By 0.7 mile, the trail is touring a drier meadow floor beneath smaller pines, juniper, and mountain mahogany. Balsamroot dots the meadow. Mileage markers tacked to the trees help hikers monitor their progress.

At 1.1 miles, the trail crosses a grass-overtaken skid road to top a small rise. The route then slowly descends into a select-cut ponderosa pine forest with an iris-spangled meadow floor—one of the finest Oregon iris displays east of the Willamette Valley.

The trail then rolls and dips, crossing small saddles, touring a fuller forest of Douglas and white fir, and passing through a meadow of false hellebore and small juniper. At 2 miles, a side path arrives from a turnout on FR 160 to the right.

Not far from the junction, the uphill grade picks up pace. A wonderful mixture of bird songs and whistles rides the morning air. In the distance, the bugling of an elk sounds a discord.

Nearing the midway point, the trail crosses over the saddle of Duncan Butte, where hikers earn their first views of the summit destination. The trail next contours an eroding slope where agates may be found.

At 4 miles, the trail reaches a log-laced knob, offering a prized view of the distant Three Sisters, Mount Washington, Three Fingered Jack, and

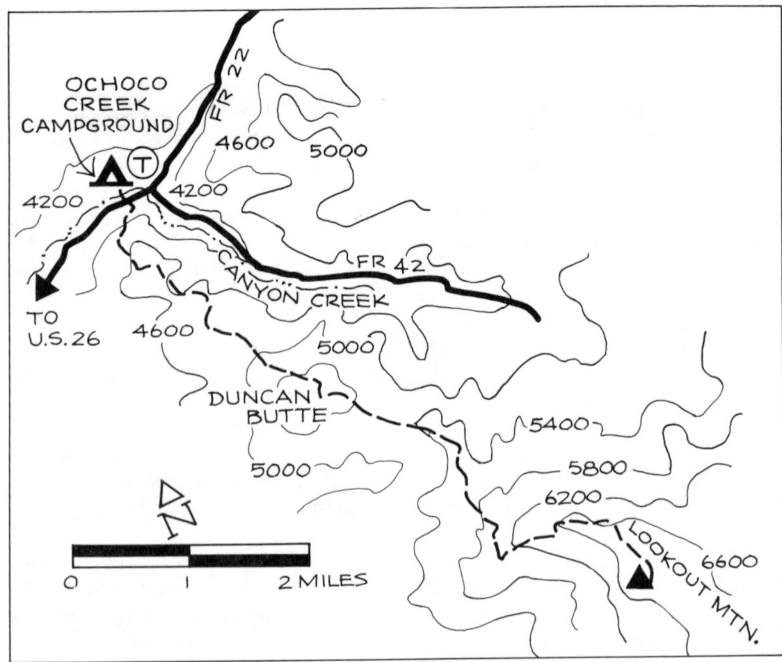

Snow fences

Black and Belknap craters. Below lies the Ochoco Creek drainage.

Rounding below a rocky ridge, touring a drier sagebrush–mountain mahogany slope, the trail affords fine looks at both Mount Jefferson and Duncan Butte. At 5.1 miles, it crosses over a small unreliable spring; plan to pack in the necessary water for a round-trip tour. Ahead, a detour off-trail to a fir-shaded rock outcrop finds another Cascade–Ochoco vista.

The trail then wriggles up through rocky, high-mountain meadows with phlox, lupine, paintbrush, and yarrow and some wind-whipped juniper. Lookout Mountain commands the view with its alternating forest and high-meadow slopes, steep cliffs, and bald summit knobs.

After tagging a grand look at the Three Sisters, the trail climbs and rounds toward the summit's North Point. Crossing to the mountain's other side, the trail travels just below the rocky ridge. Views feature Round Mountain and Big Summit Prairie. Spire-topped firs crowd the slope.

At 6.3 miles, the trail tops Lookout Mountain, with open views to the west and tree-obscured looks east. Below the trail to the west lies a big talus drop.

As the summit broadens, the trail tours the rock-plate mesa floor, following low cairns to an old jeep trail leading to the former lookout. Low sage, phlox, and parsley intersperse the rocks.

Before long, hikers find an unusual pairing of false hellebore and sagebrush. Snow fences break the plateau expanse—remnants from a research project tracking the wind's movement of snow. Yellow bells sprinkle the flat. A few clustering lodgepole pines offer shade and shelter.

Where the road splits, both forks lead to the former lookout site; a low ring of stacked rocks marks the site's perimeter. Return as you came.

81 BLACK CANYON CREEK TRAIL

Distance: 11.2 miles one way (Boeing Field to confluence)
Elevation change: 3,000 feet
Difficulty: Strenuous
Season: Late spring through fall
Map: USGS Aldrich Gulch, Wolf Mountain; USFS Ochoco
For information: Paulina Ranger District
Black Canyon Wilderness Area

This wilderness tour begins alongside Owl Creek. Upon its arrival at Black Canyon, the trail follows Black Canyon Creek downstream, criss-crossing it multiple times. It passes through ancient forest and crosses dry meadow slopes before descending into a rugged, squeezed, cliff-canyon wilderness. The hike concludes at the confluence of Black Canyon Creek and the South Fork John Day River. Wading sneakers earn their transport.

Common sightings may include deer, porcupines, grouse, and hummingbirds. Some of the trees show elk rubbings; others show signs of long-ago beaver activity.

The uppermost trailhead below Wolf Mountain Lookout requires a high-clearance vehicle; nearby Boeing Field off FR 5820 offers a standard-vehicle access.

From Paulina, follow the county highway 4 miles east and bear left at the Y-junction toward Beaver Creek and Rager Ranger Station. In 7 miles, turn right onto FR 58, and in another 1.4 miles, turn left onto improved FR 5810. In 8.7 miles, bear left off FR 5810 onto FR 5820 and follow it northeast to reach the marked Boeing Field Trailhead in a couple of miles.

For the lower trailhead, turn south off US 26 at Dayville onto County Road 42, following the South Fork John Day River. The unmarked trailhead is in 11.8 miles; pavement ends after 1.4 miles. Keep an eye to the west for the canyon mouth which signals both the confluence and the trailhead. Parking is alongside the road; the hike begins with a river fording to reach the trail start on the north bank of Black Canyon Creek.

The hiking spur from Boeing Field follows cairns across a rocky meadow and passes through forest patches to reach Black Canyon Creek Trail in 0.5 mile. To the right finds a similar 1.5-mile forest and meadow tour with one limited view en route to the trailhead below Wolf Mountain; to the left lies the main canyon tour.

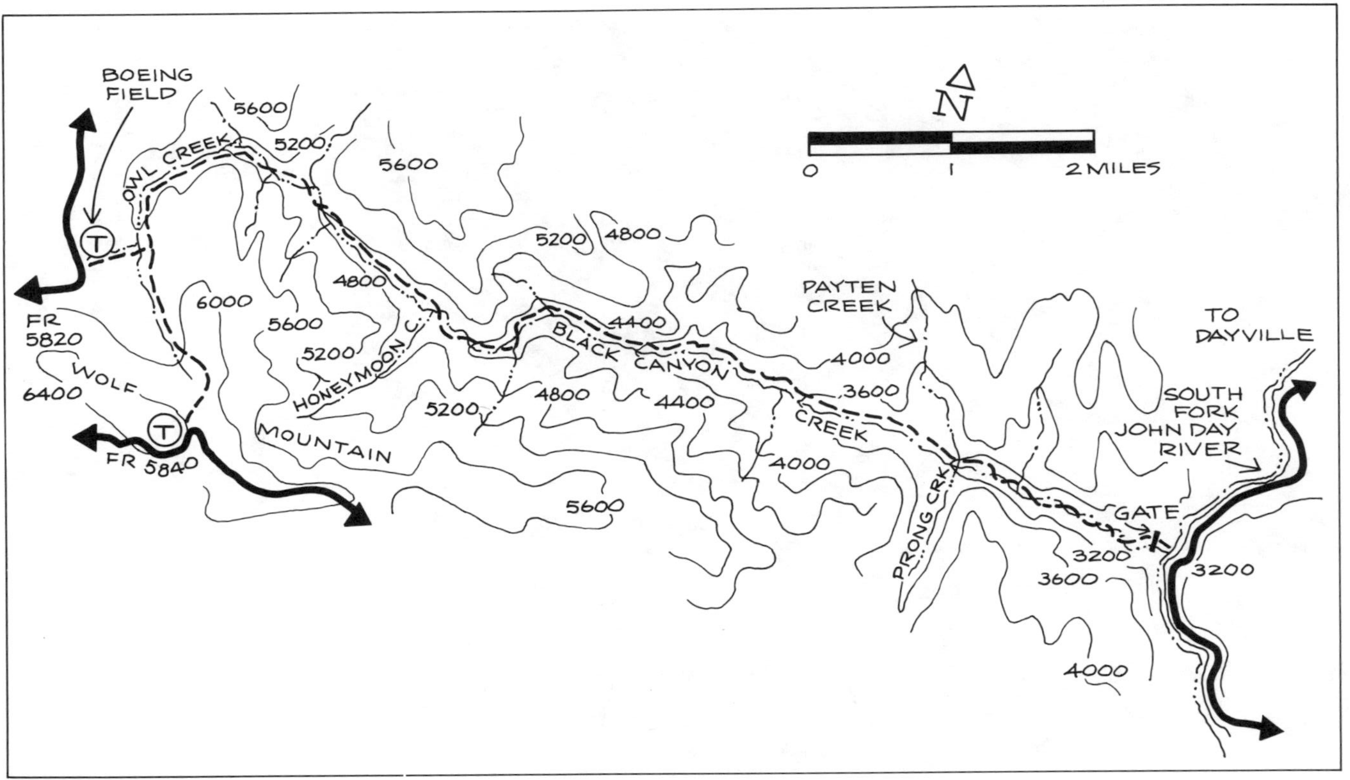
BOEING FIELD
5600
5200
OWL CREEK
5600
N
0
1
2 MILES
5200
4800
4800
6000
FR 5820
5600
5200
HONEYMOON C.
WOLF
6400
FR 5840
MOUNTAIN
4400
BLACK CANYON
PAYTEN CREEK
4000
3600
4800
5200
4400
CREEK
4000
5600
PRONG CRK
TO DAYVILLE
SOUTH FORK JOHN DAY RIVER
GATE
3200
3600
3200
4000

Ponderosa pines

The trail travels along but just away from Owl Creek, enjoying an easy downhill grade passing through open white fir–western larch forest, dry meadows, and moist false hellebore patches. Yellow bells, lungwort, waterleaf, and lupine add springtime color to the meadow floor. Numerous downed logs and snags offer wildlife habitat. At 2.5 miles, the trail crosses Owl Creek near its confluence with Black Canyon Creek.

A downstream tour of Black Canyon Creek finds a more mixed forest with twin flower, arnica, prince's pine, and dwarf huckleberry. Along the route, little-traveled secondary trails branch north and south.

Where the trail travels higher on the slope, it passes beneath old-growth ponderosa pines, larch, and some scenic snags. From the fording near Honeymoon Creek (3.9 miles), the trail briefly tours a riparian area—open, humid, and shrubby.

The crossing site at 4.1 miles is easily missed when hiking down-stream. Look for the small trail sign on the north bank. The creek is about 10 feet wide with a rocky bottom and heavily vegetated sides. Its sound provides a relaxing backdrop throughout the journey.

At 5.5 miles is a primitive camp flat with a fire ring and benches near the markers for the Wheeler–Grant county line. The trail next travels a transition habitat between the canyon-bottom forest and the open-prairie slope with balsamroot and mountain mahogany.

In another mile comes the first of a double-drainage crossing, as the trail wraps around the north canyon wall. Bracken fern meadows and springs precede the arrival at Big Ford, a large, pine-dotted grassland bench above the creek. Cones mix with the grasses.

At 8.3 miles, the trail briefly parallels a fence. Where the path fades in the prairie meadow, stay along the foot of the slope until it again reveals itself. A series of marshy springs follows. Payten Creek (9.1 miles) signals the end of the 5-mile north-bank tour and a return to the game of creek-bank tag.

By 10 miles, the open canyon floor offers views of the layered cliffs above the arid grassland slopes. Pillars, hollows, and irregular, intriguing skylines accent the rock walls. Junipers dot the rim; desert parsley adds yellow splashes to the black rock. The creek is wider, but just as clear. Plants brush the trail; darkened snags record a past fire.

With more creek crossings, the trail leaves the wilderness via a gate at 11.1 miles. The confluence just beyond marks the turnaround site or the final obstacle to a one-way shuttle tour.

In spring, beware ticks in the prairie meadow.

82 NORTH FORK JOHN DAY TRAIL

Distance: 10 miles round trip (to the Crane Creek confluence/ Wagner Gulch)
Elevation change: 700 feet
Difficulty: Moderate
Season: Spring through fall
Map: USGS Trout Meadows; USFS Umatilla
For information: North Fork John Day Ranger District
North Fork John Day Wilderness Area

This hike samples a portion of the 22.9-mile-long wilderness trail which travels the north canyon wall alongside the North Fork John Day Wild and Scenic River. The wilderness area features both historic and present-day mining cabins and claims along with its natural boasts. Gold discoveries in the 1860s first attracted Oregonians to the North Fork John Day region.

Open forest stands of lodgepole and ponderosa pines and western larch frame much of the route. The meadow floors and prairie slopes sport knee-high grasses spangled with spring and summer wildflowers: purples, whites, reds, and yellows.

In the late 1980s, fire raced through the wilderness. Its legacy lingers on the forest face, but the understory is vibrant with renewal. With the openness of the trail and the infrequent river access, carry plenty of water.

Entering from Ukiah, go 39 miles southwest on FR 52. From Granite, travel 8.4 miles north on FRs 73 and 52. The trailhead parking area lies west off FR 52, just north of the North Fork John Day Campground.

From the end of the trailhead road, a narrow path begins the hike with a log crossing of a side creek, a meadow passage, and a log-bridge crossing over the larger Trail Creek. A well-defined trail then leads the way along the north canyon wall, touring a homogeneous lodgepole pine forest with some beetle-kill, many young trees, and no shade.

At 0.5 mile, the trail travels along a river channel isolated from the main flow by a high ridge of tailings—the mining rubble of discarded rock and boulder. Here and elsewhere along the river, the volume of dislodged rock is great.

The river itself is mostly an even band of rushing water, creating small riffles and deep pools, as it spills over a rocky floor. Its scenic bends add to the beauty of the tour.

Gradually, the forest introduces more variety with ponderosa pine, larch, and spruce and with huckleberry, grasses, lupine, wild geranium,

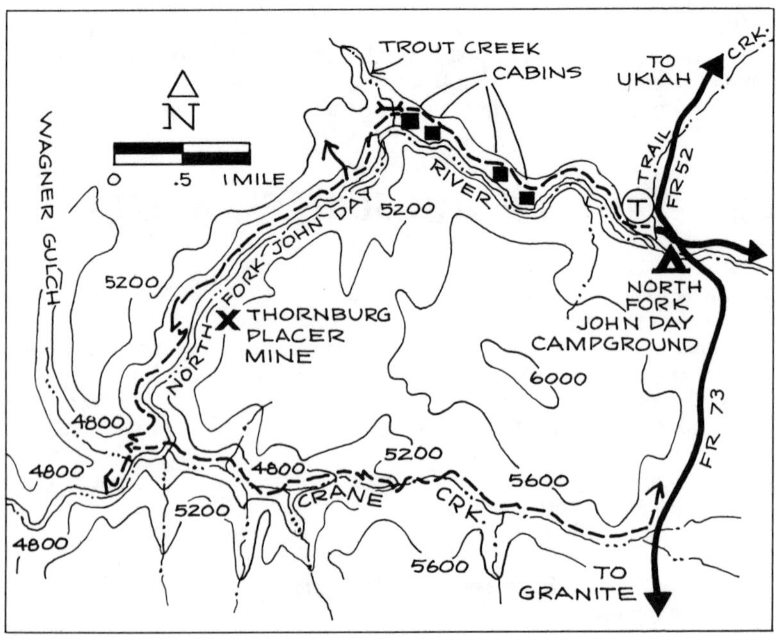

Fire zone, North Fork John Day River

columbine, and a host of other wildflowers. After descending an open slope marked by cliffs and rock outcrops, the trail begins passing the historic and present-day cabins and claims at 1 mile.

The cabins show various sizes and styles of construction and show the common household wares of the miner: makeshift seating; rusting cans, tins, and blades; fry pans and buckets; and crate shelving. Do not disturb the sites. They are either private or otherwise protected under the Antiquities Act.

The trail gently rolls along the slope occasionally offering river overlooks. Huge red larch punctuate the forest near the Trout Creek bridge at 2.6 miles. Here, the trail bids farewell to the mining cabins.

Across the bridge, the trail briefly follows an old two-track. Before long, it enters a fire zone where many of the trees retained their branches. As the trail draws deeper into the burn, the fire's impact is more complete, leaving blackened snags piercing the sky and a helter-skelter of logs.

At 3 miles, the trail reaches a campsite and a junction with old Trail #800. The river trail now bypasses more mining operations and claim markers. Much of the way, the steep slope denies easy river access.

In another mile, the trail skirts above a landslide. A few live ponderosa pines provide patchy shade. Ahead, the trail overlooks where the Thornburg Placer Mine gobbled up sections of hillside in the search for riches.

The trail levels, as it tours along an old mining ditch. Here, the burnt forest promises no shade for many years to come, but yarrow, mallow, paintbrush, and aster present a whimsey of color.

Nearing Wagner Gulch, the trail dips toward the North Fork John Day River–Crane Creek confluence (5 miles). Here, hikers have the option of following the remainder of the 22.9-mile river trail, returning as they came, or fording the North Fork John Day River for a 12.6-mile loop.

For the loop, stage the fording upstream from the North Fork–Crane Creek confluence, reaching the North Fork Crossing Camp on the opposite shore. There, the route curves left to follow the 5.1-mile Crane Creek Trail upstream. This trail is more untamed with a 1,100-foot elevation change. It crisscrosses Crane Creek touring live and burned forest, forest-meadow transition habitat, and long serial meadows.

From the Crane Creek Trail, the loop heads north via the 2.5-mile North Crane Trail. It passes through forest and meadow areas before finding the North Fork John Day River followed by the closing of the loop.

83 ELKHORN CREST–ANTHONY LAKE LOOP

Distance: 9-mile loop (13.6-mile hike adding spurs)
Elevation change: 1,100 feet
Difficulty: Strenuous
Season: Summer through fall
Map: USFS Wallowa–Whitman
For information: Baker Ranger District

This circuit develops an impressive snapshot of the spectacular scenery for which the Anthony Lakes Area is famous. The loop and its spurs travel to and overlook lush high-meadow basins, glacial cirque lakes, craggy ridges, and rugged peaks. In the summertime, alpine wildflowers color meadow, forest, and granite outcrops.

This hike samples the highest trail touring the Blues and dips into the North Fork John Day Wilderness. Celebrated vistas feature the skyline above Anthony Lake, the Grande Ronde Valley, the distant Wallowas,

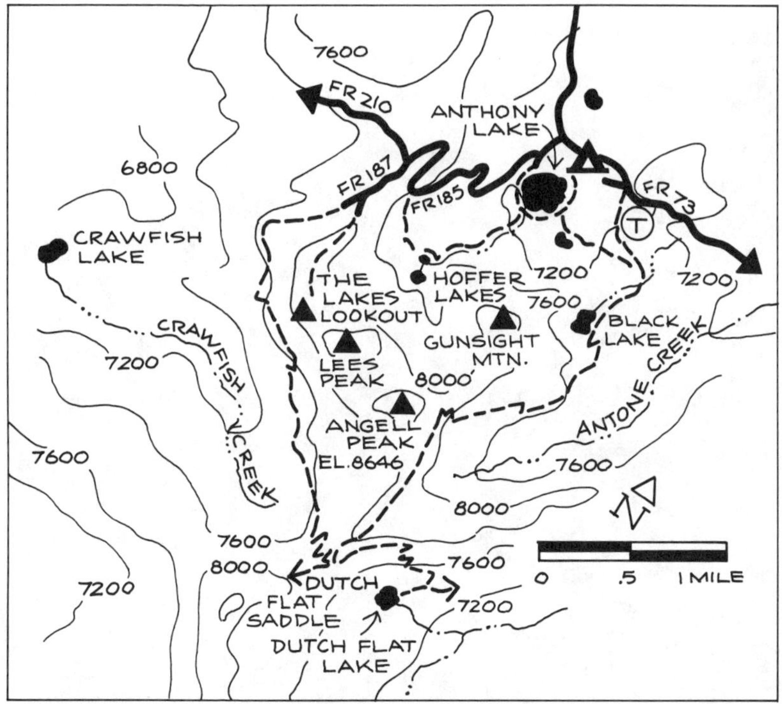

and the endless rolls of the Blue Mountains. Mountain goats live on the remote cliffs of the Elkhorn Crest.

From I-84 north of Baker City, take the North Powder/Anthony Lakes exit and head west on North Powder River Lane. At the junctions, follow the signs to Anthony Lakes, traveling county roads and FR 73 to reach the Elkhorn Crest Trailhead, 19.5 miles from the exit.

A clockwise loop follows the Elkhorn Crest Trail rolling through a boulder-studded, semi-open forest of lodgepole pine, fir, and spruce. Early views focus on Gunsight Mountain. Heather, shooting star, lily, and dwarf huckleberry adorn the meadow floor.

Stay on the Elkhorn Crest Trail; junctions are well marked. Beginning at 0.6 mile, the crest route travels upstream alongside the Black Lake outlet. At 1 mile, it overlooks the lake.

Ahead, the trail takes a couple of quick switchbacks as it begins a steady climb for the crest. Van Patten Butte fills the view, before the trail rounds the slope to travel above the Antone Creek drainage. There, it follows the side of a long granite outcrop. Aster, columbine, paintbrush, monkeyflower, penstemon, and more dot color to the rock.

A couple of brief sets of switchbacks follow as the trail travels below Angell Peak. Overall, the trail is open and sunny, so carry a good water supply. The setting grows more rugged and wild.

Nearing the crest's headwall, the trail overlooks the creek-laced

Anthony Lake and Gunsight Mountain

meadow of Antone drainage and the far-sweeping Powder River drainage. At 2.8 miles, silver snags signal the gateway for the saddle crossing.

On the other side, the southwestern stage stars the Blue Mountains; a scenic pond rests in the basin below the saddle. The trail slowly descends to enter the North Fork John Day Wilderness. Here, the whitebark pine forest shows less floral diversity, but the Clark's nutcrackers are numerous and raucous.

At 3.2 miles, the trail tags a saddle overlooking the Dutch Flat Lake basin and drainage. Ahead finds Dutch Flat Saddle and trail junction: The Elkhorn Crest Trail continues straight offering a long-distance tour, the loop bears right following the Crawfish Basin Trail, and the Dutch Flat Trail beckons a detour left.

The 1.3-mile trail to Dutch Flat Lake descends 600 feet passing through forest and prized wildflower meadows to reach the serene setting of the shallow lake rimmed by meadow, spruce forest, and granite outcrop. Small trout percolate the otherwise still waters.

Forgoing the detour, the Crawfish Basin Trail advances the loop switchbacking downslope passing through an open whitebark pine forest and dry meadows. Mid-August finds the lupine in full bloom. Elkhorn Crest and Crawfish Meadow command the view. At 3.8 miles, the trail contours the slope passing through a fuller, mixed forest interrupted by dry meadows.

At 4.3 miles, the route crosses a small drainage where hikers can usually top the water jugs. A more open lodgepole pine forest follows as the trail rolls along the slope passing below Lee's Peak and the Lakes Lookout. Following a couple of quick switchbacks, the trail leaves the wilderness area and angles up slope to the Crawfish Basin Trailhead at 6 miles.

From that trailhead, strike up the road to a T-junction with FR 187: The loop continues to the left; the Lakes Lookout summit beckons a 1-mile detour to the right. The rocky, tree-skeleton-lined Lakes Lookout Trail climbs 700 feet from FR 187 to claim a 360-degree vista overlooking Crawfish and Anthony lakes, the North Fork John Day Valley, and the Blues, the Elkhorns, and the distant Wallowas.

For the loop alone, follow FR 187 left to find a Y-junction. There, go right on FR 185 passing below the wind fences to travel the east-facing slope above the Anthony Lake Basin. In 0.5 mile, the Hoffer Lakes Trail branches to the right. Hikers may either take the trail or descend via FR 185 to Anthony Lake.

Opting for the trail, the loop descends skirting a meadow basin with views of Angell Peak and Gunsight Mountain to arrive at the two small Hoffer Lakes, situated below Lee's Peak and the Lakes Lookout.

From the lakes basin, the trail descends sharply traveling alongside stair-stepped Parker Creek to arrive at Anthony Lake at 7.7 miles. There, go right on the lakeshore trail bypassing the historic camp and crossing inlet creeks to arrive at the boat launch.

From the southeast end of its parking area leaves the Anthony Lakeshore Tie to the Elkhorn Crest Trail. The route passes through forest and meadow, skirting shallow Lilypad Lake. Gunsight Mountain looms overhead. At the 8.5 mile junction, go left retracing the Elkhorn Crest Trail to the trailhead, closing the 9-mile loop.

84 SQUAW ROCK TRAIL TO INDIAN ROCK LOOKOUT

Distance: 8.8 miles round trip
Elevation change: 1,300 feet
Difficulty: Moderate
Season: Spring through fall

Map: USGS Desolation Butte; USFS Malheur
For information: Long Creek Ranger District
Vinegar Hill–Indian Rock Scenic Area

This hike travels the Greenhorn Mountains, touring dry forest and meadow habitats to reach the top of Indian Rock (elevation 7,353 feet). The lookout affords a grand 360-degree panorama featuring Desolation Butte Lookout to the north, the immediate Vinegar Hill–Indian Rock Scenic Area, and the folded ridges of the Blue Mountain expanse. The

Meadow junction along Squaw Rock Trail

little-traveled trail offers good solitude, exercise, and discovery.

In the meadows spreading at the northern foot of Indian Rock, elk commonly browse. Sightings of deer, grouse, woodpeckers, and raptors often add to a tour. Both an advantage and a drawback to this lookout destination is that it can be accessed by vehicle. While allowing shuttle hiking, it steals from the sense of accomplishment for the round-trip hiker. The site's remoteness, however, preserves the solitude found along the trail.

At Granite, turn west off FR 73 onto FR 10, a good, graveled road. Go 18.8 miles and turn left onto FR 45, which shows a heavier-quality gravel. In 4.2 miles, at the Umatilla–Malheur national forest boundary, the Squaw Rock Trail begins on the left-hand side of the road.

Entering the scenic area, the hike briefly follows an abandoned jeep track framed by lodgepole pine, white fir, and western larch. Where the sign indicates the area is closed to motor vehicles, the foot trail begins to the right. Its mild grade allows an easy stroll.

While the forest is full, it offers only partial shade. Dwarf and low-growing true huckleberry, prince's pine, kinnikinnick, arnica, wild strawberry, and lupine embroider the path's sides. Widely scattered boulders stud the forest floor.

After a slow descent, the trail enters Horse-fly Meadow (1.25 miles), a pretty strip of lush, knee-high grasses. Tree-blazes point the way along its left side. At the end of the meadow, wild onions give the air a distinctive tang.

By 1.5 miles, the trail is traveling the spruce forest alongside the upper reaches of Big Creek; in 0.25 mile, the route crosses the creek. Lewis monkeyflowers, bog orchids, and other wildflowers accent the bank and the meadow tufts dotting the streambed.

Soon after, the trail pulls away from the drainage angling up the forested slope, maintaining a steady, moderate grade for a good cardiovascular workout. Fir with a few larch dominate the forest canopy; arnica and dwarf huckleberry are the primary understory species. When spooked by the approach of hikers, elk thunder through the forest.

At the opening at 2.5 miles, hikers snatch a quick, clear look at Squaw Rock. After which, the forest climb resumes. Nearing the ridgetop, the trail travels beside a long meadow strip. At 3.1 miles, it tops an open, barren rock and dirt outcrop which offers a square-on view of Indian Rock—the hike's destination. Yellow buckwheat and a few phlox dot the outcrop mound. For a shorter hike option, this vista site serves as a nice turnaround destination.

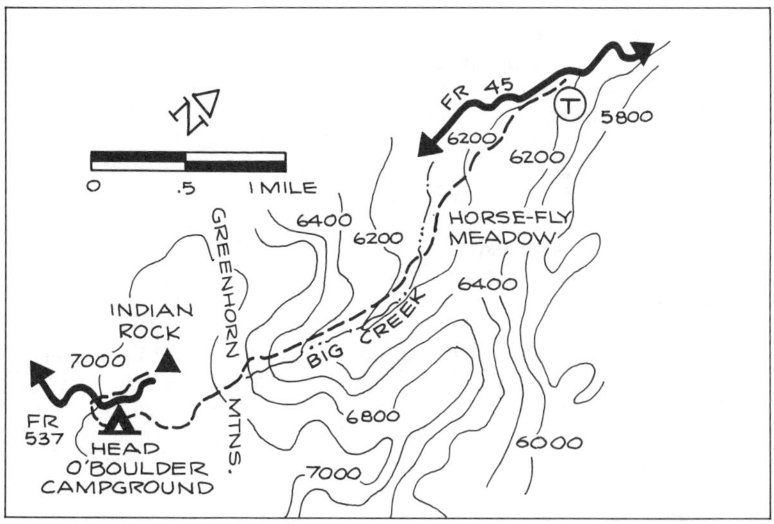

A striking skyline feature, Indian Rock shows a towering cliff outcrop with vertical, columnar-basalt walls and a talus skirt. Atop the rock sits the pale-green fire lookout.

To continue toward the lookout, follow the wooden guide posts past the barren outcrop to the meadow ridge. Here, the trail grows faint; keep an eye out for the occasional tree blazes and posts which point the way along the right-hand side of the meadow. A swath of coneflowers isolates the trail from the main meadow; mole tunnels ripple the ground.

A trail sign is at 3.5 miles. Here, the Squaw Rock Trail turns left heading toward a cairn at the far side of the meadow. To reach the lookout, bear right briefly entering the forest, following a time-softened jeep trail.

From the forest, the jeep trail continues over a rise leaving the scenic area to find the semi-primitive Head O'Boulder Camp and FR 4500.537. Follow the road uphill for 0.25 mile and take the steep 0.2-mile footpath to the summit lookout.

The trail tops Indian Rock at 4.4 miles for a sweeping Blue Mountain panorama. Sagebrush, lupine, yarrow, yellow buckwheat, and other arid plant species ornament the rocky slope. When quenched of the view or chased down by a storm, return as you came.

85 STRAWBERRY MOUNTAIN HIKE

Distance: 7.5 miles round trip
Elevation change: 1,100 feet
Difficulty: Easy to moderate
Season: Summer through fall
Map: USFS Strawberry Mountain Wilderness
For information: Prairie City Ranger District

This hike explores the wilderness skyline en route to the Strawberry Mountain summit (elevation 9,038 feet). The bald summit affords a sweeping 360-degree panorama, including the deep-canyon drainages of the wilderness, Rabbit Ears Mountain, and the expansive John Day Valley. Toward the eastern horizon, the far-reaching view finds the Greenhorn Mountains, the Elkhorn Crest, and the distant Wallowas. Haze, at the time of our visit, left the western horizon a mystery.

The forces of volcanics, faulting, and glacier action shaped this exciting wilderness terrain. Rising south above Little Strawberry Lake, the descriptively named Rabbit Ears Mountain represents the neck of one of the Miocene-era volcanos which deposited the volcanic rock that built up Strawberry Mountain.

From US 395 at Seneca, turn east onto paved FR 16. Go 14.1 miles and turn left (north) onto gravel FR 1640 for the wilderness. In 9.5 miles, the trailhead is found on the left, as the road enters a curve; look for a register and wilderness boundary sign. FR 1640 is the second highest-climbing road in Oregon; Steens Mountain Loop Road ranks first.

The hike begins following the Pine Creek Trail along an abandoned, rocky jeep trail, which surprisingly proves a pleasant wilderness entry.

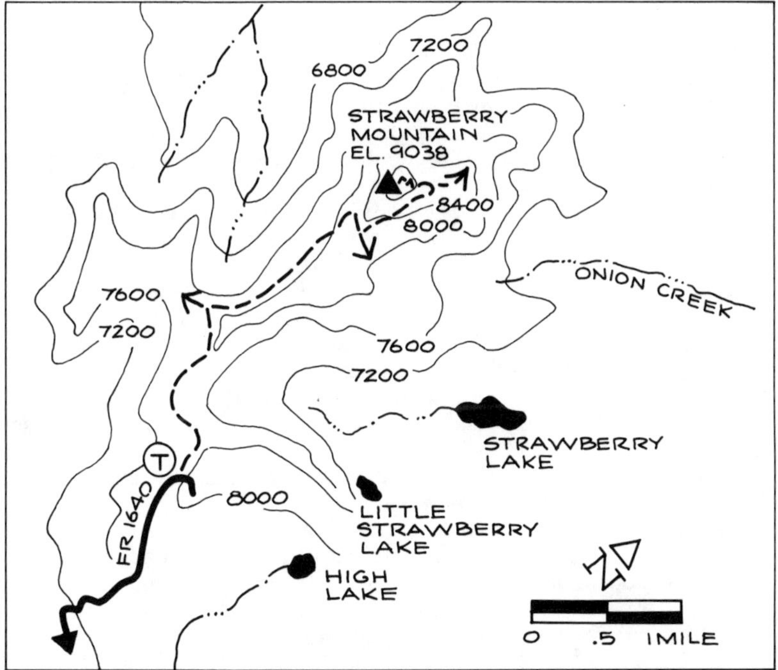

As the flat-touring trail wraps around and below a ridge, it offers an open southern view of the rolling forested hills and the expansive prairie valleys. Ahead, it finds preview looks at Strawberry Mountain and the western wilderness.

Whitebark pine and subalpine fir create an open forest; dry, alpine meadows spread between the stands. Asters, yarrow, paintbrush, lupine, yellow buckwheat, and phlox intermix with the grasses and sagebrush. At 1.2 miles, small springs muddy the slope, introducing Lewis monkeyflowers, bog orchids, columbine, and cow parsnip. For practicality though, consider this a dry trail and carry water.

At the upcoming junction, a bold look at Strawberry Mountain greets the hikers. Here, the Pine Creek Trail descends the west-facing slope; the route to Strawberry Mountain now follows the Onion Creek Trail which curves right, traveling just below the ridge. Grouse, Clark's nutcrackers, and hummingbirds can be seen.

A footpath replaces the jeep trail, as the route contours the steep, moist, west-facing slope above Indian Creek drainage. The trees show a greater girth. By 1.8 miles, talus necks interrupt the earthen path.

Openings offer looks at the rugged headwall of the Indian Creek drainage—a long, lichen-etched cliff. Ahead rises bald, conical, steep-flanked Strawberry Mountain with a look of challenge about it.

Dwarf huckleberry and arnica are the primary forest floor species with the occasional pungent patch of skunk-leafed Jacob's ladder. Approaching the saddle at 2.25 miles, the trail tours an open slope where only a few whitebark pines remain.

After taking a switchback, the trail comes to a junction at 2.7 miles: Downhill to the right lies Strawberry Lake. Striking uphill to the left continues the Strawberry Mountain route.

As the trail travels the opposite side of the saddle, views feature the meadow-drainage mosaic of Onion Creek, the Strawberry and Slide creek drainages, Rabbit Ears, and the John Day Valley far below.

By 2.8 miles, the trail begins rounding the talus middle of Strawberry Mountain. The route passes a few scattered, runty whitebark pines and low, skirted subalpine firs but finds no shade until it reaches a fuller grove of whitebarks on a side ridge at 3.25 miles. The ridge offers a nice cool-down retreat before the final assault on the summit.

It also houses the next junction. Here, the Onion Creek Trail goes right; the hike to Strawberry Mountain continues left. A detour, stepping some 40 feet away from the junction toward the open slope, finds a John Day Country panorama and a grand look at the next ridge over, rugged and cliff-tiered.

A few cairns mark the early switchbacks, as the trail ascends the rocky top of Strawberry, but the route is easy to follow. In places, it crisscrosses segments of the direct line of the old trail.

At 3.75 miles, the trail tags the summit near the site of a former lookout for a top-of-the-world view pulling together all that was seen before. Swallows circle the summit, while hikers look down upon eagles. When ready to surrender the post, retrace your steps.

86 LITTLE MALHEUR RIVER TRAIL

Distance: 16.2 miles round trip
Elevation change: 1,400 feet
Difficulty: Moderate
Season: Spring through fall
Map: USGS Bullrun Rock; USFS Malheur
For information: Prairie City Ranger District

This hike tours Monument Rock Wilderness, tracing the downstream courses of Elk Flat Creek and the creek-sized Little Malheur River. The trail seldom strays far from its watery hosts as it weaves from shore to shore, passing through lodgepole pine forest and across dry meadow habitat. The lower portion of the tour explores a multistory, mixed forest where old-growth ponderosa pine and western larch are the star features. Monument Rock Wilderness boasts one of the finest western larch stands in the state.

Platy, volcanic rock outcrops and cliffs sometimes mark the forest. The shallow-flowing Little Malheur River averages only about 15 feet wide, with most of the crossings easily managed atop stones or logs.

In Prairie City, turn south off US 26 onto Main Street. Pass Depot Park and bear left on Bridge Street to follow County Road 62 southeast out of town. In 7.8 miles, turn left onto FR 13, an improved surface and

Little Malheur River

paved route. After going 11.6 miles, turn left onto FR 1370 for the upper trailhead. In 4 miles, FR 1370 bears left. The marked trailhead lies on the right-hand side of the road in another 0.6 mile; its parking area lies just beyond.

The lower trailhead is more remote and best reached with a high-clearance vehicle. For it, from the FR 13–FR 1370 junction, continue southeast on FRs 13 and 16. Then follow FRs 1672 and 1672.457 upstream along the Little Malheur to reach the wilderness entry (some 38 miles from Prairie City).

A downstream tour begins passing through a thick lodgepole pine forest on the west side of Elk Flat Creek, which is frequently dry by midsummer. A few firs line the drainage. Dwarf huckleberry, lupine, grasses, and wild strawberry color the forest floor.

After entering the Monument Rock Wilderness, the route crosses over Elk Flat Creek at 0.3 mile. This shore shows a more open lodgepole pine forest interspersed by dry meadows of grasses, yarrow, and sagebrush. At 0.75 mile, the hike affords a downstream view of a flat rock atop a bald ridge—Bullrun Rock. Clusters of false hellebore and pockets of standing water now spot the drainage.

As the narrow path rolls along the slope, it wraps around the first outcrop of fractured, platy volcanics at 1.1 miles. A magnificent old-growth, fully branched western larch presides at the end of the outcrop.

Patches of 3- to 4-foot-tall yellow wildflowers provide striking interruptions to the forest stands. In the forest, the wild strawberries offer tasty bites of summer. By 2 miles, Elk Flat Creek loses its intermittent quality becoming a reliable, running creek.

Ahead, the trail crosses a small tributary entering from the east, climbs an open meadow slope, and crosses the Little Malheur River above its confluence with Elk Flat Creek. The forest becomes more mixed, with fir and larch. The Little Malheur proves a clearwater, gurgling companion marked by a few deep holes.

Occasionally the steepness of the slope forces the trail uphill, but it

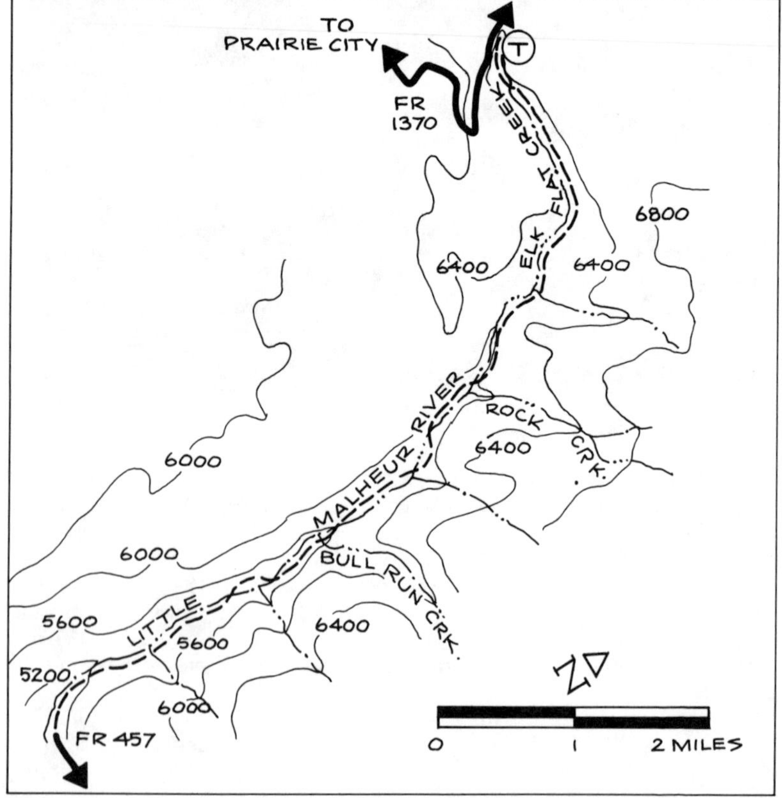

never ventures far from the river. At 2.9 miles, the trail passes below a rock outcrop with a broad talus skirt. Lichen accent the upper rock; small aspen dot the rubble base. Soon, mammoth-sized, old-growth larch trees draw the eyes skyward.

At 3.3 miles, the trail begins its crisscrossing tour of the river. As late summer wears on, the post-ripe dwarf huckleberry emit a sweet aroma. Downstream, the vegetation along shore becomes thicker.

The trail crosses Bullrun Creek at 5.3 miles, where it flows through a gulch. Large ponderosa pines grow nearby and become abundant in number and size on the east slope above the trail. In 0.5 mile, a cliff outcrop abruptly replaces the pine slope.

The trail again crosses the Little Malheur. Here, the river broadens as the valley opens up. Woodpeckers, grouse, flickers, and raptors capture the hiker's attention with flight and sound.

At 6 miles comes the final river crossing. The hike now tours the east shore and slope to reach the wilderness boundary. At 6.5 miles, resecure the gate upon passing; cows have downstream range. Although the vegetation is sparer, the forest tour remains pleasant.

The canyon slope re-emerges, with the trail pushed up on it at 7.2 miles. Small springs muddy the trail, and the forest becomes more open. The wilderness boundary and lower trailhead on FR 1672.457 are at 8.1 miles. Round-trip hikers return as you came.

87 DELINTMENT CREEK LOOP TRAIL

Distance: 5-mile loop
Elevation change: 500 feet
Difficulty: Moderate
Season: Spring through fall
Map: USFS Ochoco
For information: Snow Mountain Ranger District

Flagged in 1991, this developing trail marks the first hiking trail to be established in the Snow Mountain Ranger District. Its construction represents a major stride forward in recognizing the needs of recreationists. A possible stumble in the project occurs along the final leg of the tour: Here, a planned timber sale spills across the trail route. With nearly all the big ponderosa pines marked for removal, it would steal from the natural merit of the hike.

The loop is walkable in its pink-flagged state for a preview of the coming attraction; plans call for a 1994 completion. During the interim, the ranger plans to place some permanent markers, so the trail can be followed more easily. Obstacles include downfalls, fence crossings, and tight squeezes through congested replanted cuts. When touring the undeveloped loop, beware the eye-level dead branches on the white firs.

Delintment Lake, a one-time beaver pond enlarged by an earthen dam, launches the journey. From it, a clockwise loop strings along clear-

Ponderosa pine snag

trickling Delintment Creek, passing through premier, undisturbed stands of ponderosa pines and quiet meadow patches. The loop then swings up a pretty side canyon with a lush meadow bottom and crosses over a select-cut ridge to return to the lake near the campground. A brief shoreline stroll completes the tour.

Future plans call for building an addition to the loop which will create a 9-mile hiking option, following Delintment Creek downstream to its confluence with Silver Creek and following Silver Creek upstream to tag FR 45, west of the Delintment Lake area.

From the USFS offices in Hines, go 0.7 mile west on US 20. There, turn right onto County 127/FR 47 (Burns-Izee Road), toward Delintment and Yellowjacket lakes. The well-marked route passes through the 1990 burn area. In 11.7 miles, turn left onto FR 41 for Delintment Lake. In 26.2 miles, go left, staying on FR 41 to reach the lake in another 4 miles. The trail begins opposite the day parking area that lies next to the dam.

The hike descends a forested slope reaching the headwater springs to Delintment Creek at 0.2 mile. The route then parallels the creek downstream. The open forest floor consists of scattered cones and grasses with wild strawberry and other annuals pushing up through the needlemat.

Boulders accent the gently meandering course of Delintment Creek, a sparkling vein running through a thin meadow strip. White firs dominate the east bank, ponderosa pines the west bank. By 0.75 mile though, the pines win out, dominating both shores.

The reddish-yellow trunks of the mature ponderosas create a grand setting. Arnica spreads beneath them; in late spring and early summer, this plant's yellow bloom brightens the forest.

At 1.1 miles, the trail shows a slight rise as it passes below an impressive boulder field. A few aspens line the creek. From 1.6 to 1.8 miles, the trail crisscrosses Delintment Creek, avoiding the wet meadow sites of springs. Ahead, small meadow patches mark the route—peaceful spots for creekside repose.

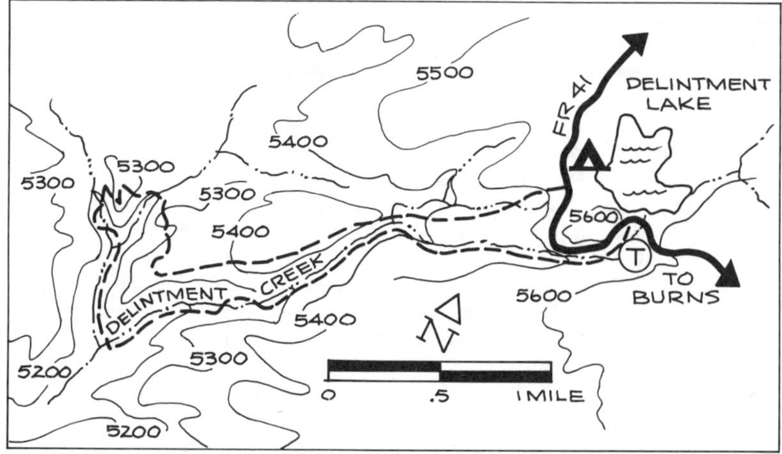

Arriving at a larger meadow, at 2.25 miles, the trail crosses to the west side of the creek. There, it traces the forest-meadow edge reaching a side-creek drainage which it follows upstream, crisscrossing the waters. The side creek is as big as, if not bigger than, the lake-reduced Delintment Creek. A multistory, old-growth pine forest lines its canyon.

At the bottom of a long meadow at 2.9 miles, the trail crosses to the east bank and switchbacks up a low ridge, topping it at 3 miles. The forest along the ridge has been marked for select cutting. The removal of the big pines will create a more open and exposed tour. Bitterbrush dots the ridge. A brief dip into a small drainage depression follows.

Where the trail returns to the ridge, the jungle of small, planted pines denies views. Tightly spaced trees continue to line the route as it travels just below the ridge above the Delintment Creek drainage. By 3.4 miles, a more mixed-age forest forms the canopy. Ahead, the trail tours above and along a boulder shelf.

At 4.1 miles, the trail follows the dividing rise between a partial-cut area and Delintment Creek. The trail then slips into a former cut, now almost meadowlike absent the big trees. Upon crossing a dry gulch, the route slowly climbs toward Delintment Lake. Gradually firs return to the mix.

The trail exits onto FR 41 near the campground. Either go right for a return via the road, or enter the camp and walk back along the shoreline to close the loop at the day parking area at 5 miles.

88 MALHEUR RIVER NATIONAL RECREATION TRAIL

Distance: 7.8 miles one way
Elevation change: 600 feet
Difficulty: Moderate
Season: Late spring through fall
Map: USGS Dollar Basin; USFS Malheur
For information: Prairie City Ranger District

This relaxing downstream tour explores the western canyon slope and forest-meadow shore along a wild segment of the Malheur Wild and Scenic River. A multistory forest of ponderosa and lodgepole pines, western larch, and white fir mounts the slope and shades the trail. The Malheur River, wide and crystalline with a changeable face—sometimes riffling, sometimes smooth and fast-rushing, invites frequent access.

Heart-leafed arnica, lupine, yarrow, waterleaf, and prairie smoke color the forest and meadow floor. Ducks, western tanagers, woodpeckers, Clark's nutcrackers, and kingfishers frequent the river corridor. Deer tracks dot the trail.

In 1826, Peter Skene Ogden of the Hudson's Bay Company dubbed this water "River au Malheur," river of misfortune. It was along this river that a band of Indians found and took the trader's stash of furs and goods.

Balsamroot

From US 395 at Seneca, turn east onto FR 16 and go 16 miles. There, turn right (south) onto FR 1643, a one-lane improved surface road. In 8.4 miles, bear left onto FR 1651 for the Malheur River. Malheur Ford Camp and the upper trailhead lie 1.2 miles ahead.

To reach the lower trailhead, from the junction of FRs 1643 and 1651, stay on FR 1643 for 6 miles. Turn left onto FR 1643.142 for the river trail. A good gravel two-track ends at the trailhead in 1.3 miles.

A downstream tour begins skirting the edge of a moist meadow flat at Malheur Ford to enter a ponderosa pine and fir forest alongside the river. The trail quickly crosses a log cattleguard, as it strings along the bank, slope, and river flat of the west shore. A few buttercups and blue violets sprinkle spring color to the grasses. The open forest affords river glimpses.

At 0.7 mile, the trail climbs and rounds a grassy slope with beautiful, large ponderosa pines. It then dips to a log-and-rock crossing of Flat Creek. A roller-coaster course follows.

River overlooks and up- and down-canyon views come with each rise. At 1.7 miles, where the trail climbs and drifts inland to round an open rocky slope, cross-river views find the high, rugged scree slope of the east canyon wall.

At 2.4 miles, the trail crosses an open talus slope affording nice river views. Where the trail again rises, it overlooks a picturesque stand of red-trunked ponderosa pines on the opposite shore. Drift logs and small meadow islands lend interest to the river course.

The trail next tours a long, narrow flat for a shady trek close to the river; venturing off trail leads to nice riverside retreats. The river maintains an even flow, creating no deep pools. The second portion of the tour is more gently rolling.

Downstream finds an earlier bloom calendar for the wildflowers. Mid-June promises the best overall show.

At 5 miles, the trail enters a burn area, which shows fire's rejuvenating quality. The arnica-meadow floor is vibrant and full, the trail remains semi-shaded, and most of the big trees remain healthy and

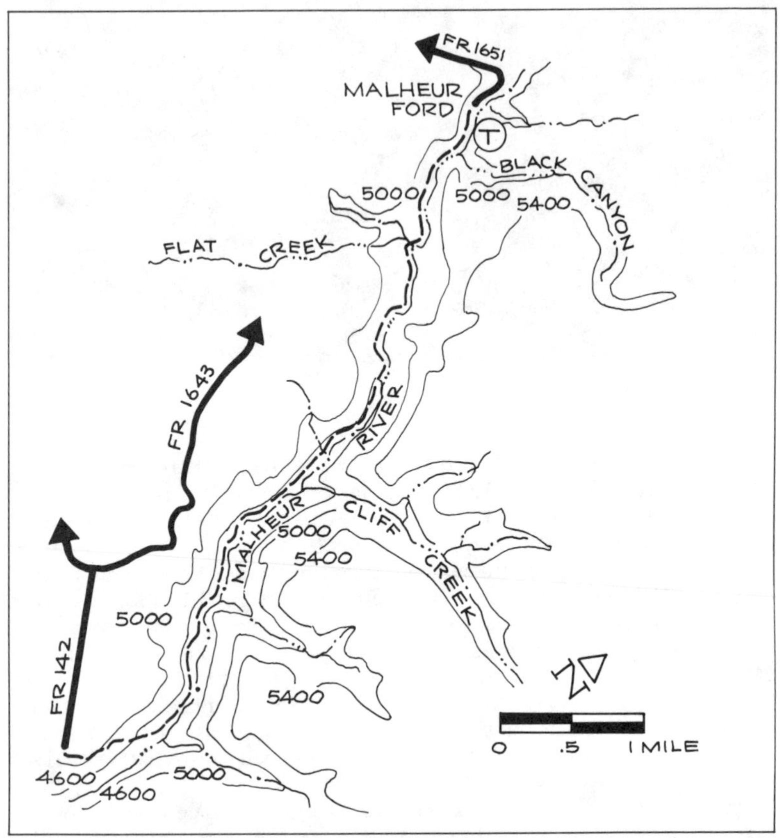

thriving, displaying only slightly darkened trunks. The small firs and pines alone were culled from the forest. At 5.7 miles, the trail leaves the burn.

Where the trail tours the meadow and open forest shore of the broad river flats, it becomes more rock-studded. Wild geraniums dash color to the forest and meadow floor, while wild roses hug the rocky river bank. Both canyon walls now show occasional rock outcrops and slides with rock rims at the crests. The river remains wide and fast-rushing.

At 6.4 miles, the trail grows faint where it passes through a meadow flat, prior to climbing to the canyon plateau. Pines and fir dot the meadow; lupine, small berry bushes, currant, and wild strawberry interweave the grasses. Round-trip hikers may choose to turn around here avoiding the uphill climb.

But the switchback course offers a comfortable ascent. It also holds the finest wildflower show of the tour, climbing from full forest to an open forest of pine, juniper, and mountain mahogany to a grassland–sage prairie slope. The upper reaches command good down-canyon views. At 7.8 miles, the trail meets FR 1643.142. Antelope range the upper plateau.

89 NINEMILE RIDGE TRAIL

Distance: 15.8 miles round trip
Elevation change: 2,700 feet
Difficulty: Strenuous
Season: Late spring through fall

Map: USFS Umatilla
For information: Walla Walla (Washington) Ranger District
North Fork Umatilla Wilderness Area

A west entrance to the wilderness, this hike ascends the southern flank of Ninemile Ridge to reach and travel its spine. The ridge is the dividing landmark between the North Fork Umatilla River and Buck Creek drainages. The west end of the tour explores the bald grassland of the summit ridge, where a few solitary ponderosa pines dot the stage. Farther east, the route alternately passes through mixed forest and grassland.

In late spring and early summer, the tour holds exceptional beauty and discovery with a bonanza of wildflower blooms and flowering shrubs. A kaleidoscope of color—red, pink, yellow, violet, and white—decorates the ridge. Familiar wildflower favorites include paintbrush, clover, lily, desert parsley, lupine, bride's bonnet, and western yarrow.

The frequent vistas encompass the Umatilla Fork drainages, the forested wilderness reaches, and the westward-rolling, bald, grassland ridges marked by deep-cut drainages. The grassland slopes of Ninemile Ridge attract deer. Hikers commonly encounter the animals as they browse or move down the slope to drink. Tracks riddle the trailbed.

From Mission Junction east of Pendleton, head east on Mission Road. At the intersections, follow the route indicated for Gibbon, continuing northeast along the Umatilla River for 27 miles to reach the Umatilla Forks Campground on FR 32. The route is mostly paved, becoming gravel. At the south end of the campground, turn left off FR 32 onto FR

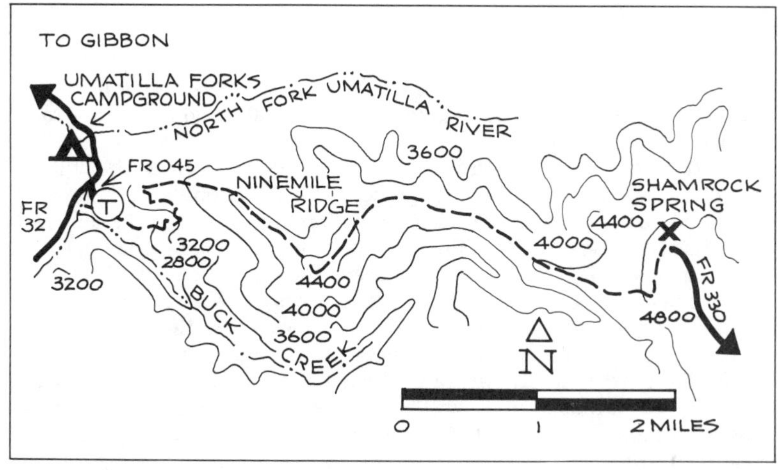

Ninemile Ridge Trail

3200.045, the road indicated for Buck Creek Trail. The Ninemile Ridge Trailhead, marked by an iron stake, lies on the left-hand side of the road just before the parking area.

This trail steps uphill with a steep, steady incline to enter the wilderness. Ocean spray, wild rose, orange honeysuckle, thimbleberry, and alder crowd its bed. At 0.3 mile lies a junction: To the left is the old trail which has been closed to halt erosion; the new trail journeys right.

A long, comfortable switchback crosses the open meadow slope. The rush of Buck Creek echoes from the valley bottom. Where the trail dips into the forested drainages, hikers find a reprieve from the sun.

Graves Butte, Bobsled Ridge, forested Buck Mountain, and the Buck Creek and South Fork Umatilla drainages combine for the early vista. Even the casual naturalist will note dozens of wildflower varieties. Ponderosa pine, fir, and larch dot the mostly bald ridge. A few rock outcrops mark the slope.

At 1.9 miles, the trail begins following the ridgeline. Each new rise offers deeper looks into the heart of the North Fork Umatilla Wilderness. In places, the uphill grade intensifies. Where the trail overlooks Ninemile's forested north face, views feature the North Fork Umatilla drainage and Grouse Mountain.

Just south off the trail at 4 miles are two summit knobs where a 360-degree view unfolds. Building upon previous views, the panorama adds the lookout tower above Spout Springs, High Ridge Lookout, and a greater expanse of the Umatilla River drainage.

The eastbound journey resumes touring the grassy ridgetop. Indian paintbrush, prairie smoke, sunflowers, cat's-ear, and other wildflowers interweave the grasses, soon hiding the trail. Follow the same general line across the broad top to relocate the path.

At 4.4 miles, the trail enters a forest. Trees now mount the slope from both the North Fork Umatilla and Buck Creek drainages stealing the views. White firs rise above a floor of pathfinder, false Solomon's seal, nettles, and wild strawberry.

Where the trail enters a meadow flat, it again vanishes amid the vegetation. Keep a sharp eye; the route descends to enter another forest stand.

Often overgrown and slightly canted, the trail rolls, either following the ridge or contouring the grassland slope of the south flank just below it. By 5.4 miles, the trail is back atop the ridge rounding behind a rock outcrop. From here to the trail's end, the route remains easy to follow.

At 5.8 miles, the trail switches over to the north slope above the North Fork Umatilla, touring a transition shrub–bunchgrass habitat. The many Douglas firs deny open views. After climbing through forest and grassland, the trail leaves the wilderness at 7.7 miles.

Ahead, the footpath gives way to a time-reclaimed two-track. Following the two-track finds a trailhead on FR 3100.330, a high-clearance-vehicle road, near Shamrock Spring (reached via FR 31 off OR 204). Round-trip hikers, return as you came.

90 WENAHA RIVER TRAIL

Distance: 19 miles round trip (to Fairview Bar)
Elevation change: 500 feet
Difficulty: Moderate
Season: Spring through fall
Map: USFS Wenaha–Tucannon Wilderness, Umatilla
For information: Pomeroy (Washington) Ranger District

Housed in a remote deep-cut canyon near the Oregon–Washington border, this upstream hike samples the offering of the long-distance companion trail to the Wenaha Wild and Scenic River. Passing through tableland country, the journey boasts arid grassland and rim-outcrop beauty, outstanding wildlife sightings, and minimal poison ivy for care-

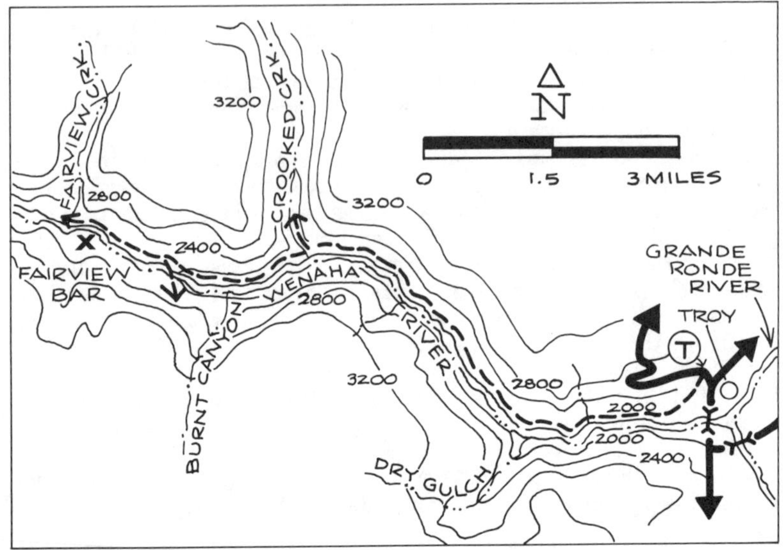

free touring. The route alternately rounds canyon wall and crosses river flats for exciting river overlooks, access, and enjoyment.

Here, hikers find one of the best opportunities anywhere to view bighorn sheep in the wild. Deer, elk, coyote, osprey, dipper, wild fish, various snakes (including rattlesnakes), and a dizzying kaleidoscope of butterflies keep the eyes darting.

From the OR 82–OR 3 junction at Enterprise, go north on OR 3 for 32.6 miles and turn left for Troy, following the well-marked, paved and good gravel route. In 15.2 miles, the route crosses a bridge entering Troy. Pass through town, taking a right toward the Wenaha Game Management Area. In 0.2 mile, turn left toward Pomeroy. The marked trailhead with pull-in parking is found on the left-hand side of the road in 0.3 mile.

The hike passes through a gate and briefly descends a grass-overtaken road to where the footpath begins on the right. The trail then contours the sometimes steep grassland slope of the north canyon wall traveling some 50 to 70 feet above the Wenaha River. Lupine, desert parsley, balsamroot, wild rose, sumac, and the occasional poison ivy plant embroider the trail's sides.

At 0.4 mile, the trail tours an open ponderosa pine flat just removed from the river; more such flats—ideal for camps—follow. Wild geraniums color the meadow. The Wenaha River flows big, wide, riffling, and clear even at flood stage. Down-canyon views stretch to the Grande Ronde River Canyon.

In another mile, the trail rounds above a big pool, passes through a shrubby corridor, and crosses an overgrown jeep track leading to another scenic flat. The north canyon wall undergoes a character change with rocky rims and cliffs parting the grasslands. Small islands divide the river.

The trail now travels some 150 feet above a cottonwood-shaded river flat. At 2.6 miles, it enters Umatilla National Forest opposite Dry Gulch, a conifer-lined drainage. Around the point finds upstream views.

The trail switchbacks to the next flat. Past the 3-mile marker, it travels the bench just above and alongside the river. Here, hikers can top the water jugs; the creeks to this point are unreliable.

The trail again alternates between river flats and pine-dotted arid slopes. At 4.5 miles, resecure the gate upon passing.

Bighorn sheep travel the cliffs and rim outcrops which now rise above the trail, so keep the binoculars handy. Ahead is a small beach opposite a cliff that gives rise to a deep pool. The route continues, touring a gravel bar along the river before entering a riparian corridor with body-brushing shrubs.

Again, the trail climbs, and scree slopes mark the south canyon wall. The river tour alternates between moist, shrubby corridors and open, dry slope. At 5.7 miles, the trail passes beneath a rock overhang. Soon it enters the Wenaha–Tucannon Wilderness.

After traveling the river bank a short while, the trail curves right entering the Crooked Creek Canyon. At 6.5 miles is the Wenaha River–Panjab trail junction. Just ahead, the river trail bears left and

Wenaha River

crosses the Crooked Creek footbridge to enter an open forest with patchy heart-leafed arnica.

Up river, the trail passes below vertical rock walls; the opposite slope is more forested. At 7.7 miles, the trail is opposite Burnt Canyon.

Ahead begins a wonderful forest tour featuring firs and pines above a floor of arnica, wild strawberry, and various other forest species. A few snags and decaying logs accent the forest. Along shore, the cottonwoods provide a pleasing setting.

At 8.3 miles, the trail rounds a point for a great up-canyon view. It then travels along a cliff and scree slope to enter a grassy flat. Hoodoo Trail branches left to cross the river and climb the south canyon wall.

At Fairview Bar (9.5 miles), ponderosa pines dot the grass and bracken fern flats that line both banks along a braided stretch of river. Fording is possible during low waters. Hikers may either continue upstream to the headwater forks or return as they came.

91 DAVIS AND SWAMP CREEKS LOOP

Distance: 19.4 miles round trip
Elevation change: 1,800 feet
Difficulty: Strenuous
Season: Late spring through fall
Map: USFS Wallowa–Whitman
For information: Wallowa Valley Ranger District

Despite paralleling two creeks, this hike is primarily a canyon-ridge tour with only a few treasured creekside moments. The hillsides unfold a fine and varied wildflower show, including one of the finest balsamroot displays in the state. The end of May and early June herald the blooms. In places, mature ponderosa pines bring an added beauty to the hike.

Vistas feature the creek drainages, Starvation and Miller ridges, the Wallowas, and an Idaho high-peak chain, the Seven Devils. Deer, coyotes, woodpeckers, grouse, and raptors number among the possible wildlife sightings.

Use care when touring this livestock-ruptured foot trail, one can easily turn an ankle. Also, be sure to resecure the gates upon passing.

From the OR 82–OR 3 junction at Enterprise, go north on OR 3 for 20.3 miles and turn right to enter an unmarked trailhead parking area with pit toilets.

From the parking area, the hike follows a jeep trail heading north, passing through a pine–fir–grassland complex. In 100 feet, bear right onto FR 3000.174. Where it forks, again go right. A trail sign marks the route as you pass through the gate.

A rocky, narrow footpath now descends the meadow slope toward Davis Creek, named in honor of the 1870s Indian interpreter, James Davis. Early views feature Starvation Ridge with the Seven Devils and high Wallowas in the distance. Desert parsley, arnica, giant-headed clo-

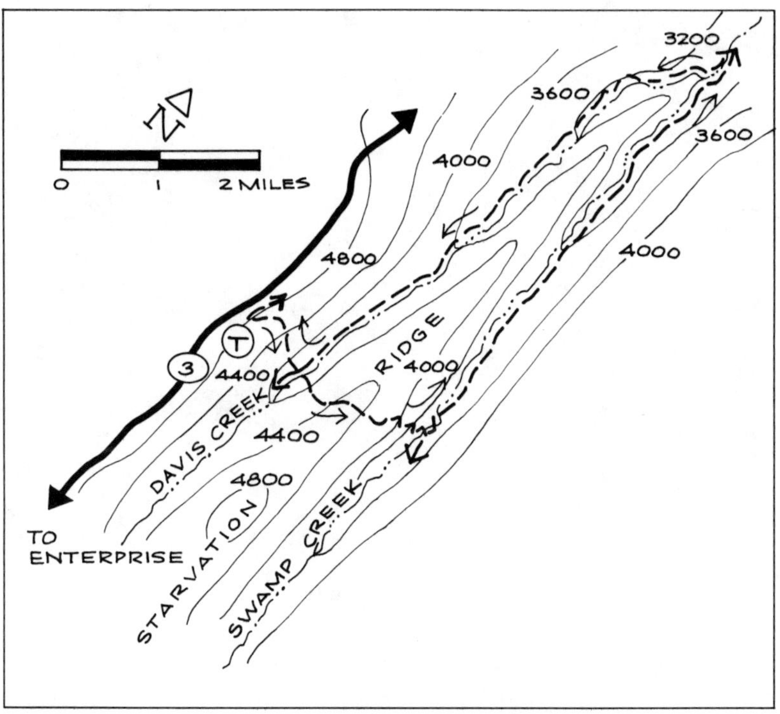

ver, lupine, and larkspur contribute to the wildflower show. The trail is sometimes overgrown, often rugged. Carry plenty of water.

After switchbacking downslope, the trail crosses a small drainage and descends through a tight forest of small white fir, larch, and a few pine. Violets and fairy slippers sprinkle the floor.

At 1.8 miles is the Chico–Davis Creek trail junction. For a counterclockwise loop, ford Davis Creek to climb Starvation Ridge.

The ridge offers an open forest and meadow tour. In 0.5 mile, the trail briefly grows faint but remains traceable. Nearing the ridgetop, at 2.7 miles, the trail meets and crosses over a jeep trail. Ridgetop views feature the Swamp and Davis creek drainages and Miller Ridge. Snags dot the neighboring hillsides hinting at past fires.

The trail then skirts a cairn, passes between two pines, and descends into the Swamp Creek drainage. In the spring, a rich green decks the slopes; by fall, they wear a golden robe.

At 3.3 miles, the trail crosses over a side ridge gaining down-canyon views and overlooks of a meandering Swamp Creek. The descent quickens as the trail approaches the forested foot of the slope.

Past the gate at 4.6 miles, the trail becomes overgrown. Head downstream following the fenceline, while keeping an eye out toward Swamp Creek for a trail sign tacked to a ponderosa pine (4.7 miles). From the sign, follow the Swamp Creek Trail downstream; the route passes through a corral to ford the creek at 5 miles.

The meadow at the confluence of Swamp and Davis creeks below Miller Ridge

At the foot of Miller Ridge, the hike now follows a fence alongside Swamp Creek. While the fence protects the streambed from grazers, it denies hikers a convenient creek and meadow access. Ahead, the route passes through a burn; most of the big trees survived. At 6.5 miles, the area of the burn grows spotty as the trail approaches a beautiful stand of red-trunked ponderosa pines. The gate at 8.3 miles signals the end to both the fence and the burn. Pines now dominate the foot of Miller Ridge.

At the north end of Starvation Ridge (10.3 miles), the hiker finds the staging site for the Swamp and Davis creek fordings. After fording Swamp Creek, ford Davis Creek slightly upstream from the confluence; look for a path streaking uphill toward a rusted, blank sign tacked to a ponderosa pine. At this dual-fording site, hikers arriving from either direction must do some scouting to stay on course.

An upstream Davis Creek tour then rounds the slope some 100 feet above the creekbed alternately touring open meadow and semi-open forest. On the opposite shore rises Starvation Ridge. Intermittent creeks slice the trail, but are not dependable water sources. Past the gate at 11.4 miles is another burn area. Before long, the trail tours some 200 feet above the creek as the slope drops steeply to the canyon floor.

By 14 miles, the trail draws closer to the creek. For a short while, it follows an old skid road, wonderfully overgrown, shaded, and welcomely flat, offering creek overlooks. In another 1.5 miles, the trail travels the flat just above the creek, alternately passing through forest and lush meadow. From the Chico–Davis Creek trail junction at 17.6 miles, strike uphill to return to the trailhead.

92 SNAKE RIVER TRAIL

Distance: 17.5 miles one way (Lookout Creek to Dug Bar, with boat-shuttle to Lookout Creek)
Elevation change: 900 feet
Difficulty: Strenuous
Season: Spring through fall
Map: USFS Hells Canyon National Recreation Area
For information: Hells Canyon National Recreation Area

This is the most untamed, rugged, and adventurous trail of the book. Exploring the west canyon wall above the Snake Wild and Scenic River, it offers tremendous solitude, spectacular arid scenery, wildlife sightings, and a look at early homestead efforts. Upstream from Dug Bar finds the historic Nez Perce Crossing, where the tribe forded a flooding Snake River without casualty, during the forced exodus of 1877.

Hot and remote, the hike explores Hells Canyon Wilderness, traveling grassland slopes dotted with prickly pear cactus and colored with wildflowers. Canyon scenery of both Oregon and Idaho can be appreciated on this hike. Raptors, deer, elk, and coyotes add excitement to the tour; snakes are a concern on the overgrown trail.

Due to the trail's condition and length (48 miles), chartering a boat trip to an upstream trailhead for a one-way hike back to Dug Bar offers the best way to see more of the trail, including riverside segments. Charters stop for hikers at Dug Bar and drop them off at points upstream

A cross-canyon view of the Snake River and the Idaho wall of Hells Canyon

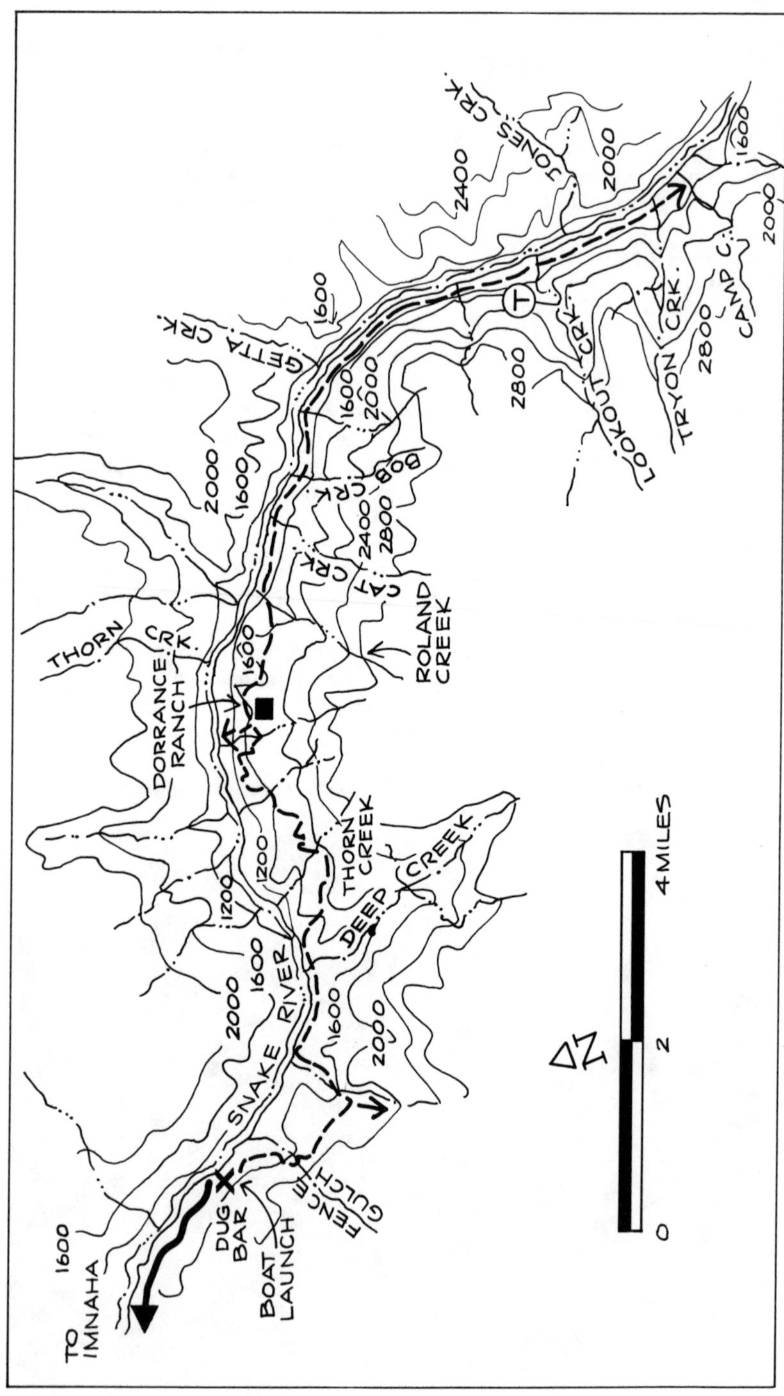
TO IMNAHA
1600
DUG BAR
BOAT LAUNCH
FENCE GULCH
SNAKE RIVER
2000
1600
1600
2000
DEEP CREEK
THORN CREEK
1200
1200
DORRANCE RANCH
THORN CRK.
1600
ROLAND CREEK
CAT CRK.
2400
2800
BOB CRK.
2000
1600
1600
2000
GETTA CRK.
1600
2800
LOOKOUT CRK.
TRYON CRK.
2800
CAMP C.
2000
1600
2400
JONES CRK.
2000
N
0
2
4 MILES

where the trail nears the river. Contact the Recreation Area headquarters or the Lewiston, Idaho Chamber of Commerce for the names of charter services.

From Imnaha, go northeast on Lower Imnaha Road, a slow, winding route not recommended for low-clearance vehicles. In 30 miles, pass through the gate to reach the Dug Bar boat launch and the Snake River Trail. From here, hikers may be picked up for their pre-arranged boat shuttle or strike uphill to the left of the corral, where the trail begins some 40 feet above a stair-stepped fence crossing.

For the shuttle option, above the gravel beach at Lookout Creek, a downstream hike begins at the Tryon Creek–Snake River trail junction. Traveling about 30 to 50 feet above the river, the often-overgrown path rounds rock outcrops and arid slopes of bunchgrass, cacti, foxtail barley, sumac, poison ivy, and wildflowers.

River views feature slow bends, riffles, and a few rapids and eddies; the shoreline is mostly rocky, marked by a few gravel bars and beaches. At 2.7 miles, the trail tops a cliff overlooking the water for a grand Snake River view.

Where the trail passes an old mining tunnel opposite the Getta Creek confluence on the Idaho shore, take the uphill path to skirt a private property; do not take the lower trail. Above the property, the trail crosses a grassy plateau. Keep a sharp eye as the path often disappears amid the tall grasses and sumac.

From the gate at 3.5 miles, cairns angle downhill pointing the way. In less than a mile, the route crosses Bob Creek. Between Lookout and Bob creeks, a few lone pines dot the slope. At the mouth of Bob, the gentle slope allows easy river access for the refilling of water jugs. The creeks to this point are unreliable.

Soon, a tree-shaded table and open-air pit toilet occupy a grassy bench above the river—a nice stop or campsite. The trail then pulls steeply uphill rounding a ranch, touring a grassland where the trail is again overgrown. At 5 miles, the more reliable waters of Cat Creek attract deer.

The trail remains far above the river. The Idaho canyon wall shows a low rim of columnar basalt. After crossing Roland Creek at 5.8 miles, the trail heads left, climbing the steep, open slope of its north bank. Elk frequent this remote canyon. The grade eases as the trail rounds the left side of a low knoll.

By 7.4 miles, the trail bypasses the outbuildings of abandoned Dorrance Ranch. At the junction on the saddle, the Snake River Trail bears left staying uphill, wrapping arid slopes and crossing unreliable creeks.

Beyond Thorn Creek, the trail tops a saddle at 10.9 miles and begins a steep descent crisscrossing Trail Gulch. With the trail's grade and surface, it's easy to lose your footing; be careful. Poison ivy further confounds the going.

In another mile, the trail again tours a slope some 50 feet above the river. Here, the Snake River is much more gorge-like with rugged canyon walls. Deep Creek, a 15-foot-wide, tumbling stream requires fording. It's a good place to rinse off any poison ivy oils. At 13 miles is another established campsite.

From the Dug Creek crossing, the Snake River Trail heads inland zigzagging up Dug Creek Canyon. Overgrown, the trail requires bushwhacking. Nettles and poison ivy add to the burden.

Departing the creek canyon at 14.4 miles, the trail again tours a grassland toward the saddle above Dug Bar. At the upcoming junction, the Lord Flat Trail heads left up canyon; the Snake River Trail climbs east to the saddle, often traveling alongside horse tracks.

After topping the saddle, the trail begins a slope-rounding, slow descent. It crosses Fence Gulch and collects upstream views before leaving the wilderness at 16.3 miles. A steep descent then leads to Dug Bar Ranch. At 17.2 miles, a stairstep over the fence at the end of the corral finds an open grassland, where the overgrown trail continues toward the boat launch and the end of the tour.

93 OREGON TRAIL–BLUE MOUNTAIN CROSSING

Distance: 0.5-mile interpretive loop, with additional mile of interlocking trail
Elevation change: Minimal
Difficulty: Easy
Season: Spring through fall
Map: USFS Wallowa–Whitman
For information: La Grande Ranger District

The merit of this hike lies not in its challenge nor in its level of adventure, but in its historical significance. This newly constructed interpretive trail (scheduled for a 1993 opening) explores a Blue Mountain remnant of one of this country's most celebrated trails—the Oregon Trail.

Time has softly touched this portion of the original overland wagon route that threw open the doors to western settlement. Here, the ruts of the ox-drawn wagons remain locked in the land. Rediscovered just a few years ago, this 4-mile segment represents some of an estimated 12 to 15 percent of the Oregon Trail that exists in a near-pristine state.

Written records indicate that between the years 1842 and 1870, some 215,000 pioneers passed along this way on their 2,000-mile-long odyssey from Independence, Missouri, to the fertile lands of Oregon's Willamette Valley.

In 1842, Doctor Elijah White and a professional guide succeeded in leading the first organized party of some 100 settlers to western Oregon, blazing the route for one of the greatest human migrations of all time. The year 1843 released the human tide.

Along the Blue Mountain passage, steep grades, a scarcity of water, muddy quagmires, and choking dust tested the trip-weary pioneers, but the rugged beauty of these forested slopes did not escape their notice. Diary entries praising the area's scenery date back to 1836 and missionary Narcissa Whitman, the first white woman to cross the plains.

Forest at Blue Mountain Crossing

The interpretive trail leads a new set of feet along the historic route, providing a physical tie to our pioneer past. It also gives note to the 1860s stage coach route which runs not a hundred yards away. In the area, remnants of log decks record the horse-team era. While not visited by the trail, they may be observed by the keen eye.

From I-84, 12 miles northwest of La Grande, take the Spring Creek Exit (248), and follow OR 30 west toward Kamela. In 0.5 mile, turn right onto FR 600. Signs for Blue Mountain Crossing now point the way to the trailhead in 2.5 miles. Where FR 600 passes under the interstate highway, there's a 13-foot clearance.

A picnic area is located 0.5 mile west of the trailhead. Restrooms and drinking water are available at both sites.

Six interpretation panels mark the all-ability Blue Mountain Crossing loop. The panels combine western art, diary excerpts, and historical records, drawing the present-day visitor back in time.

Two side loops branch from the main trail; they also travel along a portion of the Oregon National Historic Trail. To the east is the Independence Loop, which shows a slightly more difficult grade. To the west is the Oregon City Loop.

Early-day logging has transformed the modern-day trail setting from the thick ancient forests that captured the imagination of the pioneer. Small trees have invaded the trail, and the mature ponderosa pines today are less than 100 years old.

The area shows forests of spruce, fir, and larch, with much of the national historic trail traveling through a semi-open forest of ponderosa pine and fir. Grasses interwoven with wildflowers spill across the floor. In the summer, the yellow and purple blooms of the lupine unite with the yellow blooms of the arnica to create a bright hillside tapestry. Balsamroot and yarrow grow on the more open slopes.

The long depression of the Oregon Trail shows ruts 6 to 12 inches deep, with some more deeply eroded. In places, a single weather-carved trench now replaces the parallel tracks. For the protection of this fragile, irreplaceable resource, hikers are reminded to stay on the constructed paths at all times.

The sounds of I-84 drift to the site, but the forest blocks the highway from view. Elk range the surrounding hillsides; sometimes their passage takes them across the historic route.

Two other Oregon sites offer access to portions of the original overland route. Located 5 miles east of Baker City off OR 86, Flagstaff Hill overlooks the nation's longest unbroken stretch of pristine wagon ruts that are easily accessible. Keeney Pass, a Bureau of Land Management (BLM) interpretive site located 8 miles south of Vale on County Road 570, marks an Oregon Trail location where the wagon ruts have eroded, forming a deep, U-shaped gully.

South of the Keeney Pass, concrete posts mark the Oregon Trail over which modern-day Lytle Boulevard crisscrosses. Beside the road, visitors catch glimpses of the wagon wheel impressions semi-hidden by the sagebrush.

94 MAXWELL LAKE TRAIL

Distance: 8.6 miles round trip
Elevation change: 2,300 feet
Difficulty: Strenuous
Season: Summer through fall
Map: USFS Eagle Cap Wilderness
For information: Eagle Cap Ranger District

This hard-climbing, split-character trail celebrates the beauty and bounty of the Eagle Cap Wilderness. The first 3 miles climb steadily and comfortably via switchbacks. The final mileage features a steep climb followed by a quick, steep descent to reach the lake basin. Much of the way, the trail overlooks the rugged, high-walled Lostine River Canyon.

The Maxwell Lake Basin supplies a spellbinding climax to the journey. The high-mountain pool sits in a deep bowl rimmed by granite ridges, conical peaks, and steep, sliding rock slopes dotted by subalpine firs and whitebark pines.

To reach this trail, at Lostine, turn south off OR 82 at the sign for Lostine River Campgrounds. This is Lostine River Road/FR 8210, a paved and gravel route; follow it south for 16.6 miles. The trail leaves Shady Campground at the Lostine River footbridge.

Across the bridge, the trail enters a mixed fir and spruce forest with bride's bonnet and wind flower dotting the rich forest mat. At 0.1 mile lies a stone-step crossing over the creek that drains Maxwell Lake. Alders, rocky mountain maple, nettles, false hellebore, and few quaking as-

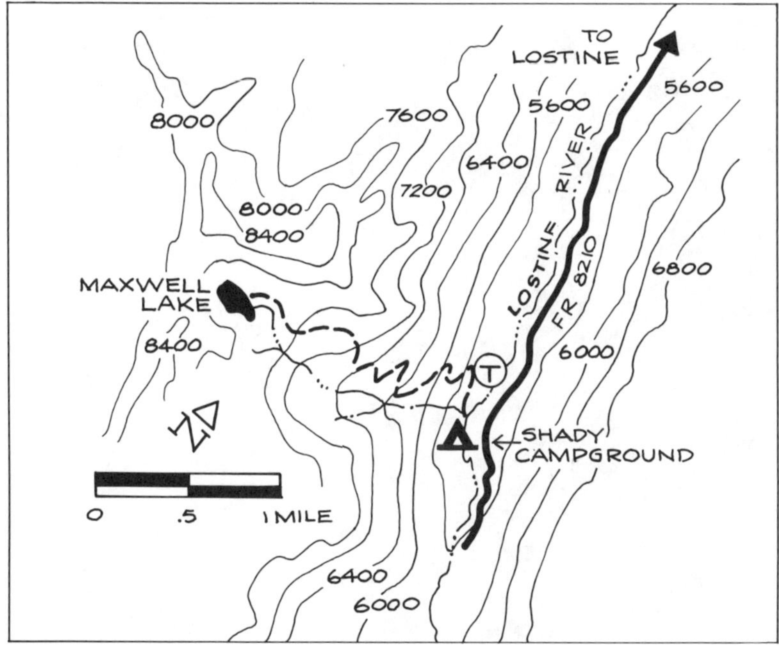

pen crowd the drainages. The zigzagging route alternates between forest stands and steep, open meadow and shrub slopes.

By 0.9 mile, up-canyon views begin to build. A few ponderosa pines intermix with the white and Douglas firs. At 1.6 miles, the trail crosses another drainage usually large enough to allow the topping of water jugs. Smaller, trickling drainages follow. At times, the trail affords glimpses of the Lostine River glistening up from its forested canyon bottom; the river's song is the hiker's companion.

By 2.5 miles, the view stretches well up the East Fork Lostine drainage; the angle prevents a west canyon view. On the steep flank of Hurricane Divide (Lostine's east canyon wall), a small drainage with a thin sparkling stream catches the eye. The forest mix undergoes a change showing more subalpine fir and lodgepole pine.

At 3 miles the trail transforms into a rugged haul. By now, the sounds of the Lostine River have quieted. At the upcoming small drainage, hikers find another reliable water source. Over-the-shoulder views find Hurricane Divide, the Lostine River drainage, the dividing ridge to the headwater forks, and the distant snow-etched peaks. Dwarf and true huckleberry and arnica color the forest floor.

The trail enters a soggy meadow at 3.5 miles, bypassing a sign for Maxwell Lake. False hellebore, pearly everlasting, and wild onion grow throughout the meadow.

Afterwards, the trail alternately travels moist meadow and open forest

Maxwell Lake

habitats. Whitebark pines and subalpine fir create the patchy cloak of the upper slope. Impressive ridges with rugged granite crests rise above the trail. Clark's nutcrackers are active at the higher reaches, where deer are commonly sighted.

The trail sharply ascends an open, boulder-studded meadow slope with white phlox, yellow buckwheat, grasses, and a few trees. At 4 miles, it tops a rise for an exciting Maxwell Lake Basin greeting. The lake, the rich meadow of its outlet drainage, and the high surrounding horseshoe ridge patched by lingering snows unite in alpine glory.

A steep descent follows, tagging the lake at 4.3 miles. A small central island accents the blue oval, while the clear waters reveal a boulder bottom. The many granite outcrops of shore limit the number of campsites, thus preserving the setting's tranquillity. Mountain heather and thin grassy tufts spot the ground beneath the low pines and firs and the silver snags.

A smaller lake lies southeast of the main lake. To reach it, cross the small outlet creek, mount the granite outcrop, and round toward the south ridge wall. Located beneath the rocky apron of the ridge, this lake's waters are deep enough to support trout.

During the short fair-weather season, pikas streak back and forth across the slope above the lake, as they gather grasses for their winter larders. Often, they halt, piping shrill commands to fellow harvesters.

When ready to leave, return as you came.

95 WEST FORK LOSTINE–BLUE LAKE TRAIL

Distance: 15 miles round trip (to Blue Lake)
Elevation change: 2,000 feet
Difficulty: Moderate
Season: Summer through fall
Map: USFS Eagle Cap Wilderness
For information: Eagle Cap Ranger District

This wilderness tour travels the forest and meadow habitats of the West Fork Lostine River drainage to visit Minam and Blue lakes. Along the way, the hiker discovers the high mountain scenery: steep-flanked ridges, spired forests, snow fields, and seasonal waterfalls.

Minam is the larger lake, a long, oval water below the aptly dubbed Brown Mountain. A small earthen dam at its south end diverted its natural drainage, but little detracts from the overall lake beauty. Blue Lake, a pretty, rounded, mid-sized lake nestled at the foot of a sharp-spined, white ridge offers the more intimate, tranquil retreat. Pockets of spire-shaped firs rim the lake and dot the ridge.

For this hike, at Lostine, turn south off OR 82 at the sign for Lostine River Campgrounds. This is Lostine River Road/FR 8210, a paved and gravel route; follow it south for 17.5 miles. The trail leaves the south end of Two Pan Campground.

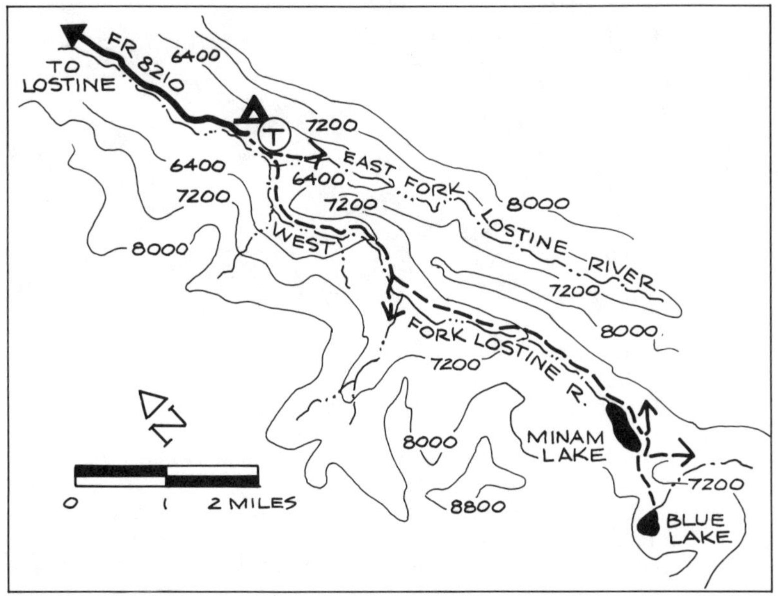

West Fork Lostine River Trail

Upon entering the Eagle Cap Wilderness, a right begins the West Fork hike. This trail crosses the East Fork Lostine River, gathers views of the West Fork, then drifts inland, climbing parallel to but removed from the river. A choked forest of thin, tall Engelmann spruce, alder, white fir, western larch, and lodgepole pine frames the path. Aster, thimbleberry, twisted stalk, and bride's bonnet mat the floor.

The trail passes granite outcrops, a boulder-littered slope with huckleberry bushes, and a mature forest stand. By 1.1 miles, it tours just above the West Fork. High Wallowa splendor enfolds the trail.

A talus slope announces the 2.8-mile junction. A right begins the Copper Creek Trail. Go left to continue the West Fork hike toward Minam and Blue lakes.

From the junction, the West Fork Trail climbs, skirting a spruce-dotted meadow. It then travels a granite boulder slope at the foot of the dividing ridge to the Lostine River forks. At times, yellow buckwheat, paintbrush, and other meadow vegetation add splashes of color to the rock. By 3.1 miles, the trail offers open views of the Copper Creek drainage, Elkhorn Peak, and the neighboring tree-studded, dome-shaped granite peaks.

With a fluctuating grade, the trail now passes in and out of the lodgepole pine–subalpine fir forest for sunnier trekking. Views come frequently. Touring a wildflower and grass meadow at 4.1 miles, the trail draws closer to the West Fork Lostine River.

Ahead is a string of stones, which normally allows a dry crossing of the now creek-sized West Fork; early season hikers may have to wade. Alternately passing through meadow and subalpine fir forest, the trail overlooks the slow-coursing upstream waters of the West Fork flowing through a long meadow.

A couple of drainage crossings follow, and at 5.3 miles, the trail again crosses the West Fork to return to a forest tour. Soon, the hike delivers the first looks at Brown Mountain; its reddish-brown volcanic crest suggests its name. At 5.8 miles, the trail reaches Minam Lake at its outlet.

In the morning, Minam Lake's glassy waters reflect Brown Mountain Ridge and the distant southern peaks. The large lake shows a varied shore with areas of forest, meadow, and white granite boulders. Its waters are surprisingly shallow.

The primary trail rounds the east slope well above the lake; camper footpaths tour closer to shore. With the forest-meadow floor being soft and moist, avoid off-trail excursions.

Near the earthen dam at 6.5 miles lies a three-way junction: To the left finds the popular lakes basin area of the Wallowas, the route straight ahead leads to the long-distance Minam River Trail, and the Blue Lake Trail crosses atop the dam and bears left.

The trail to Blue Lake climbs quickly away, heading southwest along a similar steep, open-forested slope. At 6.8 miles, it crosses a small creek drainage. Beyond lies a swath of trees tumbled by either avalanche or wind storm. The trail continues climbing.

At 7.5 miles, Blue Lake presents its deep, shimmering, cobalt waters. White granite boulders, pockets of subalpine fir, and a few weathered whitebark pines accent its shore. Rising above the basin is a striking, steep, white ridge with a razor-edged skyline and a talus skirt. Meadow drainages mark its flank.

Trout rise up through the clear waters to snap insects from the surface. Clark's nutcrackers seem to chide lake visitors. Retrace your steps when ready to return.

96 WEST FORK WALLOWA–LAKES BASIN LOOP HIKE

Distance: 30 miles round trip
Elevation change: 3,900 feet
Difficulty: Strenuous
Season: Summer through fall
Map: USFS Eagle Cap Wilderness
For information: Eagle Cap Ranger District

Among Eagle Cap's prized system of trails, this hike stands out as the premier route for discovering the Wallowa Mountain majesty. The tour takes visitors along a deep, chiseled river drainage, through high-country meadows, past six magnificent high lakes, and up and over steep, rugged ridges. Granite domes, spired forests, snow fields, alpine wildflower fields, chilly stream crossings, and snow-melt falls mark the way. Mountain goats, deer, elk, and coyotes play the cards of surprise. Despite the loop's popularity, the lakeshores remain remarkably uncrowded and pristine.

To reach the trailhead, follow OR 82 south from Joseph to the road's end in 6.5 miles. The trail begins opposite the South Day Use of Wallowa Lake State Park.

The route climbs, heading straight at the 0.25-mile junction to parallel the West Fork Wallowa River into the Eagle Cap Wilderness. As concessions conduct horse strings along the first two miles, the early route can be dusty. Mountain goats range the steep flanks of Hurwal Divide, rising to the west. Where the trail nears the river, side trails wiggle to its bank.

At the 2.8-mile junction, the West Fork Trail again heads straight, continuing up the river canyon. Beyond the Adam Creek–West Fork confluence, western views feature Craig Mountain. Traveling well above the river, the steady-climbing trail continues crossing side drainages, passing through meadows, and touring high-elevation forests of lodgepole pine, spruce, and fir.

At 6 miles, it reaches the extensive Six Mile Meadow and the lakes basin loop junction. Campsites occupy the forest edge. A cliff rises to the east.

Going straight begins a clockwise tour of the loop, still following the clear-running West Fork upstream. At 7.75 miles, the trail affords looks at the light-colored peaks at the head of the canyon. The climb picks up, with each stride drawing the hiker deeper into the high-country spell. Morning hikers may startle elk grazing in the alpine meadows.

Beginning at 8.5 miles, the trail switchbacks up slope to round a rocky ridge. It bypasses Polaris Pass Trail, skirts a cliff overlooking a West Fork gorge, and crosses the high meadow below the east canyon wall to arrive at a wet crossing of the West Fork at 9.75 miles.

The trail next switchbacks into forest as it journeys toward the canyon head. At 10.5 miles is Frazier Lake—a green, shallow pool in a scenic bowl framed by an impressive ridge. Thin chutes and snow patches mark the ridge; a smaller lake sits at its foot.

Horseshoe Lake

At the upcoming junction, the loop heads right climbing toward Glacier Pass. It tours granite boulder slopes with small tree pockets and overlooks the meadow drainage of the ribbony West Fork to the southwest. With granite domes marking the ridges, the terrain resembles the High Sierras. After 12.5 miles, Eagle Cap becomes a familiar tour landmark.

At 13 miles, the loop tags Glacier Lake, clear, deep, and blue below Eagle Cap Ridge. Fed by Benson Glacier, it's a heart-stopping beauty. Small islands punctuate the lake, which boasts an irregular shoreline. Rock slides and snowfields spill from the cliff to its waters, while wildflowers sprinkle its meadow shore. As the trail climbs away from Glacier Lake, hikers view a smaller, upper lake.

At 13.75 miles, the trail tops Glacier Pass, the high point on the trail. A sharp descent on a mostly exposed slope follows, offering down-canyon views of the East Fork Lostine River and Hurricane Creek along with

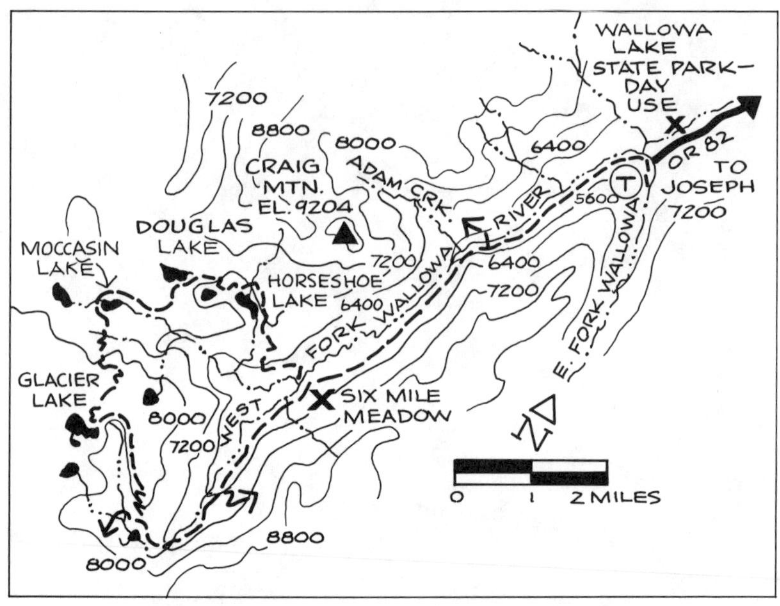

Hurricane Divide, Matterhorn, and Moccasin and Mirror lakes.

In another mile, the trail crosses a drainage to enter a series of downhill switchbacks, still steeply descending. After the next drainage, the trail strings through meadows of wildflowers and wild onion to top a rise at 16 miles. Where it dips, it finds Moccasin Lake, far larger and deeper than it appeared from above.

The lake water here and elsewhere in the basin drops sharply away from the rocky shelves of shore. All the lakes are hypnotic and blue.

Continue the loop with a crossing at the neck of the lake's two water bodies; an isthmus and a rocky walkway usually keep the feet dry. At the junction on the opposite shore, the loop curves right rounding the northwest slope above Moccasin Lake. Cross-lake views feature Eagle Cap's fractured face and Glacier Pass.

The semi-forested route then rolls between lake basins, bearing right at the junctions. It tags Douglas Lake (18 miles), Lee Lake (19 miles), and Horseshoe Lake (20 miles). After traveling the length of Horseshoe Lake, the trail begins another major descent.

Branding the steep, forested slope, a series of steady switchbacks eases the descent. Occasional views feature the West Fork Canyon. At 23.5 miles, the trail meets and follows Lake Creek downstream, passing through a stand of dead spruce. At the confluence, the route crosses the footbridges of Lake Creek and the West Fork.

The trail then edges the north end of Six Mile Meadow to close the loop at the 24-mile junction. For the return to the trailhead, go left following the West Fork Wallowa downstream for 6 miles.

97 SUMMIT RIDGE TRAIL

Distance: 16.6 miles round trip (to Lookout Mountain)
Elevation change: 1,400 feet
Difficulty: Strenuous
Season: Summer through fall
Map: USFS Hells Canyon National Recreation Area
For information: Hells Canyon National Recreation Area

Traveling the ridgeline that marks the Hells Canyon Wilderness boundary for the western rim, this trail drifts into and out of the official wilds. Along the way, it offers sweeping vistas of the deep-cut canyons of the Imnaha and Snake rivers. The neighborhood is one of flat-topped bluffs, bald, furrowed flanks, and tree-lined canyons. In the distance, hikers can see the high Wallowas to the southwest and Idaho's Seven Devils (a high-peak chain) to the east. The hike ends at the Lookout Mountain summit (elevation 6,792 feet).

The trail strings across arid grassland steppes sprinkled with wildflowers. Peak blooms arrive in early summer. By autumn, asters and Indian paintbrush alone bring color to the russet-gold grassland gone to seed. Ponderosa pine and mixed firs patch the slopes.

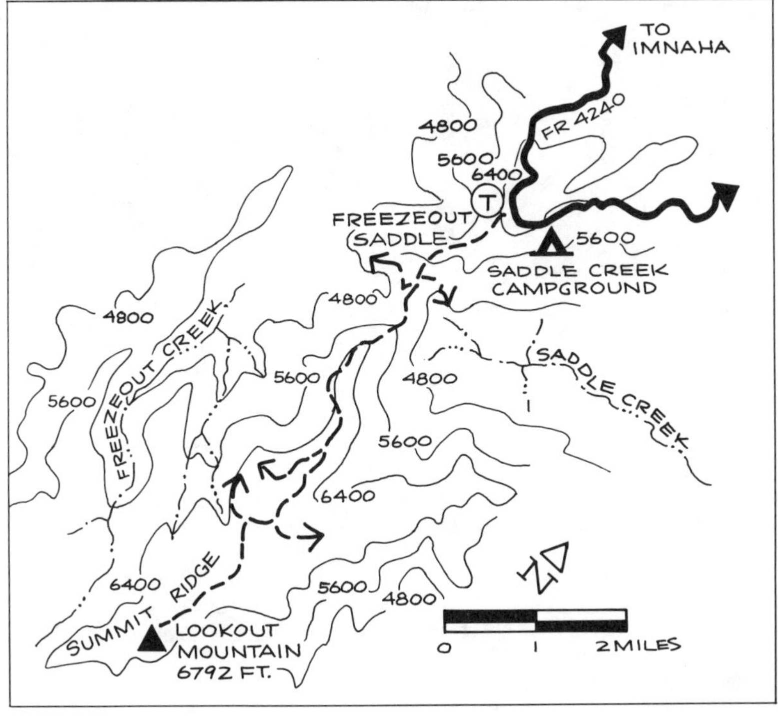

Balsamroot–bunchgrass slope

Hells Canyon, wild and remote, calls to the adventurous, not the foolhardy. Hikers should exercise the full caution warranted by this rugged terrain, and always carry plenty of water.

From Imnaha, go 16.9 miles southeast on FR 4240, Hat Point Road, to find the marked trailhead on the right, past Granny Vista. Parking is to the side of the road or uphill at Saddle Creek Camp. The single-lane gravel road with turnouts is winding and narrow, not suitable for low-clearance vehicles.

The Summit Ridge Trail, also known as the Western Rim National Recreation Trail, wraps around and down the ridge, offering early views of the Imnaha River and Freezeout Creek drainages. The open, dry slope features buckwheat, bunchgrass, and fireweed. A few fir and scenic snags dot the route.

By 0.4 mile, the view expands to include the Snake River Canyon. Keep an eye out at 0.8 mile, as the trail angles back to descend the east side of the slope overlooking the Snake. Do not take the path ahead.

At 1.4 miles, the trail crosses back onto the west side of the ridge, traveling a beautiful native bunchgrass meadow to Freezeout Saddle and its junction (2 miles). Here, one trail follows the ridge to McGraw Lookout; another heads left following Saddle Creek to the Snake River; and a third heads to the right toward Freezeout Road. The southeastern view features smooth-sided Bear Mountain and the rocky cliffs of Black Mountain. Continue straight for the ridge tour.

The trail now travels a bunchgrass–wildflower slope just below the ridge on the Freezeout Canyon side. The trail is less rocky and canted, affording more comfort. At 2.5 miles, where the ridge dips down to the trail, hikers overlook two drainages and snare a peek at Hat Point Lookout.

The trail then contours and ascends the northeast side of the ridge. While more trees enter the setting, the route remains mostly open. Rocky Mountain maple, oceanspray, and currant add to the vegetation mix.

At 3.2 miles, the trail rounds a bend exchanging views of Freezeout Saddle for views of the Freezeout Creek and Imnaha River drainages. The snowy-crowned Wallowas offer a striking skyline above the arid Imnaha rim. The trail continues alternately touring grassland and a tree–shrub transition habitat.

As the trail is again about to change direction, a superb over-the-shoulder view looks straight down Freezeout Creek to its confluence with the Imnaha River. The rugged enclosing rims present a classic Hells Canyon image. Around the bend, views feature the Western Rim.

Beginning at 4.9 miles, the trail travels below an old burn marked by standing snags and scattered young evergreens. Near a large ponderosa pine, the trail passes through a fence opening. At 5.1 miles is the junction with trail #1763; the rim trail continues straight ahead. Here, too, hikers find a prized view of Idaho's Seven Devils rising up behind Bear Mountain.

The trail then crosses over to the west slope, touring just below the ridge. The fire's impact lingers with snags and downed logs. Sprouting groves of aspen dot the way.

At the 6.1-mile junction, the Bear Mountain Trail heads left; the Summit Ridge Trail bears right. Below the junction, a seasonal spring feeds a greener area with false hellebore and buttercups.

Soon, an old jeep trail continues the journey, entering an area logged prior to the fire. At 6.4 miles, it meets another jeep trail: Downhill to the right is Mark's Cabin; the ridge route continues bearing left. By 6.9 miles, the rolling tour returns to an undisturbed grassland with lilies, sagebrush, and lupine; high-elevation firs and spruce mark its edge.

With a gentle ascent, the trail claims the Lookout Mountain summit at 8.3 miles. A radio tower occupies this mostly tree-flanked site. Although the trees deny a 360-degree view, the top does afford a fine Hells Canyon look. Return as you came.

98 MAIN EAGLE TRAIL

Distance: 15 miles round trip
Elevation change: 2,500 feet
Difficulty: Strenuous
Season: Summer through fall
Map: USFS Eagle Cap Wilderness
For information: Eagle Cap Ranger District

While this southern gateway to the Eagle Cap Wilderness finds a slightly different alpine wilderness from that seen along the trails entering from the north, the mountain splendor is not diminished. The trail passes through forest and open meadow-shrub habitats offering grand vistas of the rugged cliffs, granite peaks, and high, hanging lake basins.

Climax to the hike, the Eagle Lake Basin is nothing short of spectacular: bold, wild, rugged, and exposed. Sparkling up from the bowl is gem-like Eagle Lake—big, clear, and blue-green, but the rock dam at its outlet steals from the naturalness of its stage. Cloud changes bring an added excitement to the setting.

From Medical Springs on OR 203, turn southeast on Collins Road/Eagle Creek Drive, heading toward Boulder Park. The route soon changes to a wide, good gravel surface. After going 1.6 miles, turn left onto FR 67 and go 13.5 miles. There, turn left onto FR 77 and follow FRs 77 and 7755 north reaching the trailhead at the end of FR 7755 in another 4.1 miles.

The re-routed trail travels 0.25 mile along an abandoned road skirting a landslide that scoured the wall of a nearby peak. This slide altered the

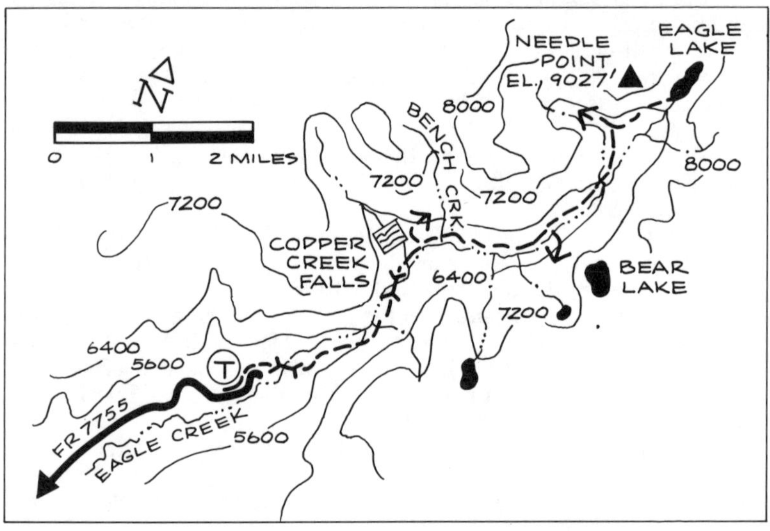

Copper Creek Falls

flow of Eagle Creek, broadening and slowing its stream and flooding the bases of living trees.

Ahead, forest and meadow interlock, and wonderful views of the Wallowa ridges greet the hiker. Evergreen spires, lingering snowfields, and seasonal falls contribute to the high-rise splendor.

The trail crosses the boulder rubble from the slide to reach an Eagle Creek bridge at 0.75 mile. Upstream from the bridge, two broad, fast-rushing cascades mark the creek course. Ahead, the trail climbs and parallels the creek, alternately touring a Douglas fir–Engelmann spruce forest and a deciduous shrub corridor. Beware of nettles when passing through the body-brushing shrubs.

After entering Eagle Cap Wilderness, the trail crosses over small side creeks to travel the length of two narrow meadows beside Eagle Creek. False hellebore and a wildflower myriad interweave the grasses.

Shortly after the second Eagle Creek bridge comes the fording of Copper Creek—a broad waterway following the snow melt. Where the trail offers a Copper Creek Falls view at 3 miles, a short off-trail scramble up the slope finds an informal path leading to an even better falls vista atop the rocks below and beside the unruly, tumbling chute.

The Main Eagle Trail next bypasses the Bench Canyon Trail and crosses Bench Creek. Alders line the creeks; thick patches of alder and aspen mark the boulder-studded meadow slope. With much of the trail exposed, carry plenty of water.

Soon, stands of subalpine fir dot the canyon bottom; the trail grows rockier. Where the trail rounds the slope at 4.5 miles, it affords a grand view of Eagle Creek lazily slipping through a lush, green meadow. Morning hikers often surprise meadow-grazing deer.

Just ahead lies a trail junction: Passing down through the meadow to the right is the route to Bear and Lookingglass lakes. Bearing left toward Trail Creek continues the Main Eagle hike. A hub for the high-lake trails, this large creekside meadow is the ideal base camp for area exploration.

Now, the canyon grows more defined, and the trail travels the flat closer to its watery host. Indian paintbrush, mariposa lily, and pearly everlasting provide showy displays. At 5.75 miles, the route ducks into a high-elevation forest with some big spruce.

Where it ascends a low meadow ridge between Eagle Creek and a side drainage, hikers find square-on views of Needle Point (elevation 8,022 feet). At 6 miles, the trail begins its switchbacking assault on the Eagle Lake Basin. The thick vegetation on the open, boulder-studded slope makes for a humid climb.

At the cairn marking the 6.5-mile trail junction, the route to Eagle Lake branches right. The open slope offers exciting canyon overlooks and down-canyon views featuring Hummingbird Mountain. The canyon floor unites spired firs; lush meadow grasses; low, clustering alders; granite boulders; and a sparkling creek ribbon in a wonderful wilderness tapestry, full of texture, shade, and contrast.

The final 0.3 mile of the ascent rounds and switchbacks up a granite ridge arriving at the lake outlet and dam at 7.5 miles. The high mountain bowl features steep sloping sides that defy vegetation and camps. Near the outlet, hikers can usually find a "flat" suitable for a tent, but the meadow at 4.6 miles remains the preferred camp area.

With minimal shade, the high elevation, and the reflecting lake waters, hikers who stay at Eagle Lake will want sunscreen and sunglasses. Return as you came.

99 UPPER LESLIE GULCH HIKE

Distance: 4 miles round trip
Elevation change: 500 feet
Difficulty: Moderate
Season: Spring through fall
Map: USGS Bannock Ridge, Rooster Comb
For information: Vale District BLM

Named for a pioneer struck by lightning here in 1882 (Hiram Leslie), Leslie Gulch enfolds the beauty of erosion-carved volcanic-ash cliffs and captures the isolation and romance of the wilderness. The canyon wash of Upper Leslie Gulch, a wilderness study area, provides a natural avenue for discovery.

Massive flows, dikes, fissures, and elemental sculpting create a canyon rich in character. Many of the sheer walls and pitted towers represent the weathered formations of Leslie Gulch tuff—a solidified volcanic ash unique to the Owyhee region. In places, the tuff measures some 2,000 feet thick.

Red- and orange-hued walls and isolated plates frame the route; a dark desert varnish streaks some of the rock faces. Junipers dot the sagebrush floor, while wildflowers adorn the rock niches and canyon bottom.

The movements of golden eagles, jackrabbits, and chukars attract the eye. The keen observer may even spy a bighorn sheep traveling up the rocks. Leslie Gulch with its adjacent canyons is one of the region's four primary viewing sites for bighorn sheep; Spring and Slocum creeks and Juniper Gulch are the other three.

At night, bats scour the canyons for insects, coyotes serenade the moon, and stars pepper the sky.

As always in desert canyon country where snakes reside, be alert; look before you reach, sit, or stride. Such areas call for common sense, not alarm.

The highly scenic Succor Creek–Leslie Gulch National Back Country Byway accesses this canyon hike. From OR 201 8 miles south of Adrian, go southwest on Succor Creek Road for 26 miles and turn right onto Leslie Gulch Road. Continue 8.9 miles on Leslie Gulch Road to reach the mouth of Upper Leslie Gulch Canyon and a parking turnout, both on the left. If you pass Dago Gulch Road and a cabin you've gone 0.2 mile too far.

A well-tracked, informal footpath travels the belly of the gulch, crisscrossing the wash. The drainage itself offers an alternative path, although near the mouth, it proves more difficult to follow.

The footpath weaves amid the 4- to 6-foot-high sagebrush, parted by rabbitbrush, sweet clover, and a few juniper. In May and early June, fleabane, phlox, paintbrush, milk vetch, geraniums, and balsamroot add their floral signatures.

At 0.25 mile, the canyon shows a gradual bend. The west wall features rounded, rock outcrop-dotted bunchgrass slopes; the opposite wall shows rugged, spire-topped cliffs rising some 300 to 400 feet above the canyon bottom. The rocks reveal honeycomb hollows, pockmarks, and shelves.

Upper Leslie Gulch

Where the footpath forks, stay right to continue up the canyon.

Side drainages, mostly shallow and dead-end in nature, invite additional exploration. The industrious may mount the gentler slopes for canyon overlooks.

By 0.75 mile, the path affords a look at a main-canyon fork; a cone-shaped grassland hill topped by a lone chimney rock isolates the canyon arms. Beyond it lies an eye-catching view: a series of rocky shields protruding from a grassland ridge like the platy spine of a dinosaur. Tree-covered hills rise in the backdrop.

Approaching the canyon-dividing hillside at 0.9 mile, the footpath dies. The drainage now guides the upper canyon tour. Go left following the main wash. It measures some 20 feet wide and presents a bed of small rocks and coarse sand for easy walking. Heavy rains, however, may alter its condition over time.

The wash remains relatively wide with brief squeezed segments, as it travels between the grassy slope of the drainage-dividing hillside and the picturesque cliffs of the east wall. The cliffs conjure up various images and moods, with lighting and weather animating the setting.

At 1.4 miles, the trail arrives below a mountain mahogany stand on the hillside. A great monolith reigns at the head of the canyon, while above and to the left sits a scenic hanging basin with a dark-varnished bottom. Clumps of wild rye now dot the wash.

Bluebirds, western tanagers, and olive-colored songbirds flit amid the brush. At 1.8 miles, the route approaches the base of the slope housing the large monolith. Follow the main canyon as it curves left.

Imposing rock walls straddle the pinched canyon as the hike draws to a close. Leafy bushes thrive in this moister gorge. Where it dead-ends at 2 miles, return as you came.

100 COFFEEPOT CRATER HIKING

Distance: 1 mile of exploration
Elevation change: 100 feet
Difficulty: Easy to moderate
Season: Spring through fall (dry weather destination)
Map: BLM Sheaville 30-minute quadrangle (for roads)
For information: Vale District BLM

Occupying the northwest corner of Jordan Craters Research Natural Area, Coffeepot Crater introduces some of the wonders found in this 5,000- to 6,000-year-old geologic flow. One of the youngest flows in the United States, the formations provide a nearly perfect record of the volcanic event. Time, weathering, human presence, and vegetation have little altered the features. Only a few lichens and mosses cling to the rock.

Northwest of Jordan Valley, the Jordan Craters lava flow spills over a 27-square-mile area; the flow is part of a greater area proprosed for wilderness designation. The area's remoteness and broken topography allow ample opportunity for solitude. Here, one finds spatter cones, cinder cones, lava tubes, and various surface-flow patterns to explore. Domes, cracks, and sinks punctuate the flow. Arid, rolling plains and hills of sagebrush and bunchgrass form its border.

With no formal hiking trails, the touring of this lava land is cross-country. Boots are a necessity; flashlights come in handy for peeking into the lava tube entrances and looking under rocky shelves.

When traveling across this sharp, crusty terrain, use care, and when exploring the caves or tubes, be aware of the possibility of rock falls. In the remote caves of the Jordan Craters flow, the rare Townsend's big-eared bat finds suitable habitat. This species receives both state and federal protective listing.

A high-clearance vehicle is recommended for this trip. From Jordan Valley, go 7 miles north on US 95 and turn west (left) at the sign for Jordan Craters. In 11 miles, go right, now traveling a dirt road of lesser quality. Stay on it for about 13 miles, journeying generally northwest following the signs. It passes through open range to arrive at an unmarked junction past Blowout and Coffeepot reservoirs.

A left leads to Coffeepot Crater in 2 miles; the road dead-ends a short distance from the crater's base. Wilderness Study Management restricts vehicle travel to existing roads.

While much of the route is marked, the numerous side roads may still introduce confusion. Before attempting an outing, it's best to purchase a map with the route highlighted on it from the Bureau of Land Management (BLM).

To begin the exploration, mounting the back of Coffeepot Crater for an overview of the flow and a look into the crater cavity is a natural calling. The neighboring small spatter cones likewise suggest a closer examination. Otherwise, hikers are on their own to poke around and satisfy their curiosity.

The black cinder cone of Coffeepot Crater towers over this corner of the flow. When mounting it, stay on the tried path; the fragile cinder slopes scar easily.

From the crater rim, the spectacle of the blow-out zone reveals the power of volcanism, as does the deep fissure cut into the flank of the cone. The crater core features dramatic, vertical reddish-black cliffs with a black cinder slope spilling at the base. The crater top holds exciting over-

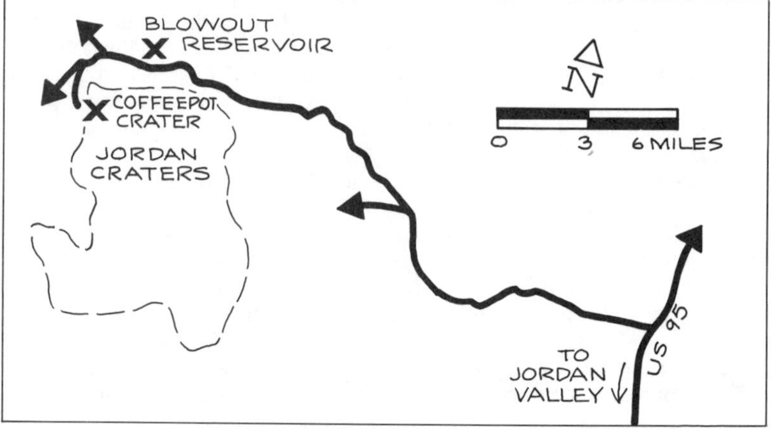

Coffeepot Crater

views of the extensive flow, its arid setting, and two smaller craters to the east.

When ready to surrender the lofty post, the pahoehoe (rope-like lava) surface in the immediate crater area affords fairly easy touring. Across the flow, fractures create a tile-like surface of plates. At the spatter cones, the texture tells the story of their creation: how the vents spit out the molten rock, splashing layer upon layer to build up the cones.

Mini lava tubes riddle the expanse. Some have collapsed; some sport yawning galleries where the ceilings are high enough and the rooms deep enough to invite a stooped entry. But, beware when exploring around any collapsed vent holes; some have thin edges. Sometimes only a few inches of lava separate you from a 40-foot drop. Use proper care and common sense.

Low-impact techniques help ensure the continuance of this outstanding primitive recreation experience. When touring lava country, leave all glass bottles in the vehicle. The danger presented by broken glass in the dark hollows is particularly great. As always, pack it in/pack it out.

Hikers should also remember that the black lava absorbs and radiates a great deal of heat; carry plenty of water even for short excursions. Early-morning tours, before the ground has had a chance to heat up, provide the greatest comfort.

Indian pipe

ADDRESSES

Applegate Ranger District
6941 Upper Applegate Road
Jacksonville, OR 97530
(503) 899-1812

Baker Ranger District
3165 10th Street
Baker City, OR 97814
(503) 523-4476

Barlow Ranger District
P.O. Box 67
Dufur, OR 97021
(503) 467-2291

Bear Springs Ranger District
Route 1, Box 222
Maupin, OR 97037
(503) 328-6211

Bend Ranger District
1230 NE 3rd
Bend, OR 97701
(503) 388-5664

Big Summit Ranger District
348855 Ochocho Ranger Station
Prineville, OR 97754
(503) 447-9645

Blue River Ranger District
P.O. Box 199
Blue River, OR 97413
(503) 822-3317

Bly Ranger District
Bly, OR 97622
(503) 353-2427

Burns District, BLM
HC 74-12533, Highway 20 West
Hines, OR 97738
(503) 573-5241

Chemult Ranger District
P.O. Box 150
Chemult, OR 97731
(503) 365-2229

Chetco Ranger District
555 Fifth Street
Brookings, OR 97415
(503) 469-2196

Clackamas Ranger District
61431 East Highway 224
Estacada, OR 97023
(503) 630-4256

Columbia Gorge Ranger District
31520 SE Woodard Road
Troutdale, OR 97060
(503) 695-2276

Coos Bay District, BLM
1300 Airport Lane
North Bend, OR 97459
(503) 756-0100

Crater Lake National Park
P.O. Box 7
Crater Lake, OR 97604
(503) 594-2211

Detroit Ranger District
HC 73, Box 320
Mill City, OR 97360
(503) 854-3366

Diamond Lake Ranger District
HC 60, Box 101
Idleyld Park, OR 97447
(503) 498-2531

Eagle Cap Ranger District
Rt. 1, Box 270A
Enterprise, OR 97828
(503) 426-4978

Estacada Ranger District
595 NW Industrial Way
Estacada, OR 97023
(503) 630-6861

Fort Rock Ranger District
1230 NE 3rd
Bend, OR 97701
(503) 388-5664

Galice Ranger District
1465 NE 7th Street
Grants Pass, OR 97526
(503) 476-3830

Gold Beach Ranger District
1225 South Ellensburg-Box 7
Gold Beach, OR 97444
(503) 247-6651

Hart Mountain National Antelope Refuge
P.O. Box 111
Lakeview, OR 97630
(503) 947-3315

Hebo Ranger District
Hebo, OR 97122
(503) 392-3161

Hells Canyon National Recreation Area
P.O. Box 270A
Enterprise, OR 97828
(503) 426-4978

John Day Fossil Beds National Monument
420 West Main
John Day, OR 97845
(503) 987-2333

Klamath Ranger District
1936 California Avenue
Klamath Falls, OR 97601
(503) 883-6824

La Grande Ranger District
3502 Highway 30
La Grande, OR 97850
(503) 963-7186

Lakeview District, BLM
1000 Ninth Street South
Lakeview, OR 97630
(503) 947-2177

Lakeview Ranger District
HC 64, Box 60
Lakeview, OR 97630
(503) 947-3334

Lane County Parks Division
3040 North Delta Highway
Eugene, OR 97401
(503) 341-6900

Long Creek Ranger District
528 East Main Street
John Day, OR 97845
(503) 575-2110

Lowell Ranger District
60 Pioneer Street
Lowell, OR 97452
(503) 937-2129

Mapleton Ranger District
Mapleton, OR 97453
(503) 268-4473

McKenzie Ranger District
McKenzie Bridge, OR 97413
(503) 822-3381

Medford District, BLM
3040 Biddle Road
Medford, OR 97504
(503) 770-2200

North Fork John Day Ranger District
P.O. Box 158
Ukiah, OR 97880
(503) 427-3231

North Umpqua Ranger District
18782 North Umpqua Highway
Glide, OR 97443
(503) 496-3532

Oakridge Ranger District
46375 Highway 58
Westfir, OR 97492
(503) 782-2291

Oregon Department of Fish and Wildlife
2501 SW 1st Avenue
Portland, OR 97207
(503) 229-5400

Oregon Dunes National Recreation Area
855 Highway Avenue
Reedsport, OR 97467
(503) 271-3611

Pacific Northwest Regional Office
United States Forest Service
319 SW Pine Street
Portland, OR 97208
(503) 221-2877

Paulina Ranger District
171500 Beaver Creek Road
Paulina, OR 97751
(503) 477-3713

Pomeroy (Washington) Ranger District
Rt. 1, Box 53F
Pomeroy, WA 99347
(509) 843-1891

Portland Parks and Recreation Department
Hoyt Arboretum
4000 SW Fairview Boulevard
Portland, OR 97221
(503) 823-3655

Prairie City Ranger District
327 Southwest Front Street
Prairie City, OR 97869
(503) 820-3311

Prineville District, BLM
185 East Fourth Street
Prineville, OR 97754
(503) 447-4115

Prineville Ranger District
155 North Quartz
Prineville, OR 97754
(503) 447-9641

Prospect Ranger District
Prospect, OR 97536
(503) 560-3623

Rigdon Ranger District
49098 Salmon Creek Road
Oakridge, OR 97463
(503) 782-2283

Roseburg District, BLM
777 NW Garden Valley Boulevard
Roseburg, OR 97470
(503) 672-4491

Salem District, BLM
1717 Fabry Road, SE
Salem, OR 97306
(503) 375-5646

Silver Lake Ranger District
Silver Lake, OR 97638
(503) 576-2169

Sisters Ranger District
P.O. Box 249
Sisters, OR 97759
(503) 549-2111

Snow Mountain Ranger District
HC-74, Box 12870
Hines, OR 97738
(503) 573-7292

South Slough National Estuarine Reserve
P.O. Box 5417
Charleston, OR 97420
(503) 888-5558

State Parks and Recreation Division, Salem
525 Trade Street SE
Salem, OR 97310
(503) 378-6305

State Parks, Bend Regional Office
P.O. Box 5309
Bend, OR 97708
(503) 388-6211

State Parks, Coos Bay Regional Office
365 North 4th Street, Ste. A
Coos Bay, OR 97420
(503) 269-9410

State Parks, Portland Regional Office
3554 SE 82nd Avenue
Portland, OR 97266
(503) 238-7491

State Parks, Tillamook Regional Office
416 Pacific
Tillamook, OR 97141
(503) 842-5501

Sweet Home Ranger District
3225 Highway 20
Sweet Home, OR 97386
(503) 367-5168

Tiller Ranger District
27812 Tiller-Trail Highway
Tiller, OR 97484
(503) 825-3201

Vale District, BLM
100 Oregon Street
Vale, OR 97918
(503) 473-3144

Waldport Ranger District
Waldport, OR 97394
(503) 563-3211

Walla Walla (Washington) Ranger District
1415 West Rose Avenue
Walla Walla, WA 99362
(509) 522-6290

Wallowa Valley Ranger District
Rt. 1, Box 270A
Enterprise, OR 97828
(503) 426-4978

William L. Finley National Wildlife Refuge
26208 Finley Refuge Road
Corvallis, OR 97333
(503) 757-7236

Zigzag Ranger District
70220 East Highway 26
Zigzag, OR 97049
(503) 622-3191

INDEX

Other books you may enjoy from The Mountaineers:

Columbia River Gorge: A Complete Guide, Jones, editor. Practical information on superb hiking, cycling, windsurfing, boating, camping, and photography opportunities. Background on history, weather, geology, flora and fauna.

Best Hikes With Children in Western and Central Oregon, Henderson. 100 easily accessible hikes, many lesser-known, with detailed trail information. Tips on hiking with kids, safety, and wilderness ethics.

Day Hikes From Oregon's Campgrounds, Ostertag. Guide to campgrounds that access the best hikes and nature walks in Oregon. Facilities, hike descriptions, more.

50 Hikes in Oregon's Coast Range and Siskiyous, Ostertag. Hikes in mountain corridor between I-5 and Highway 101, from ½-mile walks to 47-mile backpacks.

Exploring Oregon's Wild Areas: A Guide for Hikers, Backpackers, X-C Skiers & Paddlers, Sullivan. Detail-stuffed guidebook to Oregon's 65 wilderness areas, wildlife refuges, nature preserves, and state parks.

Bicycling the Backroads of Northwest Oregon, Jones. Descriptions, maps, mileage logs for 40 trips in Willamette Valley, from Portland south to Eugene.

A Pedestrian's Portland, Whitehill. Features 1- to 5-mile walks in and around 40 Portland, Oregon parks and neighborhoods.

Canoe Routes: Northwest Oregon, Jones. Details, maps, photos for 50 one-day flatwater trips in Lower Columbia River and Willamette Valley, north ocean coast. For all skill levels.

The 100 Hikes Series
Washington's Alpine Lakes, Spring, Manning & Spring.
Washington's North Cascades: Glacier Peak Region, Spring & Manning.
Washington's North Cascades National Park Region, Spring & Manning.
Washington's South Cascades and Olympics, Spring & Manning.
Inland Northwest, Landers & Dolphin.

50 Hikes in Mount Rainier National Park, Spring & Manning.

55 Hikes in Central Washington, Spring & Manning.

Available from your local bookstore or outdoor store, or from The Mountaineers Books, 1011 SW Klickitat Way, Suite 107, Seattle, WA 98134. Or call for a catalog of over 200 outdoor books: 1-800-553-4453.

The MOUNTAINEERS, founded in 1906, is a non-profit outdoor activity and conservation club, whose mission is "to explore, study, preserve and enjoy the natural beauty of the outdoors . . ." Based in Seattle, Washington, the club is now the third largest such organization in the United States, with 12,000 members and four branches throughout Washington State.

The Mountaineers sponsors both classes and year-round outdoor activities in the Pacific Northwest, which include hiking, mountain climbing, ski-touring, snowshoeing, bicycling, camping, kayaking and canoeing, nature study, sailing, and adventure travel. The club's conservation division supports environmental causes through educational activities, sponsoring legislation, and presenting informational programs. All club activities are led by skilled, experienced volunteers, who are dedicated to promoting safe and responsible enjoyment and preservation of the outdoors.

The Mountaineers Books, an active, non-profit publishing program of the club, produces guidebooks, instructional texts, historical works, natural history guides, and works on environmental conservation. All books produced by The Mountaineers are aimed at fulfilling the club's mission.

If you would like to participate in these organized outdoor activities or the club's programs, consider a membership in The Mountaineers. For information and an application, write or call The Mountaineers, Club Headquarters, 300 Third Avenue West, Seattle, Washington 98119; (206) 284-6310.

About the authors:

Salem, Oregon residents, Rhonda (author) and George (photographer) Ostertag have spent more than a decade hiking extensively in the western states. Rhonda is a free-lance writer specializing in travel, outdoor recreation, and nature topics. George has participated in several environmental-impact studies, including the California Desert Bill. The Ostertags have been published in *The Los Angeles Times, Newsday, Backpacker,* and more. They are the author/photographer team of *50 Hikes in Oregon's Coast Range and Siskiyous* and *Day Hikes From Oregon Campgrounds* (The Mountaineers).